CONTENT WARNING: Images and descriptions of genocide, gender violence, state torture & brutality, racial injustice, child labor exploitation, cultural appropriation, explicit language, territorial dispossession, dehumanization, mass murder, white supremacy, and intergenerational trauma.

"Since the beginning of our life as a people, this territory has been our supermarket, our pharmacy, our hardware store. Our ancestors were born and buried here. Our connection to this place is deeper than the state's. We should be managing it and protecting it."

Alex Lucitante (Kofan)
"When Conservation Became Colonialism"
Foreign Policy
(2018)

From germ theory to plantation logic, this 529-year timeline charts the legacy left behind by extractivist forces of colonial powers in the violent search for the elusive *Cinchona plant*. Originally known as the *fever tree* since time immemorial, Cinchona is a plant that grows in-between worlds—from the lower reaches of the Andean Mountains to the upper headwaters of the Amazonian River Valley—constantly resisting and fighting attempts at its substitution, simulation, or synthesization. Yet the Cinchona plant is more than a tree though: it is a map of soils, airs, climates, temperatures, territories, histories, and peoples. Stolen by the Spanish Jesuits in the 17th century, smuggled abroad by the British and Dutch during the 18th century, mapped by Humboldt in the 19th century, and patented by global pharma in the 20th century, the story of the Cinchona plant whose bark lies at the base of global drug production is not only a story of the search for the cure for malaria; it is a story captured by the quintessential capsule of quinine as we know it today.

In a wide-ranging way, this little pill is not only the product of removing bark from a tree; it is the dangerous precedent that was set in an imperial attempt to remove the plant from its peoples and its systems; systems of governance, of knowledge, of healing, of history, of life. It is a story of human violence, land dispossession, and cultural erasure, through more than five hundred years of chemical abstraction.

For thousands of years, Indigenous Peoples of Kechwa Nations through the Central Andes have cared for, cultivated, and nurtured the medicinal knowledge of quinine and the geographic intelligence of the Cinchona plant by respecting and honoring its sovereignty. Its very existence has come under threat of extinction by an array of foreign invasions: over-harvesting, industrial logging, deforestation, missionary expeditions, infrastructural development, road building, pipeline corridors, land seizures, mining, extraction, rampant tourism, unregulated trade, pharmaceutical dumping, proliferating chemical synthesis, intellectual property patenting, child labor exploitation, global trade deregulation. In other words, the basis of western industrial capitalism of the North—a bountiful world, free of malaria—is primarily, if not entirely premised on the wasting of the South, specifically rampaging Andean and Amazonian environments that have been inhabited for multi-millennia generations. From Amazon gift cards to Expedia eco-tourism, the benevolent eurocentric image of greenness that masks global capitalism is actually pillaging the region with foreign intervention.

As witnessed by the enduring legacy of the Cinchona plant, there is an overlooked territorial conflict belying the transnational world; frictions resulting from the invasive penetration into the Andes and rampant extraction of the Amazon: the oppression, exploitation, and elimination of Indigenous Peoples. As a declaration of sovereignty, this timeline thus proposes the mapping of a counter-cartography that transcends the historical divide between the colonial metropolis and resource hinterlands of a capitalist cosmos: one that centers Indigenous struggles instead of fragmenting or opposing them, positioning futures in parallel with that of the Cinchona plant and the urgently needed deindustrialization of the global production of quinine.

From fact to fiction to fable, the scientific and taxonomic epistemologies of the Cinchona plant are rooted in longstanding forms of imperial conquest and economic appropriation, as well as cultural construction and scientific misinterpretation. And to be sure, the dehumanizing holism of German explorer Alexander von Humboldt's hegemonic universalism, his trite naturalism, performative humanism, regional romance, equatorial fetish, and missionary lust lie at its very core.

Extracted from its territory and stolen from its peoples, this is the story of a plant whose myths have been, and continue to be, instrumentalized in the name of economic domination and capitalist accumulation mapped onto the nation-state. It is a story of empire-building and the resistance to its near hegemonic power. With miners as the new missionaries and conservationists as the new capitalists, the difference today is that you can destroy the rainforest with a click of a button instead of a bible; prime, modern-day conquistadors cloaked as point-accumulating consumers and saint-like conservationists.

As a political legacy whose intergenerational history is one of resilience and resurgence of self-determination, the botanical timeline of this book thus functions as a counter-map to the discourses on so-called civilization and urbanization. Through a layering of rebellions and resistance movements, the book proposes a way to rebuild relations with the Quino tree, by acknowledging its territories and honoring its peoples. The destruction of which continues to expand amidst coercive measures of conservation of the countryside; sociopolitical pressures that hide behind the veil of nature protection, rainforest preservation, or sustainable development. By challenging the all-encompassing nationalization of nature inherent to the ideologies of conservation, not only does this book ask how national histories should be challenged through the lens of a single plant, but how the capitalist world can be transformed and how alternative worlds can be re-imagined by dismantling the structures of settler-colonialism and by debunking the western myths of science and nature; myths that persist supposedly in service of humanity, so long as it is malaria-free.

Considered as a treaty then, this timeline acknowledges that until the systems and structures of dispossession and dehumanization—including targeted gendered violence, contradictory regional conservation measures, unchecked extraction infrastructures, non-consensual national land policies, unsanctioned foreign scientific interventions, unjust international patent laws, and uneven transnational trade agreements—are completely dismantled that the process of decolonization cannot take place. The legacy and reality of racial injustices, spatial inequalities, and environmental inhumanities of the past five centuries exist between the map and the territory, but they are embodied. Indigenous Peoples from the Andes and the Amazon—from the Indigenous Nations of *Awá, Chachis, Épera, Tsa'chila, Achuar, Andoa, Kofan, Waorani, Secoya, Shiwiar, Shuar, Siona, Zápara, Kichwa*, and Pueblos of *Chibuleo, Cañarí, Karanki, Cayambi, Kisapincha, Kitukara, Panzaleo, Natabuela, Otavalo, Puruwá, Palta, Salasaka, Saraguro, Waranka, Huancavilca, Secoya, Siona*, to *Afro-Ecuadorian Peoples*—are involuntary prisoners of settler-colonialism and inheritors of a spectrum of violence that must end.

Like the fresh waters that flow downwards, the cloudy atmospheres that rise up, the animals that roam across, and the soils it replenishes, the living, political, and historical biota of the Cinchona plant has always been in reciprocal relation with Indigenous Peoples. It always has, and always will.

John Phillips, *Hydroxychloroquine Sulfate*, 2020

andicola (Palmier)
Rubus alp.
Thibaudi
Régi
Nerteria
Salviæ
Limite super. des gr
tetrandra
Mutisia clematit
Lobeliæ
Arnica
Maratrum
a Mut.
Passiflores en arbres
Alchemilla
Hydrocotile
argemonoides
Oxalis edul
Tr
Solanum
Région
Styrax
Besleriæ
natisp. Cav.
Cinchona cordifolia Mut.
(Qu. jaune)
suvium
Fuchsiæ
Xyris
de 700 m à 2900 m
des Cinchona
Morus escul
Coffea occid.
Freziera canescens
Portulac
Polypodium
Krameria
Loasa triphylla
locos rosea
Porleria hygrometrica
Cinchona ovalif
(Qu. blanc)
yen
Calyplectus
Hydrolea trigyna
Lu
Freziera chryso
Freziera sericea
Molinæ
Lythrum ciliat
Cissus
Melastomes à grandes fleurs
Cantua (Periphragm.)
rostichum
Calicarpa

goff

a botany of violence

~~across 529 Years of Resistance & Resurgence~~

pierre bélanger · ghazal jafari · pablo escudero

produced on Lands of Kichwa Nations
Imbabura Territory (Andes)

Published by Goff Books, an Imprint of ORO Editions.
Executive publisher: Gordon Goff.

www.goffbooks.com
info@goffbooks.com

USA, EUROPE, ASIA, MIDDLE EAST, SOUTH AMERICA

Authors: Pierre Bélanger, Ghazal Jafari, Pablo Escudero
Book Design: OPSYS Media, LA MINGA, NOT YOUR AMAZON
Project Manager: Alejandro Guzman-Avila
Managing Editor: Jake Anderson

10 9 8 7 6 5 4 3 2 1 First Edition. World Rights: available.

ISBN: 978-1-951541-93-4

Library of Congress Control Number: 2021906697
Catalog-In-Publication Data available upon request.

Color Separations and Printing: ORO Group Ltd.
Printed in China.

Text of this book was set in D-DIN / Bahnschrift typefaces.

International distribution: www.goffbooks.com/distribution

ORO Editions makes a continuous effort to minimize the overall carbon footprint of its publications. As part of this goal, ORO Editions, in association with Global ReLeaf, arranges to plant trees to replace those used in the manufacturing of the paper produced for its books. Global ReLeaf is an international campaign run by American Forests, one of the world's oldest nonprofit conservation organizations. Global ReLeaf is American Forests' education and action program that helps individuals, organizations, agencies, and corporations improve the local and global environment by planting and caring for trees.

“qhipnayra uñtasis sarnaqapxañani”

Silvia Rivera Cusicanqui

Sociología de la Imagen: Miradas Ch'ixi Desde la Historia Andina

(2015)

529 Years of Resistance & Resurgence

a field note on the image & evidence of violence

On October 12th, 2019, at 3:51 pm in the city of Quito, a photograph taken by Mestizo photojournalist David Diaz Arcos captured a historic moment in the long legacy of political resistance in the region. As Indigenous-led activists and demonstrators came together from across the mountainous nation of Ecuador, they descended upon the country's capital and gathered to protest sanctions from the IMF (International Monetary Fund) and austerity measures that were imposed overnight by then Ecuadorian President Lenín Moreno. During the political uprisings that shook the city for several weeks, organized street marches symbolically converged at the intersection of 12 de Octubre and Madrid Avenues, location of the commemorative statue of Isabel la Católica.

Erected in 1990, the statue exclusively serves the Latin American élite of European descent ('colonos') and its sympathizers as site of colonial commemoration of the 500-year anniversary of the so-called 'Discovery of the Americas.' Flanking the scarlet-dripping statue of the Queen of Castile on this day were two self-determined Indigenous women from Kechwa Nations, each respectively coming from the mountainous region of the Andes and the highlands of the Amazon. Each one was holding the ceremonial concha in one hand and, in the other, a flag-like banner screen-printed with the portrait of another Indigenous activist: Dolores Cacuango. As a symbol of centuries-long Indigenous self-determination, Cacuango was born on October 26th, 1881, thirty years after the Monroe Doctrine was imposed on Latin America. Also known as Mamá Dulu, Cacuango was a radical feminist organizer and Indigenous warrior from the Andes who lived through most of the 20th century to see, lead, and inspire revolutionary change for Indigenous women and tribal nations against settler-colonialism, militarism, extractivism, and neoliberalism; until the day she passed away on April 23rd, 1971. Covering the face and crown of Isabel la Católica, the symbolic dethroning or decapitation of the statue was met with anoth-

David Díaz Arcos, *Indigenous Uprising* (Quito), 12 October 2019

er gesture. Rising behind the statue, a third and no-less undeterred Indigenous woman lifting and holding up another banner. The backface of a brown, unfolded cardboard box-turned-protest sign spelling out in bold, black, spray-painted, capital letters: *RESISTENCIA*.

Drenched in red paint, the statue was not only a symbolic rallying point for demonstrators that day; but it was also a revolutionary moment in longstanding legacies of Indigenous resistance across the Andes. Planned for the day that many western nations celebrate Columbus Day on October 12th—when white minority élites paradoxically celebrate the arrival of a genocidal murderer and slave trader on the shores of the Americas every year—the rallying point at the statue was particularly strategic. Protesting austerity measures and spiking fuel prices, the uprising was carefully orchestrated and coordinated as an assembly of over 10,000 Indigenous, Afro-Ecuadorian, Mestizo/a citizens converging on what was a long history of 529 years of oppression originally imposed by the staunch Catholic ruler of the 15th century Spanish Empire, Queen Isabel la Católica, in 1492. As the demonstrations in 2019 and centuries-long legacy of resistance show, anti-colonial struggles have arguably never ended. Not only did the Spanish Monarchy commission and bankroll the voyages of Christopher Columbus to 'discover the New World,' but the Queen of Castile and King Ferdinand II of Spain sanctioned and legitimated campaigns of violence, rape, looting, theft, assimilation, evangelization, and exploitation that left Indigenous Peoples and enslaved Black Peoples of the South American continent ruined and devastated.

The 17th-century chronicles of violent dispossession and cultural genocide drafted by Andean nobleman Felipe Guamán Poma de Ayala in his 1615 *El Primer Nueva Corónica y Buen Gobierno* (*The First New Chronicle and Good Government*) is groundbreaking testimony of that blood-soaked history. The front lines of colonization as depicted by Guamán Poma de Ayala in the early 17th century are as important as the embodied work on front lines today that are recorded by photojournalists such as David Diaz Arcos and several others. Fearless, unrelenting Indigenous organizers such as Nemonte Nenquimo—co-founder of the CEIBO Alliance that bring together Peoples of Siona, Siekopai, A'i Kofan, and Waorani Nations of the Upper Amazon region of Ecuador—is one of many fighting to protect their lands and waters against the ravages of extractive multinational corporations, Christian evangelical missions, and autocratic government regimes.

The capital city of Quito has long been the symbolic, geographic, and administrative center of these campaigns of political control and economic domination. Since the Treaty of Tordesillas in 1494 which unilaterally split the world in the most prepotent act between the two empires of Spain and Portugal, *La Real Audiencia de Quito* (*The Royal Court of Quito*) not only occupied one of the highest elevations along the Earth's Equator of any city in the world, but it marked the western edge of Spain's ruling territory that once spanned the extremities of the continent, from the mouth of the Amazon River on the Atlantic Ocean to the peak of the Chimborazo Volcano in the Andes towards the Pacific.

Amidst the turmoil of the demonstrations, the symbolic takeover of the statue by Indigenous feminist activists captured in Arcos' photograph is a metaphor for the occupation of Quito, the capital city. As confrontations with state and local police forces drew closer to the government's National Assembly and Presidential Quarters at Carondelet Palace in Quito, President Moreno cowardly retreated from the federal administrative center in the northern part of the country and escaped to the port city of Guayaquil in the south. The political event brings into sharp relief the power of Indigenous resistance and the deep-seated significance of confrontations and clashing with forces of colonialism, capitalism, and globalization intersecting with the nation-state. As a semiotic representation, the image is thus a strong if not monumental and contemporary reflection of Indigenous resistance and self-determination led by Indigenous Peoples for over 500 years.

As one of the more than 250 'history-images' contained in this book, Arcos' photograph not only captures a revolutionary moment in time, but provides a cross-section of a deep-running, anti-colonial movement led by Indigenous women in the fight against structures of settler-colonialism for justice, equality, land, and sovereignty. The photograph offers a story within a story, a powerful image that presents a political pretext for understanding and revealing historical struggles that converge and coalesce in different ways. Its significance is further found in the form of a counter-representation that challenges the counterfactual images circulated by white settler-media. As anthropologist Maximilian Viatori explains in their 2014 essay "Indigenous Threats and White Counterfactuals: The Semiotics of Race in Elite Print Media Coverage of Ecuador's 1990 Indigenous Uprising":

> "The image of a threatening other plays a critical role in the execution and legitimation of modern forms of power."

Counter-representations are especially important, as Ecuadorian anthropologist Lourdes Endara Tomaselli observed back in their 1989 book, *El Marciano de la Esquina: Imagen del Indio en la Prensa Ecuatoriana Durante el Levantamiento de 1990* (*The Martian in the Margins: Image of the Indian in the Ecuadorian Press during the 1990 Uprising*):

> "In contemporary Ecuadorian society . . . the Indian is seen as a cannibal because he symbolically attacks Spanish-speaking humankind. It is not a real aggression (here corporeality does not matter), but an attack on the legitimacy of Hispanic-American culture, its institutions, its economic model, etc."

As a timeline made of interwoven images, these counter-representations bring forth visual evidence of deeper, more hidden realities. They reveal the often less visible conflict in daily life and overwhelming oppression in the friction with the globalized economy of Ecuador whose control is in the hands of a minority of settlers and foreigners. A colony in all but name, Ecuador was forced to abandon its own currency—the sucre that circulated since 1884 after Independence—for the US dollar on March 9, 2000. That financialized economy premised on structures of racialized capitalism, is also based on an economy of appearances unequally controlled by white settler-media.

As an image within an image, Arcos' photograph (like many others in the book) is like a map tracing a complex cartographic context; a time in a place that brings together tribal nations, ancestral traditions, lived experiences, and Indigenous sovereignties through embodied action. Far more than rhetoric or illustrative diagram, the photographic image as sociological representation is reflective, inflective, and projective. As Indigenous scholar Silvia Rivera Cusicanqui observed in a 2009 lecture, *Sociology of the Image: A View from Andean History*:

> "I have differentiated myself from visual anthropology that uses images to see the other as an exotic animal. Same with historiography, that uses the image to corroborate written sources, or at worst as a mere illustration."

As a visual, territorial, and political field then, the medium of the photograph is a confrontation whose political image is primed with sweat and tears. And just like the statue on October 12th, 2019, that confrontation is still dripping with fresh blood.

Convergence & Confrontation. Greatly influenced and shaped by the revolutionary nature of this moment and by the legacy of anticolonial writers, the idea for this book project was conceived not uncoincidentally at the same time as the political uprisings and demonstrations in Ecuador were taking place in 2019. Inspired by the graphic bombardment of protest images and the vividness of the long history unfolding in front of us, the intention of this book is to tell a deeper story of environmental and spatial injustices across the past 500 years beyond (and behind) the façade of vivid images from current affairs. For this reason, we bring together a series of stories, photographs, and maps laid out as a multi-layered timeline telling the lesser-known story about Ecuador's past and present. The contours of transnational research are as much along the boundaries and borders of settler-spaces as they are along ridges, forests, mountains, volcanos, peaks, plains, plateaux, valleys, rivers, and bodies of water they are imposed on.

Part timeline, part atlas, and part essay, the book's format is purposely designed to combine multiple forms of spatial, visual, and archival media—from art, text, video, and voice—to overcome the unevenness of conventional state histories and the flatness of official state maps. Views from above that most often pass through the colonial gaze, the overseers whom Afro-Caribbean author and political theorist Aimé Césaire refers to in his 1950 book *Discours sur le Colonialisme* as:

> "The decisive actors of colonization: the adventurer and the pirate, the wholesale grocer and the shipowner, the gold digger and the merchant, appetite and force, and behind them, the baleful projected shadow of a form of civilization which, at a certain point in its history, finds itself obliged, for internal reasons, to extend to a world-scale the competition of its antagonistic economies."

While the chronological layout of the book may appear to be linear at first glance, its organization is multi-layered, stratified, and recursive. That layout confronts colonial conventions of visual anthropology and social sciences by drawing systemic connections and grounding events in their territorial milieux; geographic contexts and historical patterns that are often fragmented and atomized by scientific specialization, or whitewashed and obscured by technocratic abstraction. Weaving subtle yet sometimes banal images with new, alternative, and jarring information, the visual juxtapositions in the book are intended to disrupt and displace the colonial gaze by grounding the alternative realities and lived experiences of the oppressed. Again, from her anti-colonial vantage point, Silvia Rivera Cusicanqui sheds light on visceral relations and connections grounded in land through the practices that embody the sociology of the image as a critique of visual anthropology:

> "In visual anthropology, we need to familiarize ourselves with the culture, the language, and the territory of other societies, different from the Eurocentric and urban society that researchers often represent. On the contrary, the sociology of the image supposes a defamiliarization, a distance with the well-known, enhanced by the immediacy of routine and habit. Visual anthropology is based on participant observation, where the researcher participates in order

to observe. On the other hand, the sociology of the image observes what it already participates in; participation is not an instrument at the service of observation but its economy, although it is necessary to problematize it in its colonialism/unconscious élitism... Another difference between the sociology of the image and visual anthropology is that the latter is oriented primarily to the record (photographic, videographic, filmic) of the societies it studies to show them before an urban and academic audience. That is, above all, a practice of representation. On the other hand, the sociology of the image considers all representational practices as your focus of attention; addresses the entire visual world, from advertising, press photography, image archives, pictorial art, drawing and textiles, as well as other more collective representations such as the structure of urban space and the historical traces that become visible in it."

Image & Evidence. More than just a compilation of illustrations, the archive of photographs, paintings, maps, marginalia, advertisements, diagrams, and other media that this book brings together seeks to transgress the romanticized picturesque of imperial conquest; those images rendered legible through colonial categories and vocabularies of settler representation. This multimedia compilation delineates histories of struggle and scales of conflict through their own interpretive language—that is, visual and spatial. The interplay of different scales and temporalities—from the global and continental to the human and botanical—is vital. Serving two purposes, this scalar interplay acts as a language with dual meanings. First, this interplay cuts through long and short periods of time, transcending a multitude of misrepresentations and seemingly disconnected or unrelated events. Second, this interplay reconnects these events in a manner that reclaims the significance and impacts of these representations whether related to systems of sustenance or governance—from river waters to resource policies. This double language thus offers a discernible lens that sees through the opacity of the sophistication of neoliberal statecraft; a craft that plays out in a paper world of settler-jurisprudence and corporate colonialism while it skews, distorts, and exploits the realities, rights, and spaces that exist between the map and the territory. This language opens a lens and sheds light on complex capitalist flows and trade policies that cast shadows on human rights and environmental justices; flows and policies aimed at exploiting, suppressing, marginalizing, erasing, and wiping humanity literally off the official state map.

What crosses the borders of official maps? What lies on their edges? What is left out? The spatial forms and historical periods of representation in this book intersect with these questions, yet they are specifically grounded in the shared struggle against dehumanization and racial domination as they argue for freedom from settler-colonialism, state nationalism, and global capitalism—pressures that have persisted for over five hundred years since first contact with Jesuit missionaries and Spanish colonizers. As a cypher, the organization of the book decodes and disentangles overlapping histories of oppression and intertwined geographies of domination to reveal and confront the hidden and dark underbelly of territorial dispossession. It ultimately seeks to weaken images that normalize exploitation and naturalize domination by a society of settlers. By doing so, it aspires to challenge and confront the extractivism that underlies the production, conservation, and reproduction of territorial injustices through the unchecked circulation of the image of the nation-state of Ecuador, past and present.

Guiding this book, Silvia Rivera Cusicanqui's work on the sociology of the image from her 2015 book *Sociología de la Imagen* is especially instructive. The Aymaran aphorism borrowed from Cusicanqui's words at the onset of this introduction—"qhipnayra uñtasis sarnaqapxañani"—offer a compelling understanding and call to action in dismantling the systems of oppression that continue to dispossess today:

> "by looking back and forth (future-past), we can walk in the present-future."

Forensic Botany & Systems of Oppression

The following chronology doesn't just start with an industrial white pill nor with global conservation policy. Beyond the boundaries of the nation-state, it begins with the geopolitical transformation of the only known natural cure for malaria, the complex compound of *quinine*. Its endemic geography may trace a historical territory of tradition between the lowlands of the Andean Mountain Range and the highlands of the Amazon River Basin, but the global complex of plantations inscribe and entrench a space of technological violence and domination. These are traditional lands of Kechwa Nations that underlie the boundaries territories of Ecuador, a nation whose colonial administrative space once stretched a massive region mirroring the watershed of the Amazon River, from the Atlantic to the Pacific, geometrically paralleling the cartographic line of the Equator. This territorial history also goes beyond the geography of quinine production to delineate the political trajectory of the *Cinchona plant* whose potent and precious bark has been—and, still is—the object of scientific expeditions, industrial secrecy, pharmaceutical exploitation, and corporate colonialism. If the plant is a media that carries a message, then it is a political medium of the forces—past, present, and future—that shape its environment. To map the plant is thus to reveal its enduring power shaped by legacies of historical struggle and contemporary conflicts. Mapping the contours of the dominant structures of power associated with the Cinchona plant reveals how political control is exercised at different levels and how the image of authority and the narrative of the omnipresent nation-state are projected at different scales. Here, the nation-state is, according to Peruvian sociologist and scholar of the *coloniality of power* Aníbal Quijano, "a society where, within a space of domination, power is organized with some important degree of democratic relations... basically in the control of labor, resources, products, and public authority." To understand the imperative for decolonizing the global and national discourse on conservation (specifically, through land cessions and reparations) that shapes these lands and waters today, it is essential to understand how these power structures are historically entrenched in a dominant system of settler-colonialism formed by European policies of spatial, racial, and economic domination—the basis of empire-building and white supremacy. How the inequalities and injustices of the Cinchona plant's history emerge from the original *civilizing mission* of the Spanish Empire, sanctioned by the Catholic Church and its papal bulls (*Doctrine of Discovery*) over the past five centuries is paramount in understanding the significance and influence movements of resistance, patterns of resurgence, and struggles for self-determination today.

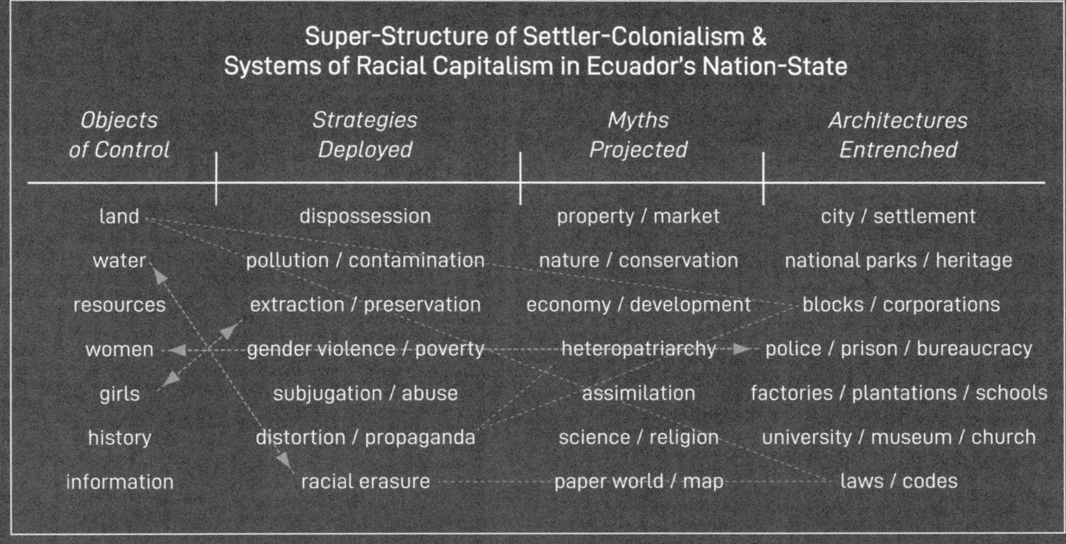

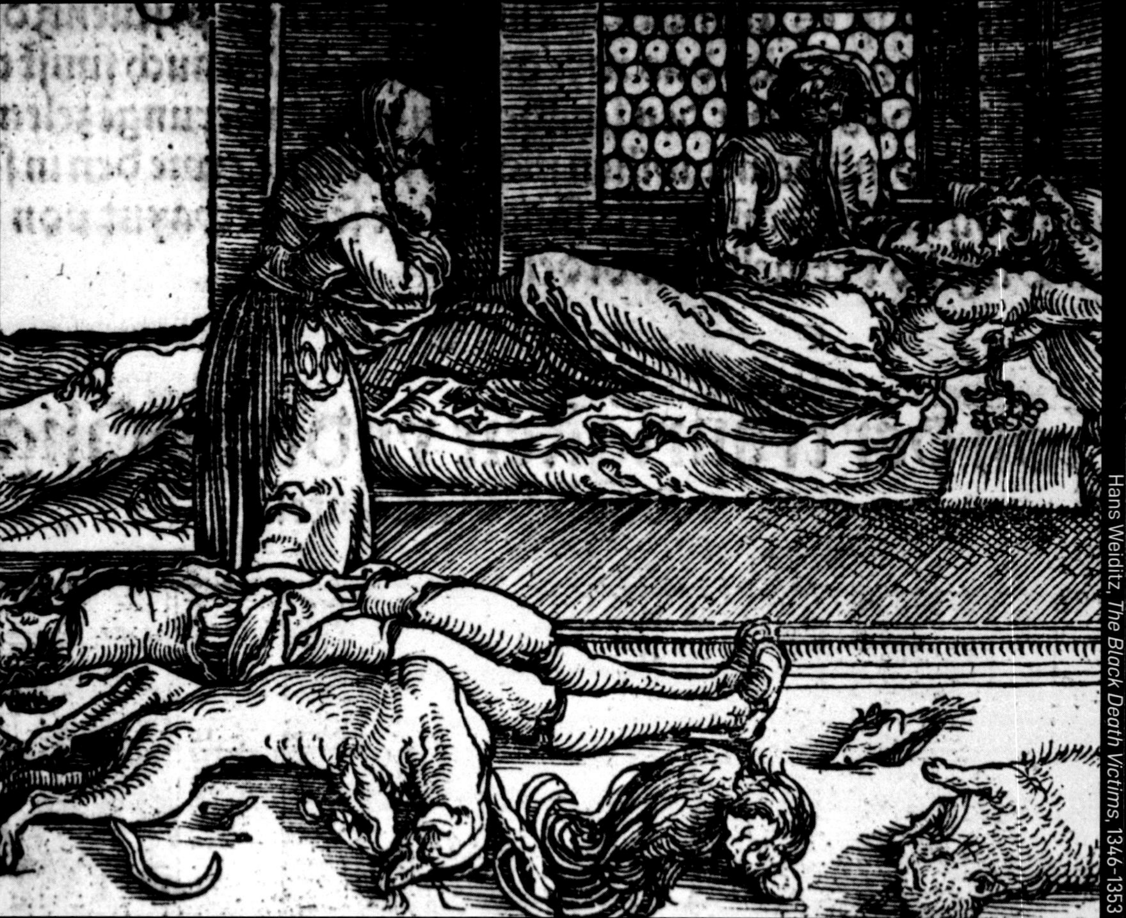

Hans Weiditz, *The Black Death Victims*, 1346-1353

460-377 BCE: Contagion

As the primary explanation of diseases in Greco-Roman Antiquity and likely cause of the Fall of the Roman Empire in the 4th century AD, the concept of *bad air* (most often from decaying organic matter) prevails in the Western World as the cause of disease, plague, and death. In 5th century BCE, Hippocrates' rejection of the supernatural world and formulation of environmental theory leads to *contagion theory*, later called the *miasma theory of disease*, laying down foundations of the Renaissance and medical science, in a global search for the cure to *mal'aria* (bad, air) that hit imperial powers hard with the Great Plague of the 14th century. In his *De Morbis Popularibus* (*Of Epidemics*), Hippocrates writes of the classic effects of the Plasmodium falciparum mosquito, whose effects range from 9 to 14 days with symptoms including shaking chills, high fevers, sweating, headaches, nausea and vomiting, anemia, and diarrhea. With the attendant colonization of other territories for 'new' resources and medicines, 'The Age of Discovery' (including that of *medical discovery*) irreversibly begins.

DE CORTICE PERVVIAE.

Continens Ortum Corticis, qualitates, Causas, aliaque his Confinia.

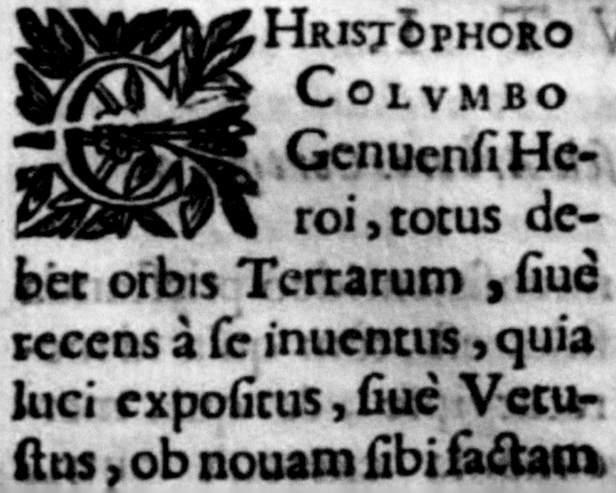

CHRISTOPHORO COLVMBO Genuensi Heroi, totus debet orbis Terrarum, siuè recens à se inuentus, quia luci expositus, siuè Vetustus, ob nouam sibi factam *tot millium capitum* accessionem, & incrementum; debet, *ob tot rerum* acquisitionem in eo orbe repertarum, *ob auri, & argenti* immensas planè fodinas, quibus Regum *Gazæ* implentur, vt planè in *aurum*

1492: Delirium

Lost, hungry, sick, mad? Christopher Columbus and his crew aboard the Santa María may have been said to have discovered the 'New World,' but if they did, it was by accident. Scouting a new spice route, or new land? Whatever the truth is, Europeans were suffering from centuries of incurable malaria that especially infected Mediterranean regions; fevers that even Hippocrates studied centuries earlier. In a strange twist of universal history, the feverish lust for gold so rampant in imperial narratives of conquest was likely the mask of a darker reality. Desperate and destitute, Europeans were on a rabid hunt for the elusive, mythologized plant in faraway lands beyond their reach, until the Genoese navigator ran ashore. Most likely, when Columbus was reportedly sent by the Spanish Empire to find gold and silver, his most sizable and lethal contribution was the injection of colonizers across the soon to be named Americas, the enslavement of Black Peoples, and the genocidal havoc they would wreak; but later, the extraction of a special plant with special powers by those following in his footsteps. At the intersection of the Andes and the Amazon, the highlands that were opened by force to access lands that held a secret to solve the age-old European problem of finding the cure to malaria for their own kind. Greater than gold or silver, they sought a tree called *fever*.

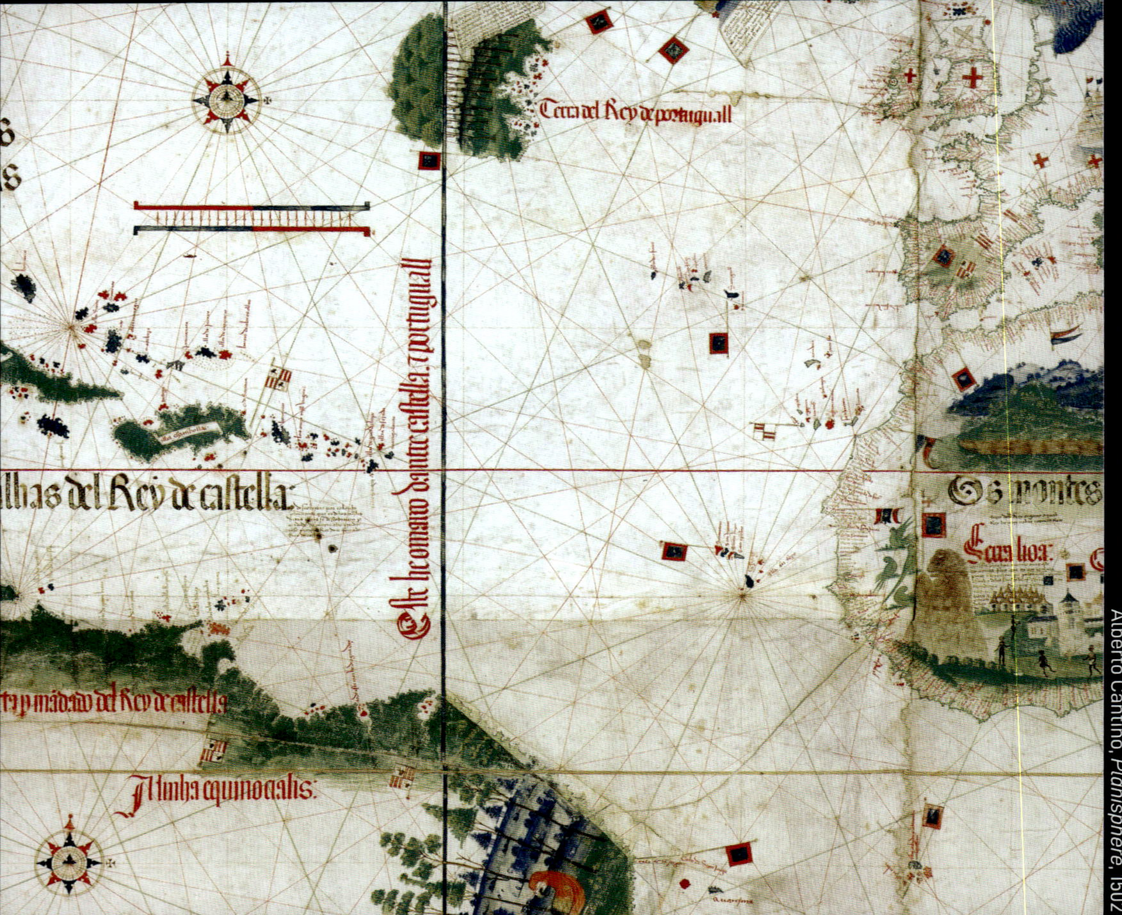

Alberto Cantino, *Planisphere*, 1502

1494: Territory & Terrorism

In one of the most defining geopolitical acts to define the planet, the Portuguese and Spanish Empires split the surface of the world into two realms: the East and the West. Any 'newly discovered lands' beyond shores of the homelands become captive territories, along the dividing line of meridian 370 leagues west of Cape Verde as boundary: the invisible line of the Treaty of Tordesillas. Sealing decisions from previous Papal Bulls, namely *Dum Diversas* by Pope Nicholas V in 1456 and *Inter Caetera* by Pope Alexander VI in 1493, an era of violent missions and predatory quests is launched on lands deemed *terra nullius* by the Holy See where non-Christians are either assimilated and civilized, enslaved and oppressed, or maimed and murdered. The interiorization of Indigenous lands and the terrorization of Indigenous Peoples begins.

Circulus articus
Oceanus occidentalis
Terra del Rey de portuguall
Has antilhas del Rey de castella
Os montes claros em africa
Serra lioa
Castello damina
Mare oceanus
Tropicus capricorni

Circulus articus:
Circulus articus:
Tropicus cancri
Oceanus orientalis:
Linha equinocialis:
Mare barbaricus:
Oceanus yndicus meridionalis:
Circulus capricorni
Oceanus yndicus meridionalis:

1532-85: Foreign Invasions

At the precise moment that Francis Bacon begins writing his three *Essays* on "Nature," "Science," and "Empire," the pillaging of the Andean region now associated with Ecuador, Peru, and Colombia are in full force. Spanish conquistador Francisco Pizarro traps and tricks Incan Emperor Atahualpa Capac, massacres thousands of Incan warriors—women and men—assimilating and indoctrinating remaining Indigenous survivors into Christianity. Not uncoincidentally, "dominion over nature," as Bacon proclaims, implies supreme colonial power, control over land, and elimination of Natives deemed "savages."

AMAZON.

Penthesilea, Queen of the Amazonas, 1862

1532: Avenge of the Amazonas

After Spanish conquistador Francisco Pizarro battles Inca Emperor Atahualpa Capac (1532) in his quest to secure points of territorial penetration into the continent, another colonizing navigator, Francisco de Orellana Bejarano Pizarro y Torres de Altamirano, founds port of Guayaquil a few years later (1538), to later fight off Tapuya Nations during his 4,000-mile river journey, where he coins the resilient and powerful warrior women, *the Amazonas*. Over time, their name is politically, culturally, etymologically, and mythologically adopted as the name of the region itself: *Amazonia* (*The Amazon*). Yet, the given name of 'the Amazon' is also a colonial surrogate. Here, the massive river region that designates the cross-continental space of Indigenous matriarchy, long prevalent in the region since time immemorial, substitutes the heterogeneity of lands and peoples whereby 'the' Amazon stands in as a monolithic, homogeneous, seemingly mappable, and captive space for European conquest and consumption in the image and imagination of untouched nature. In the dehumanizing nomenclature of the Amazon, Indigenous Peoples and Tribal Nations become the involuntary prisoners of Spanish settler-colonialism.

1542: Gendering Violence

As a result of the accounts of Dominican Friar Bartolomé de la Casas in his 1542 book *A Short Account of the Destruction of the Indies* (regarding the atrocities committed by Spanish conquistadors in New Spain), the *New Laws of the Indies for the Good Treatment & Preservation of the Indians* are drafted by Charles V, King of Spain, in 1542 to bring an end to the atrocities of Spanish colonizers on Indigenous Populations. The King's imperial reforms, namely the new *encomienda* system of labor, actually result in the enslavement of Indigenous Peoples. Through the ensuing process of Christian assimilation, the heteropatriarchal power that underlies colonial governance institutes a structure of political domination and subjugation. These brutal powers are specifically unleashed through forms of gendered violence that target Indigenous women and girls at the core of matriarchal societies.

Bartolomé de las Casas, *A Short Account of the Destruction of the Indies*, 1578

REPÚBLICA
SEÑORES
TONIO FLORES.
trabajos propios del autor.
eron consultados todos
isten sobre el territorio
o, Velasco, Humboldt, del
ateriales importantisimos
tes colindantes del Perú),
ncuentran en la obra que
zig.
P A C Í F I C
ESMERALDAS
P. Gorda
Rio verde
P. Verde
La Tola
S. Lorenzo
Concepcion
Cayapas
Playa de oro
Atacames
P. Galera
S. Francisco
Cabo de S. Francisco
Muisne
Montañas de Atacames
Montañas de Mompiche
Montañas de Cojimies
Lago y pantanos de Sade
Cord. de Cayapas
Cord. de Toisan
Rio Guaillabamba
Rio Blanco
Pedernales
P. Pedernales
P. Palmar
P. Surones
Cojimies
L.y P. de Zapotal
P. Portete
Bahia de Ancon de Sardinas
Gualea
Nanegal
P R O V. D E E S M E R A L D A S

1553: Afro-Indigenous Insurgency

In the Spanish quest to conquer lands of the Esmeraldas and to subvert the Jesuit reign across South America, one of many ships en route to Peru from New Spain (Mexico) runs ashore in treacherous waters off the Pacific coast. Twenty-three *Cimarrones* (maroons), as Black runaway slaves would later be called, survive the shipwreck and escape to high ground into the rainforest highlands where they find allyship with Indigenous tribes—the traditional home of the Chachi Nation. Staving off countless coastal confrontations from colonists on their way to Lima notwithstanding the future pressures of *mestizaje* (race mixing) and *blanqueamiento* (whitewashing), Cimarrones establish *palenques*, fortified settlements of mixed Indigenous and Black Peoples throughout the mountain-valley region of Ríos Guayllabamba and Chota. Building a legendary regional image of anti-colonial resistance (that would survive for five centuries) and as a stronghold against the Spaniards, the land of the Emeralds solidifies as a republic of Free Blacks and harbor steeped in Afro-Indigenous traditions; Esmeraldas becomes the go-to safe haven for slaves and oppressed Black Peoples escaping treacherous conditions in gold mines and plantations from Colombia in the north.

Real Audiencia de Quito, 1546

1563: Penetration I

King Philip II of Spain decrees the *Real Audiencia de Quito (Province of Quito)* as the administrative district from the Atlantic to the Pacific Ocean, an area encompassing current day Brazil, Colombia, Peru, Venezuela, and Ecuador. Traversed by the Amazon River system (with its thousands of tributaries) and bounded to the east by the Treaty of Tordesillas of 1494, the treaty was promulgated by Pope Alexander VI and signed by the kingdoms of Castille and Portugal. In the most hegemonic act in global history, the entire surface of the planet is divided into two halves, splitting the spoils of stolen lands between two European empires, thus creating east-to-west divisions that still remain—albeit highly contested—in place today.

EL GRAN RIO
MARAÑON, o AMAZONAS
Con la Mission de la Compañia de IESVS
Geograficamente delineado
Por el Pe. Samuel FRITZ Missionero conti nuo en este Rio.
A LA CATOLICA Y REAL MAGESTAD
DEL REYN. S. D. FELIPE V.
LA PROVINCIA DE QUITO DE LA COMPa. DE IESUS
OFRECE, Y DEDICA
en eterno reconocimiento
ESTE MAPA DEL GRAN RIO MARAÑON
CON SU MISSION APOSTOLICA
COMO A SU SOBERANO PATRON, Y MANTENEDOR
POR MANO
DE SU REAL AUDIENCIA
DE QUITO
MAR DEL SUR
MAR DEL NORTE
Cabo de Norte
Sta. Fe de Bogota
Rio Orinoco
Popayan
Pasto
Linea Equinoccial
Parime Lago
Rio Negro
Rio Napo
Quito
Cuenca
Lima
Callao
Cuzco
Para
Norte
Sur
Leste
Oeste
Leguas Castellanas
Mission de la Compañia de IESVS
Ad maiorem Dei gloriam.

Samuel Fritz, El Gran Rio Marañon o Amazonas con la Mision de la Compañia de Jesus, 1707

QVITO
Baeza
Archidona
Latacunga
Quijos
Ambato
Riobamba
Patate
Napo
Encabellados
Sucumbios
Chiŭs
Rio Ica, o Putumayo
Icates
Parianas
Yacariuaras
Rio Napo
Abijiras
R. Curaray
Andoas
Aunalas
Rio Tigre
Roamaynas
Rio Pastaça
R. Chambira
Punta de Sta Helena
Guayaquil
la Puna
Cuenca
R. Paute
R. de Zamora
Zamora
Loxa
Xibaros
Santiago
Borja
Payta
Piura
Valladolid
Chirinos
Iaen
Punta de Aguja
R. Tamborapa
Tomependa
R. Guancabamba
Saña
Chota
Cocota
Norte
Guanchaco
Truxillo
Guañape
Santa
Calcas
Contumaca
Cascamarca
R. Nieva
Chillaos
Lamas
Rio Gualaga
Pachitea
Cunivos
Mananabobas
R. Amenguaca
Vcayale
Lagunas
Xeberos
Capanauras
Auaranateos
Huahuratates
Ticunas
Omaguas
Guarecicus
Curinas
S. Miguel de Yarapa
Rio Yutay
Leste
Sur
Guarmey
Guaura
Chancay
Piros
Cambas
Guanuco
Lag. Lauricocha
R. Perene
R. Paucartambo
Chinchacocha
LIMA
Callao
Pachacama
Mala
Xauxa
Guamanga
Guancabelica
R. de Vrcos
CUZCO
Leguas Castellanas.
10 20 30 40 50 60 70 80 90 100
Este famoso
nas, ya de Orellan
mografos desde s
guna Lauricoch
1800 leguas, hasta
de Borja tiene
guas de largo de
y otra ribera de
vegable, hasta el
ras de todos colore
vo para guisados,
Vaca Marina, o Pe
de las orillas; y la
tissimo de Tortu
Culebras tan dis
roces Tigres, Ja
de Animales, con
innumerables b
este Mapa) singu
les tienen fama
algunas Poblac
Miss
Tiene la Compañ
bajosa, y Aposto

nto Descubierto, que llaman ya de Amazo=
Marañon; nombre, que le dan los mejores Cos=
as sus Provincias Superiores. Nace de la La=
udad de Guánuco en el Reyno del Perú. Corre
lel Norte con 84 de Voca. Junto a la Ciud.
nbrado el Pongo de 25 v.s de ancho, y 3 le=
, que se navega en un quarto de hora. Vna
de Iaen de Bracamoros (desde donde es na=
bladas de altissima arboleda. Tiene made=
o, Zarza parrilla, y corteza, que llaman de Cla=
s innumerables Peces el mas singular es la
dicho por la semejanza: sustentase con yerva
cria con leche a sus hijuelos. Es abundã=
os, Lagartos, o Cocodrilos; y tiene algunas
tragan a un hombre. En sus montañas ay fe=
dancia Dantas, y otras muchas especies
colores en sus Vegas. Está pobladissimo de
ones (las de mas nombre van notadas en
os Rios que le entran: algunos de los qua
. Los Portugueses posseen azia la Voca
de Rio Negro und Fortaleza.

Compañia de IESVS.

n este gran Rio una muy dilatada, tra=
en que entró año 1638: cuya Cabeza
la Ciu.d de S. Fran.co de Borja Provincia de los Maynas distãte de Quito 300 leguas
y se estiende por los Rios de Pastaza, Guallaga, y Ucayale hasta el fin de la Prov
de Omaguas. Vase a ella por tres caminos asperissimos, y en gran parte a pie: por d
en Patate, y Archidona: en cuyos Puertos se embarcan los Missioneros en Canoas,
navegando largas, y peligrosas distãcias hasta sus Reducciones. Han muerto en ellas los Barbaros a lo
siguientes Padres (en cuyas muertes huvo sucessos prodigiosos): al V.P. Frã.co de Figue
roa en la voca del Rio Apena junto a Guallaga año 1666: al V.P. Pedro Suarez en Abijira
año 1667: al V.P. Agustin Hurtado en Roamaynas año 1677: al V.P. Henriq. Ricter en Piros año 16
y en este año de 1707 ha llegado repetida la noticia de que en Gayes mataron los Barbaros
al V.P. Nicolas Durango. Los sitios de sus muertes van señalados con esta ✝. Tãbiẽ mu
ahogado por tã gloriosa causa el V.P. Raymũdo de S.ta Cruz navegãdo el Rio de Bobonaza
año 1662. Tiene la Comp.a en esta Missiõ (a mas del Curato de Borja, y sus Anejos) en 4 Par
dos 39 Pueblos fũdados cõ su sudor, y por la mayor parte a sus expẽsas: en el Partido d
Xeberos, la Cõcep.n de Xeberos, y 5 Anejos de Paranapuras, Chayavitas, Cahuapanas, M
niches, y Otanapis. En el Partido de la Laguna, S. Tiago de Gitipos, y Cocamas, y 3 Anejos
Chamicuros, Tibilos, y Aguanos. En el Partido de Gayes, S. Xavier de Gayes, y 5 Anejos de
Roamaynas, Pavas, Pinches, Andoas, y Semigayes. En el Partido de Omaguas, S
Ioachin de Omaguas, y 22 Anejos de Yarapas, Omaguas, y Yurimaguas. En l
quales Partidos, y Pueblos ay hasta Veinte, y seis Mil almas reducidas, y bau
zadas por los Padres Missioneros: que al presente son diez, y seis Sacerdote
(de mas de otros dos, que assisten en la Mission de Colorados). Y a mas de
los dichos Pueblos estan amistadas varias Naciones numerosas, de qui
nes se espera la Conversion: y grandes aumentos de esta Mission, con la Rea
Magnifisencia, y Proteccion de su Magestad.

Ad maiorem Dei gloriam

Antonio de Ulloa & Jorge Juan, Spanish Colonial Impressions of Pre-Contact Quito 1735

QVATRO LIBROS.

DE LA NATVRALEZA, Y VIRTVDES DE LAS

plantas, y animales que eſtan receuidos en el vſo de Medicina en la Nueua Eſpaña, y la Methodo, y correccion, y preparacion, que para adminiſtrallas ſe requiere con lo que el Doctor Franciſco Hernandez eſcriuio en lengua Latina.

MVY VTIL PARA TODO GENERO DE gente q̃ viue en eſtãcias y Pueblos, do no ay Medicos, ni Botica.

¶ Traduzido, y aumentados muchos ſimples, y Compueſtos y otros muchos ſecretos curatiuos, por Fr. Franciſco Ximenez, hijo del Conuento de S. Domingo de Mexico, Natural de la Villa de Luna del Reyno de Aragon.

¶ *A Nr̃o R. P. Maeſtro Fr. Hernando Bazan, Prior Prouincial de la Prouincia de Sãctiago de Mexico, de la Orden de los Predicadores,*

1570: Naturalizing Supremacy

In response to the need for systematic communication and information from and across the colonies, the Spanish Empire sponsors physician Francisco Hernández to develop a project involving a systematic exploration and appropriation of geographic, anthropological, and Indigenous knowledge about medicinal plants. All knowledge from the "Geographic Relations Project" is stored in *La Casa de la Contratación de las Indias* in Seville (*House of Trade of the Indies*), an institution established by the Spanish Crown of Castile to impose and secure the royal monopoly on commercial trade across the entire Americas. The claiming of species through classification, identification, and naming will become the subject of considerable controversy and competition between warring scientific empires and colonial classes.

Diego Rivera, *The Arrival of Cortés*, 1951

CORTES
Ca Tenemos
corazón,
con
mal de
enfermedad
ello

Diego Rivera, *The Arrival of Cortés*, 1951

Guaman Poma, *Nueva Cronica y Buen Gobierno*, 1615

1575: Matriarchy & Resistance

Denouncing the atrocities and oppressive injustices of Spanish conquistadors and Jesuit missionaries against Indigenous Peoples of Andean Nations, Kechwan scholar Felipe Guamán Poma de Ayala produces the monumental *Nueva Crónica y Buen Gobierno (New Chronicle & Good Government)* for King Philip II of Spain. The chronicles are an exhaustive 1,200–page volume written in the form of a letter, documents atrocities that specifically target Indigenous families: women and children are torn apart, forced labor imposed, political indoctrination installed, Christian assimilation en masse, cultural practices forbidden, rampant torture, and countless murders. Secretly shared between mother and daughter, traditional knowledge (herbal, medicinal, agricultural) is passed down across generations as an embodied form of resistance, often practiced covertly to transgress colonial prohibitions. Pressing and urgent, Guamán Poma's monumental work however will never be read nor recognized by the monarchy whose atrocities will not only continue but worsen.

Guaman Poma, *Nueva Crónica y Buen Gobierno*, 1615

DON FRAN. DE AROBE. 56.

1599: Subject & Subjugation

Commissioned by Quito colonial official Juan del Barrio de Sepúlveda for the King of Spain Philip III to gloat of his gubernatorial might, the friar-trained Mestizo painter Andrés Sánchez Gallque depicts the supreme sign of cross-continental conquest in the subjugation of Afro-Ecuadorians on the west coast of colonial Latin America on canvas. Simultaneously dressed in royal garb (Spanish-style neck ruff), African hunting gear (spear), and adorned with Incan tradition (gold jewelry, loose poncho) as symbols of nobility, Don Francisco de Arobe, the Governor of a small Ecuadorian coastal town, flanked by his son (Don Pedro) and another young man (Don Domingo) stand as representative emblems of a reluctantly faithful yet fiercely proud patriarch; colonialism on canvas.

DON P.º ZZA S.º
DON

DEAROBE. 56. A
DŌDOMINGO. 18. A
PHILIPPO. 3. CATHOLICO
REGI. HISPANIAR
INDIAR Q DÑO. SVO
DOCTOR. IOÃNES. DEL. BARRIO
A SEPVLVEDA. AVDITOR. SVÆ
CANCELLARIÆ. DEL. QVITO
SVIS EXPENSIS. FIERI.
CVRAVIT
ANNO. 1599
AR SHS. GAL

conserua, y carbon para hale
que tienen se esta referidos, y
del arbol Quinaquina se saca
odorifera y saludable, con su
y reumas de Cabeza, con esta
heridas, y llagas, y el mismo
de sus pepitas, y es con mas effic
hermoso, y su madera muy o
blanca, o leonado a vetas. ~

1628: Errata, Quina-Quina?

A mysterious tree of the Andes whose bark (known to cure fevers) is the object of intrigue and missionary expeditions, but first becomes subject of mistaken identity. In the early 17th century, another species is incorrectly identified by Spanish explorers as 'fever tree.' Confusion dates back to the early work of Carmelite Fray Antonio Vásquez de Espinoza whose treatise on the *Quina-Quina* plant claims its bark can cure fevers and other ills. As it turns out, 'Quina-Quina' is actually the Kechwan name for an entirely different though morphologically similar plant: the *Peruvian Balsam* (later used by the Holy Chrism of the Church in America). Completely ineffective, no one will be cured from malarial fevers from the collected bark of Quina-Quina for centuries to come as a result of this ongoing dendrologic error and semantic mistake up until and into the 20th century. The other species still remains evasive.

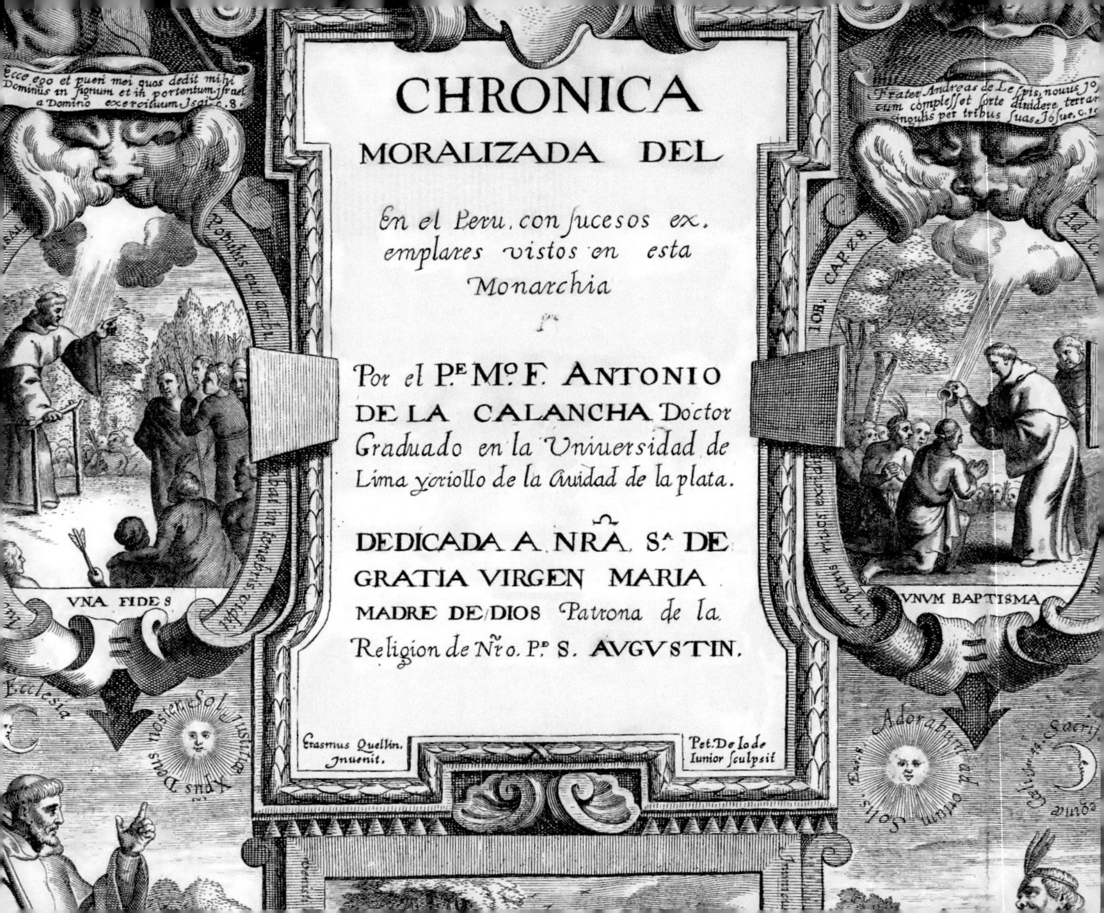

CHRONICA
MORALIZADA DEL
En el Peru, con sucesos ex.
emplares vistos en esta
Monarchia
Por el P.e M.o F. ANTONIO
DE LA CALANCHA Doctor
Graduado en la Uniuersidad de
Lima y criollo de la Ciudad de la plata.
DEDICADA A NRA. S.a DE
GRATIA VIRGEN MARIA
MADRE DE DIOS Patrona de la
Religion de Nro. P.o S. AVGVSTIN.
Ecce ego et pueri mei quos dedit mihi Dominus in signum et in portentum Israel a Domino exercituum Isai. c. 8.
VNA FIDES
VNVM BAPTISMA
Erasmus Quellin. Inuenit.
Pet. De Iode Iunior sculpsit

1633: Wonder Drug? Miracle Plant?

In the next decades and centuries, and following the first arrival of Jesuits in the administrative capital of Quito around 1586, Friar Antonio de la Calancha writes during his travels across South America in his *Chronicles of St. Augustine* in the early decades of the 17th century: "of a tree which they call the *fever tree* whose bark made into a powder—amounting to the weight of two small silver coins—and given as a beverage, cures fevers and tertians." Speculation across imperial scientific communities about this miracle cure and mystery tree sets off campaigns of scientific exploration and botanical expeditions programs across the colonial territories of the Andes and the Amazon that will endure for centuries.

1637: Territorial Dispossession

At the height of Europe's so-called *Scientific Revolution*, Kechwa Peoples living across Incan lands of the Central Andes are brutally forced out of their territory, pushed away from their resources, and tricked by the Jesuits. The missionaries make it their mission to steal medicinal plant knowledge specifically about a fever tree, a plant (yet to be named by Europeans in spite of widespread knowledge of its efficacy by Kechwa Peoples in the Andes and Amazonas for multiple millennia) whose precious bark contains a rare alkaloid later to be named and identified as quinine, the only medical solution and cure to Europe's rampant spread of malaria.

1638: Hoax, or Appropriation?

In the so-called first recorded account of the European use of quinine—known then as the *Countess' Powder*—the life of the Countess of Chinchón (named after a town in Spain's Capital of Madrid), the wife of Spanish Viceroy Luis Jerónimo de Cabrera is reportedly saved. Medication comes on the recommendation of a miracle drug from the Loja Region, called the region of rivers, Kechwan territory of the Saraguro Peoples in the Central Andes of Peru (now southern Ecuador). Like the myth and lie of this story that becomes colonial legend (that still persists into the 21st century), the theft and appropriation of sacred knowledge from traditional healers—*Hampiyachakkuna* (kechwa for "wise keeper of medicinal knowledge") or *Yurakhampiyachak* ("knowledge keeper of healing plants")—begins its journey across the colonial empire of Spain and to the Holy See at the Vatican.

Pope Urban VIII & Cardinal Juan de Lugo, 1625–1633

1640: Pope, Power, Powder

Spanish Jesuit Juan de Lugo y Quiroga, Cardinal to then Pope Urban VIII, champions *quinine* (reportedly with the aid of Jesuit Barnabé Cobo) as a miracle cure of malarial fevers. In spite of widespread anti-Catholic sentiment and Protestant resistance across Europe, official dosages of the bark extract held by the Catholics—"devil's powder" to Protestants—are listed in the 1649 *Schedula Romana*. An exponent of Jesuit Missions, the Pope had issued a few years earlier in 1638 the papal bull *Commissum Nobis* to regulate missionary work in South America while breaking up its monopoly in China and Japan.

Vicente Albán, *Señora Principal con su Negra Esclava*, 1783

1648: Black Labor Extraction

Following the first ship of enslaved persons in 1533 off the Pacific shores of Ecuador, exploitation of Black labor forced to settle in the Provinces of Esmeraldas and Imbabura along rivers Chota and Mira reaches its height in the 17th century with nearly 2 million West Africans taken and stolen from their homelands. For the next 300 years, African slaves are forced into lives of hard labor and servitude to the dominant, albeit minority Spanish colonial elite of Criollos. In spite of abolition in 1851, Afro-Ecuadorians will continue to suffer from extreme forms of economic and racial injustices for nearly four more centuries, pressed under the thumb of plantation owners and their descendants, now visibly exploited by merchants and traders in big cities like Guayaquil and Quito, as well as Ibarra.

1648: Midwifery & Resistance

Seeking to free herself from slavery that began in 1553 off the coast of Esmeraldas, Afro-Ecuadorian María del Tránsito Sorroza fights for her emancipation and is granted freedom from slavery using her ancestral knowledge as a midwife to build a small community in the Port City of Guayaquil. Nicknamed *Manos de Seda* (*silk hands*) for her unique ability to attend to complicated deliveries, the revered midwife purchases enslaved or abandoned Afro-descendant girls to, in turn, grant them freedom and share with them her great knowledge and ability in ancestral medicine. Pathways of liberation are charted towards better lives for young Afro-Ecuadorian women while ensuring the preservation of maternal knowledge, where guardians of the art of midwifery can nurture future generations. But it would take another two centuries before slavery is abolished in Ecuador (1852) and another three and a half centuries before Afro-Ecuadorian communities begin to repatriate rights to ancestral lands through *Circunscripciones Territoriales Afroecuatorianas* in 1998.

1648: Tricks & Traps

Secret operations and targeted missions are initiated by *The Society of Jesus* (c.1540) in search of the elusive cure for bad fevers, a plague that haunted the seat of the Catholic Church and Italy as a whole, ever since the fall of the Roman Empire. "To dare the vile contagion of the night," as Shakespeare recounted in *The Tragedy of Julius Caesar* (1599), "and tempt the rheumy and unpurged air." Through overt Christianization missions, the bark of the notorious *fever tree* is covertly extracted from Kechwan territories in the Andean mountains by Jesuit missionary envoys such as Padres Venegas and Messia. Appropriated and swindled by the black robes, bark from the forests of Loja is packed, bundled, and routed to Spain and other European destinations via port cities like Payta in Peru and Guayaquil in Ecuador. No known compensation from the Spanish Monarchy nor acknowledgment from the Holy See is made to the traditional knowledge bearers from Kechwan Nations that make the so-called discovery of the bark by the Jesuit missionaries possible; a form of corporate dispossession that would persist for centuries.

Debret & Motte, *Sauvages Civilises & Soldats Indiens Ramenant des Sauvages Prisonnières*, 1839

ITALIA
HISPANIA
EGO AVTEM SICVT OLIVA FRVCTIFERA IN DOMO DEI.
Psal. 51.
Pater Iohannes Nugnesius
Pater Franciscus Borgia
Robertus Bell.
P. Euerard,
P. Claudi. Aquaviva

1650: Jesuit's Bark

Quinine, the active ingredient in the bark extract of the *fever tree* that will be isolated later in the 20th century, is identified as this potent substance by *The Society of Jesus*. Its new, assigned name is a conflation of territory and property: *Jesuit's Bark*. Promoting themselves as carriers of good morals and civilized knowledge, the Society of Jesus is the first incarnation of the modern corporation masquerading under the dubious banner of humility and benevolence that is Psalm 52:8, "ego autem, sicut oliva fructifera in domo Dei" ("I am like a green olive tree in the House of God"). As precursors of predatory corporate practice, the financialized organization of Jesuits weaponizes religious Christian ideology in order to access, assimilate, and extract resources from foreign lands. Their work is cloaked in political secrecy and scientific elitism, operating throughout the colonial world prior to the official colonizing campaigns of conquistadors; missionaries dressed in black and brown bearing the ultimate symbol of God-fearing might: the Holy Christian Cross.

Sanctus Pater IGNATIUS de Loiola Societatis IESV Fundator, et Generalis primus
Societas IESV á 1538. in cepta primum a Paulo III. ac deni a Successorib. SS.PP. approbatur Confirmatur privilegiis donatur á Conc. Trid. Comendatur
IHS
DEUS Pater Commendat filio suo IGNATIUM & socios unde origo appellationis societatis IESV.
S. Pater Franciscus Xaverius unus ex decem primis Patribus Indiæ & Iaponicæ Apostolus.
P. Alphonsus Salmeronius ex primis X.
NOMEN DOMINI IN OMNI
Arbitramur Idem Abbas super nubem tamen in eo quod candidam signari Iustorum cui datum sit perfecte Sabere linguam eruditam ad Evangelizandum in arcam Domini ultimam messem Et hi Viri Viro Christi et Apostolorum servantium Vitam Christi ibidem. Rut. Benzon ibidem.
BRASILIÆ Socy 280
Reg. Sinarum Socy 30.
PHILIPINÆ Socy 100.
MEXICANÆ Socy 340.
IAPONIÆ Socy 130
GRANATENSIS Socy 100
Peraquaviæ Socy 116
PERUANÆ Socy 370.
MALABARICÆ Socy 150.
GOANÆ Socy 280.
INDIA
LITHVANIÆ Socy 336
POLONIA Socy 859
BELGICA
Gallo-Belg. Socy 652
Flandro-Belgicæ Socy 617
Austriæ Socy 553
Germaniæ Superior Socy 546
GERMANIA
Franciæ So. 358
Tolosanæ Socy 310
Campaniæ Socy 226
Aquitaniæ

A SOLIS ORI
FORVM
EGO AVTEM SICVT OLIVA FRVCTIFERA IN DOMO DEI.
Psal. 51.
HISPANIA
ITALIA
LVSITANIÆ
Castel lanæ
Toletanæ
Sardinia
Siculæ
Venetæ
Neapolitana
Mediolanensis
Romana
Franciscus Toletus Cardinalis.
Robertus Bellarminus Cardinalis Archiepiscopus Capuanus.
Pater Iohannes Nugnesius Æthiopiæ Patriarcha primus.
P.Pater Franciscus Borgia Dux Gandiæ Generalis III.
P. Claudi. Aquaviva Ducis Atriæ filius Gn. V.
In tibi, benevole lector, arborem fructiferam, cum primis fœcundatam et dilatatam, oculisq. exhibentem India et progressum Doma

1663: Rumors & Murmurs

In one of the first written accounts about the uses of Jesuit's Bark in Latin America, Genoese physician Sebastiano Bado describes that the bark is not only well known but also used extensively by Indigenous Peoples throughout the Loja Region in the Ecuadorian Andes to cure febrile diseases, including malaria. Future scholarship will locate Loja as the geographic and historic center of the region's long tradition of Indigenous medicinal knowledge, practiced by *Curanderos* (*healers*) and *Yerbateras* (*herbalists*) in the Loja Region. Nevertheless, boastful claims are made in the 900 pages of testimonials and extensive description of miraculous recoveries filling the pages of Bado's tome. Suspiciously, one of its most often repeated: "Peruvian bark as greater than gold, or silver, to civilization." In scientific circles, Dr. Bado's claims become an often-repeated refrain befittingly capturing the riches of a distant land and the remedial romance of the fever tree, as if to create interest and speculation about the plant and to raise capital for more colonial campaigns from the captive audience of Jesuits and Spanish Royalty: "Peru keeps it in her arms, how very rich the bark of her trees."

71. CINCHONA.

QUINQUINA. *Condam. Act. paris.* 1738.

Loc: Loxa Peruviæ.

PHARM: CHINÆ Cortex ℥j. *Essentia*

QUAL: tenacissime amara.

VIS: carnes amaritie inficiens, roborans, ~~sublaxan~~

USUS: Febres criticæ, Anorexia, Calculus, Oe

Hysteria.

COMP:

Carl Linnaeus, *Materia Medica*, First Notes on Cinchona, 1747

1663: Errata, <u>C</u>inchona or <u>Ch</u>inchona?

In Carl Linnaeus' 1753 *Species Plantarum*, the world-renowned Swedish botanist will immortalize the name "Cinchona" for the "fever tree" species, a misspelled derivative from the legendary Countess of Chinchón, allegedly cured by the miraculous bark extract. The species name will be picked up from Sebastiano Bado's 1663 account in his *Anastasis Corticis Peruviae* that honors yet deceptively perpetuates the Countess' tale. Not until the mid 20th century, does the scientific and historical communities prove that Dr. Bado's account was incorrect and that, in fact, the story is fake. As it turns out, the Countess of Chinchón never traveled to Latin America, let alone to Peru. She never even suffered from malaria. In Bado's own confusion between Italian and Spanish orthography, he nevertheless omits the "h" in "Chinchón," a mistake that will prove to be irreversible. Thanks to the widespread scientific authority of Linnean taxonomic nomenclature, the Latin genus of the plant belonging to the Rubiaceae family of flowering plants is entrenched as *Cinchona*. The nomenclature will remain, as it is today, an epistemic, etymological metaphor for the blatant colonial error and scientific lie serving to mask any and all Indigenous cosmologies from the Andes.

DE
CINA CINA,
SEV
PVLVERE AD FEBRES
Syntagma Phyſiologicum.

AVCTORE

GAVDENTIO BRVNACIO
Doctore Romano.

Ad Illuſtriſs. & Excellentiſs. Dominum
ANTONIVM BERNARDVM
D. Marci Procuratorem Meritiſſimum.

Gaudentio Brunacio, *De Cina Cina seu Pulvere ad Febres*, 1661

ANASTASIS CORTICIS PERVVIÆ,

SEV

CHINÆ CHINÆ

DEFENSIO,

SEBASTIANI BADI GENVENSIS

Patrij vtriuſque Noſochomij olim Medici,

Et

Publicæ Sanitatis in Ciuitate Conſultoris.

Contrà

VENTILATIONES

IOANNIS IACOBI CHIFLETII,

GEMITVSQVE

VOPISCI FORTVNATI PLEMPII,

Illuſtrium Medicorum.

Opus in tres libros diſtinctum, & in eis Documenta

Sebastiani Badi, *Anastasis Corticis Peruuiae, seu Chinae Chinae defensio*, 1663

Henri Testelin, *King Louis XIV at the Academy of Sciences* (detail), 1666–1667

1679: State Secrets

On the recommendation of King Charles II of England, King Louis XIV of France finds a new supply source of Cinchona bark to break up the global monopoly held by the Jesuits while also receiving the secret pharmacological formula for preparing the quinine solution from the King's physician, Dr. Robert Talbor. France in turn becomes the northern trade epicenter of all quinine products for the next century until the bark is over-harvested in the Loja Region and explosive demands from Europe lead to more forceful and more extractive measures by colonial powers in the coming century.

Henri Testelin, *King Louis XIV at the Academy of Sciences* (detail), 1666–1681

POËME DU QUINQUINA.

A MADAME LA DUCHESSE DE BOUILLON.

CHANT PREMIER.

E ne voulois chanter que les Heros d'Eſope.
Pour eux ſeuls en mes Vers j'invoquois Calliope.
Meſme j'allois ceſſer, & regardois le port.

Jean de la Fontaine, *Poëme du Quinquina*, 1682

1682: Rush

In reference to the extremely valuable nature of the Cinchona bark (also referenced here as *Quina*) throughout European Empires and their growing colonies, Colombian Professor of Medicine Jaime Jaramillo-Arango proposes in his 1949 book on the *Basic Facts in the History of Cinchona* "that the discovery of Quina was far more valuable than the treasures that the Spaniards were so anxiously searching for in the New World, treasures upon which, we could add, by one of fate's ironies, the conquistadores were never able to lay their hands." Citing Jean La Fontaine's illustrious poem, *Le Poème du Quinquina (The Poem of the Cinchona)*, is of particular relevance: "Cent machines sur l'onde, Promenaient l'avarice en tous les coins du monde: L'or entouré d'écueils avait des poursuivants; Nos mains l'allaient chercher au sein de sa patrie, Le Quina vint s'offrir à nous en même temps. Plus digne mille fois de notre idolâtrie." "Driven by greed, hundreds gathered from around the world, in pursuit of a cursed gold. Reaching into the depths of empire, Quina manifests itself to us, all in the same time, more worthy and honorable than our own self-adulation."

FEBRIS
Simplex
Putrida
Continua
Intermittens
Remittens
Subintrans
Periodica
Erratica
Quartana
Tertiana
Proporcionata
Continens
Essentialis
Officialis
Privata
Com pli cata
Solitaria
Comitata
Lactea
Alba
Fixa
Vaga
Synochus
Ephemera
Maligna
Benigna
Complicata
Hemi tri tæus.
Quotidiana
Terciana
Quartana
Duplex
Triplex
Simplex
Acuta
Causon
Assodes
Helodes
Hectica
Lenta
Verminosa
Scorbutica
Venerea
Ulcerosa
Pustulosa
Tabida
Cachectica
Secundaria
Primaria
Quas jugulat Cortex in Ramis Cortice tectis
Inspicias Febres. Quas jugulare nequit
In deliberatis. Media quæ sorte fruuntur
Dimidio obductus Cortice Ramus habet
LIGNUM FEBRIUM.

1712: Fever Tree

Preempting the sciences of systemic botany, pharmacology, and biochemistry, the famous Italian physician Francesco Torti illustrates the growing understanding of the diversity of fevers, each one corresponding in various ways to different treatments composed and formulated from different bark species. In his now-classic treatise, *Therapeutice Specialis*, Torti's graphic illustration of the "Tree of Fevers" (*Lignum Febrium*) maps out the range of therapeutic trials that are needed for different bark species. While considerable attention and space is granted throughout the 700-page volume to the various forms and types of fevers found to be treatable by the *Peruvian Bark* (*Cortex Peruviae*) as seen on the left side of his "febris" diagram, only one mention is made of the fever tree's (palo de las calenturas) provenance in the distant, colonial hinterlands of Spain: the region of Loja (Loxa). With the widespread distribution of Torti's treatise across Europe, rampant campaigns and expeditions in search of the miracle bark would continue until the near exhaustion of Cinchona trees in the region during the next century.

Mapa del Partido de Vilcabamba (Loja), 1735–178

1735: Race to the Equator

While measuring the arc of the equatorial meridian in Latin America to determine the shape of the Earth on a westward journey from Martinique on the Atlantic Coast to what is now Ecuador on the Pacific Coast (via Saint-Domingue, Panama, and Colombia), the French colonial explorer, mathematician, and naturalist Charles Marie de La Condamine will abandon his royal geographic survey team (after years of discord and internal dissent) and will soon return eastward traveling down the course of a massive river system towards French Guiana. Before setting sail across the Amazon River, La Condamine makes a detour to Lima (Peru) to collect funds for his return journey to France but, along the way, he ends up fulfilling the mission's unofficial and unintentional objective for the King: he crosses paths with and collects seeds and seedlings from the now-famed 'fever tree' called *Cinchona* in the Andean region of Loja. Located in the southern part of current-day Ecuador, in mid-altitudes of the Andes, the millennial-old pathways that La Condamine travels on will soon lead through the area of Vilcabamba, 'land of the sacred trees.'

ſemble, que les obſervations faites à Aléxandrie, ne prouvent aucunement que la hauteur du Pole ait changé, ou, du moins, que les obſervations de Ptolomée ne ſont pas ſuffiſantes pour décider cette queſtion.

SUR L'ARBRE DU QUINQUINA

Par Mr. DE LA CONDAMINE*.

MON voyage de *Quito* à *Lima* ayant été jugé néceſſaire pour les affaires de la Com-

* 29 Mai 1737.

1738: Science of Erasure

Widely celebrated by the Royal Academy of Sciences in France, Charles Marie de La Condamine's commemorative book on the Cinchona plant, *Sur l'Arbre du Quinquina* (*On the Quina-Quina Tree*, in reference to the term designating the bark) receives instant recognition upon his return to Paris and publication of his findings. However, when La Condamine previously traveled to Malacatos in the southern Loja Region to study Cinchona trees, he had no ability at all to correctly identify the species. Completely and violently omitting the sources of his botanical knowledge originating from Mestizo guide (and likely herbalist) Fernando de la Vega and his close relations with the Saraguro Peoples of Loja (traditional Kechwan communities in the South Central Andes), La Condamine claims all the knowledge from these natural worlds to himself.

C
B
b
C
C
C
C
B
B
C
D
D
D
D
D

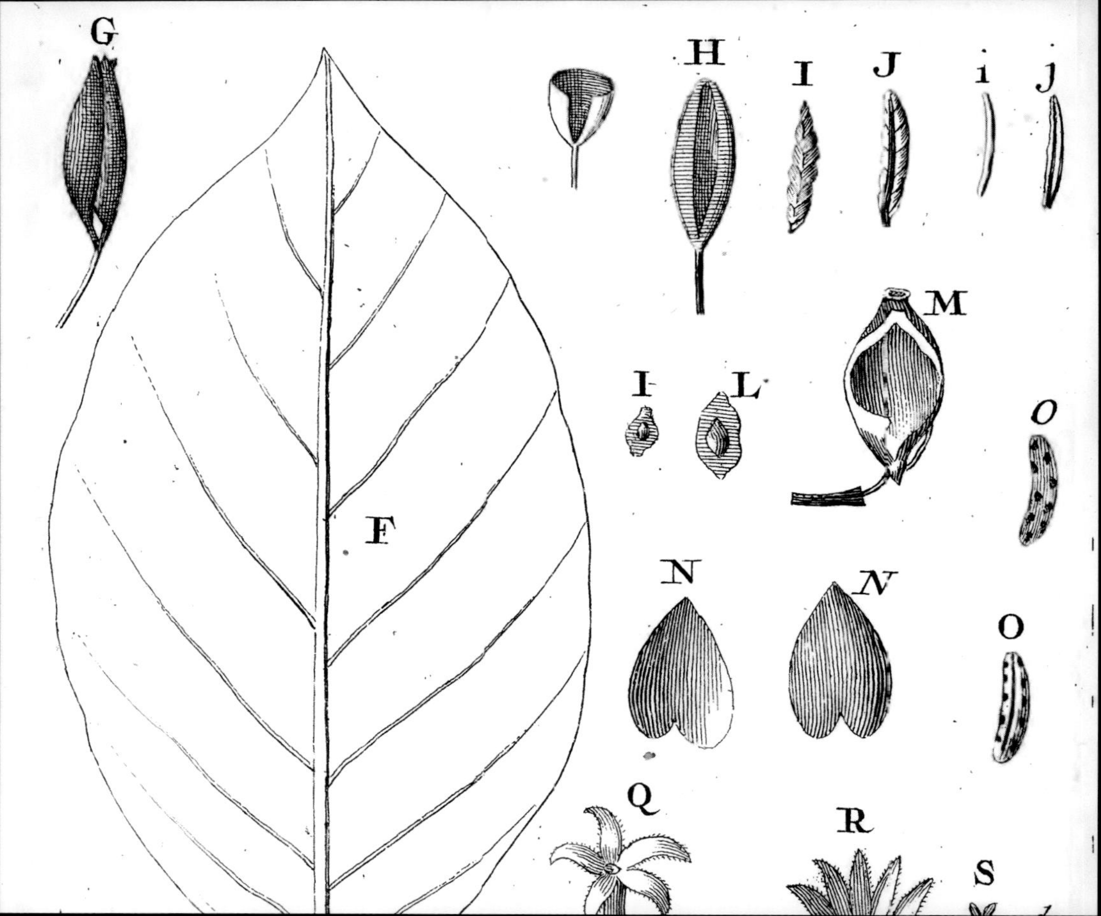

Charles Marie de La Condamine, *Sur l'Arbre du Quinquina*, 1738

1738: Errata, Quinquina?

In July 1738, La Condamine's work *Sur l'Arbre du Quinquina* is not only read but revered by the French Royal Academy of Sciences. La Condamine suggests the name is derived from Kechwan term *Quina-ai*, meaning *cape* or *shawl*... a word from an old 1614 Kechwan dictionary from Lima (Peru). Under the pretense of a "very limited vocabulary of the Kechwan language," La Condamine argues that the term *Quina-ai* was analogical, referring to what covers or wraps the tree (eg. *bark*) in the same way that a cape covers a body. In a later rebuttal of La Condamine's facts and of Haggis' later revisionism in 1941, Colombian scholar Jaime Jaramillo Arango counter-argues in 1949 (note here that "Quichua" refers to "Kechwa"): "To come back to La Condamine, he must have felt wherein lay the weak point of his argument, for he excuses it by asserting that the *Quichua vocabulary* was very limited.

In judging the Indians incapable of assigning an individual and distinctive term to the Balsam Tree, Haggis by implication follows him in this. As a matter of interest, we have personally computed the number of words in Fray Juan Martinez's "Quichua Vocabulary:" it contains 5,008 words. And that of Father Diego Gonzalez Holguin from the Company of Jesus, also edited in the *City of the Kings* (Lima) in 1608 by Francisco del Canto, contains some 12,000. The average vocabulary of a well-educated Englishman contains some 5,000 words; of a writer or professor some 10,000 words; basic English is founded on 850; and English has one of the richest vocabularies in the world. From this comparison it will be manifestly seen that the inferences of La Condamine and of Haggis, implicating paucity of Quichua vocabulary, have no real weight nor basis."

Mappa Geographica
exhibens
Provincias, Oppida, Sacella &c
quæ Mensibus Novembri ac Decembri
anni 1751 et Januario Februario
et Martio anni 1752 peragravit
ad Indorum Chilensium terras
excurrens P. Bernardus
Havestadt è Soc. JESU
Missionarius.

Liûcura
5
V. Diarium
Grùleuvu
6
7
Tocuman fl.
8
Caicaien
loca periculosissima
Rutuhue
V. Dia
Uñodquin
Pire Vutan
Mapu
La Laxa V. de
3
Callaqui
Lolco
Viltucura
Cura
Mah
5
10
20
Leucæ 3000 passuum

1740: Maps, Missions, Missionaries

Conceived by Portuguese ruling monarchies in their quest to assimilate by Christianizing Muslims of the East, the so-called "Civilizing Mission" of the imperial project (starting with Portugal and Spain and evolving to France and Britain), becomes the central policy and underlying ideological framework at the onslaught of colonization and conquest of foreign lands—*terra incognita* as the Vatican dubbed it. Equating what Aimé Césaire referred to in his 1950 *Discours sur le Colonialisme* as the false equivalencies of *Christian pedantry*: "Christianity = civilization, paganism = savagery." The projection of civilization through culture and science (art, literature, math, chemistry) by evangelical missionaries is the assimilation project of Indigenous Peoples in plain sight as the so-called European gift to the 'savages' of the world.

Fig: 1:

Tab: 2:

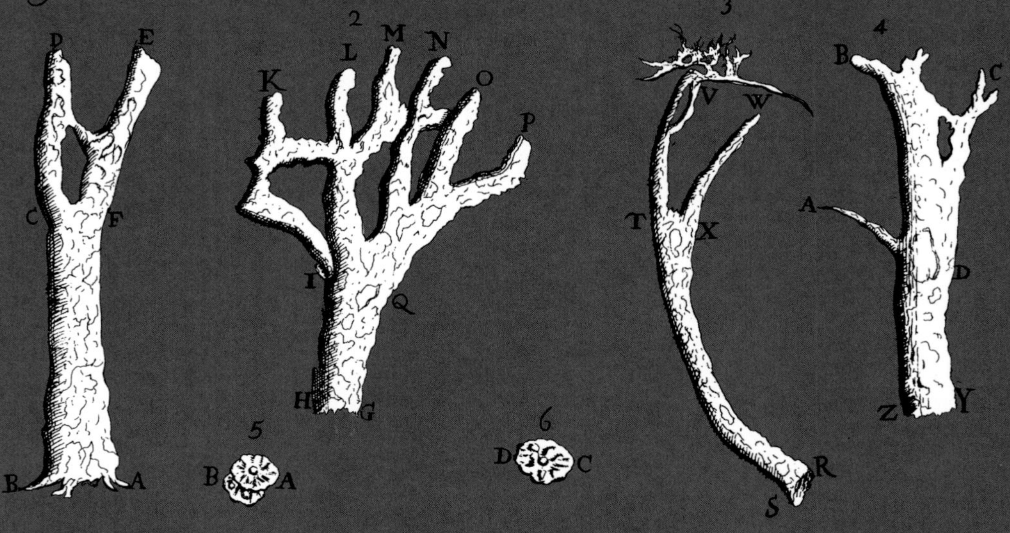

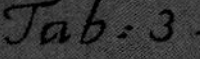

Fig: 1.

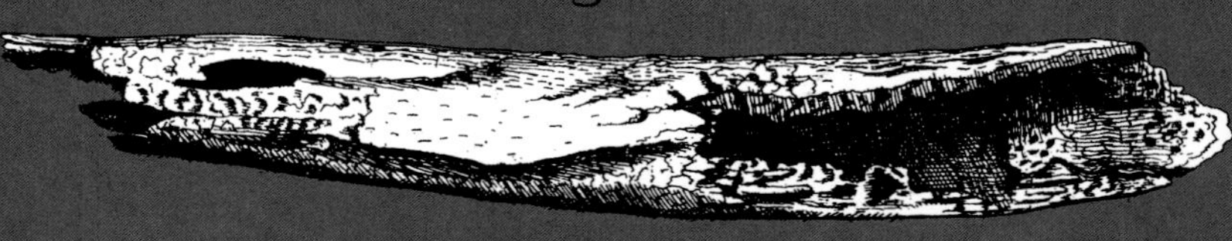

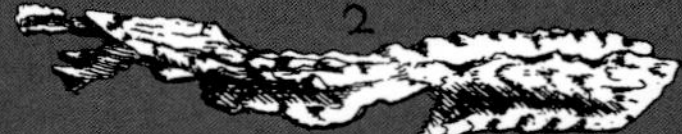

1742: Maiming by Naming

Swedish naturalist Carl Linnaeus names *Cinchona v. officinalis* in honor of the Spanish Viceroy's wife, the Countess of Chinchón, who reportedly was cured of malaria by the plant taken from the Curanderos, originating from Kechwa territory up in the Andes, back in the 1630s. That myth is a factual error that will be passed down to generations across the following centuries. Although that blatant imperial lie will be hotly debated as well as contested by a handful of Cinchona historians and quinologists in the mid 20th century, Linnaeus' taxonomic nomenclature will remain in place. Given the opportunistic, affirmative, imperial lineage of the Cinchona, the Spanish State (or the Spanish Academy of scientists and scholars) will avoid the revocation or revision of that faulty nomenclature and false narrative well into the 21st century.

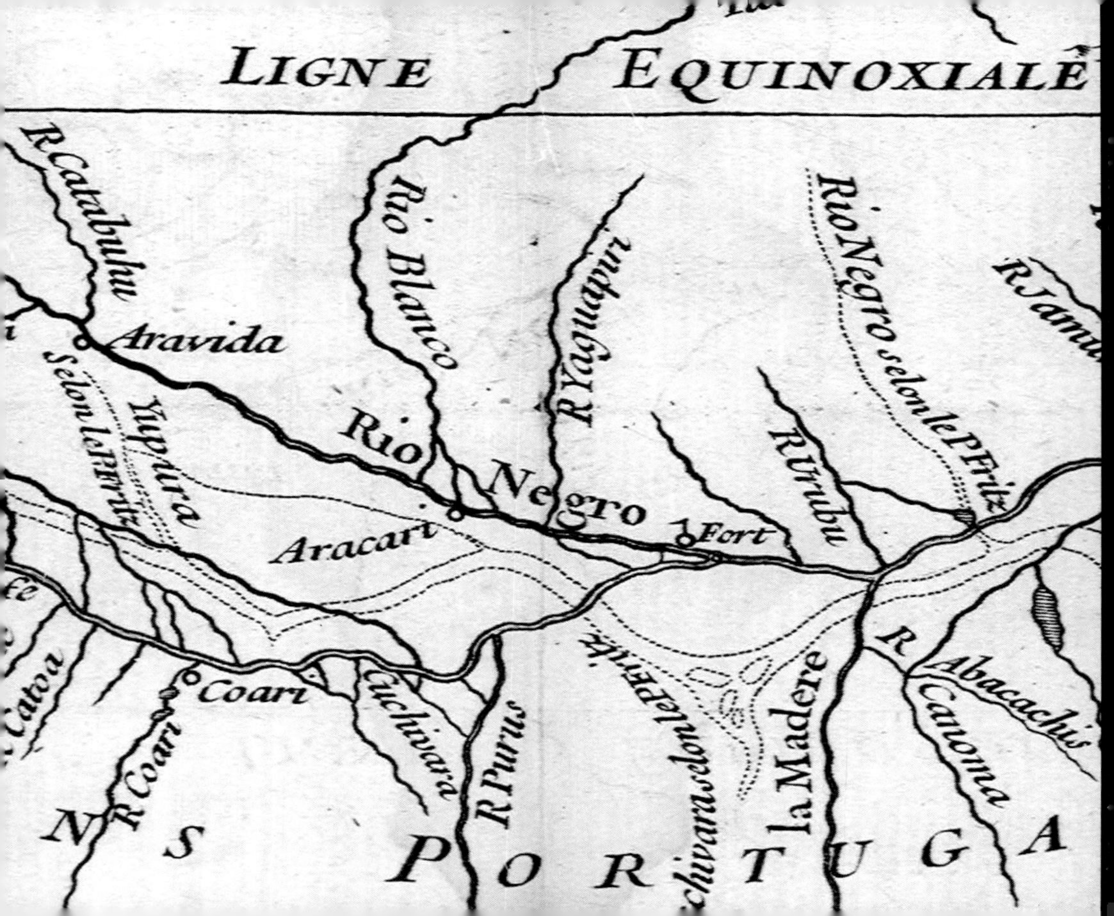

LIGNE EQUINOXIALE

R. Catabuhu

Rio Blanco

R. Yaguapiri

Rio Negro selon le P. Fritz

R. Jamu

Aravida

Yupura

Selon le P. Fritz

Rio Negro

Aracari

Fort

R. Urubu

R. Abacachis

R. Canoma

Coari

R. Coari

Catoa

Cuchivara

R. Purus

Cuchivara selon le P. Fritz

la Madere

N S

PORTUGA

1743: Amazonia

A century after the establishment of evangelical missions in the Province of Quito, Spanish and Portuguese explorers *cursed by the hunger for gold* (*auri sacra fames*) overcome the seemingly impenetrable landscape of massive river systems. Missionary expeditions map out a more manageable identity for dueling hydrographic missions of Franciscans and Jesuits: *The Amazon River*, or more accurately *Amazonas (Amazonia)*. Part-river, part-forest, part-passage, part-territory, part-myth, the singularity of 'the' Amazon registers almost irreversibly on the colonial imagination of explorers, merchants, and settlers. La Condamine's fluvial memory of Amazonian voyages between 1743 and 1744 defines the colonial map on which the imperial imagination and colonial gaze of Europeans imprints itself for the next three centuries.

CARTE DU COURS DU MARAGNON OU DE L

Dans sa partie navigable depuis Jaen de Bracamoros jusqu'à son Embouchure et qui comprend

Levée en 1743 et 1744 et assujettie aux Observations Astr

Augmentée du Cours de la Riviére Noire et d'autres détails tirés de div

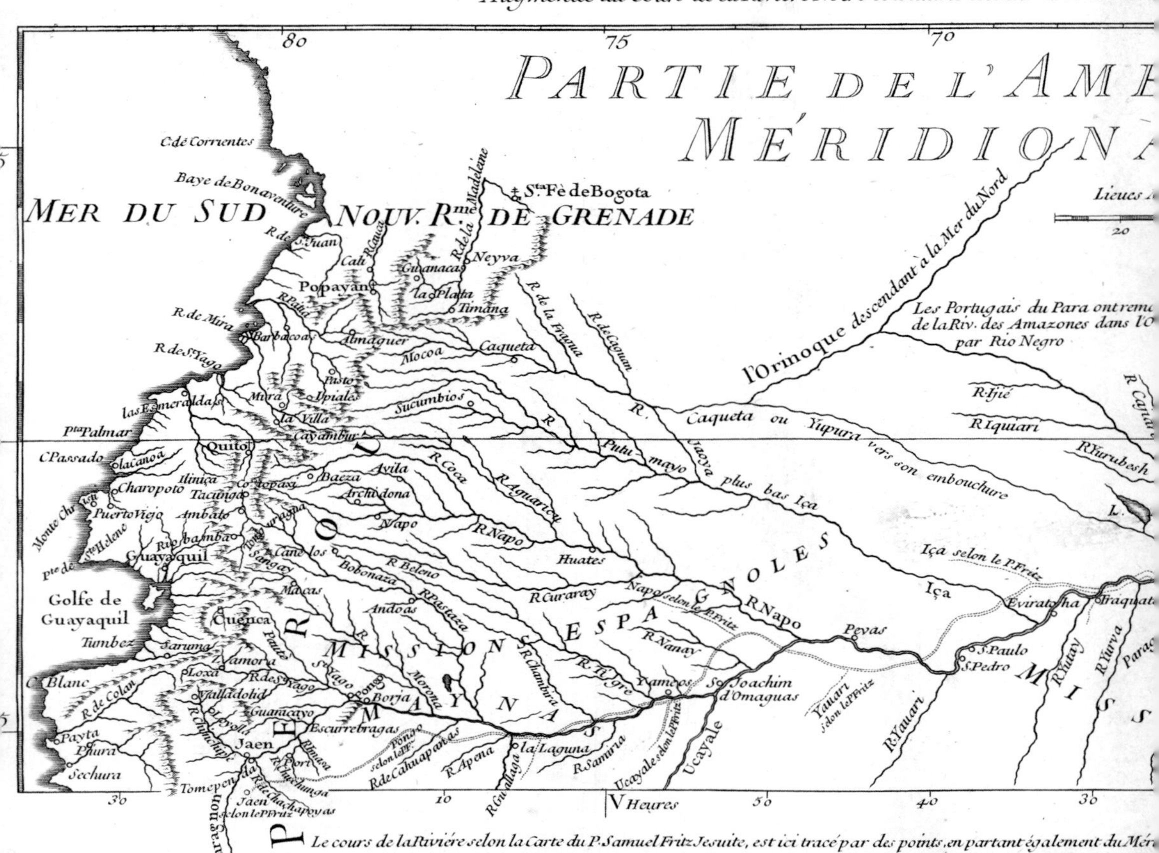

NDE RIVIERE DES AMAZONES

QUITO, et la Côte de la GUIANE depuis le Cap de Nord jusqu'à Essequebè

ar M. DE LA CONDAMINE de l'Ac. R[le] des Sc.

outiers manuscrits de Voyageurs modernes .

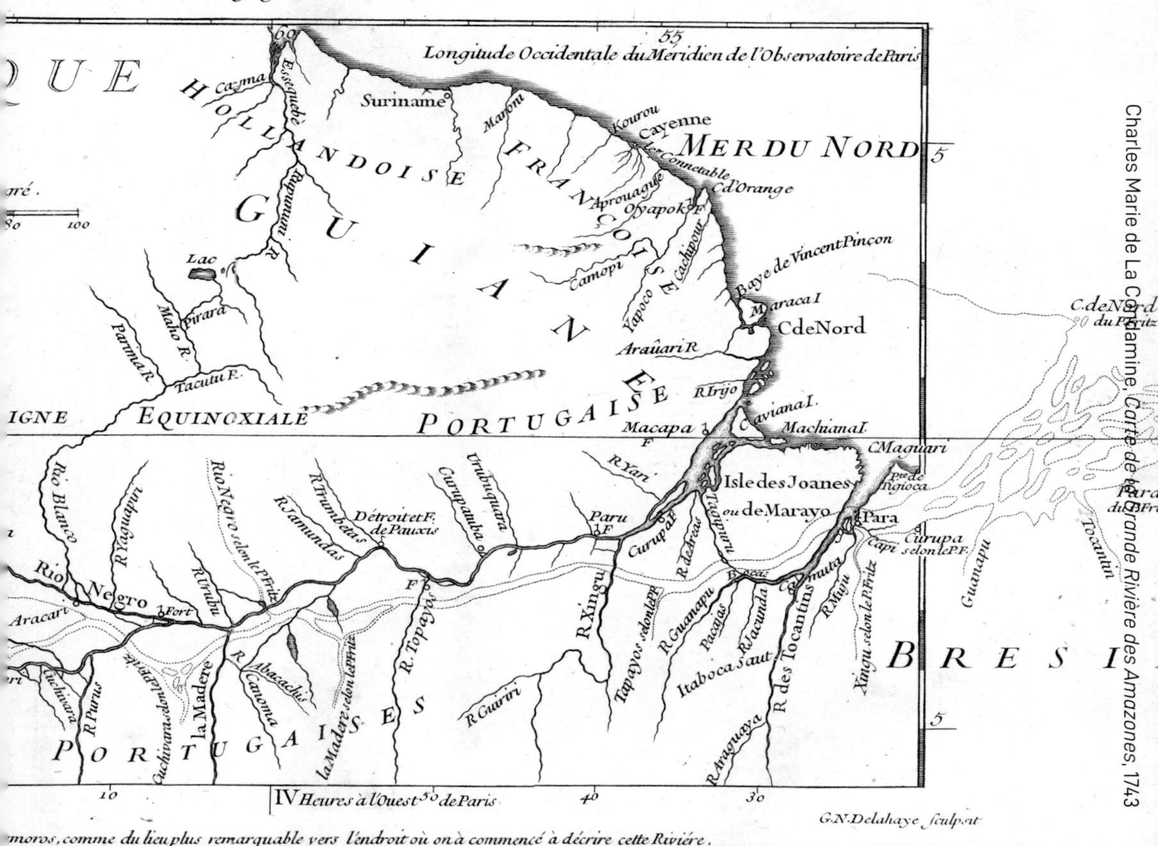

Charles Marie de La Condamine, *Carte de la Grande Rivière des Amazones*, 1743

MAPA

Que comprende todo el distrito de la

AUDIENCIA DE QUITO

En que se manifiesta con la maior individualidad Los Pueblos y Naciones barbaras que hay por el Rio Marañon y demas que en el entran

Para acompañar

A la Descripcion del nuebo Obispado que se proyecta en

MAYNAS

Construido

De Orden del Sr. Dn. Josef García de Leon y Pizarro Presidte. Regte. Comandte. y Visitador Gral. de la misma Audiencia

Por Dn. Francisco Requena Yngeniero Ordinario Governador de Maynas y Primer Comisario de Limites

el Año de 1779

Caracteres de este MAPA

- Curato
- Anejo
- Naciones de Gentiles
- \+ Poblaciones antiguas de Españoles destruidas.
- Fortalezas.
- Cº Cabo.
- Pta. Punta.
- Y. Ysla.
- R. Rio
- C. Ciudad.
- O. Obispado.
- ⚓ Embarcaderos en los Rios
- .... Caminos

Nota

La longitud de este Mapa se deve contar desde el Meridiano de Quito que se ve en el trazado, y cada grado de Veinte legs. de a 2840 Tuesas cada una, que hazen 56800 ts. por el Valor de los grados en el Equador segun las ultimas observaciones y estando como estan los que este Mapa contiene inmediatos a la Linea Equinoccial se les deve dar esta medida de esta suerte cada legua de la de veinte y cinco a grado debe baler 2272 Tuesas yguales a 5301 baras y un pie y de las leguas de Ordenanza de a 5000 baras

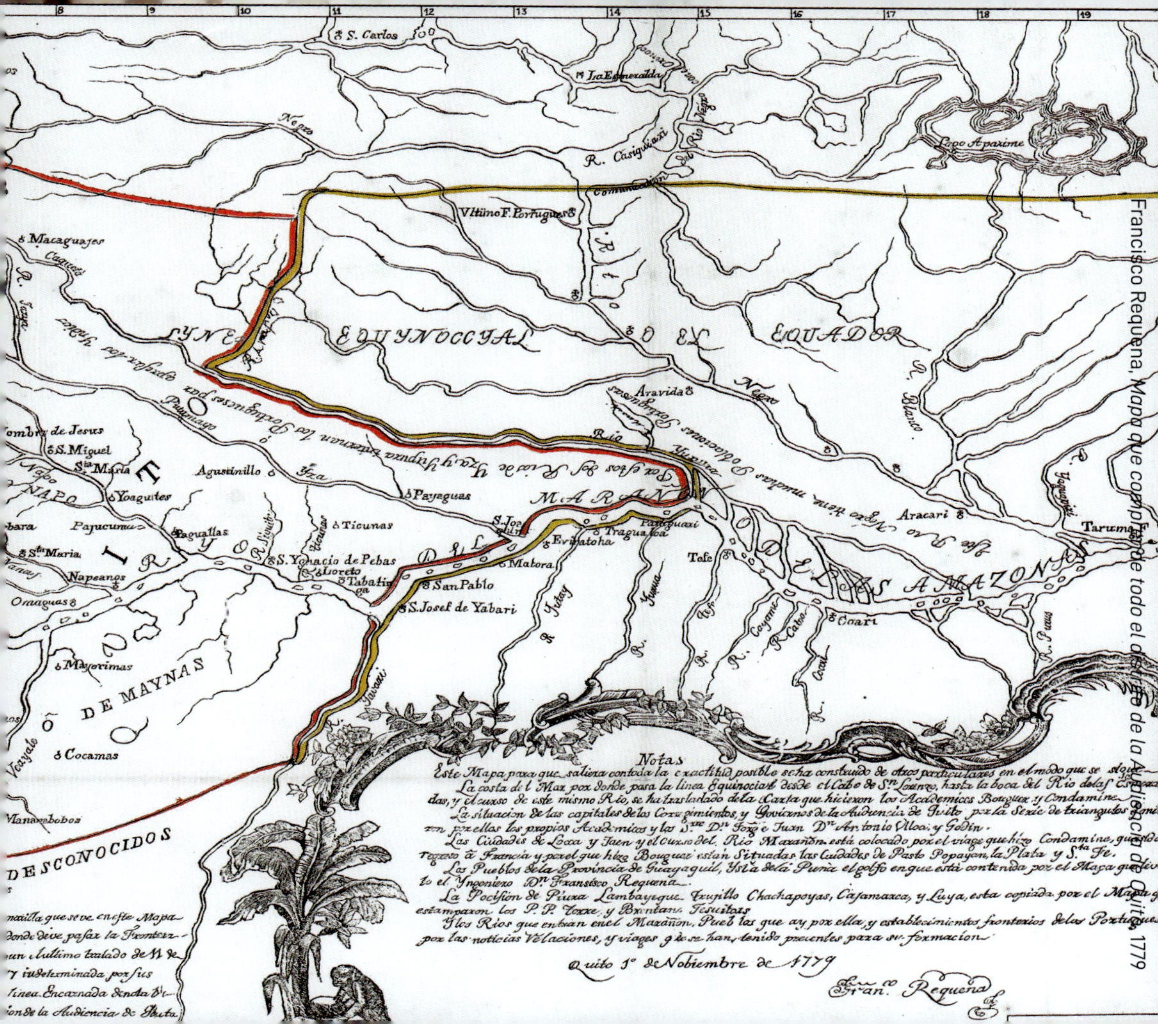

Francisco Requena, Mapa que comprende todo el distrito de la Audiencia de Quito 1779

COLECCION

DEL REAL DECRETO

DE 27. DE FEBRERO DE 1767.

PARA LA EGECUCION

del Estrañamiento de los Regulares de la Compañia, cometido por S. M. al Excmo. Señor Conde de Aranda, como Presidente del Consejo: de las Instrucciones, y Ordenes succesivas dadas por S. E. en el cumplimiento; y de la Real Pragmática Sancion de 27. de Marzo, en fuerza de Ley, para su observancia.

Año 1767.

1750: Preservation as Appropriation

The Spanish Crown officially claims and declares the bark of the Cinchona plant as a "natural resource of the empire." The monarchy invokes a colonial strategy of territorial appropriation by converting the forests and sequestering lands around the Loja Region—the herbal and medicinal epicenter of the Andes—into a royal reserve (*estanco*) to secure a constant, annual uninterrupted supply of Cinchona bark shipments to the Crown in Spain by order of Royal Decree. In its most literal sense, the royal reserve is a mine, and its so-called strategy of *preservation* is more precisely characterized as *extraction without any form of consent* nor benefit to the Saraguro Peoples of the Loja Region, homelands of the Kechwa Nation.

C
D
D
D
D
D
D
A

1753: Errata, <u>C</u>inchona or <u>Ch</u>inchona?

So-called "father of modern taxonomy," Carl Linnaeus not only indulges in the art of classifying plants according to a novel binomial nomenclature, but he also revels in the science of 'fine-tuning' Indigenous knowledge with scientific foot soldiers of his own. Having never set foot in Latin America, he names *Cinchona officinalis* in his massive 1753 volume *Species Plantarum* with drawings taken from geographer La Condamine's *1737 Loja Expedition*. No mention is made to signal the involvement of Fernando de la Vega (guide and curandero to La Condamine's expedition) nor to the lands of the Saraguro Peoples. Linnaeus' appropriation is symptomatic of his remote and self-indulgent botanical imperialism. As Professor-Rector at Uppsala University, his early experience in Lapland with Sami Peoples primes the dispatching of his students on often deadly, highly extractive expeditions around the globe. In 71 years of worldwide research on the kingdoms of natural systems, Linnaeus would never set foot outside of Sweden.

In Pentandria monogynia poſt GENIPAM *Num.* 168.

1021. CINCHONA. Quinquina *Condamin Act. Gall.* 1738.

CAL. *Perianthium* monophyllum, quinquefidum, minimum, perſiſtens.
COR. monopetala, infundibuliformis. *Tubus* cylindraceus, lougus. *Limbus* patulus, quinquefidus, ſerratus, acutus.
STAM. *Filamenta* quinque, miniina. *Antheræ* oblongæ, intra tubum corollæ.
PIST. *Germen* ſubrotundum, infra receptaculum floris. *Stylus* longitudine corollæ. *Stigma* craſſiuſculum, oblongum, ſimplex.
PER. *Capſula* ſubrotunda, calyce coronata, bilocularis, a baſi verſus apicem bifariam dohiſcens.
SEM. plurima, oblonga, compreſſa, marginata.

ERRATA

F I N I S.

1753: Errata, Linnaeus' Misspelling?

A decade after Linnaeus' original misspelling of the Cinchona plant back in 1738 as *Cinchona v. officinalis* (L.) is later corrected as "Chinchona" in honor of the Spanish Viceroy's wife—the Countess of Chinchón is registered in an addendum to his Baedeker-like tome *Systema Naturae*. Nevertheless, Linnaeus' mistake sticks and, to this day, the widespread use of "Cinchona" (no matter its contested origins) remains the misspelled albeit original version. His binomial nomenclature and the taxonomic system would essentially legitimize the European race for objectifying, classifying, inventorying, and essentially dominating the way to see plants and other living beings through a scientific, elitist, and institutional lens that was universalized by colonial science in the name of progress and modernity.

TOMO. I
DE LA COLECCION DE
ANIMALES Y MONSTRUOS
DEL REAL GABINETE DE HISTORIA NATURAL
DE MADRID.
DEDICADO
AL EXMO. Sr. CONDE DE FLORIDABLANCA
Del Consejo de Estado de S.M. y su primer
Secretario de Estado y Gracia y Justicia,
POR
Juan Bautista Brú
Pintor y Disecador de dicho
Real Gabinete,
y Socio de Merito de la
Real Sociedad de Madrid.
De Orden Superior
AÑO DE
1784.

1755: Colonies & Collections

Under the Bourbons, the Spanish Crown becomes a royal sponsor of the emerging colonial sciences of botany and natural history in order to bring profit and prestige to the Bourbon dynasty at a period of all-time opposition across Europe. New institutions mobilized the natural sciences at large (from geology and mineralogy to botany and zoology) across a landscape of looted foods and colonial trophies displayed in exhibition halls, entire buildings, and even gardens. In 1755, the Crown cements its institutional prowess with the construction and establishment of two new facilities in the nation's capital of Madrid: the Royal Botanical Garden in 1772, and a decade later, the Royal Cabinet of Natural History.

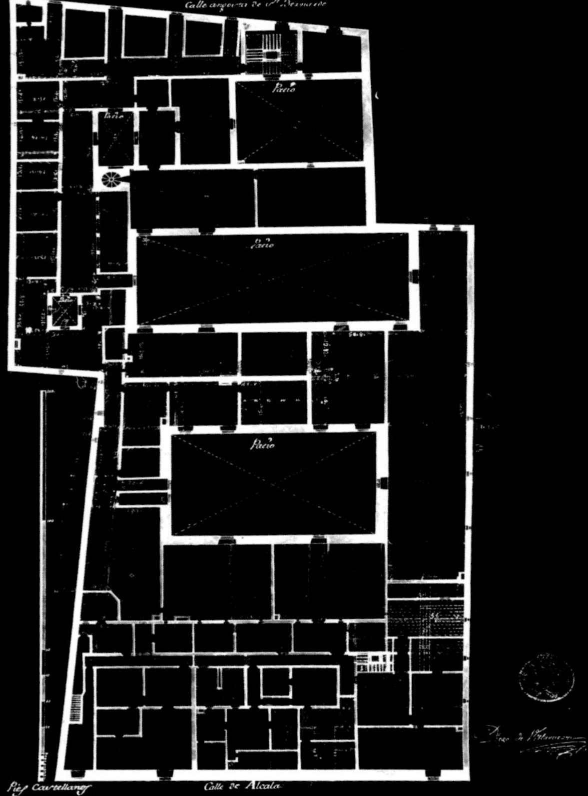

Real Gabinete de Historia Natural, 1771

PLANO DEL JARDIN BOTÁNICO DE MADRID INAUGURADO

Real Jardín Botánico de Madrid, 1781

Miguel Colmeiro y Penido, *Real Jardín Botánico de Madrid*, 1781

1768: Pharmacopeia

The Royal Pharmacy in Madrid becomes the clearinghouse for seeds and samples from all of the Cinchona species in the world coming from Ecuador and Peru. Samples are first collected and cataloged at the Royal Reserve created a few decades earlier in the Cinchona-rich region of Loja. Spanning a three to six-month journey, goods were then transported from South America to Europe via the Port of Guayaquil (and the southern port of Piura) on the Pacific Coast, then bound for the Spanish port City of Cadiz, off the Atlantic Coast. Far before the first official College of Pharmacy is established in 1845, the "Pharmacy" securitizes bark storage for dispensation from select Cinchona species according to both quality (concentration of quinine) and destination (class economy): the best quality reserved for the Royal Family first and foremost, for the Royal Pharmacy second, then for hospitals, churches, convents, troops third, and finally, individuals last.

1776: Rage, Rebellion, Revenge

On November 10th 1776, the King of Spain and Catholic Church release a Royal Decree for a new National Census, a general population accounting in the colony preempting the imposition of new taxes across the Real Audiencia de Quito. Retrospectively recognized as the 'Guano Rebellion' in the Andean region of Chimborazo Province just south of the Capital City of Quito, Indigenous leaders Manuela and Baltazara Chivisa lead a fierce rebellion of citizens and workers in the small town of Guano (Ecuador) against colonial authorities. Surprising and shaming the State, the forceful resistance is nevertheless arrested and Baltazara captured. In a violent sign of state vengeance and as a warning to the populace, her head and hands are chopped off and sent across the region to the colonial administrative center (teniente) & sub-court (corregidor).

1778: Imperial Insecurities

Responding to growing discontent and resentment across the Spanish Empire at the height of American Independence, the 1778 Reforms of the Bourbon Dynasty include a policy of free trade between the Americas and the Spanish motherland. Decentralizing the main port cities of Lima/Callao, Veracruz, Cartagena, and Panama, the economic and regulatory reforms not only secure but expand the Spanish monopoly on commercial trade by establishing thirteen new imperial ports in Spain and nine additional ones throughout Central and South America on both sides of the colonized continent. The reforms increase royal powers of economic control by racializing administration and centralizing logistical distribution through Spanish control. Extraction of natural resources intensifies altogether, ultimately excludeing Criollos from the offices of colonial governance.

1779: Competition & Confusion

Amidst growing competition in the search to secure constant supplies of bark from Cinchona trees, hasty explorers and uninformed brokers misidentify the Cinchona plant with far less potent varieties or under-performing plants with similar visual features. One of the customs officials in Guayaquil, Miguel García de Cáceres, argues that so-called European 'experts' (including physicians and pharmacists) incorrectly focus on the aesthetic qualities of Cinchona for its identification—such as coloration, odor, and flavor—to determine therapeutic efficacy and commercial value. It would not be until much later in the late 19th century that anatomical differences are better indicators of quinine-rich varieties bearing higher concentrations of active alkaloids needed to fight off malarial fevers.

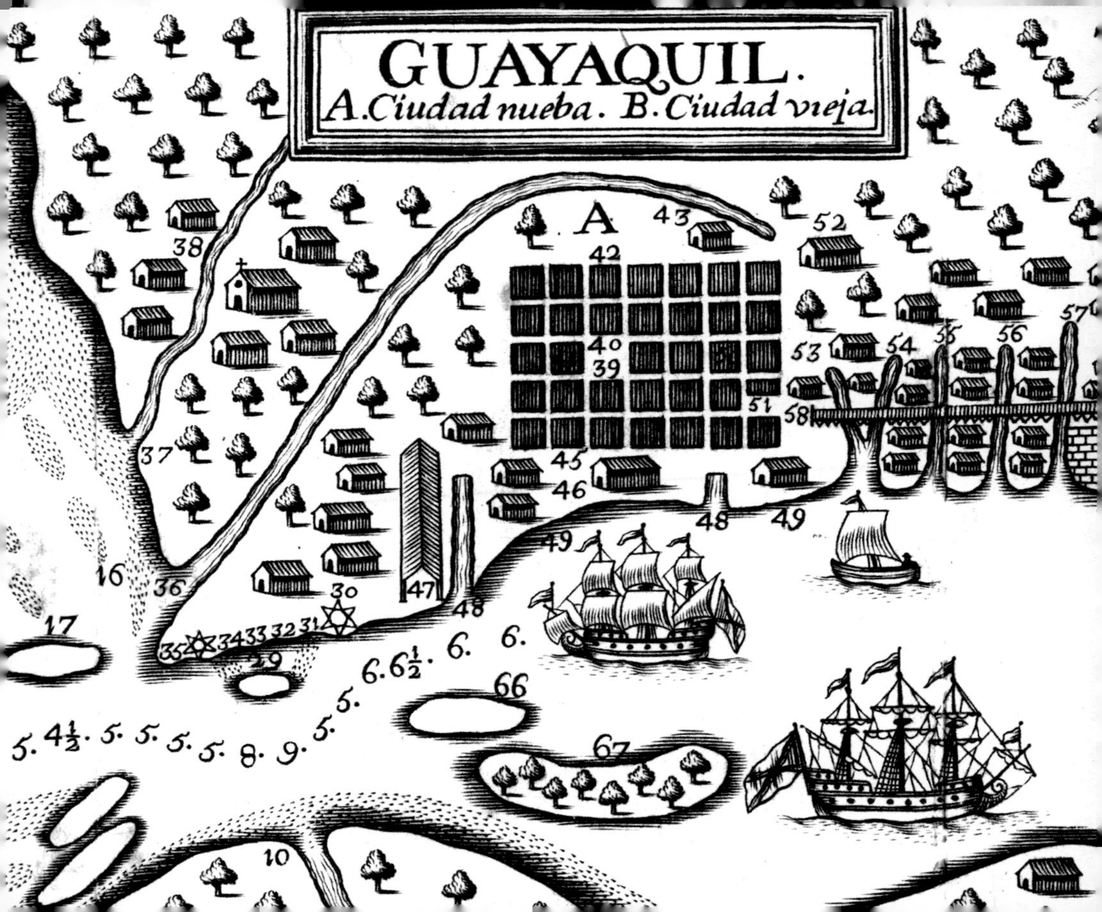
GUAYAQUIL.
A. Ciudad nueba. B. Ciudad vieja.
A
43
42
52
38
40
39
53
54
55
56
57
51
58
37
45
46
48
49
49
16
36
30
47
48
17
35 34 33 32 31
29
6.
6.
6.6½.
66
5.
5.
5.
5. 4½. 5. 5. 5. 5. 8. 9.
67
10

1780: Empire's Extract

With town planning ordinances for the colonies, missions, and presidios ordered by King of Spain Philip II, his 1573 *Laws of the Indies* implement a spatial order on Indigenous land to control and administer access, flow, and extraction. Serving as main hubs for Cinchona bark exports on the Pacific West Coast of South America, the growing port cities of Payta (Peru) and Guayaquil (Ecuador) drain the Andean region of Loja of their natural supply for more than a century afterward without any long-term plans for reforestation to address growing scarcities amidst warring factions between imperialist comptrollers, colonial administrators, trade companies, enslaved labor, and local Indigenous populations. Located at the mouth of a deep water estuary and massive watershed of the River Guayas whose inland tributary practically reaches the administrative capital of Quito, the extractive and now entrenched infrastructure of Guayaquil expands the city grid by extending the dominant system of plantations run by the Jesuits for over a century before getting kicked out by the Spaniards at the end of the 18th century.

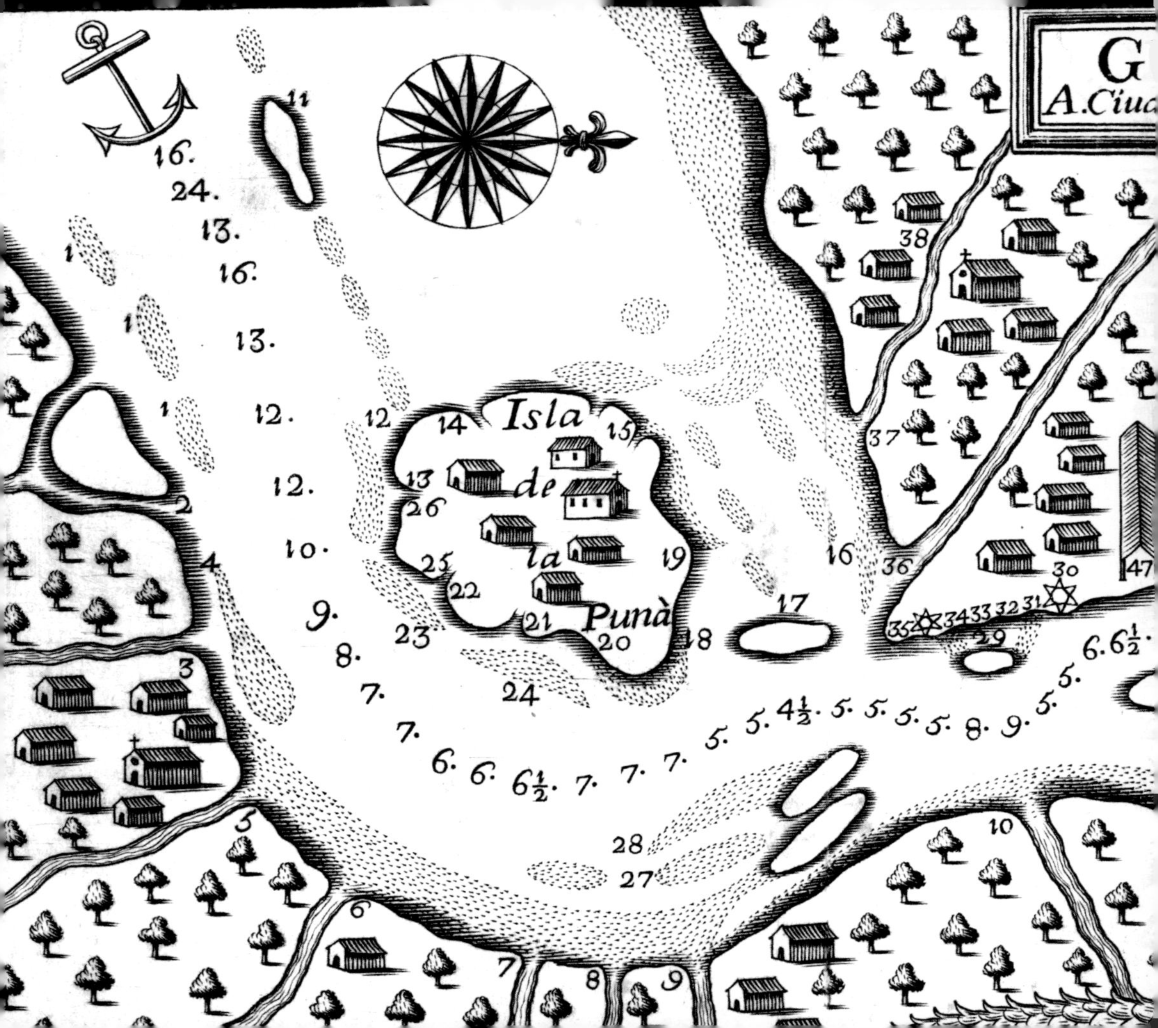
Isla de la Punà

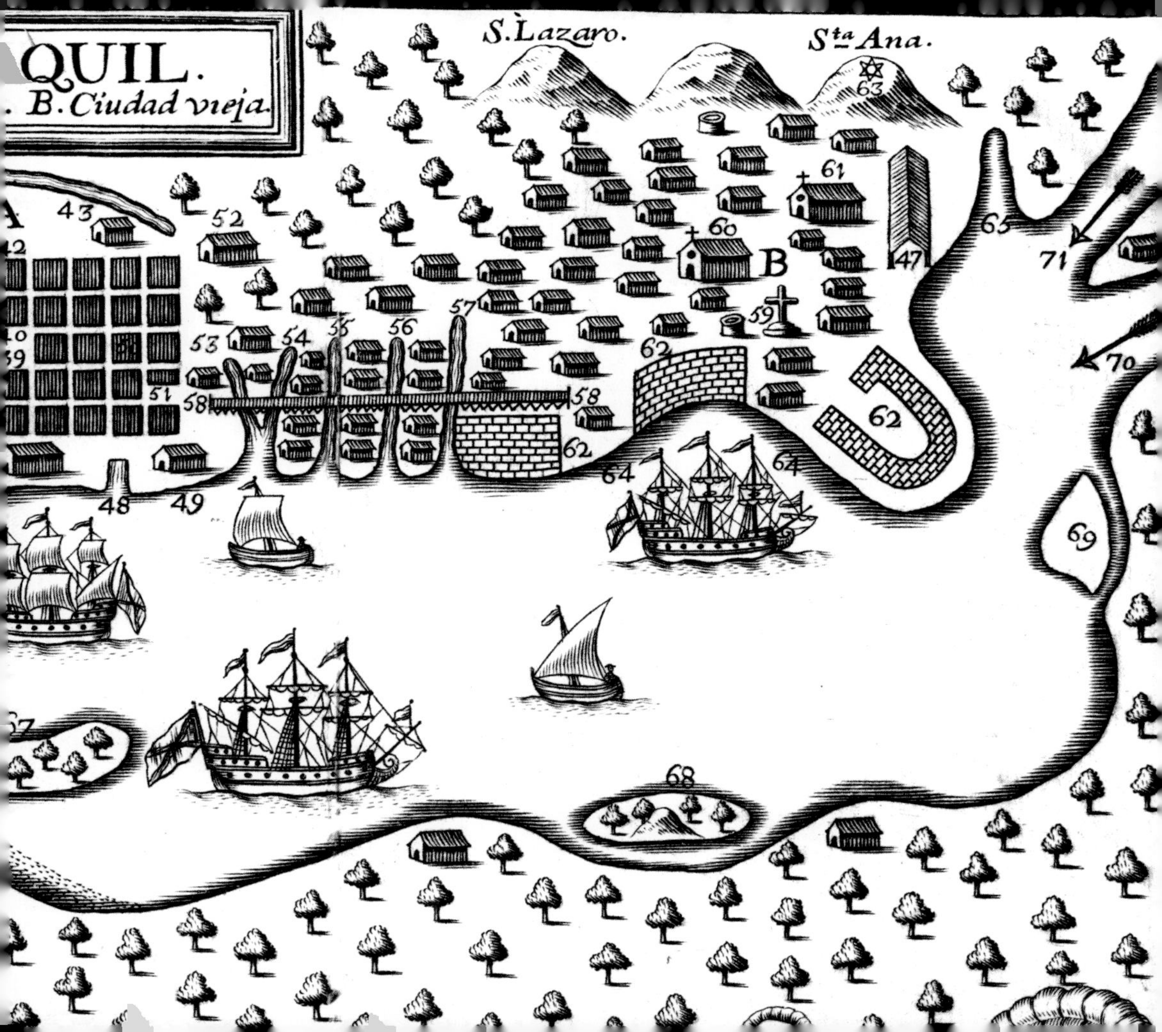

QUIL.
B. Ciudad vieja.
S. Lazaro.
Sta Ana.
63
61
60
B
65
47
71
70
43
42
52
53
54
55
56
57
58
58
59
62
62
62
64
64
51
48
49
69
67
68

28
27
7
8
9
. Punta de Chuches.
. Eſtero del Gallo.
. Punta de Arenas.
25. La otr
26. Rio de
27. Bajos

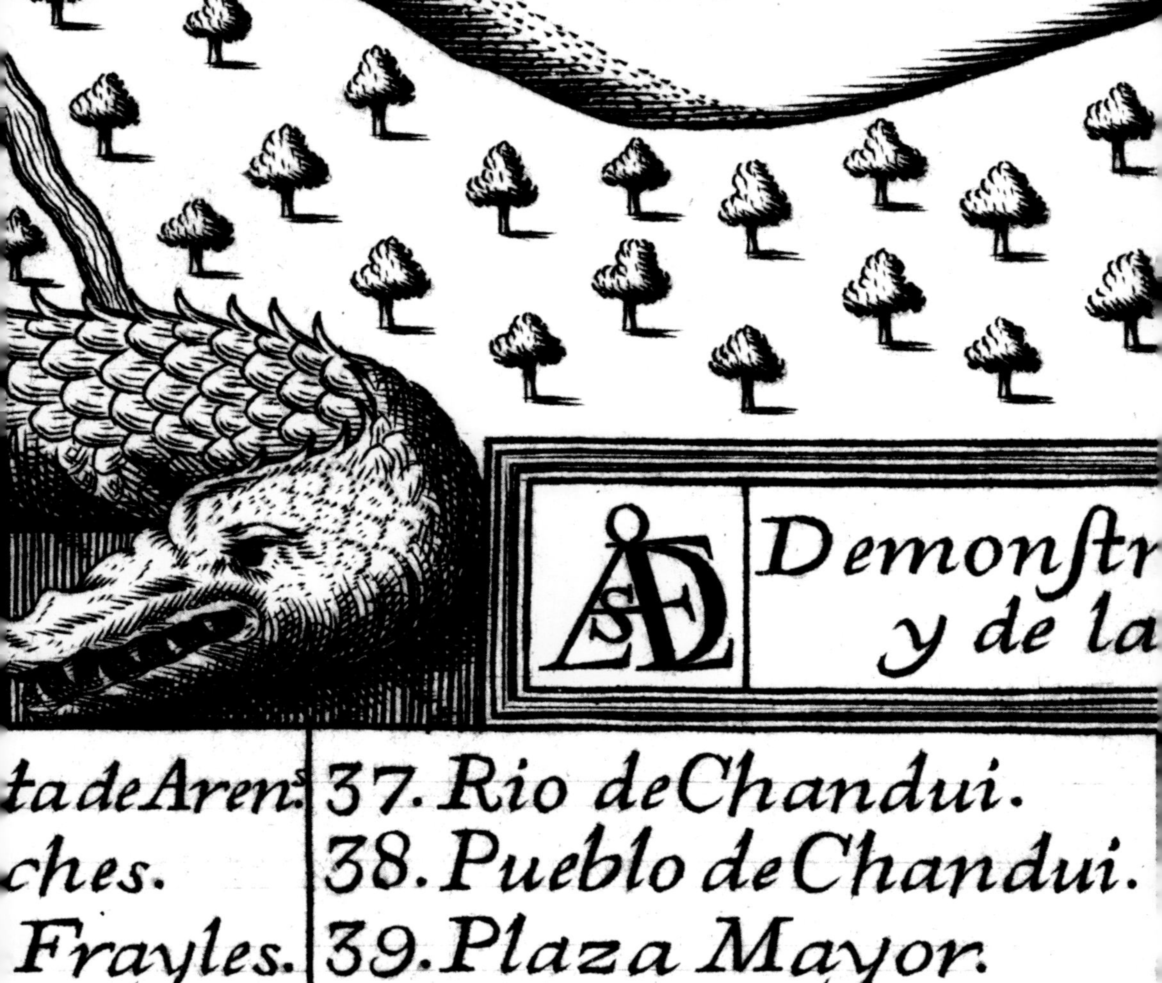
ASDE
Demonstr
y de la
ta de Aren:
ches.
Frayles.
37. Rio de Chandui.
38. Pueblo de Chandui.
39. Plaza Mayor.

1780: Planning for Extinction

After more than a century of intensive exploitation, the supply of Cinchona trees from the Loja Region begins to dwindle and showing signs of scarcity with varieties and species as a result of over-harvesting as demand from Europe grows and grows, outpacing re-planting efforts that are lagging behind. Out of surging demand and desperation for new bark sources, Catholic clergy-scientist and botanist José Celestino Mutis describes the study of the Cinchona plant as the exclusive objective of the *Royal Botanical Expedition of the New World in New Granada* (now modern-day Ecuador, Colombia, and Venezuela). The executive powers of the Archbishop Viceroy of New Granada Antonio Caballero y Góngora requisitioned trees, seeds, and bark while ignoring ever more the knowledge of Kechwa herbalists and healers of the Loja Region.

1780: Unhinging Heteropatriarchy

Confronting and combating heteropatriarchal systems of control embedded in the Monarchy and Spanish colonies, Indigenous leaders and warriors Martina Gomes and Rosa Señapanta lead major uprisings in what is recognized today as the "Shaved Women's Rebellion." Irrespective of the shame and torture they will suffer, they both lead an insurgence to oppose the legal and fiscal abuses of the Crown imposing taxes and regulations on goods; rules that solely benefit of the ruling colonial élite and Spanish Crown. Often characterized as insubordinates by colonial scholars, Gomes and Señapanta both establish legacies of self-determination and assertion of sovereignty as Indigenous warriors. Through planned resistance and organized rebellions, another example is set for Indigenous women throughout the Andes to lead massive revolts that will continue to persist into the 21st century.

TE HACEMOS
PASEAR POR
LAS CALLES
COMO REINA
Y LUEGO A
PATIBULO

X
N
d
R
L
K
O
P
m
V
e
18
11
Loma

1784: Metropolitanization I
Top of the World, Middle of the Earth

With the highest elevation in the world at over 2,800 meters above sea level, the city of Quito is planned by the Spaniards as a near-perfect 100 x 100 meter grid on a large plateau, amidst a valley of volcanic formations. Centrally aligned to look north-south over the Andes along the "Avenue of the Volcanoes" as dubbed by Alexander von Humboldt, and east-west towards the headwaters of the Amazon. Outward looking, the administrative center of Quito in the middle of the Spanish Kingdom that encompasses Peru, Ecuador, and northern Brazil, from the Pacific to the Atlantic, is founded on heavily guarded functions and buildings of colonial control: schools, churches, and prisons (the architectural essence of parishes) built on the back of enslaved and converted Indigenous labor. Administered and ruled by provincial governors and their functionaries, the central plan of Quito serves as a territorial and theological template for other colonial spaces, each one literally centering around the open space plaza of a Roman Catholic church.

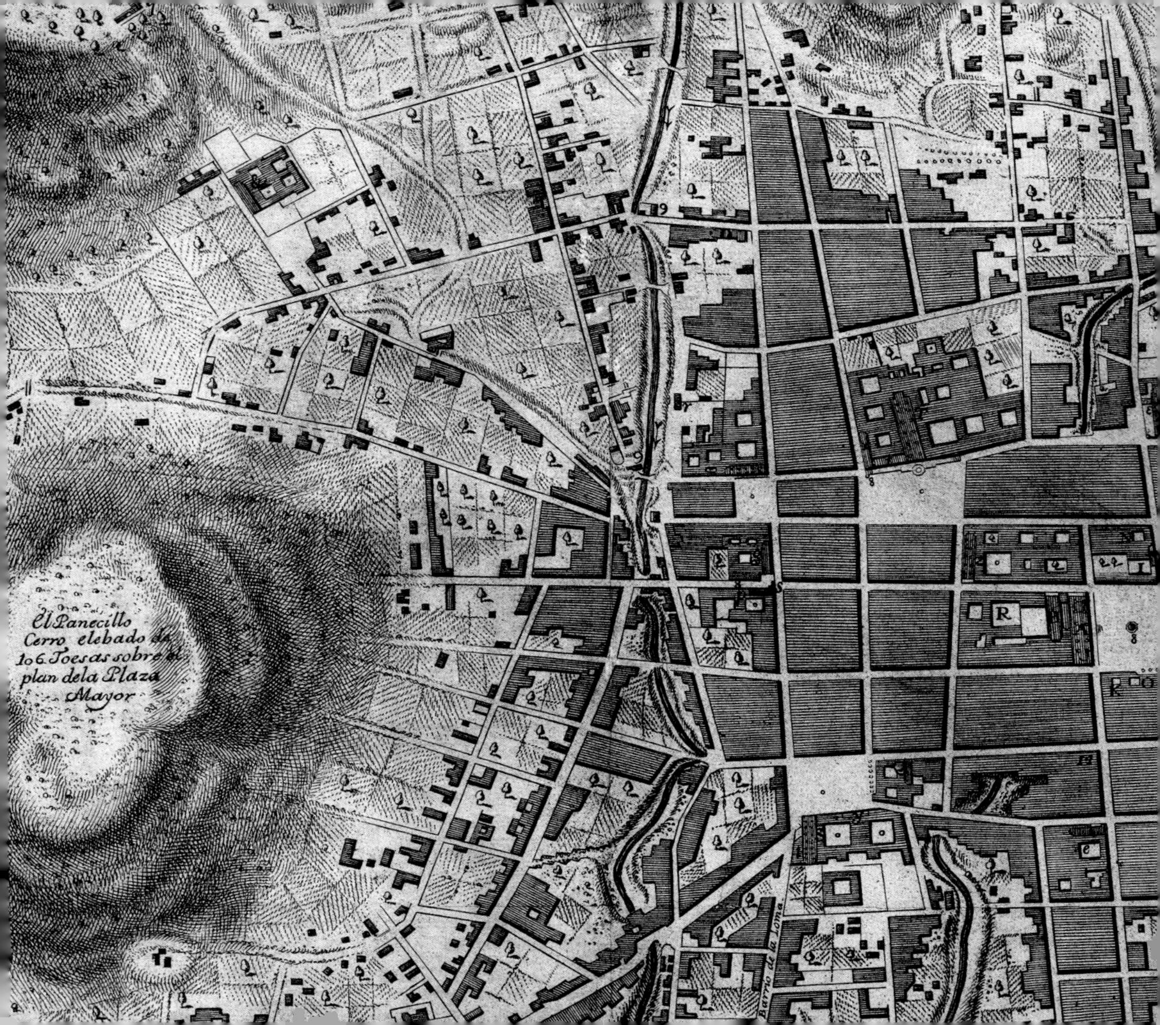
El Panecillo
Cerro elebado de
106 Toesas sobre el
plan dela Plaza
Mayor
Barrio de la Loma.
R
K

PLANO DE LA CIUD. DE
S. FRAN.CO DEL QUITO
Situada en los 00. g. 13 1/3 min de Latitud
Meridional, y en los 81° 45.' de
Longitud contada acia el Oeste, to-
mando por primer Meridiano el
Observatorio de Paris.

E. Parroquia de S. Sebastian.
F. Parroquia de S. Marcos.
G. Parroquia de S. Blas.
H. Parroquia de S.a Prisca.
I. Palacio de la R. Audiencia.
K. Casa de Cavildo.
L. Palacio Episcopal.
M. Capilla Real.
N. Carcel de Corte.
O. Carcel comun.
P. S.ta Marta Carcel de Mugeres.
Q. Iglesia y Colegio R.l d. S. Fern.do
R. Colegio de S. Luis.
S. S.to Domingo.
T. S. Francisco.
V. S. Agustin.
X. la Merced.
Z. la Compañia de Jesus.
&. S. Diego.
a. Recoletos de S.to Domingo.
b. Recoletos de la Merced
d. Monjas de la Concepcion
e. Monjas de S.ta Catherina
f. Monjas de S.ta Clara
g. Carmelitas de Quito.

q. Hermita de N. S.a de Illes
r. Capilla de Jerusalem
s. Capilla de la Reyna de los An
t. Iglesia de S. Buena Vent
x. Capilla de N. S.a de Cantur
y. Capilla de los naturales ó In
1. Capilla de N. S.a de los Desam
2. Hermita del S.to Christo de la
3. Capilla de S. Juan de Petr
4. Hermita de N. S.a de la Conso
5. El S.to Christo de la Paz.
6. Hermita de la Vera Cru
7. Iglesia de N. S.a de Bethlem
8. Fuentes.
9. Molinos.
10. Batan.
11. Caniceria.
12. El Rollo.
13. Casa donde se hicieron l
meras Observaciones de l
y de Obliquidad de la Eclip
14. Casa donde se hicieron la
gundas Observaciones de.

Meridiana

Laguna q. suele secarse

Barrio de Gutumbia

Potrero del Rey

onio de Ulloa & Jorge Juan, Plano de la Ciudad de San Francisco del Quito (detail), 178

LIST of EXAMINED and APPROVED
SIR DREARY DROPSICAL
DOCTOR GLISTERPIPE
DOCr S
SIR JAUNDICE JOLLOP
BALLOON THICKSKULL Esqr
BENJAMIN BOWELESS
PAUL PURGE
DAVID PUKE
DOCT
NIC. NERVOUS
SCURVY
TWISTUM
ABRAHAM
GABRIEL
SAMUEL

1785: Myths & Methods

Illustrating a group of British surgeons (Dr. Peter Putrid, Dr. Gleet, Dr. Glisterpipe,...) attempting a prophylactic amputation, British satirist Thomas Rowlandson's retrospectively depicts the near lunacy of the medical profession with the assumed remedy to malarial fevers: limb removal, purging, blood-letting, herbal administration, rest, massage, hydrotherapy, fasting, and other dietary control. The persistence of such medical and procedural myths cast light on the dramatic and contrasting significance that the role of Cinchona bark will increasingly take on as a natural, organic, non-invasive cure for malaria. The enigmatic plant whose active ingredient is shrouded in scientific mystery and pharmacological wonder; its materia medica continues to evade knowledge of even the most accomplished European physicians and chemists. The remedial use of Cinchona bark will require a cognitive shift and scientific acceptance of Indigenous medicines and botanical methods for those in foreign, colonial territories and metropolitan centers where imperial science and so-called medical innovation are reliant on aggressive remedies and more invasive techniques that are often ineffectual.

1790: Conservation as Exclusion

By order of the Spanish Monarchy, the Director of the Royal Reserve of Quina Vicente Olmedo oversees the task of *surveying* and *mapping* all of its Cinchona plants in the Loja Region, from seedlings to trees. Under the auspices of resource conservation primarily in the interest of the Empire and the Royal Pharmacy in Spain more specifically, the quinological information is to be shared among the scientific élite to "develop and conserve Cinchona trees" in the wake of dwindling supplies and over-harvesting in the region driven by white merchants. While incapable of seeking alternatives to the Cinchona bark, the botanist-chemist Olmedo and his superiors overlook alternative sources of remedial plants from other bark extracts such as Cascarilla, well known among Indigenous herbalists and healers, according to Matthew James Crawford's research on the Cinchona plant and limits of imperial botany published in *The Andean Wonder Drug*. In a dismissive but-all-too-common perception regarding substitutes and over-harvesting when "many European observers of the eighteenth-century Americas commented on the ignorance of the indigenous peoples," the botanical bureaucrat Olmedo observed that those "natives who lack intelligence, are poorly endowed with little rationality, and are unable to accept instruction contrary to their erroneous maxims."

1794: Plantation, Preservation, Power

Working for the Spanish Crown, the imperial botanist and chemist Vicente Olmedo manages to establish the first prototype of a plantation of the Cinchona plant in the Loja region. While the Spanish Crown keeps pushing new, supplementary regulations for the "reproduction of good Quina" (as the bark was referred to then and increasingly a commodity, dismembered from its tree source) as an "object of great importance and necessity for the empire." Following the publication of the definitive treatise on the Cinchona plant in 1972 by Crown botanist Hipólito Ruiz López (after a decade of royal expeditions with botanist José Pavón), *Quinologia ó Tratado del Árbol de la Quina ó Cascarilla,* the Spanish Crown proposes and funds the transition from economies of wild harvesting to managed cultivation in the sierras south of Quito. Focused on Loja, the Crown's goal: to replenish reserves, restore damaged forests, intensify bark production, control distribution, and monopolize the market. In the foreground of exploiting local Indigenous labor, the transition from an economy of pure extraction to the labor-intensive and scientifically-managed plantation is launched. Established by imperial scientists and botanical bureaucrats, the model for global Cinchona plantations will soon explode with looming competition from Dutch and British colonial enterprises.

PERUVIAN BARK TREE PLANTATIONS IN THE NEILGHERRY HILLS, INDIA: SIR W.

SON, GOVERNOR OF MADRAS, PLANTING THE FIRST TREE IN A NEW PLANTATION,

1779-1829: Smuggling Seeds

Despite tight export restrictions imposed by central government administrations of Peru, Ecuador, Bolivia, and Colombia, British alpaca trader and wool broker Charles Ledger steals Cinchona seeds out of Ecuador, Bolivia, and Peru for resale to the British and Dutch governments, at tremendous costs to the lives of Indigenous guides and Mestizo traders involved in dangerous and covert smuggling operations out of Andean forests. Ledger's closest servant and most experienced bark collector, the Aymaran guide Manuel Incra Mamani, perishes at the hands of authorities. In the process, a 13-pound bag of Cinchona seeds soon makes its way into the hands of the Dutch and eventually the British for new plantation prospects. According to Kew Gardens, the estimated value of Ledger's burlap seed sack is in its yield: 20,000 seeds, enough to grow 4 million plants. Soon after, Great Britain and the Netherlands set up their own formal Quina cartels through a series of plantations in regions of similar tropical and humid climates in colonial outposts of India and Indonesia, not only to secure trade routes but ultimately to control global trade of the precious Cinchona bark extract.

1800: Dispossession & Dehumanization

Mapping the Church's missionary zeal and aggrandizing the propagandistic benevolence of the Spanish Monarchy, painter of the ruling class élite José Cortez de Alcocer depicts the complicity of the Jesuit Mission with the ruling Minister of State and Conquistador Pizarro wrapped in celestial contemplation from the Divine Christian God. In a rather bizarre neo-Baroque, pre-Humboldtian gesture, the mural portrays a day at Hospital San Juan de Dios making claims to the universal humanity of the *civilizing mission* of Indigenous and Afro-Ecuadorian Peoples. Dispossessed from the territory as a source of medicine, the colonized are assimilated under its banner wrapped in 2nd-century biblical scripture: "Gloria in altissimis Deo et in terra pax hominibus bonae voluntatis" ("Glory to God in the highest, and on Earth peace, good will toward men"). Although the Jesuits are expelled and suppressed across the dominions of the Spanish Empire, their influence will persist into the 21st century as foreign agents of religious conversion and cultural assimilation using language, education, food and technology as cover to conduct more extractive and exploitative operations at larger, territorial scales.

José Cortez Alcocer, *Betlemitas del San Juan de Dios* (detail), c.1800

instinto de opresores y tiranos. Tubón y Lorenza Huamanay fueron apresados entre otros cabecillas; muchísimos fugaron por distintas direcciones, metiéndose en las serranías y en las selvas; mas aquellos pagaron en la horca su atentado. La feroz Huamanay, supersticiosa cuanto feroz, había sacado los ojos á un español y guardádolos en el cinto, creyendo tener en ellos un poderoso talismán; pero viéndose al pie del patíbulo, se los tiró con despecho á la cara del al-

guacil que mandaba la ejecución, diciéndole: «¡Tómalos! Pensé con esos ojos librarme de la muerte, y de nada me han servido.»

1803: Indigenous Uprisings

In the massive rebellion in Guamote—between the capital of Quito and the economic port of Guayaquil—Indigenous uprisings are led by Lorenza Peña, Jacinta Juaréz, and Lorenza Avemañay in the fight against labor abuses and taxation imposed by the Crown's colonial administration. Indigenous tactics co-opt military strategies of surprise by attacking the Spanish élite and ruling class on the day of a Catholic mass, Sunday February 27th. Captured, Avemañay is tied and dragged through the streets by horseback and then violently hanged in humiliating retribution. Chronicled in the Ecuadorian classic *Cumandá ó un Drama entre Salvajes*, author Juan León Mera recognizes in 1837 the long Amazonian and Andean tradition of Indigenous women's resistance, a tradition personified and emblematized by Avemañay's iconic heroism: "...the terrible conspirator, a name famous in the traditions of our peoples."

Profile of Mount Chimborazo in Humboldt's Physical Tableau of the Andes, 1804

1807: Humboldt's Extractivism

Prior to writing the entire book on the Cinchona plant, German naturalist and explorer Alexander von Humboldt writes the definitive treatise "An Essay on the Geography of Plants" with the illustrious "Physical Tableau of Equatorial Regions." Based on travels throughout the Andes from 1799 to 1803 (following the footsteps of Charles Marie de La Condamine, Hipólito Ruiz, and José Pavón), Humboldt establishes a genre of romantic travel writing that combines science with emotion and universal wonder combined with scientific fact while providing a basis for modern ecology and biogeography as it is practiced today in the 21st century. Largely ignored by historians, scientists, and geographers, and mostly overshadowed by his so-called 'discovery' of guano off the Pacific coast of Latin America, Humboldt's work was far more importantly focused on the altitudinal distribution, geographic locations, and environmental studies of a special medicinal plant from the central Andes: *Cinchona*. Staking his claim on the widespread distribution (yet rapidly depleting) forest resources of the Cinchona plant, Humboldt's map purposely 'botanizes' the way for other expeditions—excursions for extraction—in the following century by the precursors of Cinchona plantations in other European colonies: Hugh Weddell, Clements Markham, Charles Ledger, and Richard Spruce.

Swertia quadr. Pitcarnia Embothrium emarginatum Gentianes

Région des Wintera Escallonia

Limite supérieure des Cinchona

Ancistrum

Styrax Escallonia myrtill. Symplocos Alstonia Margyricarpus Dichondra Vallea

Niérembergia Castilleja integrifol. Passiflora cuprea Ceroxylon andicola (Palmier) Spermacoce Rubus alp.

Région du Barnadesia

Solanum Columella Piper Piper paras Nerteria Salviæ Limite

Clusia tetrandra Cinchona lanceifolia Mut. (Qu. Orangé) Mutisia clematit Lobeliæ Arni

Chenopodium Weinmaniæ Hydrocotile Passiflores en arbres

Quercus granat. Lich. melanoleucos Loasa argemonoides Oxalis édul

Citrosma Solanum Styrax

Viburnum Cinchona condaminea (Qu. de Caxanuma) Passifl. pinnatisp. Cav. Cinchona cord (Qu. jaune)

Limite sup. des Mimoses irrit.

Sesuvium Fuchsiæ

Gunnera Pinguicula loxensis Achyranthes

Région des Cinchona de 700.m à 2900.m

Melastomes à fleurs bleues Psidium Morus escul Coffea

Freziera canescens

Fragaria vesca Juglans granat. Colletia Portulac Krameria

Abondance d'Epidendrum Bocconia Loasa triphylla

anthus Oxalis Freziera nervosa Symplocos rosea Porleria hygrometrica

Hypericum cayen Hydrolea trigyna

Salviæ Rapanea Calyplectus

Vaccinium merid. Urticæ Freziera sericea

Bytneria Molinæ Lythrum ciliat

Erithroxyl. peruvian Cissus

Voyra cærulea Cantua (Periphragm.) Melastomes à gran

Acrostichum

orsten drak Ægmaetia carañifera

Région des Fougères en arbres de 400.m à 1500.m

Calicarpa Killingiæ

Comelina hexandra Jussieua sedioides (Fragaria chil)

Piper en grands arbres

Paullimiæ Hydrobium nat. Mut Heterandiera (Plury

Euphorbia cotinifolia Pitcarnia Matisia cordata

Daphne merid. Diandher

Clusia alba Melastoma villosa

Région des Palmiers et des Scitaminées de 0.m à 900.m

Jriartea Tillandsia Cinchona lo

Carloludovica

Basella
Escallon. tubar
Vaccinium
Berberis
ta Ellisii
Quinquina orange
Castilleja fissifolia
dia uvifera
Polymnia
Passiflora mixta
Palmier à Cire de Quindiu
grands arbres
Bubon apio
Calceolaria
um fluviat
Valeriana
Oxalis
da aphanoid
Begonia
Acæna
Taxus
Tropæolum
Polypod. calaguala
2800 m
Urticæ
Salix pol.
Piper parasit.
Datura
Altstrœmeriæ
Ayenia
Andromeda
Hyperic. bacciferum
Loasa
Clusia alba
Schinus molle
Région de 1800 m à
Barbulæ
Añona reticul.
Thalictrum
a arbor.
Xyris
Tillandsia
Thelephora glabra
Aristidæ
Andromeda
Abondance de musci frond
Pourretia
Palmier à Cire
Solanum
Freziera reticulata
Norantea
Paspalum
Foveolaria
Lich. Cinchonæ
Dorsteniæ
sophylla
Polygalæ
Freziera nervosa
Passiflora tomentosa
Equiset
Nicotianæ
Pontederia
Cinchona oblongifolia Mut.
(Qu. rouge)
Pothos
Phyllanth
Lantana
Cassiæ
Cyperi
Tecomæ
Daphne lagetto
Dolichos
Solidago
Schinus molle
Celsia
Cucullaria grandifl.
clastoma longifolia
Eugenia
Cytisus viol
ylla
Smilax
Ruellia violacea
Voyra rosea
Melastoma micran
Polygonum
Caryocar amygdalif.
a
Sisyrinchium
Myristica granat.
Comocladia
Bocconia
Bauhinia
Parthen. hysterophor.
Thibaudia
Cucullaria rochy
Manettia
Prunus occid.
Andira
Camacha Mut.
Limite inférieure des Cinchona
Martinezia
Godoya
mbago
caverva

Profile of Mount Chimborazo in Humboldt's *Physical Tableau of the Andes* (detail), 1804

ESQUISSE DES PRINCIPALES HAUTEURS DES DEUX CONTINENS

dressée par

Mr de Göthe, Conseiller intime du Duc de Saxe Weimar

d'après l'ouvrage de Mr de Humboldt, publié en 1807 sous le titre d'Essai sur la Géographie des plantes.

Note: Cette esquisse est copiée sur celle que renferme le 41me volume des Ephémérides géographiques de Mr Bertuch à Weimar. On y a ajouté quelques sites importants. Les neiges perpétuelles, dont la limite inférieure sous l'équateur est de 2460 toises (4794 mètres), descendent en Suisse et dans les Pyrenées jusqu'à 1350 toises (2630 mètres) et en Norwège jusqu'à 700 toises (1364 mètres) de hauteur au dessus du niveau de l'Océan. Tout ce qui a rapport à la Géographie des plantes et aux phénomènes géologiques et météorologi-

4 … *Chimborazo 3358 T.*
Le Condor (vulturgryphus)
3 *plane souvent à 3300 T.*
2
Hauteur qui a été atteinte par
1 *M. M. de Humboldt et Bonpland*
… *3032 T: le 23 Juin 1802*
3000
… *Volcan du Cotopaxi 2952 T.*
9 *Limite superieure des plantes*
… *lirheneuses 2850 T.*
8 *Mont St. Elie 2829 T.*
7
6
… *Tungurahua 2544 T.*
5 *Limite inferieure les neiges*
perpetuelles sous l'Equateur
4 … *2460 T.*

Johann W. von Goethe, *Höhen Der Alten Und Neuen Welt*, 1813

F.G. Weitsch, *Von Humboldt und Bonpland am Fuß des Vulkans Chimborazo*, 1806

F. Gerard Inv. Del. Voy. de Humb. et Bonpl. *Bt. Roger Sculp.*

HUMANITAS. LITERÆ. FRUGES.

Plin. jun. L. VIII. Ep. 24.

1814: Humboldt’s Civilizing Science

In the self-adulating adventures and fantastic travels of Humboldt, the cover of the book *Atlas Géographique et Physique des Régions Équinoxiales du Nouveau Continent* appears a rather bizarre and utterly delusional historical depiction of the "Arts" and "Commerce" consoling the "Conquest of the Americas." Commissioned by Humboldt and illustrated by French artist and engraver François Baron Gérard, the book's frontispiece presents the reluctant vanquishing of the ‘Indigenous’ to the Roman deities Athena, the Goddess of War, and Mercury, the God of Commerce. The illusion of Indigenous submission is a seemingly peaceful surrender to European colonial powers of science, knowledge, and trade, set in the foreground of Humboldt’s lifelong infatuation with the foreboding summit and snow peak of Mount Chimborazo. Entrenching Humboldt’s distinctive brand of primitivism, the neo-classical engraving by Gérard featured as the volume’s opening page comes with the positivist, Pliny-esque, caption "Humanitas, Liteae, Fruges." The bold and outlined capitalization of "Civilization, Literature, Prosperity" marks another moment in Humboldt's career where Indigenous knowledge is suppressed and technology denied, as well as where Indigenous governance is depoliticized and Indigenous Peoples are dehumanized.

François Baron Gérard, *Voyages de Humboldt et Bonpland* (detail), 1815

1845: Humboldt's Colonial Gaze

Notwithstanding the erasure of centuries-old technical and medicinal knowledge, Humboldt's perspectives are almost entirely if not completely contingent on the violent elimination and dehumanization of Indigenous presence as well as the deceitful appropriation of Indigenous world views. The principles that structure Humboldt's mammoth-sized, magnum opus and scientific swan song published in his 1845 book *Cosmos* are the result of inherited privilege. His so-called gift to the European world of colonial science and Anglo-American bourgeoisie filled readers with travel-envy and prompted artists to follow in his footsteps and represent the beauty of Central and South America. In the wake of France's massive *Exposition du Système du Monde* that took the intellectual élite by storm in 1796, the zeal of his mid-19th century manifesto on "Nature" crystallizes settler-colonialism across the arts and sciences: empirical imperialism as a naturally dominant world view, where nature is universalized, depoliticized, and romanticized. In the representation of "Naturgemälde," the implied sense of unity or wholeness of the universe that was conditional, it relied on the exclusion of Indigenous and Black bodies.

Julius Schrader, *Baron Alexander von Humboldt*, 1859

1845: Humboldt's Inhumanity

Humboldt's *Cosmos* is both a travel romance with the 'New Continent' of Jefferson's *America* after the 1776 Revolution, as much as it is a manic missionary fetishization of 'worldly' travels of Jesuits to their so-called 'New World.' Humboldt was not only motivated by the same imperial impulse, colonial fantasy, and moralistic desire; his own artistic and scientific missions oddly shared similarities with the Jesuit code: *Natura ad majorem gloriam Dei (Nature for the glory of God). Cosmos* is precisely Humboldt's own version of the new world. *Cosmos* is Humboldt's 'Nuevo Mundo,' the shiny, stylized, bourgeois version of two, earlier, canonical texts: Padre Acosta's 1590 Jesuit account of the 'New World' in his *Moral & Natural History of the Indies* and of Padre Bernabé Cobo's 1653 *Historia del Nuevo Mundo*. For the next 150 years, Humboldt's intellectual hegemony, much like the 19th-century landscape paintings that Humboldt inspires (including the Hudson River School of landscape painting) relegates the Indigenous (people, culture, and governance) to the far-distant and remote background, to clear the way for Linnaen universalism, 20th-century environmentalism, new age Gaia theory, and modern 21st-century ecology steeped in the settler gaze that persists throughout the capitalist world today. Like settler-colonialism, Humboldt's *Cosmos* too is universally dependent on the elimination and erasure of Indigenous humanity, sovereignty, and territoriality—an exoticized world view where so-called modern economies are built entirely on stolen Indigenous lands with the labor exploitation of Black Peoples.

immortal poet has said, in our own tongue—Amid ceaseless change seeks the unchanging pole.*

[In order to trace to its primitive source the enjoyment derived from the exercise of thought, it is sufficient to cast a rapid glance on the earliest dawnings of the philosophy of nature, or of the ancient doctrine of the *Cosmos*. We find even amongst the most savage nations (as my own travels enable me to attest), a certain vague, terror-stricken sense of the all-powerful unity of natural forces, and of the existence of an invisible, spiritual essence manifested in these forces, whether in unfolding the flower and maturing the fruit of the nutrient tree, in upheaving the soil of the forest, or in rending the clouds with the might of the storm. We may here trace the revelation of a bond of union, linking together the visible world and that higher spiritual world which escapes the grasp of the senses. The two become unconsciously blended together, developing in the mind of man, as a simple product of ideal conception, and independently of the aid of observation, the first germ of a *Philosophy of Nature*.]

[Amongst nations least advanced in civilisation, the imagination revels in strange and fantastic creations; and by its predilection for symbols, alike influences ideas and language.] Instead of examining, men are led to conjecture, dogmatize, and interpret supposed facts that have never been observed.

to the present. Thus deeply rooted in the innermost nature of man, and even enjoined upon him by his highest tendencies—the recognition of the bond of humanity becomes one of the noblest leading principles in the history of mankind."*

With these words which draw their charm from the depths of feeling, let a brother be permitted to close this general description of the natural phenomena of the universe. From the remotest nebulæ and from the revolving double stars, we have descended to the minutest organisms of animal creation, whether manifested in the depths of ocean, or on the surface of our globe, and to the delicate vegetable germs which clothe the naked declivity of the ice-crowned mountain summit; and here we have been able to arrange these phenomena according to partially known laws; but other laws of a more mysterious nature rule the higher spheres of the organic world, in which is comprised the human species in all its varied conformation, its creative intellectual power, and the languages to which it has given existence. A physical delineation of nature terminates at the point where the sphere of intellect begins, and a new world of mind is opened to our view. It marks the limit but does not pass it.

Alexander von Humboldt, *Cosmos*, 1845–1861

1820: Colonizing Science

With seeds and plants illegally obtained from Ecuador and Peru, the Cinchona plant's active alkaloid—*quinine*—is finally isolated by French chemists Pierre-Joseph Pelletier and Joseph Bienaimé Caventou preempting Louis Pasteur's chemical discovery of quinidine, another synthetic extract from Cinchona bark, a few years later. Enabling the industrial production of the bark's active alkaloid as a chemical drug, supplies of quinine can now be mass-produced for European armies and manufactured in colonies where protection against malaria is essential for longer term, settler-colonial operations; now made possible without the reliance on plants or bark sources from the politically-charged, conflict-ridden, and increasingly militant regions of Latin America.

C. Laplante Gathering & Drying of Cinchona bark in a Forest Clearing in Quechua Territory, 1867

Caribbean Sea
500km
Mosquito Coast
ATLANTIC OCEAN
Department of Venezuela
GRAN COLOMBIA (1820)
Gulf of Panama
Department of Cundinamarca
Equator
0°
Quito
Department of Quito
Disputed Territory
Amazon River
Real Audiencia De Quito (former 1563 boundary)
BRAZIL
Peru
PACIFIC OCEAN

1820: Re-Territorialization

Once a great centralization of governed departments and districts forming the royally-claimed territory of *Gran Colombia*, its disintegration in the early 19th century with the advent of the Madrid Treaty leads to the formation of the nation-states of *Panama, Venezuela, Colombia,* and *Ecuador*. The geopolitical fallout sees the majority of the Amazon region taken over by Portuguese colonial powers, to become the official nation-state of *Brazil*, 'land of the redwood trees,' after it gains independence a few years later, in 1822. Wedged in between the converging waters of Marañón (Ecuador-Peru) and Putumayo (Ecuador-Colombia) leading to the Amazon River, river courses are now the center-lines of conflict that delineate major boundaries and sources of geopolitical dispute between emerging nation-states. Ecuador subsequently experiences a major and forceful seizure of its eastern territory (including residual lands where the Cinchona plant is found and later major oil reserves) by the neighboring giant to the south, Peru. As Gran Colombia falls apart and new nation-states gain independence, the transnational and logistical instrumentality of corporations amidst global trade will begin to rise.

Delineada en vista de las cartas de DON PEDRO MALDONADO, el BARON DE HUMBOLDT Mr. WISSE, la de las sontas de las costas por M.M. FILZROY i H. KELLET, i las particulares del autor
Destinada á servir de complemento á la obra de geografia del Ecuador publicada del mismo autor

Doctor Manuel Villavicencio.

Esta carta es dedicada á la juventud ecuatoriana, año de 1858.

1:350,000

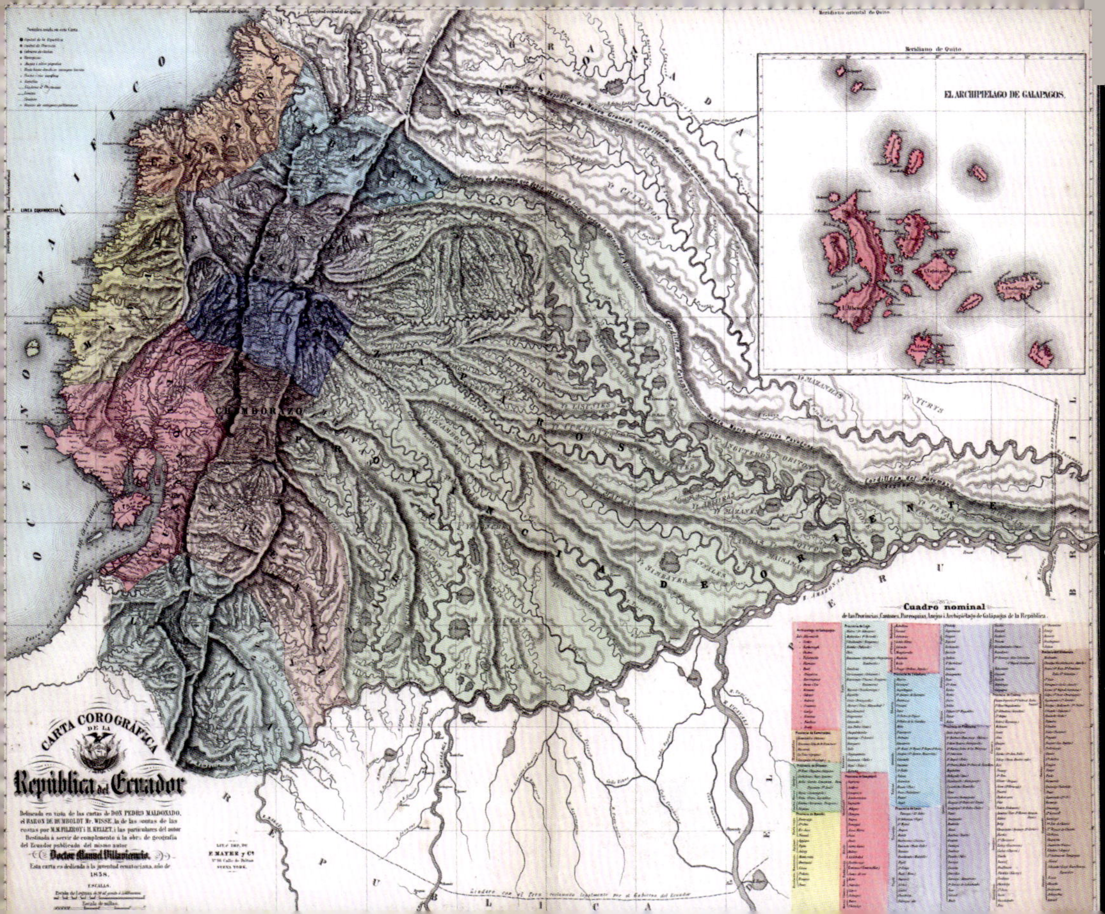

CARTA COROGRÁFICA
DE LA
República del Ecuador
Delineada en vista de las cartas de DON PEDRO MALDONADO, el BARON DE HUMBOLDT Mr. WISSE, la de las costas de las costas por M.M. FILZROY i H. KELLET, i las particulares del autor
Destinada á servir de complemento á la obra de geografía del Ecuador publicado del mismo autor
Doctor Manuel Villavicencio.
Esta carta es dedicada á la juventud ecuatoriana, año de 1858.
ESCALAS.
Escala de millas.
F. MAYER y Cº
EL ARCHIPIELAGO DE GALAPAGOS.
Meridiano de Quito
Cuadro nominal
de las Provincias, Cantones, Parroquias, Anejos i Archipielago de Galápagos de la República.
LINEA EQUINOCCIAL
CHIMBORAZO
OCEANO PACIFICO
NUEVA GRANADA
PROVINCIA DE ORIENTE
R. NAPO
R. TIGRE
R. PASTAZA
R. MORONA
R. YURYS
R. AMAZONAS
PERU
BRASIL

1835: Counter-Insurgency

Exiled in Venezuela, Jamaica, and Peru until her death in 1856, the South American heroine Manuela Sáenz is called to be expelled twice from Ecuador by President Vicente Rocafuerte for fomenting the revolutionary spirit of the nation's underclass and Indigenous Peoples. At a critical moment in Ecuador's emancipation movement, Rocafuerte compares Sáenz's influence to French political theorist, novelist, and agitator Germaine de Staël during the French Revolution. According to Ecuadorian lawyer, historian, and biographer Ketty Romo-Leroux, the Ecuadorian President makes a foreboding comment in correspondence with rival and former Ecuadorian President Juan José Flores on the radical and anarchist body-politic that Sáenz and her allies represent: "*Doña Rosa Gangotena has returned from Cumbal and is working to revive the revolutionary spirit. Women are always the ones who foster the spirit of anarchy in these countries. Preempting your belated recommendation, the knowledge of this truth, of her radicalism, has prompted government ministers to order the expulsion of Manuela Sáenz from the territory of Ecuador.*"

Popayan
Almaguer
R. Patia
C. LANCIFOLIA
Pasto
R. Putumayo
0
QUITO
IV
Chimborazo
20.697 Ft
Huaranda
RED BARK
E C U A D O R
C. SUCCIROBRA
C. S. Helena
Guayaquil
III
Puna I.
Gulf of
Guayaquil
Cuenca
C. OFFICINALIS
Loxa
R. Caquetà or Japurá
River Marañon
5
Payta
R. Yavari
R
Lambayeque
R. Ucayali
Pacasmayo Pt.
P
R. Huallaga
B
Truxillo
River
Huamalies
Monzon
Cuchero
II

1840: Cartographic Conservation

Between the map and the territory, English geographer Clements Robert Markham initiates a long era of mapping the world according to the Cinchona plant, much like the race for measuring the world that led to the founding of Quito along the Equator a century earlier. Soon after, the country would bear the name of this line—Ecuador—the centerline of the Earth's sphere that so many European explorers have fetishized and fantasized about. Here, the convergence of the Amazon headwaters and the Andean foothills come together to form ideal climatic conditions, between Loja to the south and Quito to the north, for the mid-altitude ecology of the Cinchona plant. The potent, red-bark variety of the Cinchona plant species would be sought after by European powers once Ecuador, Peru, Bolivia, and Colombia criminalize the export of Cinchona in the late 19th century. Thwarted by anti-export policies and heavily controlled trade, the economic repercussions of Cinchona sanctions by the Andean countries eventually push rogue smuggling operations abroad. Risks and dangers associated with the illicit trade of Peruvian bark (including prohibited seeds and seedlings) eventually leads towards a project of global colonial expansion. Dispossession takes on a planetary dimension with the planning of Cinchona plantations in tropical, mountainous regions.

MER DES ANTILLES
la Hacha
Ste Marta
la Cienaga
Cartagena
Rio Magdalena
Tenerife
Tolu
Chagres
Porto Bello
Maracaybo
G. de Venezuela
Coro
Porto Cabello
Lac de Maracaybo
Mompox
Panama
Baie de Panama
Tamalameque
VENEZUELA
Merida
Saragoza
Caceres
NOUVELLE GRENADE
Pamplona
Giron
Rio Apure
Remedios
Rio Cauca
Socorro
Velez
Rio Meta
Antioquia
Medellin
Rio Magdalena
Muzo
Mariquita
Honda
Tunja
Pore
Novita
Guaduas
Cartago
BOGOTA
Buga
Cali
Rio Guaviare
Neyva
Pitayo
Popayan
la Plata
R. Patia
Barbacoas
Almaguer
Pasto
Tacames
Tuquerres
Otobalo
Equateur
QUITO
Mt. Antisana
Mt. Cotopaxi
EQUADOR
Mt. Chimborazo
Rio Bamba
Rio
Caqueta
S. Elena
Guayaquil
Rio
Patomayo
Asuay
Rio
Napo
Cuenca
de Guayaquil

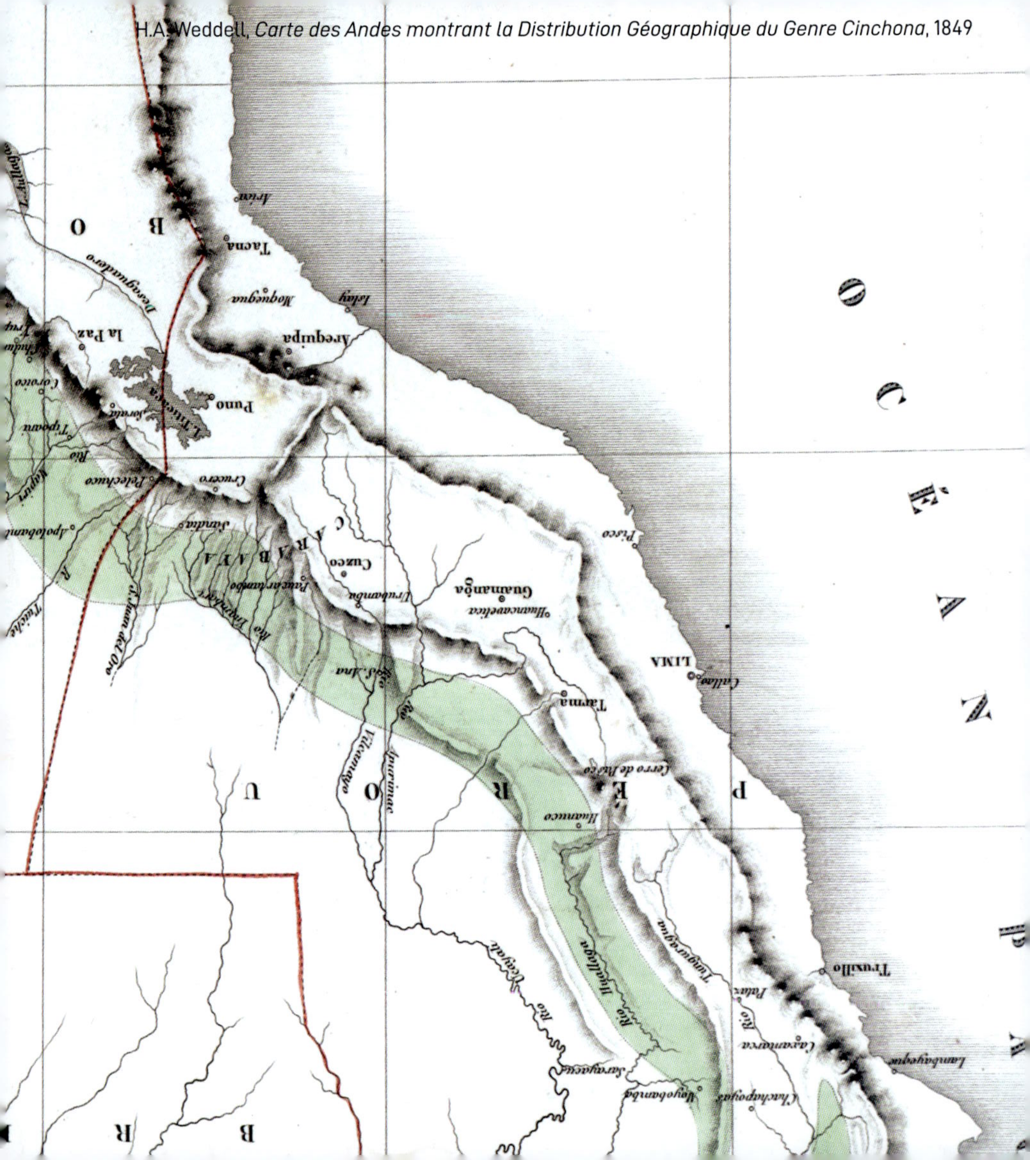

H.A. Weddell, *Carte des Andes montrant la Distribution Géographique du Genre Cinchona*, 1849

1
2
3
4
5
6

1840: Economic Botany

Asserting its intellectual dominance in the botanical sciences of the British Empire, the Royal Botanic Gardens at Kew (England) contribute to the overall strength and medical resilience of colonial forces by contributing life-saving knowledge on the production and supply of quinine. As a cheap, fast, and effective medicine for Britain's imperial soldiers in colonial theaters of war, botanical scientists at Kew conceive and plan strategic resource replenishment of quinine through the economic and entirely exploitative model of Cinchona plantations in British colonies. By undervaluing Indian labor and by exploiting women and children, labor divisions and occupational economies possible in the eastern region of the country, and southern region of the Himalayas, with altitudes of 1500–2000m ASL, makes the agricultural region of West Bengal for example a favorable location for early Cinchona plantation experiments. Quinine was evermore important "in the occupation and safe administration of tropical colonies." According to Norman Taylor in *Quinine: The Story of Cinchona (1943)* the Dutch and the British "became alarmed anout the last century because each had highly malarious colonies and both feared that exhaustion of the dwindling bark supplies would spell disaster." Despite early failures, quinine's role is now extractive and operational.

A MAP OF
INDIA
WITH
THE CHINCHONA PLANTATIONS
AND
THE LINES OF RAINFALL.
Scale of English Statute Miles.
AFGHANISTAN
BALUCHISTAN
Plateau of Tibet
LESS THAN 10 INCHES
The Thur or Indian Desert
RAJPUTANA
The Punjab
Mouths of the Indus
Haidarabad
BOMBAY
Plain of Guzerat
Kattywar
GULF OF CAMBAY
SURAT
BOMBAY
Mahabaleshwar Hills
Ratnagiri
GOA
ARABIAN SEA
Laccadive Islands
Maldive Islands
Mangalore
Cannanore
Nilagiri
Calicut
Palghat
Anamallé Hills
Palnai Hills
Madura
C. Comorin
MYSORE
Nagar
MADRAS
ABOVE 40 INCHES
Pulicat L.
Kaveri R.
CEYLON
COLOMBO
PT. DE GALLE
HAIDARABAD
CENTRAL INDIA
CENTRAL PROVINCES
BERAR
NAGPORE
Plain of Chotesgarh
LESS THAN 50 INCHES
BENGAL
CALCUTTA
Mouths of the Ganges
Mouths of the Mahanuddy
Mouths of the Godavery
Mouths of the Kistnah
BAY OF BENGAL
AGRA
OUDE
LUCKNOW
NORTH WEST PROVINCES
Dehra Dun
LASSA
BHUTAN
BURMA
BRITISH BURMA
MANDELAY
BAMO
RANGOON
MOULMEIN
Negrais
Mouths of the Irawaddy
SIAM
BANKOK
GULF OF SIAM
Andaman Islands
Nicobar Islands
YUEN KIANG
KIANG HUNG
BATANG
TALI
YUNNAN

1851: Weaponization

Strengthening stockpiles of Cinchona bark far beyond South American sources, Great Britain identifies quinine as essential for colonial administrations and troops. Weaponized and militarized, the Cinchona plant is not only labeled as 'strategic resource' but becomes the object of central research for massive plantation projects in tropical and equatorial climates throughout the Empire. Markham's maps are the result of a triple expedition in the Andes to extract *Cinchona officinalis* from Peru, *Cinchona succirubra* from Ecuador, and *Cinchona calisaya* from Bolivia for plantations in their colonial surrogates: the lower Himalayan mountain region of Darjeeling in East India (West Bengal) and the upper Nilgiri mountains in Southern India (Western Ghats). Kew is botanical epicenter of Cinchona knowledge for the next colonial wave in Asia and Africa where quinine is essential. Royal Botanic Gardens director and botanist Sir William Hooker reflects on the global imperative in 1861: "*the means adopted for introducing Cinchonas (trees yielding quinine) into the East Indies and our Tropical Colonies, rank first in point of interest and importance of the works of the past year*." From India to Indonesia, the dramatic expansion of production of Cinchona bark is the result of rampant yet unspoken exploitation of labor of women and girls in British and Dutch plantations.

Gendered child labor in Cinchona bark collecting & bark stripping (West Java, Indonesia), c.1905–191

REPUB. PERUANA. CUZCO. 8 R.
G
1830

1852: Botanical Nationalism

In a bid to historically secure and nationally claim the territorial origins of quinine, Peru officially inscribes and entrenches the image of the Cinchona plant as a national emblem in the flag of the New Republic, whereby replacing the formerly nationalized Chonta tree. Although bark from the Cinchona plant is still consistently yet incorrectly identified by staunch nationalists as 'Peruvian,' its true Andean homelands remain in the mountainous border region of Loja, north of Peru (now part of Ecuador), lands of the Saraguro Peoples and Kechwa Nations. The alarm sounded over a hundred years of dwindling forest reserves of the Cinchona tree from over-harvesting for exports to Spain and Italy was ironically seeing its inevitable fate. As Spanish scientist and explorer Antonio de Ulloa reported back in 1735 in this re-published 1931 statement from Kew: "*the habit of cutting down the trees in the forests of Loxa and afterwards barking them without taking the precaution of replanting would undoubtedly cause their complete extirpation.*" With dwindling populations of the lama-like Vicuña from three centuries of over-hunting by Spanish colonizers, the depletion of national resources contradicts the central image of the nation's bounty and cornucopia of treasures. By the mid-19th century, Peru is more accurately an exhausted and expired hinterland.

1855: Seed Money

With the growing need for seedlings in colonial plantations, the Royal Botanic Gardens at Kew in England quickly become a global, imperial center of economic botany. Under the leadership of botanist and financier Sir William Hooker, the so-called *Cinchona Transfer Program* is created with the assistance of botanist Dr. Robert Spruce. Smuggling an initial collection of live specimens and seeds from Ecuador, new greenhouses are built at Kew as a strategic conservatory of biological materials and seedling production; Spruce establishes a massive 15,0000-acre area of plantations in less than 20 years in Southern India. With low-cost and reliable labor, Spruce yields consistent supplies of high-volume bark with high-concentrate quinine for the British Army left scrambling after the 1857 Rebellion in India and upcoming raids in Southern Africa. Preparations are now being made for successive establishment of plantations in West Bengal, one after the other: Mungpoo (1862), Mangpoo (1864), Munsong (1901), and then much later, Rongo (1938), Latpanchor (1943), and Ambotia (1977).

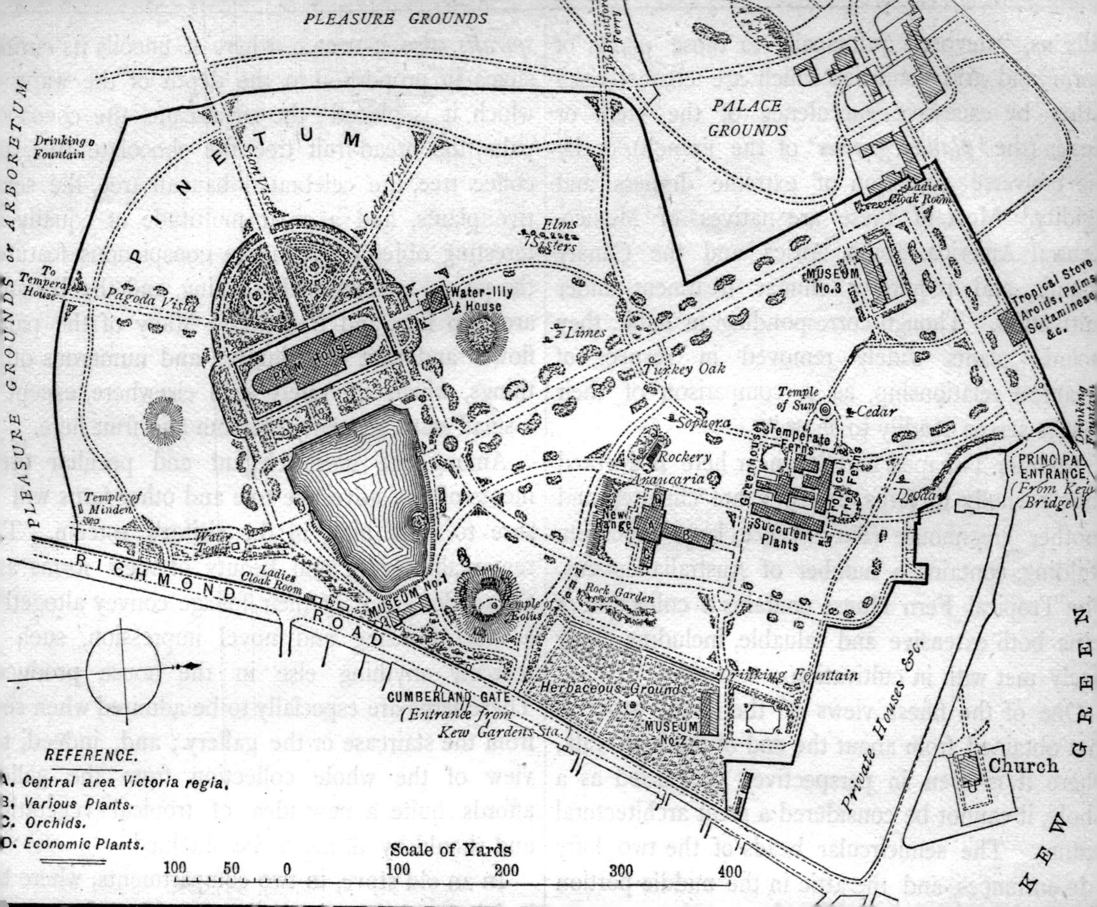
PLEASURE GROUNDS
To Brentford Ferry
PALACE GROUNDS
PLEASURE GROUNDS or ARBORETUM
Drinking Fountain
PINETUM
Sion Vista
Cedar Vista
Elms
7 Sisters
To Temperate House
Pagoda Vista
Water-lily House
PALM HOUSE
2 Limes
Turkey Oak
Ladies Cloak Room
MUSEUM No.3
Tropical Stove Aroids, Palms Scitamineae &c.
Temple of Sun
Cedar
Sophora
Temperate Ferns
Greenhouse
Tropical Tree Ferns
Rockery
Araucaria
New Range
A
B
C
D
Succulent Plants
PRINCIPAL ENTRANCE (From Kew Bridge)
Drinking Fountain
Deodar
Temple of Minden
Water Tower
Ladies Cloak Room
RICHMOND ROAD
MUSEUM No.1
Temple of Æolus
Rock Garden
Drinking Fountain
Herbaceous Grounds
CUMBERLAND GATE (Entrance from Kew Gardens Sta.)
MUSEUM No.2
Private Houses &c.
Church
KEW GREEN
REFERENCE.
A. Central area Victoria regia.
B. Various Plants.
C. Orchids.
D. Economic Plants.
Scale of Yards
100 50 0 100 200 300 400

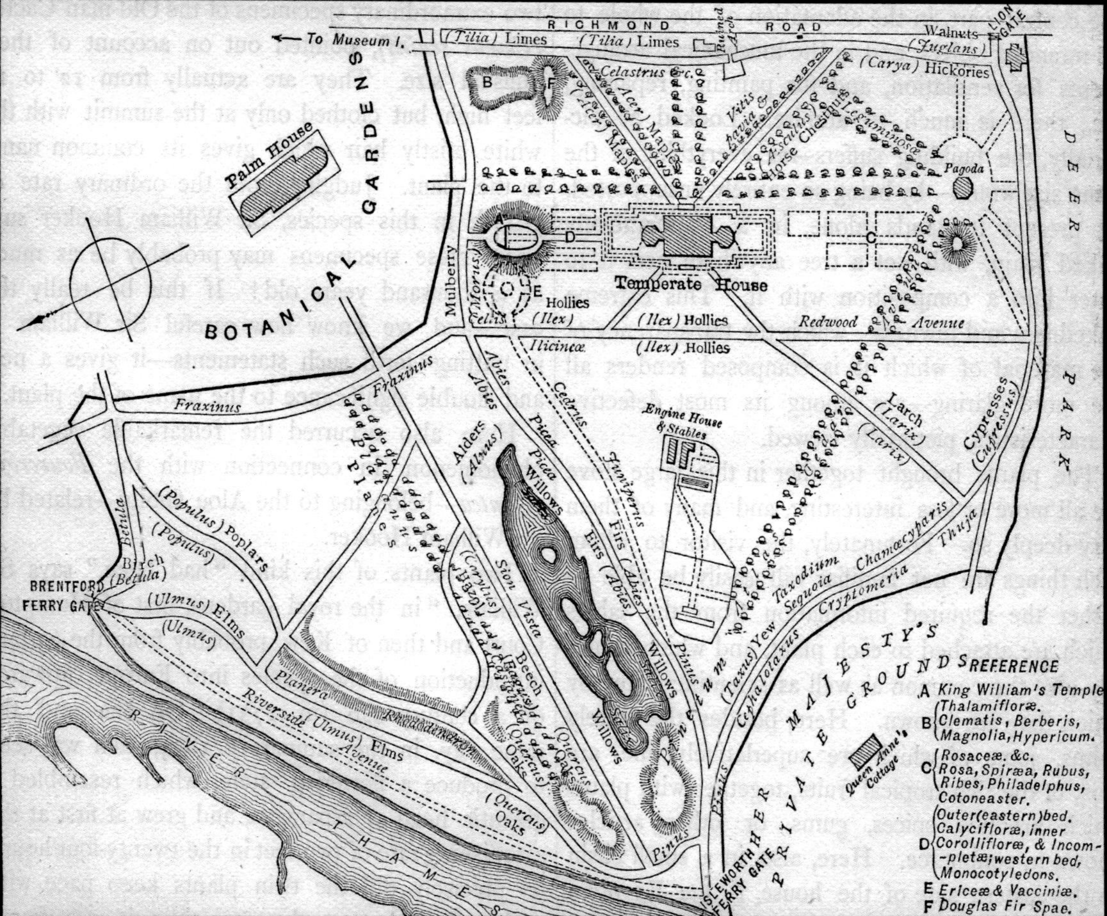

RICHMOND ROAD

BOTANICAL GARDENS

DEER PARK

HER MAJESTY'S PRIVATE GROUNDS

REFERENCE

A King William's Temple

B (Thalamifloræ. Clematis, Berberis, Magnolia, Hypericum.

C (Rosaceæ. &c. Rosa, Spiræa, Rubus, Ribes, Philadelphus, Cotoneaster.

D (Outer (eastern) bed. Calycifloræ, inner Corollifloræ, & Incom-pletæ; western bed, Monocotyledons.

E Ericeæ & Vacciniæ.

F Douglas Fir Spae.

Edward Walford, *Plan of Kew Gardens* (London, England), 1888

Frederic Edwin Church, *Heart of the Andes* (US Sanitary Commission Metropolitan Fair), 1864

1859: Tyranny of the Picturesque

Following the footsteps of Alexander von Humboldt's expeditions, American painter Frederic Edwin Church travels to equatorial South America to find inspiration and pay homage to the Prussian explorer with a massive panorama of Mount Chimborazo after parachuting into the region for two months. A huge sensation when launched in 1859, the 5' x 10' Heart of the Andes scene draws thousands of visitors, seeking to 'experience' it for a quarter. Later exhibited at the U.S. Sanitary Commission's Metropolitan Fair to aid the Union Army during the Civil War, Church is hailed as one of the most important painters of the 19th century. Heart of the Andes comes to represent the nationalism of nature itself, whose huge frame is flanked and crowned by portraits of the first US Presidents. More than a picture, Church's work fuels an era of realism where picturesque painting from the Hudson River School propagates signature traits of scientific 'naturalism.' The colonial gaze of Anglo-American art serves as the cover for the erasure of Indigenous territoriality and humanity; its legacy bolsters the myth of the 'new continent' of Humboldt's coming, according to Simón Bolívar, as "the Second Columbus."

Frederic Edwin Church, *Heart of the Andes*, 1859

1862: Plantation Logic

To destabilize and displace the monopoly of Indigenous sources of Cinchona bark in the Latin American countries and Andean regions of Ecuador, Peru, and Colombia, the Dutch begin to usurp South American supplies through the establishment of Cinchona plantations in Indonesia. The *Kinabureau* is formed in 1913 as a central administrative unit of the Dutch government focused on the global management of cartels, markets, producers, and plantations across Dutch colonies. Three key botanical explorers and ambitious plantsmen coalesce their efforts in the fertile Preanger region (West Java): Johannes Elias Teijsmann, Justus Carl Hasskarl, and Franz Wilhelm Junghuhn. By their arrival in the mid 19th century, one of the world's largest megacorporation—the *Dutch East India Company* (VOC)—had already been operating in the region for well over 200 years, suppressing any and all Indigenous influence—namely Sundanese and Javanese Peoples of West Java. According to genocide scholar Dirk Moses, "*from the outset, violence was intrinsic to Dutch colonial exploits in the Indonesian archipelago. The VOC used extreme force to build up its trade empire in the seventeenth century.*" By the late 19th century, the Dutch are producing more than 20 million pounds of Cinchona bark annually, enough to supply 97% of the world's demand for quinine.

Planting Seeds of Cinchona Succirubra in British Sikkim (Munsong Plantation, Bengal), c.1860–1975

Kinabureau, *Clearing Virgin Forest in West Java for Cinchona plantations* (Indonesia), c.1905–1920

Cinchona Nursery on Munsong Plantation (West Bengal, India), c.1905–1920

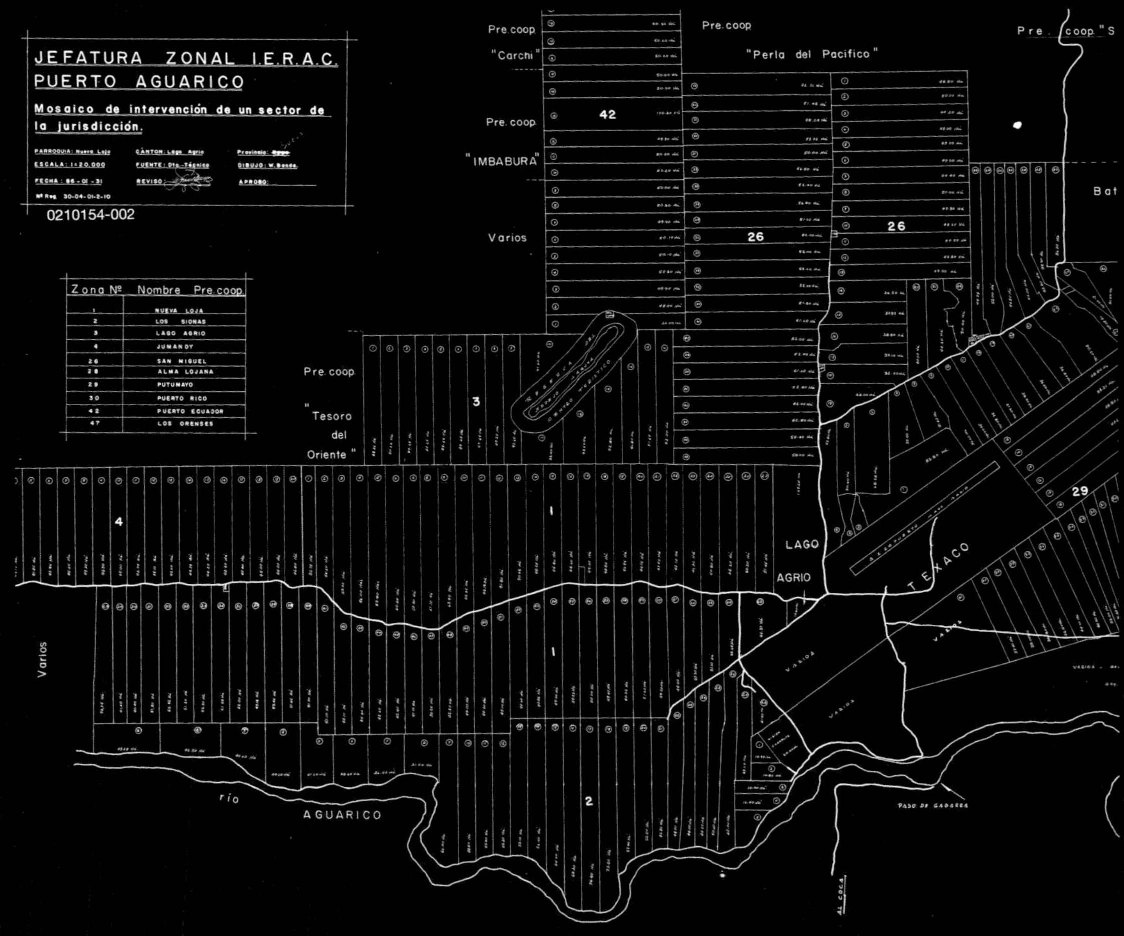

Zona Nº	Nombre Pre.coop.
1	NUEVA LOJA
2	LOS SIONAS
3	LAGO AGRIO
4	JUMANDY
26	SAN MIGUEL
28	ALMA LOJANA
29	PUTUMAYO
30	PUERTO RICO
42	PUERTO ECUADOR
47	LOS ORENSES

1870: Delineating Dispossession

Alexander von Humboldt admonishes uncontrolled deforestation occurring in the Andes—one of the planet's most biologically productive tropical ecosystems—for the harvesting of Cinchona bark, logging of exotic hardwoods, and cattle farming. Humboldt's *Views on Nature* (1807) is a retrospective on rampant destruction, "*to procure the small supply of 11,000 Spanish pounds of bark, no less than 800 or 900 Cinchina trees were cut down every year... the older and thicker stems are becoming more and more scarce.*" As settler-colonialism advances, European-based agriculture organizes the destruction of forests through colonial plans of river access and industrial operations of extraction, as secondary processes of territorial dispossession take place. As a precursor to modern (eurocentric) forms of conservation (and environmentalism), Humboldt's observations set in motion the reservation of public lands based on emerging conservation ideologies while allocating other areas (in familiar grids, and granular patterns) for private land ownership. In the shadow of conservation is the creation of boomtowms that regions like Loja once were. In spite of benevolent efforts, extractive industries will continue unchecked under the premise of 'development' operating at a rampant and exacerbated pace well into the 21st century.

1871: Confronting the Nation-State

In the Yaruquí Rebellion near Quito, thousands of people organize and mobilize in the Ecuadorian Province of Chimborazo, to protest and fight against the centralized imposition of abusive taxes from the Catholic Church and the violent state-building policies of Ecuadorian President Gabriel García Moreno. Targeting the diezmos (state tax system and collection agencies), the uprising is led by Manuela León and Fernando Daquilema, both eventually executed in the public squares of Riobamba and Yaruquí in bloody and violent displays of state-sanctioned torture, brutality, and murder. In spite of the show of state supremacy and military might, as well as the administrative erasure of their historical archive (no public record of their execution exists today), León and Daquilema will remain the faces of the people's revolution. As the power of their stories increases over time, they become icons of resistance against state oppression.

Un costado del Parque "Calde

El desesperado pueblo a una sola voz

SAL! SAL! SAL!......

Manuel Jesús Serrano, *Salt Uprising* (Cuenca), 1925

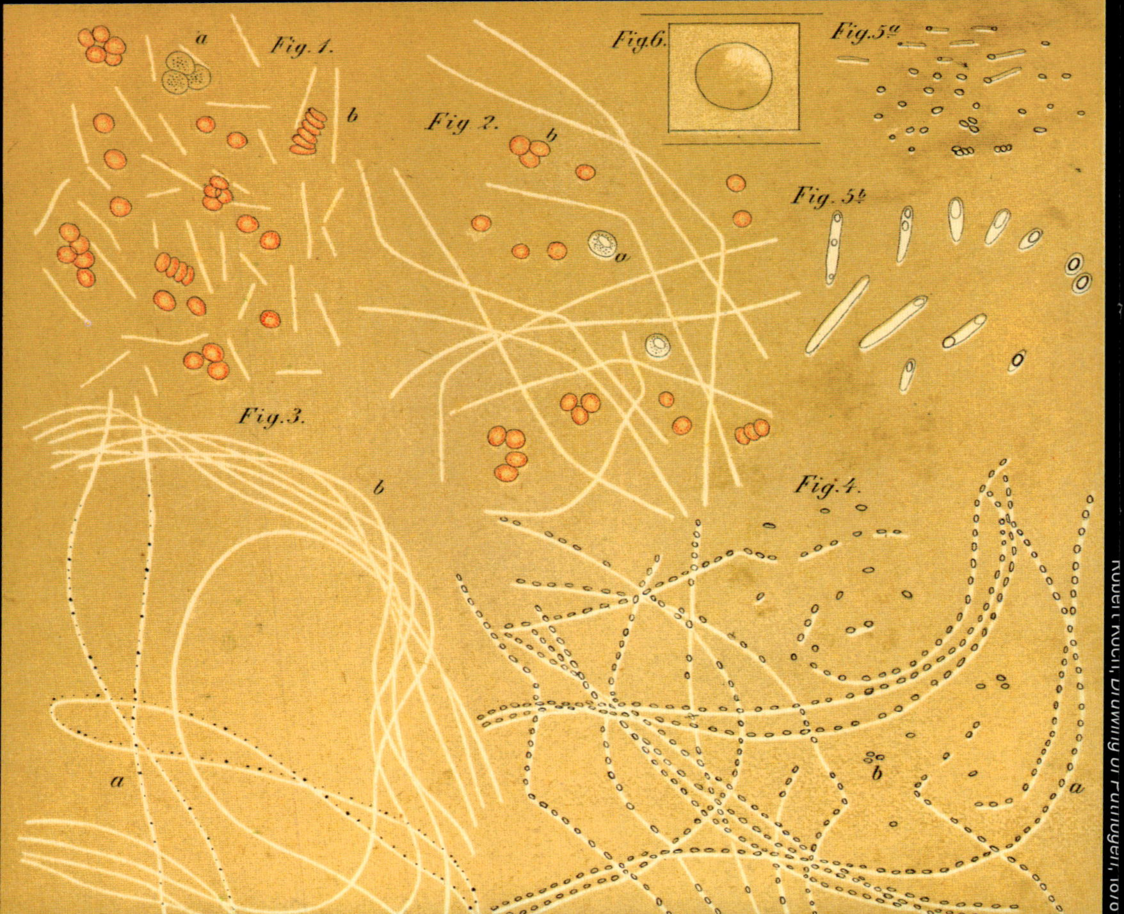

Robert Koch, Drawing of Pathogen, 1876

1878: Germ Theory

On the coattail of the early discovery of bacteria by Antonie van Leeuwenhoek in 1676, French scientist Louis Pasteur and later German doctor Robert Koch, theorize the origins of disease—germs—by incriminating microorganisms as leading causes, pathogens, and vectors of infectious diseases. Together, they debunk the theory of miasma as caused by *bad air*, long held since Antiquity. While imperial science and pharmaceutical research make advances in Europe to close in on the transmission vectors of malarial diseases, the European search for the root cause of malaria intensifies with the attendant pressure of another colonial demand on the near horizon: the supply of quinine in colonial theaters of operation in Africa... a looming scramble for resources is about to radically take place after fourteen European nations meet in Berlin to partition a continent three times the size of Europe.

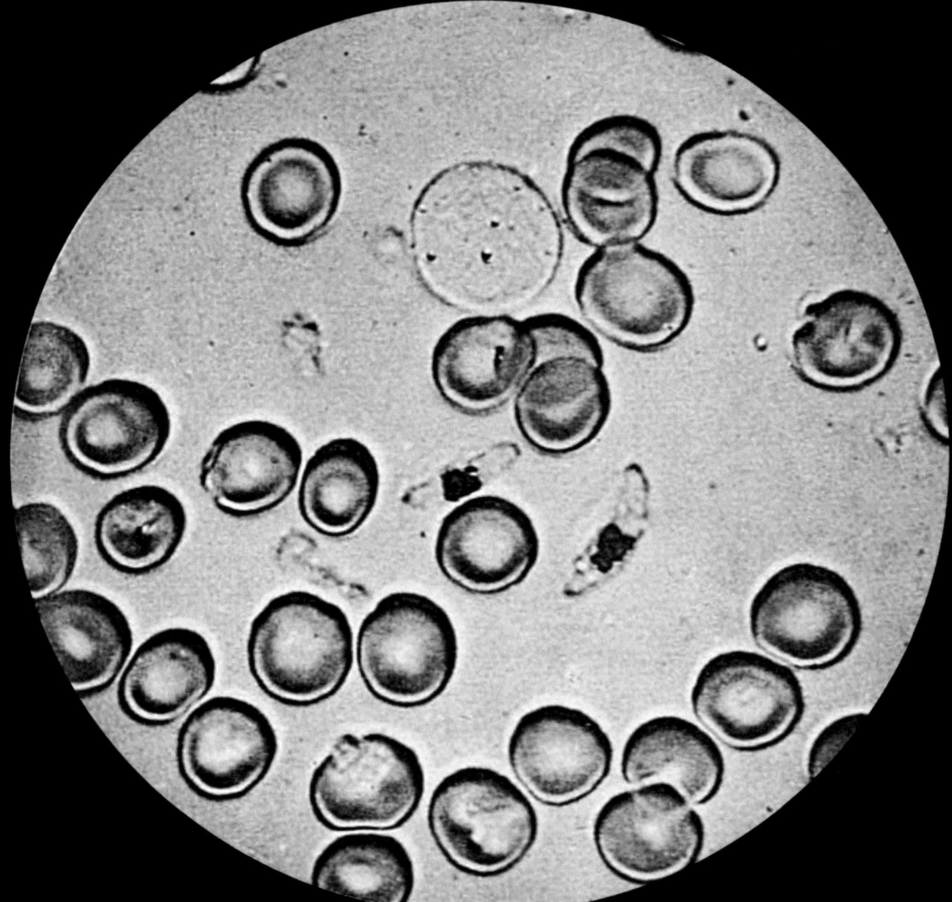

1880: Vector

Dr. Alphonse Laveran, a military doctor in *France's Service de Santé des Armées* ('Health Service of the Armed Forces') discovers the parasite at the root cause of malaria: mosquitoes of the genus *Anopheles*. Following the malaria transmission theory of the *mosquito of the lowlands* a half-century earlier by Dr. Josiah Nott (Mobile, Alabama) in 1848, the Anglo-American Physician & Professor Albert A.F. King proposes, in a series of 19 concise principles, one of the most thorough and comprehensive theories of malaria transmission—the mosquito as the vector of disease—irreversibly debunking centuries-old theories of miasma and infectious bad airs. Yet, the original Latin designation of the disease—*malaria*—will persist. Revered by colonial forces based in Algiers, the role of military medicine would be central campaigns to any and all campaigns on the Africa continent where 7 out of 10 soldiers from the East Africa Company perished from malaria back in the early 19th century. After recently leading a malaria expedition to West Africa, a young lecturer at the Liverpool School of Tropical Diseases—Major Ronald Ross—would claim, "the coming century the success of Imperialism would depend largely upon success with the microscope." Quinine, quite conceivably, would be the colonizer's cure.

On the hurricane deck of a mule

1880: Global Pharma's Ground Zero

Increasingly worried by dwindling, unreliable sources of Cinchona bark from South America, Anglo-American entrepreneur Henry Wellcome undertakes a reconnaissance mission to Ecuador and Peru between 1878 and 1879 to check in on Cinchona forest reserves and track down new herbal remedies and plant-based medicines throughout the rainforests. Mirrorring Humboldt's Andean journey to the forests of Loja with a Thomas Church-lust for the *Heart of the Andes*, Wellcome observes from the promontory of *Popular Science Monthly* on the extreme risks of cascarilleros and their squads in bark harvesting: "the almost continuous revolutions and wars in those South American countries so unsettle everything as to render investments hazardous; the roads and ports are sometimes blockaded for months, preventing shipments of barks... Mules and servants are engaged for the journey to the mountains. Wheeled vehicles are useless, for want of roads, and all transportation is done on the backs of beasts or Indians... The skeletons of hundreds of wretched peons can be seen in the far depths of the chasms below of some of the older trails, suggestive of lurking dangers." By privileging supply over territory, Wellcome's career will explode as a pharmaceutical entrepreneur, medical innovator, and precursor to the multinational corporation bearing his name.

NORTHERN NIGERIA
CAMEROON
FRENCH CONGO
GABUN
BELGIAN CONGO
ANGOLA
(PORTUG. WEST AFRICA)
ANGLO-EGYPTIAN SUDAN
ABYSSINIA
UGANDA PROT.
BRITISH EAST AFRICA
GERMAN EAST AFRICA
RHODESIA
BRIT. SOMAL
FRENCH SOMALI
ITALIAN
Bight of Biafra
Fernando Po
Princes I.
Thomas
EQUATO
Kordofan
Darfur
Wadai
Bornu
Kanem
Kuka
Zinder
Kano
Sokoto
Zaria
Bauchi
Zungeru
Bida
Yola
Ngaundere
Calabar
Buea
Duala
Batanga
Carnot
Bangi
Fᵗ Archambault
Fᵗ Crampel
Fᵗ de Possel
Dar Runga
Dar Banda
Shari
Chad
Katuaka
Dem Zobeir
Bahr el Ghazal
Meshra-er Rek
Ghaba Shambe
Bor
Lado
Gondokoro
Fashoda
Khartum
Sennar
El Obeid
El Fasher
Shakka
Hofrat en-Nehas
Ain Medob
Bir Alali
Agadem
Abeshr
Dar Tokonavi
Kassala
Adua
Gojam
Debra Tabor
Adis Ababa
Harrar
Berbera
Aden
Jibuti
Zaila
Sheikh Husein
Ogaden
Lugh
Bardera
Brava
Kismayu
Gobwen
Port Durnford
Lamu
Malindi
Mombasa
Wanga
Pemba
Tanga
Zanzibar
Dar-es-Salaam
Mafia
Kilwa-Kivinje
Lindi
Mikindani
C. Delgado
Comoro Is.
Aldabra
Mozambique
Quilimane
Chinde
Zambezi
Mahajamba B.
Analalava
Maintirano
Mayotte
Marsabit
Rudolf L.
Stefanie L.
Elgon
Kenya
Nairobi
Kilimanjaro
Victoria Nyanza
Entebbe
Albert Nyanza
Albert Edward Nyanza
Ruwenzori
Kivu
Usumbura
Ujiji
Tabora
Karema
Bismarckbg.
Langenburg
Nyasa
Blantyre
Zumba
Tete
Sena
Salisbury
Mashona
Broken Hill
Kalomo
Barotseland
Lialui
Mpashi
Ovamboland
Otavi
Kunene
C. Frio
Mossamedes
Port Alexander
Humpata
Benguella
Bihe
Loanda
Novo Redondo
Ambriz
Cacongo
Kabinda
Banana
Boma
Matadi
Congo
S. Salvador
Loango
Mayumba
Setté Cama
Libreville
C. Lopez
Franceville
Brazzaville
Léopoldville
Stanley Pool
Bolobo
Coquilhatville
Lukolela
New Antwerp
Stanleyville
Upoto
Mobeka
Banzyville
Mobaye
Yakoma
Nyangara
Wadelai
Vankerckhovenville
Avakubi
Ponthierville
Nyangwe
Kasongo
Albertville
Baudouinville
Lusambo
Luebo
Lunda
Kabinda
Malanje
Mosiko
Kabemba
Lukafu
Bangweulu
Kazembe
Chitambo
Serenje
Livingstone
Victoria Falls
Bulawayo

1884: Blood Money

Almost a half-century after the Abolition Act (1833) in Great Britain, deep economic depression hits European countries with a burgeoning demand for raw materials (gold, rubber, oil, cotton, copper...) from the push-and-pull of the Industrial Revolution. Using the alibi of another civilizing mission through Christianization, the race to partition the continent of Africa is officially kicked off in Berlin at a conference in 1884–85 without a single African representative present. In less than fifty years between 1870 and 1910, over 90% of the continent would be partitioned between 7 European nations: Britain, France, Germany, Spain, Italy, Portugal, and Belgium. Also called the *Congo Conference*, for the sweeping powers assumed by King Leopold II claiming a territory of over 70 times the size of Belgium. The 'Scramble for Africa,' as the London Times coined it in 1884 would see the control of resources, territories, and governments shift at a breakneck pace with the level of brutality in colonial campaigns, unprecedented. "The violence," according to Pan-African historian Dr. Ama Biney, "should be seen on a spectrum and a continuum of plunder, pillage, and rape that all European powers engaged in, at varying degrees and varying levels...and the most horrific exemplar of the violence of colonialism is Congo." The vast, metropolitan wealth of Europe: built on a massive land grab.

DEMARCAÇÃO DOS LOTES COLONIAIS EM 1890

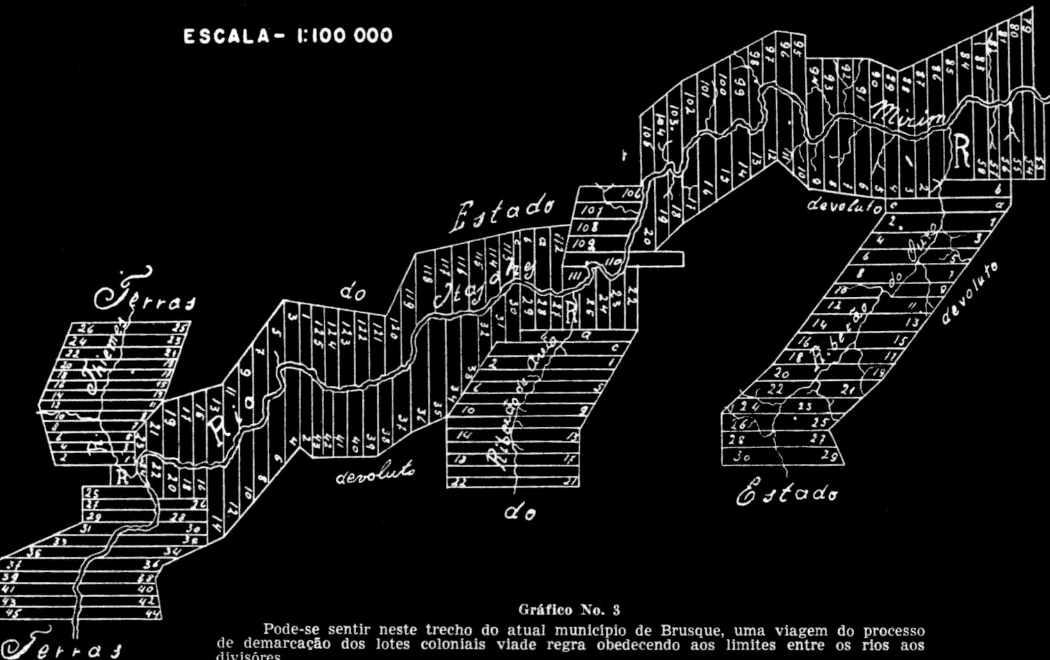

Gráfico No. 3

Pode-se sentir neste trecho do atual município de Brusque, uma viagem do processo de demarcação dos lotes coloniais viade regra obedecendo aos limites entre os rios aos divisôres.

1890: Penetration II

As the bones of a future Trans-Amazonian project, the colonial planning and land settlement of cities and towns in Eastern Brazil sets up a distinctive, spatial template of property partition, subdivision, and allocation by the State. Tributaries serve *a priori* as penetrative devices into the massive rainforest regions then as organization devices fo settlement and occupation. Continuing Francisco Pizarro's imperial dreams and plans of an intercoastal infrastructure—its main goal is to extract resources from South American territories for export the Spanish homeland—the sacking and pillaging of Indigenous lands as *hinterlands* and *settlements* soon takes place through Indigenous erasure and assimilation. Through the creation of a massive transcontinental infrastructure where roads, lots, cut blocks, and mines, criss-cross a gridded terrain that preempts settler-colonialism. Under the guise of cultural protection in Brazil, the National Indian Service (SPI, *Serviço de Proteção ao Índio* later called *Fundação Nacional do Índio*, FUNAI) is created and headed by Amazonian explorer and Field Marshal Cândido Rondon. Led by white administrators and ruled by settler-colonial jurisprudence, the intended and unintended consequences of cultural preservation smoothen and will amplify the path towards extractivism.

1902: Monster

Praised for identifying mosquitoes as vectors of malarial transmission, the India-born British-trained physician Ronald Ross defines the racist project of tropical colonization in his Nobel Prize speech: "Malarial fever is important, not only because of the misery which it inflicts on mankind, but because of the serious opposition which it has always given to the march of civilization in the tropics. Unlike many diseases, it is essentially endemic, a local malady; and one which unfortunately haunts more especially the fertile, well-watered and luxuriant tracts—precisely those which are of the greatest value to man. There it strikes down, not only the Indigenous barbaric population, but, with still greater certainty, the pioneers of civilization—the planter, the trader, the missionary, the soldier. It is therefore the *principal and gigantic ally of Barbarism*. No wild deserts, no savage races, no geographical difficulties have proved so inimical to civilization as this disease. We may almost say that it has withheld an entire continent from humanity—the immense and fertile tracts of Africa; what we call the Dark Continent should be called the Malarious Continent; and for centuries the successive waves of civilization, which have flooded and fertilized Europe, and America, have broken themselves in vain upon its deadly shores."

CAN SCIENCE COLONIZE THE TROPICS?

The colonization of the tropics by white men is one of the vast potentialities of science and commerce. For generations, the two mosquitoes which carry the germs of malaria and yellow fever have held Panama in their grip, as our artist has suggested here, but at last, science is protecting people from these diseases, which have entirely disappeared from the Panama Canal works. Science, in other words, is opening the gates of the tropics once more to wealth, civilization, and population.

Harmsworth Popular Science, *Can Science Colonize the Tropics?*, 1911

1915: Transplantations

As South American Nations struggle for independence, the foreign empires of Great Britain, Holland, and Spain develop routes for the illicit trade of Cinchona bark and the smuggling of seeds from Ecuador, Colombia, Peru, and Bolivia to establish plantations in colonies of India, Indonesia, and later in Africa. At a period of heightened territorial insecurity and the scramble for Africa by European nations, the role of Royal Botanic Gardens at Kew is crucial for safeguarding botanical data and collections from around the colonial world. However, Kew's epicenter will soon be usurped by the *Dutch Kinabureau* with the 'discovery' of a more potent form of Cinchona species and thus far superior quality quinine with higher concentration levels. To increase yields, accelerate growth, and abate disease, sophisticated grafting, inoculation, and harvesting techniques are de rigueur across the family of Rubiaceae varieties. Going beyond techniques of seed sorting and plant layering, cuttings from *Cinchona ledgeriana* (Ledger Bark, 1881) grafted onto the hardier rootstock of *Cinchona succirubra* (Red Bark, 1857) to produce a colonial hybrid highly sought-after for some of the most potent alkaloid-producing plantations in the world.

Investor Dr. L.Ph. de Bussy Inspecting Cinchona Seedbeds at Tjinjiroean Plantation (West-Java), 1927

Kinabureau, *Grafting Cinchona ledgeriana/succirubra (Tjinjiroean Plantation, West Java)*, c.1920

Removing the Bark of a Cinchona tree with a Bendo (West Java) c.1945

Cleaning and Packing Bark of Cinchona Succiruba on the Tjinjiroean Plantation (West-Java), 1907

Women Working on the Fields of the Ramawatie Plantation (Parahyangan, West-Java), c.1900

1919: Workers' Rebellion

In response to colonial land reform policies that disproportionately target and largely dispossess Indigenous Peoples through settler control by Criollos across the country, community leader Dolores Cacuango leads the first Indigenous demonstration and protest in contemporary Ecuador against labor exploitation by large landowners (*hacendados*) at the Pesillo Hacienda in the city of Cayambe, Indigenous territory of the Kayambi Peoples. The protest results in the creation and drafting of workers' rights and national legislation of fair wages. Cacuango later forms the communist-based Indigenous organization *Federación Ecuatoriana de Indios* (the Ecuadorian Federation of Indigenous Peoples) and becomes one of the earliest and main forerunners in the creation of a national program of bilingual education that places Kechwa side-by-side with the 100-year old Spanish-based system.

¡¡ABAJO!

1922: Labor Revolutions

Under the thumb of a major export-based cocoa oligarchy whose crops are devastated by disease, the Republic of Ecuador sees the rise of over 30,000 workers from the port city of Guayaquil, where a powerful group of Black and Indigenous women joined by Mestizas lead a massive demonstration on Wednesday, November 15th, demanding improvement to working conditions and better salaries. Aided and abetted by the Government and the Army, the cacao companies open fire on the crowd killing thousands and then throwing dead bodies into the river as a warning. Once labeled as vandals and terrorists, some of the key activists and women warriors in the line of fire on that bloody Wednesday, November 15th, are now recognized almost annualy in national news media like El Commercio: Tomasa Garces, la *Negra Julia*, Esther Balbina Rivera, Ángela Meza, Asunción Ramos, Balvina de Pausan, Ceferina Romero, Francisca Casanova, Mercedes de Silva, Manuela Guzmán, María Mayorga, María Morán, Otilia Gonzabay.

Can Nature be equalled by Synthesis in Malaria?

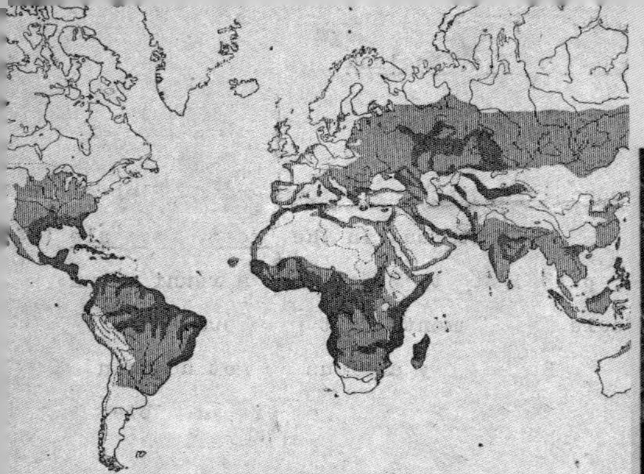

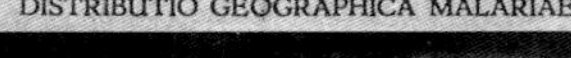

The Short Quinine Treatment and The New Synthetic Antimalarials

Bureau for propagating the Use of Quinine
Amsterdam (W.) – Holland 1936

1930: Global Monopoly

In spite of trade regulations, the Netherlands secures a monopoly on the production of 97% of the world's supply of quinine drug by the 1930s through the inception and hyper-administration of the *Kinabureau* (Dutch Cinchona Bureau). Thanks to the cultivation of high-grade and high-concentrate hybrid varieties of Cinchona plants grown in Javanese colonies and sophisticated grafting techniques, Dutch yields almost completely quash competition from previously dominant plantations in Ceylon and West Bengal. Notwithstanding the highly performative graft of *Cinchona ledgeriana* x *Cinchona succirubra* with 14–16% quinine, a range of different varieties at different altitudes demonstrate the superiority of Dutch botanical simulations to reproduce the most ideal, Andean-like growing conditions for Cinchona in the Preanger Region (Parahyangan) of West Java. The Dutch botanical arsenal also included a vast array of other Cinchona species: *calisaya Javanica, caloptera, cordifolia, Hasskarliana, Josephiana, lancifolia, micrantha, ovata, officinalis, Pahudiana, Pitayensis, pubescens*. With bark demand topping 2 million pounds a year "to eradicate malaria as an economic problem" as the Kinabureau referred to in its annual *Chininum* compendium, bark shipments were destined for the major western markets in London, Paris, and New York.

REAU TOT BEVORDERING VAN HET KININE-GEBI

D'ENCOURAGEMENT POUR
MPLOI DE LA QUININE

REAU FOR INCREASING
HE USE OF QUININE

LEGR.: ARATROQUINA
LEF.: 44841

BÜRO ZUR FÖRDERUN
CHININGEBRAUCH

OFICINA PARA EL DESAR
EMPLEO DE LA QUIN

AMSTERDAM-W.,
DE WITTENKADE 48

1932: Corporate Colonialism

Underscoring the military necessity for medicine in the colonial field, a new motto is developed by French military physician Dr. Eugène Battarel in theaters of war. Adapting the famous Latin slogan *ense et aratro*, the farmer-soldier metaphor of Algerian Governor (1834–1847) Général Thomas-Robert Bougeaud. For the General in charge of brutal campaigns: "to serve country, the citizen—in times of peace—must be willing and able to farm land, with plough in hand, and to protect the motherland in times of war, ready to take up arms—the sword, and be a soldier." Thus, sword and plough. Weaponizing quinine, the necessary technology for winning wars in malarial regions, Dr. Battarel makes a necessary adaptation: *ense, aratro et quina* ("sword, plough, and quinine"). A few years later, the Kinabureau (Dutch Cinchona Bureau) working with Spain, Great Britain, United States, and France (unsuccessful in their colonial plantations), appropriate and abbreviate the French military motto for their corporate logo: *aratro et quina* ("plough & quinine"). In their version, the sword is removed, all is left is: quinine... Thus, the world as global plantation to manage civilization. For the so-called pacifist Dutch, either plantation owners, quinine producers, and kina capitalist: Cinchona is the new sword.

QUINTO GRADO
21 OCT. 1986
EL LIBRO
DEL ESCOLAR ECUATORIANO
SEXTO GRADO
EL LIBRO
DEL ESCOLAR ECUATORIANO

1935: Indoctrination

Through the publication of mandatory schoolbooks, the State operates as a civilizing agent through the pedagogical propaganda machine of Ecuador's Ministry of Education—once the exclusive authority of the Roman Catholic Church dating back to 1863. The *El Libro Del Escolar Ecuatoriano* becomes the mandatory history book for every student in every school across the country. To this day, the book remains the official educational textbook throughout the second half of the 20th century. Absent of any Indigenous or Afro-Ecuadorian representation, the cover page stages a white mestizo farmer in the background without shoes, and an urban looking white-blonde boy in the front holding an open book in his hands ("del escolar ecuatoriano") next to the Ecuadorian flag; although white people only represent 6% of the total Ecuadorian population.

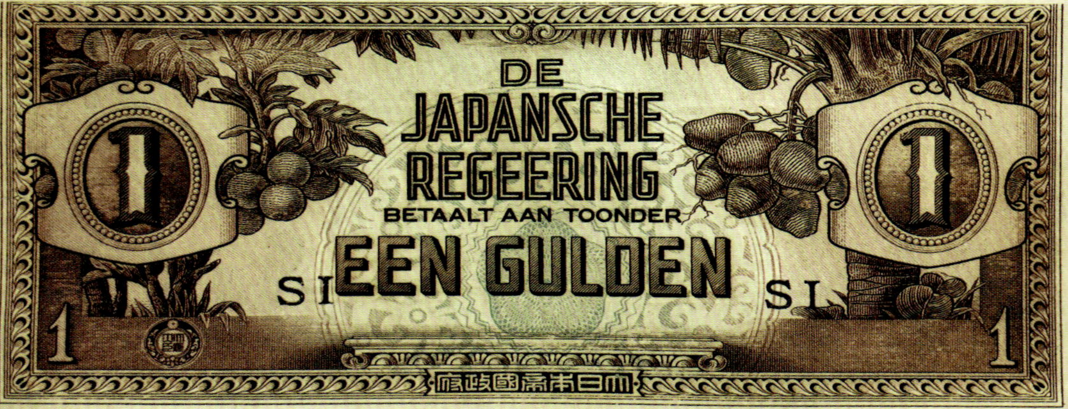

DE
JAPANSCHE
REGEERING
BETAALT AAN TOONDER
EEN GULDEN

SI 1 SI 1

大日本帝國政府

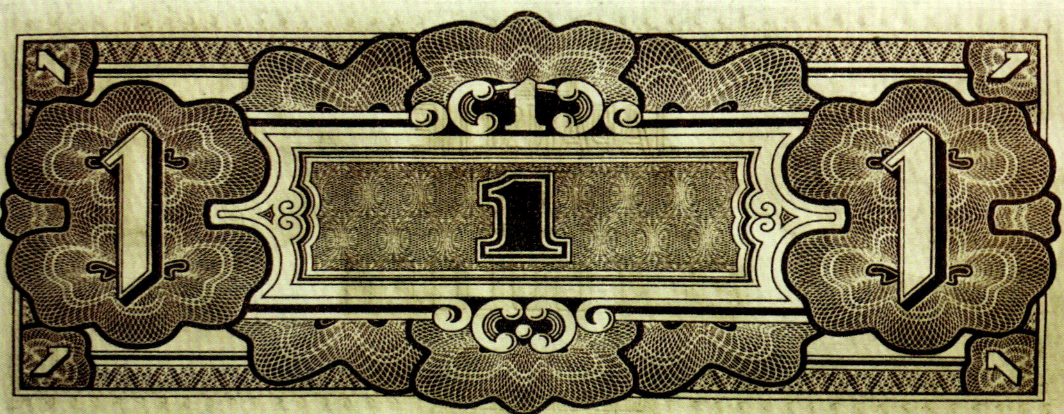

1

1

1942: Blockage

During the Second World War, Japan occupies the Dutch Indies—with a heavy presence in Java—cutting off the Allies' supply of quinine which, by then, accounted for more than 90% of the world drug supply. The Dutch global monopoly was enjoyed for decades was now its weak spot. With Indonesian Independence looming on the horizon with bloody confrontations with troops and an internal civil war across the islands, the political and economic reign of over 250 years of colonial occupation by the Netherlands comes to an end. While Dutch capitalists will maintain their grip on resource exploitation, the Dutch Cinchona Bureau explores investments in Africa with France and Germany along the Equator. Mid to high tropical altitudes, namely in the center of the continent, and low-wage labor supply for new plantations are needed to maintain control of global production and supply of quinine. In recognition of quinine's distinct military advantage in colonial theaters of operations, the U.S. Board of Economic Warfare initiates a Cinchona-procurement program for new sources of bark. In the spirit of their European predecessors, the Americans initiate new expeditions and fact-finding missions to South America now that Cinchona forests are showing evidence of regeneration after centuries of rampant logging and harvesting by the Spanish Empire.

250km
COLOMBIA
Equator
0°
Quito
ECUADOR
Putumayo River
MAYNAS
Territory claimed
by Ecuador
to Rio Protocol 1942
Amazon River
Present
Border
Marañon River
BRAZIL
Peru
Andes
PACIFIC
OCEAN

1942: De-Territorialization

As the independent Republic of Ecuador grows in population, its territory dramatically dwindles. With increasing pressure from neighboring states, Ecuador reluctantly cedes disputed territories to Peru after signing the *Rio de Janeiro Protocol* while maintaining claims to "free and sovereign access to the Marañón-Amazonas," an agreement signed under duress that it will dispute later, in 1960. At the center of the conflict is the resource-rich, Amazonian side of Ecuador, east of the Andes with battles over access to the Amazon through Marañón and Putumayo Rivers. The region, called 'Oriente' (eastern valley in the headwaters of the Amazon River basin) is split down the middle, north to south, cutting through seven key tributaries in the headwaters of the Amazon River: Río Putumayo, Río Napo, Río Tigre, Río Pastaza, Río Santiago, Río Chinchipe, and Río Huancabamba. As a border region and intense source of dispute from warring colonies ever since 1770–1820, the national guarantors of the Rio Protocol (United States, Brazil, Argentina, Chile)—on the heels of the pan-American *Organization of American States* in 1948—will continue to see the politicization of border conflict at the center of national struggles for autonomy. The 170-year old conflict over the northern, eastern, and southern boundaries will not be re-negotiated until a half-century later, in 1998.

1942: American Missionaries

During what is dubbed the *Cinchona Program*, American survey missions sponsored by the U.S. Bureau of Economic Warfare for 'exploration and discovery' are conducted by American scientists including a crew of anthropologists, botanists, biologists, and lawyers. According to Ecuadorian historian Nicolás Cuvi, "the program for the extraction of a single medicinal plant, apart from representing a new model of scientific imperialism (subsequently renamed by the US Government as 'scientific cooperation') was the most intensive and extensive scientific exploration of a single medicinal plant in the history of mankind." Producing and exporting 40 million pounds of Cinchona bark, the short two-year lifespan of the U.S. Cinchona Program would be cut short in 1945 when natural and botanical supplies of quinine would soon be usurped by synthetic and chemical substitutes.

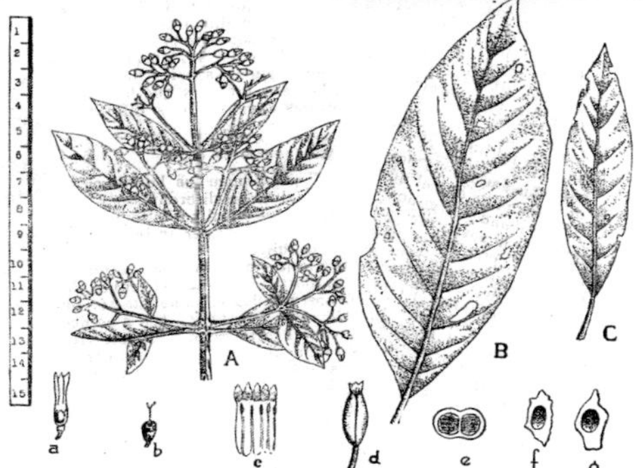

Cinchona officinalis L. («fina costrona») de la cordillera Oriental de las Provs. de Cañar. Azuay y Loja. Dibujo hecho con especímenes de las áreas del Oriente del Pan, Prov. del Azuay.
Fila superior: A rama floral; B hoja adulta; C hoja joven.—Tamaño ½
Fila inferior: a flor; b la misma sacada la corola; c corola abierta; d cápsula joven; e cápsula vista en corte transversal ampliado; f y g semillas aladas.—Tamaño: a. b, c, d: 1/1; e 2/1; f y g 3/1

DESARROLLO Y HABITO DE LAS CINCHONAS

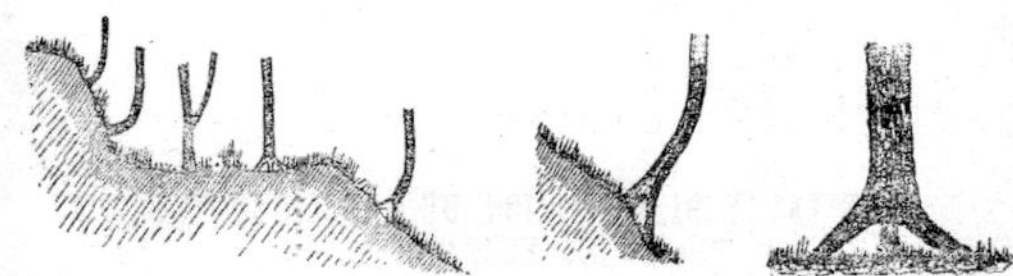

Hábito y desarrollo de los troncos de *Cinchona pubescens* Vahl. o *C. succirubra* en los bosques subandinos, cerca de Chillanes, en «Urcu-corral», de los 2.600 a los 2.950 m.s.m.

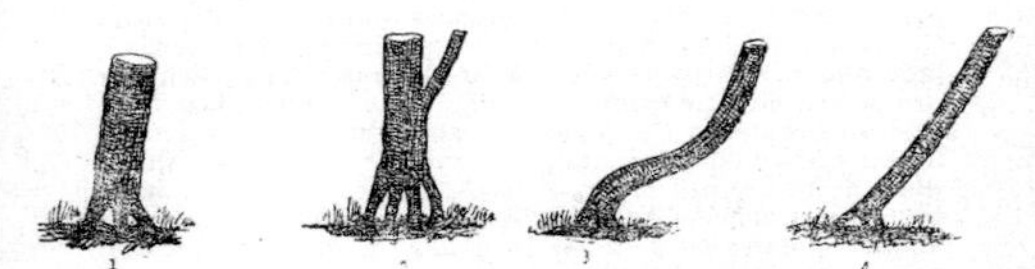

Hábito y desarrollo de *C. pubescens* Vahl. de los bosques de «La Hamaca», en Cotacocha, Prov. de Loja, de los 1.800 a los 2.000 m.s.m.

LAMINA XXXIX

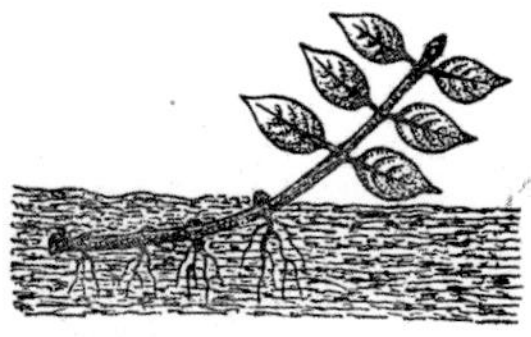

Ejemplo gráfico de la propagación vegetativa de la *Cinchona succirubra* hecha en los valles equinocciales de la Provincia de Bolívar. Una rama con guías es plantada en el suelo y ella después produce retoños o «hijuelos».

Un modelo de almácigo de Cinchona, utilizado en Java, el techo es de paja u hojas.

Injertación de la Cinchona.—A, patrón de C. succirubra, arreglado para ser injertado; B. ramita vegetativa injerto de *C. Ledgeriana*, lista para juntarse al patrón A; C, joven planta ya injertada.

LAMINA XXX

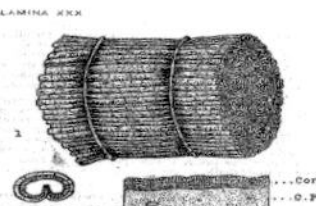

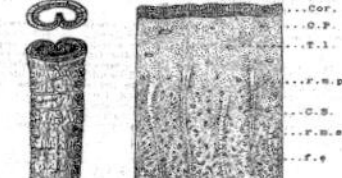

1.—«Carga» de corteza de «cascarilla roja», tal como empacan en las áreas de Limón y Telimbela (Prov. Bolívar), para la exportación; tamaño 1/10.
2.—Un pedazo de corteza de Cinchona roja; tamaño 1/6
3.—Corte transversal de la corteza, visto a 20 diámetros de aumento.
Leyenda:
Cor. corcho o súber; C. P. corteza primaria; T. 1. tubos laticíferos; r. m. p. radios medulares primarios; C. S. corteza secundaria; r. m. s. radios medulares secundarios; f. e. fibras esclerenquimáticas.

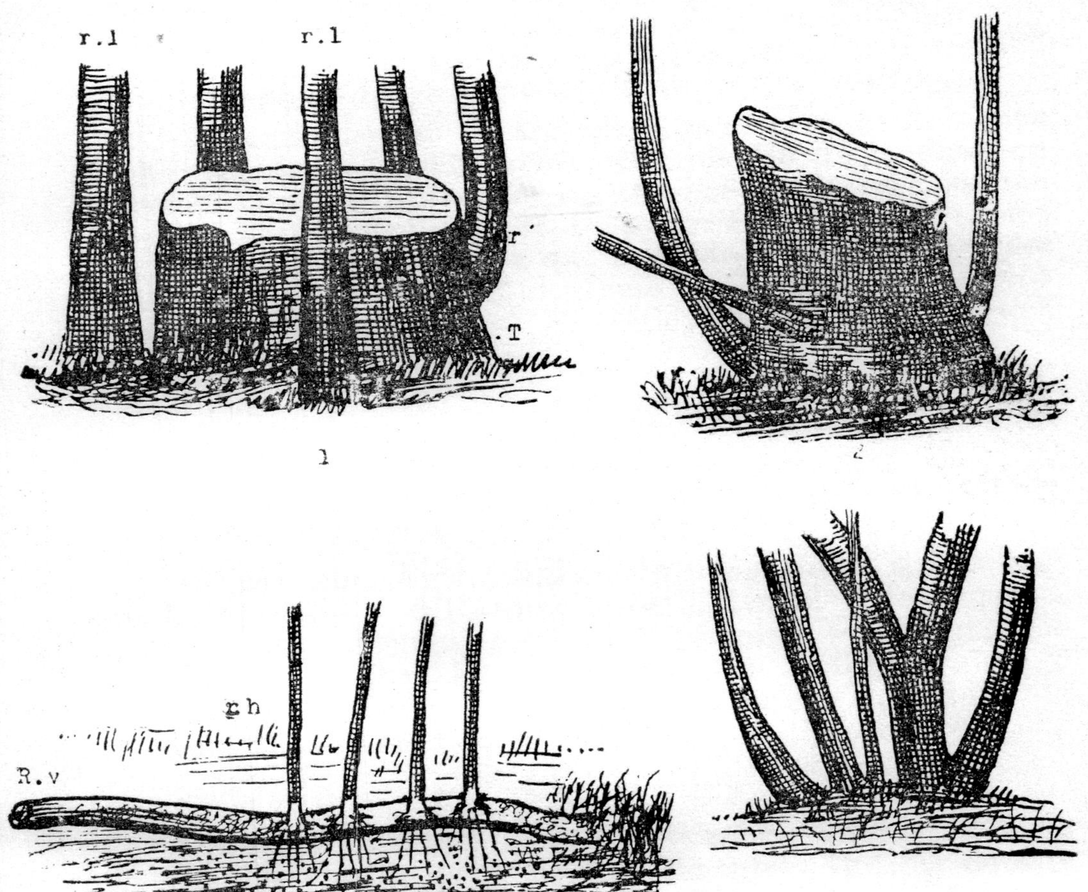

r.1
r.1
r
T
1
2
rh
R.v
3
4

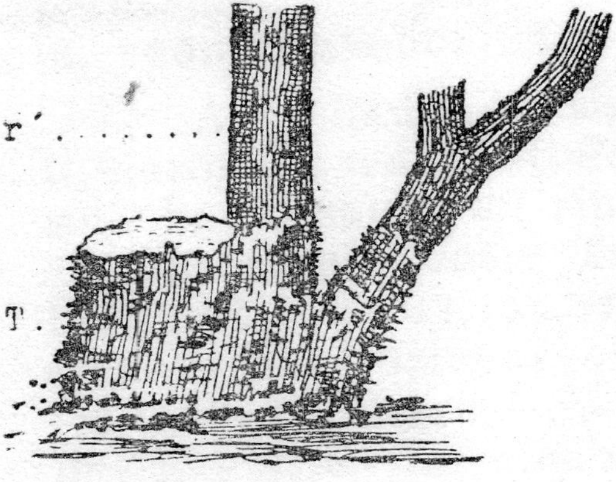

r´
T.

1

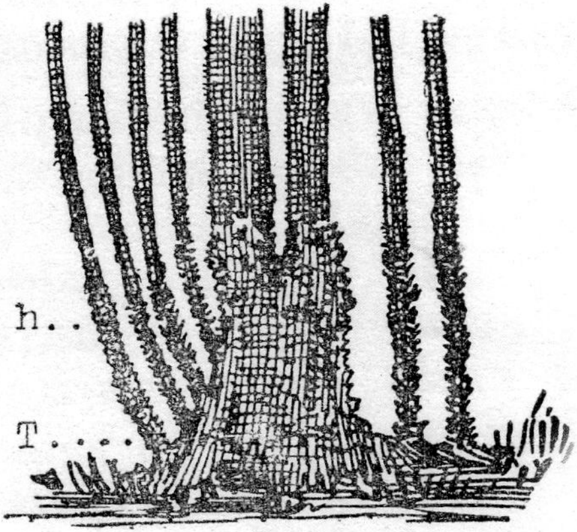

h..
T...

2

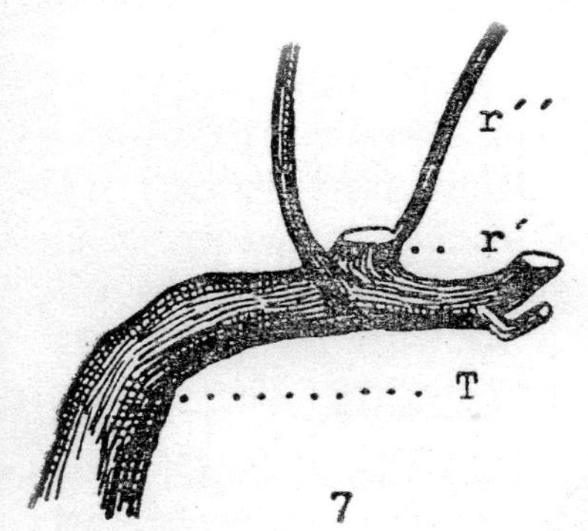

7

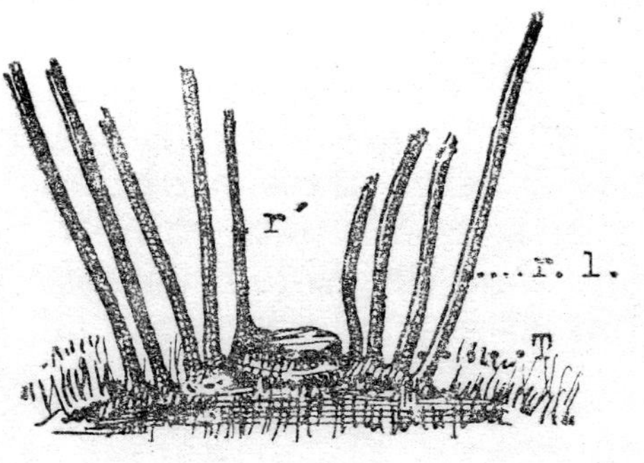

8

Misael Acosta-Solís, *Notas sobre la Propagación Vegetativa de la Misión de Cinchona*, 1944

1944: Jungle Fever

With global supply cut off by Japanese forces during WWII and imminent fights against communism to follow, the quinine alkaloid $C^{20}H^{24}N^{2}O^{2}$ is finally synthesized for the first time by Harvard chemists William von Eggers Doering and Robert Burns Woodward. New York Times reporter William Laurence hails their discovery as one of the "greatest scientific achievements" in a century, a major step in delivering anti-malarial drugs to US soldiers in South Asia and Central America. In spite of the massive cost differential in manufacturing costs for synthetic quinine ($1,500/kg vs. $8/kg for natural quinine), the chemical substitute offers a strategic and locational advantage: organic chemistry decouples from conflicted geographies of production in South Asian plantations or political instabilities of Latin American countries. From this 'territorial untethering,' original supply chains of bark from the U.S. Cinchona Program are cut off shut and research networks shut down. U.S. imports from Ecuador and Peru plummet. The availability of synthetic quinine for troops precipitates another development in the fight against malarial-borne mosquitoes: the spraying of tropical forests with Dichlorodiphenyltrichloroethane (DDT). Using fast combat aircraft, the mixture of motor oil with DDT is held as "indispensable insecticide" in the new entomology of death.

1944: Territorial Resistance

As the most revered and respected Indigenous women in Ecuadorian history, Dolores Cacuango and Tránsito Amaguaña found the first plurinational Indigenous organization in Latin America on January 30th from Cayambe: *the Ecuadorian Federation of Indigenous Peoples* (FEI, *La Federación Ecuatoriana de Indios*). With strong ties to labor organizations and Indigenous rebellions of the 1920s and 30s, their vision is focused on statutes of self-empowerment, self-determination, and solidarity to overcome legacies of exclusion and exploitation of Indigenous Peoples, primarily persecuted by the State and its minority of white settlers. According to historian Marc Becker (scholar of US surveillance in Latin America and leftist-socialist movements in Ecuador), the FEI (later called FIE, *Federación Indígena del Ecuador)* "issued a blunt statement in one of the organization's first statements made only weeks after its founding. Dolores Cacuango denounces an attack against Doctor Ricardo Paredes in the city of Esmeraldas, the dignified functional representative for the Indigenous race in the Honorable Constituent Assembly, cowardly and entirely outraged by Pablo Simón Plata." Denigrated as criminal and bolsheviks, the FEI will issue and publish legally statements in nation-to-nation correspondence to assert human rights, land rights, and demands for restorative justice.

List II—Continued

Material	Commerce Import Class No.	Governing date
Pulpwood	4500.000 - 4596.000 inc.	1/12/44
Punga fiber	N. S. C.	3/5/43
Quinine salts or alkaloids from cinchona bark:		
Quinine sulphate	8102. 000	3/5/43
Quinine alkaloid	8103. 200	3/5/43
Other salts and derivatives of quinine	8103. 300	3/5/43
Cinchonidine and its salts	8103. 400	3/5/43
Cinchonine and its salts	8103. 500	3/5/43
Quinidine and its salts	8103. 600	3/5/43
Totaquine and totaquine compounds	N. S. C.	3/5/43
Raffia, unmanufactured	3409. 500	

Alfal
Ancl
oil
Ancl
sub
Ann
App
rat
Apri
eva
Argo
cru
Bala

1944: IP as Territory

The scientific and industrial process of synthesization leads to the first international patenting of quinine as a chemical compound and pharmaceutical drug. Since American and European patent laws do not recognize oral traditions (such as Indigenous knowledge or technology), Indigenous rights are excluded and shut out of the financialization of the global drug market namely by German, French, British, and American manufacturers. The intellectual property (IP) of the active alkaloid in the Cinchona plant, known and used for time immemorial by Andean Peoples (and their related Amazonian Nations), is effectively (but not irreversibly) stolen. Traditional herbal experts from Ecuador and medicinal healers of the Loja Region are not only excluded from the rights to royalties, but they are left dispossessed amongst the ruins of colonial extraction throughout the Cinchona forests of the Central Andes. Centuries of over-harvesting leave livelihoods of Kechwan Nations with few vestiges of Cinchona trees, notwithstanding depleted reserves of food sources and medicines. Forced out of traditional territories and fragmented across urban regions, tribal populations are displaced to the fringes of settler economies seeking expensive, industrial products and chemical, synthetic substitutes in metropolitan areas dominated by white merchants and traders.

THIS IS Ann.. . . . she drinks blood!

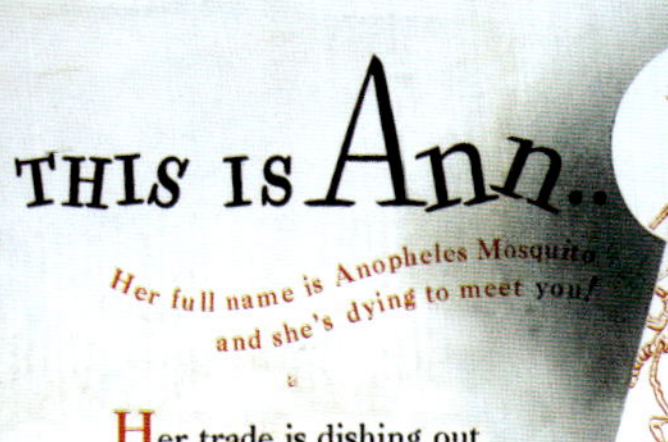

Her full name is Anopheles Mosquito and she's dying to meet you!

Her trade is dishing out MALARIA! If you'll take a look at the map below you can see where she hangs out.

She can knock you flat so you're no good to your country, your outfit or yourself. You've got the dope, the nets and stuff to lick her if you will USE IT.

Use a little horse sense and you can lick Ann. Get sloppy and careless about her and she'll bat you down just as surely as a bomb, a bullet or a shell.

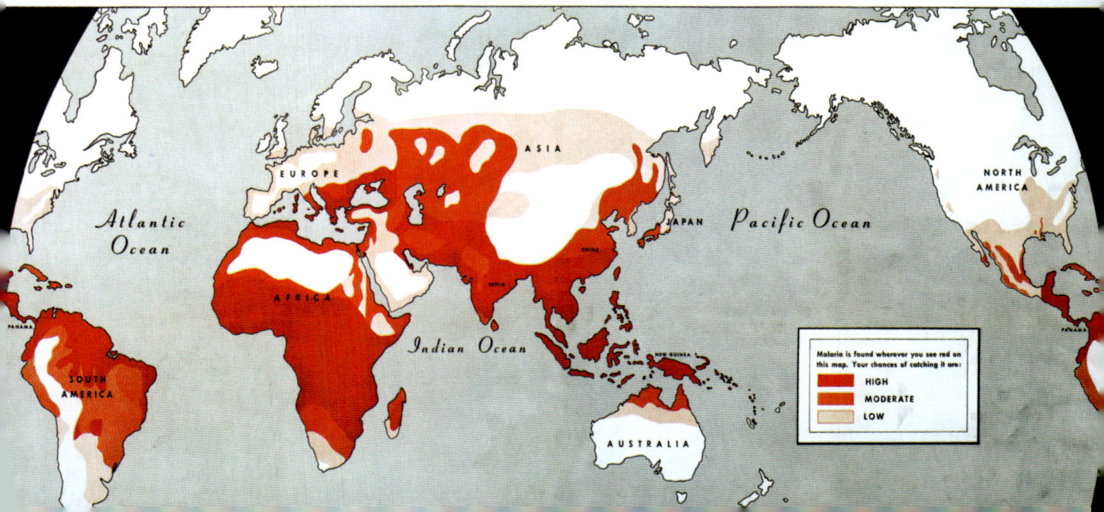

Atlantic Ocean

Pacific Ocean

Indian Ocean

EUROPE

ASIA

AFRICA

INDIA

CHINA

JAPAN

NEW GUINEA

AUSTRALIA

NORTH AMERICA

SOUTH AMERICA

PANAMA

Malaria is found wherever you see red on this map. Your chances of catching it are:

HIGH

MODERATE

LOW

1945–1957: Chemical Resistance

In a relatively short period of time, the antimalarial drug *chloroquine* is introduced for civilian consumption for the first time across countries of the West, while no sooner than twelve years later, the first case of malaria resistance against the synthetic drug will be identified. A host of other synthetic substitutes are developed (mainly for wartime purposes associated with the pending Vietnam War) and introduced later. The range of new synthetic drugs include *hydroxychloroquine, malarone, mefloquine,* and *quinine sulfate* as more resistant strains of malaria emerge. As the physical and mental side effects of anti-malarial drugs (fatigue, depression, hallucination, psychosis) are hotly debated and widely divergent, questions soon arise regarding the medical effectiveness of chemical substitutes versus the broad spectrum properties of traditional medicines and botanical sources. As chemical technology develops, the synthetic 'distancing' from the traditional, biological, and organic values of heirloom Cinchona bark extracts from plants endemic to the Loja Region in the Central Andes will prompt an expeditionary return of scientists during the second half of the 20th century and a renewed interest in tropical plantations.

1950–57: *LOST*, A Missionary Mystery

In a highly coveted missionary expedition sanctioned by the Protestant Church and funded by *Shell Oil Company* during the 1950s, "Operation Auca" sees the unsolved death of five Christian missionaries from the United States—a selfless band of interdenominational evangelists according to LIFE Magazine—who crash-land in Waorani Territory of Ecuador's Amazon while on an evangelical mission-turned-international mystery. Piloted by Nathaniel Saint of Mission Aviation Fellowship (a Christian organization founded in 1945 that according to them, "provides aviation, communications, and learning technology services to more than 1,000 Christian and humanitarian agencies, as well as thousands of isolated missionaries and indigenous villagers in the world's most remote areas"), the 5 missionaries were reportedly murdered on "Palm Beach," by nameless "savages". Never are they acknowledged as trespassers on sovereign Auca territory. Dramatized by one of the missionary widows, Elizabeth Elliott, in her best-selling book/film *Through the Gates of Splendor*, countless missions into the so-called darkness of the jungle and fog of the highlands continue into the next decades in a Christian quest to mobilize and civilize 'savages' on missionary reservations and make way for unimpeded oil extraction in so-called *tierras baldías,* the wastelands of colonization.

THE FIVE WIDOWS, who had been waiting at the Shell Mera, Ecuador mission station hear the agonizing account of discovery of their husbands' bodies in the jungle from fellow missionary Dr. Arthur Johnston (*foreground*) who went along with the overland search party. The listeners are (*left to right*) Marilou McCully, Barbara Youderian holding her 21-month-old son Jerry Lee, little Stephen Saint, Marjorie Saint holding one-year-old Philip, Olive Fleming and Elisabeth Elliot.

'GO YE AND PREACH THE GOSPEL' FIVE DO AND DIE

In the jungles of eastern Ecuador lives a tribe of Stone Age Indians called Aucas, little known even to anthropologists and until less than a month ago never photographed in their native surroundings. The young American missionary who took the picture on the opposite page is dead —murdered by the Aucas. His widow and four other bereaved wives are shown above as they heard how their husbands were martyred.

The five dead men formed a selfless band of interdenominational evangelists. James Elliot, Peter Fleming and Edward McCully had been sponsored by the Christian Missions in Many Lands. Roger Youderian belonged to the Gospel Missionary Union. Nathanael Saint was pilot and missionary with the Missionary Aviation Fellowship. They learned about the Aucas as they and their wives were ministering to Quechua-speaking and Jivaro Indians. The Aucas had killed all strangers for centuries. Other Indians feared them but the missionaries were determined to reach them. Said Elliot, "Our orders are: the Gospel to every creature."

They found the Aucas by flying over their territory in Nate Saint's small plane. For weeks they dropped presents to make friends. They finally touched down on a sand beach in the Curaray River and made face-to-face contact with the Aucas. The messages and diaries they shuttled back to their operations base were full of hope. Then, on January 8, they were set upon and speared to death. When the wives heard, they joined in a hymn their husbands had sung before entering Auca territory:

We rest on Thee, our Shield and our Defender
Thine is the battle, Thine shall be the praise
When passing through the gates of pearly splendor
Victors, we rest with Thee through endless days.

On these pages is the first complete story of the missionaries' martyrdom, brought to LIFE by Photographer-Correspondent Cornell Capa. It is told partly in their own photographs and diaries and partly in pictures by Capa. It is the story of five men who poignantly subscribed to the words which one of them, James Elliot, wrote in a diary five years ago: "When it comes time to die, make sure all you have to do is die."

'WE PRAISE GOD FOR HIS LEADING AND CARE'

Missionaries' diaries tell of good works to win friendship, leading up to fateful meeting on the beach

Among the effects of the missionaries whose bodies were found in the Curaray River were three diaries in which the men had recorded, step by step, the progress of their mission. LIFE herewith excerpts two of those diaries. One is by Nathanael Saint, pilot of the mission's plane and the other is by Peter Fleming. Saint's account starts by describing the scene at Shell Mera, the missionaries' base camp, in an entry dated Oct. 2, 1955.

Last night Ed McCully, Jim Elliot, Johnny Keenan and I were on the living room floor on elbows and knees poring over a map of the eastern jungles of Ecuador. We had just decided that it was the Lord's time to try to contact the savage Auca tribe located somewhere east of Ed's Quechua Indian mission station.

Later in the kitchen, over a midnight cup of cocoa, we decided that our efforts should be carried forward as secretly as practical so as to avoid inciting other nonmissionary groups to competitive efforts that would undoubtedly employ a heavily armed invasion party action overland. This we fear might set back the missionary effort among these Stone Age people for decades.

The actual search did not get under way until one morning in September. It was around 8:30 a.m., as I recall, and the river valleys, which are usually camouflaged by light-haze-foliage combinations, were clear in the distance. I'd been eying a blemish, barely discernible on the jungle, maybe five miles away. The blemish grew into a good-sized clearing. This was it. All told we must have seen about 15 clearings and a few houses. It was an exciting old time . . . a time we'd waited for.

A couple of weeks later we flew down a little river and spotted a half dozen big houses with smaller ones around them. The most significant part of it was not the information gained but the fact that after so much fruitless searching we had located the first group and then a couple of weeks later we practically stumbled over the other group. It seemed to mean that now was the Lord's time to do something about it. We agreed to be praying about it and compare notes later.

They decided that the first move was to fly over the Auca compounds and drop gifts. They planned to do this by circling slowly while suspending the gift on a long line which would be held stationary by gravitational pull. This they planned to do once a week, in the hope that the Aucas would come to welcome the regular visits.

The first gift was a small aluminum kettle with a lid. Inside we put about 20 brightly colored buttons, obviously not for their clothes since they don't wear any, but they do make good ornaments. To these things we attached about 15 brightly colored ribbon streamers about a yard long.

Fifteen minutes' flying brought us over the first clearings. About 15 minutes more assured us that we were over the house that interested us. We were about 3,000 feet above the ground. We could not see anyone on the ground, yet every indication showed clearly that the house was occupied. The house was about 40 yards from the edge of the stream and had a nice beach in front of it. A path showed that they used the *playa* [beach] frequently. The *playa* would be our target.

We slowed the plane down to 55 mph and held the gifts over the side and hooked up the automatic release mechanism. Then we slowly lowered it until well clear of the plane. We allowed the air speed to come up to 65 and began reeling out the line. All went well and we began circling at about 65 mph until the gift was drifting in a small, lazy circle below us, ribbons fluttering nicely. Still no sign of life below. The gift seemed pretty high so we started spiraling down.

Finally it looked pretty close to the trees below. Time for the attempt. A couple of times it seemed that we snatched [the gift] upward just in the nick of time to keep it out of trees bordering the beach. We made about six attempts at this elevation. Then we held our breath while [the gift] lowered toward the earth. It wouldn't be ideal for it to hit the water and it was heading close . . . close . . . closer . . . plunk! It hit about two or three feet from the water, directly in line with the path to the house. They couldn't miss it since they probably got their water for cooking right at that spot.

We had delivered the first gospel message by sign language to a people who were a quarter of a mile away vertically but, in a sense, 50 miles horizontally, and in a more real sense they were continents and wide seas away, for they had never been contacted by the outside world.

May God continue to put His good hand on the project and may we drop it when not fully assured of His direction. At present we feel unanimously that God is in it. May the praise be His and may it be that some Auca, clothed in the righteousness of Jesus Christ, will be with us as we lift our voice in praise before His throne. Amen.

The following Friday the plane went out again, with a machete as a gift.

Our plan was to check the beach where we left the gift last week. The gift was gone. We started to circle 2,500 feet above the house. Ed all of a sudden let out a yell. We were seeing our first Auca. Pretty soon there were three of them, watching the prize that dangled below the plane. We let on down. Then splash . . . and a bigger splash. The machete had released OK and an Auca had dived in for it.

The men still worried over the possibility of outside interference that might upset their delicate mission. To mask their activities they took circuitous routes in their flights over the Auca settlements. They adopted such code names as "Terminal City" for the Auca clearing. Meanwhile the air drops went on regularly, one each week. In all, some 10 machetes, 8 kettles, 6 shirts, 3 pairs of trousers and uncounted colored buttons and other trinkets were dropped in the 13 gift visits. The shirts, especially red-checked and pink ones, seemed to appeal particularly to the leaders of the community. One of the most ingenious air drops took place on Nov. 26 when the men tried littering the treetops so that the Indians would chop the trees down and make it easier for the plane to fly low over the settlement.

In rummaging in the emergency kit we found a roll of Waldorf [toilet tissue]. We thought it might help to get those tall trees down and it would seem easy to drape it in the treetops. However, it rolled out about six feet and then the wind tore off that length and then the process would be repeated until there was a white dotted line floating down into the trees.

On the ninth gift flight, Dec. 3, Saint and McCully got their first close look at an Auca.

We checked the hilltop clearing. I could see someone was there. They turned out to be two women, young. We passed within 50 feet of them and for the first time looked full into an Auca face. She was good looking, with hair cropped to bangs in front.

Meanwhile the missionaries had been learning some rudimentary phrases in the Auca language. And on another visit the Indians gave a gift in return.

This morning we took off at about 9:15 with gift-wrapped machetes, axes and small knives and plastic items. [Over the clearing] we made a low pass to drop an axhead. We spotted the boss man in the red-checked

AUCA HUT, part of village which the missionaries called "Terminal City," was photographed by Saint.

Flanked by a row of unw[...] in a clearing beside a trib[...]

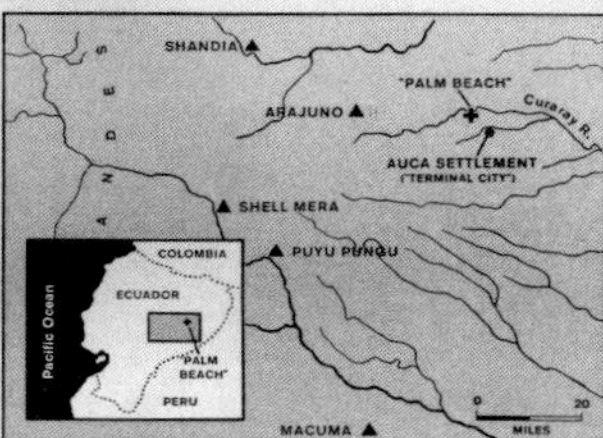

SETTING FOR TRAGEDY in Ecuador is shown in maps above. Big map shows same region as green area in small map. Cross marks "Palm Beach" in Curaray River near Auca Village. Youderian came from mission at Macuma, Fleming from Puyu Pungu, Saint from Shell Mera, Elliot from Shandia, McCully from Arajuno.

FOUR MARTYRED MISSIONARIES were *(left to right)* James Elliot, 28, from Portland, Ore.; Nate Saint, 32, of Huntingdon Valley, Pa.; Roger Youderian, 31,

from Lewistown, Mont., and Edward McCully, 28, from Milwaukee, Wis. Portraits like these, which show missionaries with combs and headdresses—gifts of

LIFE, *Go Ye and Preach the Gospel*, January 30th 1956

TED GIFTS, including a festooned kettle, by Saint in front of mission's Piper plane.

AUCA OFFERING was a girl brought to camp to be used as barter. The missionaries named her Delilah.

TREE HOUSE was built in jungle 30 yards from Palm Beach out of boards and aluminum which had been flown in. Picture shows McCully (*top*) and Elliot.

t in a basket
ith a partially

g and care.

heir portraits,
ot understand
me had come
Curaray River
They gave it
and supplies.

two minutes
under it and
checked the

the trees in a
came to the
of the water
ft sand—too
he softer spot
r came.
nd down the
moving sticks
-off position.
the wheels,
hung on and
eing over wa-
o gain speed

and took in-
tely essential
gested soften-

nce, checked
t tires stayed
ings out.
iority boards
s and boards
d the alumi-
for.
seen yester-
hat any man

had joined the

eing watched.
had a lighted

lantern "to keep the target well lit." At 5 a.m. they shined the flashlight down on the *playa* to check a gift machete left the night before. It was gone! For the next 15 minutes the jungles rang with Auca phrases—perhaps with a Midwestern accent. Then they shined the light for a closer look. A leaf had fallen on the knife so as to hide it. Tough!

Except for 47 billion flying insects of every sort this place is a little paradise. With the help of smoke and repellent we are all enjoying the experience immensely. Jim just pulled in a 15-inch catfish a little while ago. It is roasting over the fire now.

We find we have a friendlier feeling for these fellows all the time. We must not let that lead us to carelessness. It is no small thing to try to bridge between Twentieth Century and the Stone Age. God help us to take care.

The climax of the mission, the confrontation of Auca and white man, was written down most fully by the last man to join the group, Peter Fleming. His account of Jan. 6, 1956, follows:

This is a great day for the advance of the gospel of Christ in Ecuador. Ed was at one end of the beach, Jim on the other and Roger, Nate and I in the center near the shack—all of us shouting phrases periodically. Suddenly from directly across the river a strong masculine voice began jabbering at Ed and immediately three Aucas stepped out into the open on the opposite bank, two women and a man. My heart jumped and thumped wildly as we walked slowly to join Ed and to shout phrases with him. We shouted "*puinani*" (come) and he replied lengthily, pointing frequently to the girl (of about 15–16) as perhaps willing to trade her for some knives. Jim started wading across the shallow, 20-yard-wide river.

The Aucas were a little afraid but as Jim gradually approached them, the girl began to edge toward the water and stepped off a log into the water with the fellow following her slowly and last of all the other woman. Jim caught them by the hand and began leading them across to our side. They were uneasy but did not seem terrified as they stepped out on our side and we all laughed, smiled and told them they had come well and not to be afraid.

The man was a young fellow of 20 or so, the girl younger and the woman perhaps 30 or so. They were completely naked except for a G-string worn around the waist. We walked toward the plane and showed it to them, explaining by sign language how the propeller worked. By then the Aucas were relaxed and showed no signs of fear, jabbered happily to themselves and to us, seemingly with little idea that we didn't understand them. The young girl was still childish though physically mature, seemed dreamy, rubbing her body against the plane and waving her hands in the air imitating the plane's movements.

Soon the fellow began to show interest in the plane and we guessed from his talk that he was willing to go to his house to call his comrades. We put a shirt on him and he climbed in the plane with no sign of any emotion except eagerness to do his part. Nate taxied down the strip and took off while the fellow shouted all the way. After circling and shouting briefly Nate landed again, thinking to give the fellow a rest before making the flight to Terminal City. Nothing doing! He was ready to go right then—I guess he shouted all the way over and back and thoroughly enjoyed his trip.

My theory is that he had been sent with the girl and her mother (?) to give us the girl in exchange for paring knives and beads. We are praying that the others will come over and invite us to go over to their place—this fellow has seemed reluctant whenever we mentioned the subject and it may be he lacks the authority to invite us on his own.

Their curiosity apparently satisfied, the three Aucas melted back into the jungle. What then happened is suggested by the cryptic notes, evidently made in preparation for later diary entries, by Pilot Saint:

Heart heavy that they fear us.

Saturday night I was wide awake at 1 a.m., thinking of the many ways we might have tried to keep our visitors around on Friday. I guess the thrill of being with them and of their casualness quite disarmed us of keen constructive thinking. Perhaps it is the Lord's goodness that we had a quiet day yesterday (Saturday).

Song and prayer service. Spirits high on *playa*. Put beans on to cook.
Arrange shack for company.
Arrange "sand table."
Eat lunch.
Song and prayer service.
Short flight—no men at *chacra* [compound] now.
Going for bath now.

This note, apparently scrawled out at noon on Jan. 8, was the last record made of the mission to the Aucas before disaster struck. Half an hour later Saint was talking to the base camp over the plane's radio. "We are hoping for visitors at about 2:30," he said. "I'll call you again at 4:35."

He did not call back at 4:35. When his speared body was found in the river by the search party five days later, his watch had stopped at 3:12.

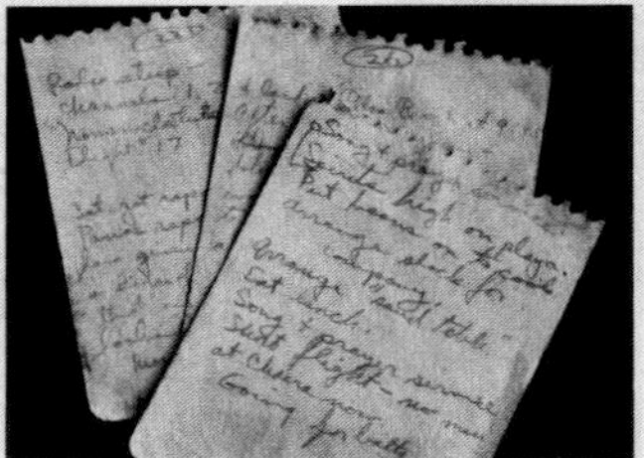

LAST WORDS of Saint's diary were found by search party in waterlogged notebook recovered from Saint's body. The body was found 440 yards downstream.

SAINT'S LAST PICTURES were developed from film in his camera, found in shallow river five days after death. Top pictures show Delilah on Palm Beach. In center she holds drink while older woman fingers ribbons attached to gift kettle previously lowered from plane. Emulsion of last picture was damaged by water.

SEARCH PARTY RENDEZVOUS near stripped plane (*left center*) occurs as helicopter (*center*) lands Major Nurnberg. At same time rescue party disembarks from canoes on Palm Beach to recover bodies. Tree house was just beyond beach.

HALF-SUBMERGED BODY of Elliot was found downstream in tangle of debris. Nurnberg made this picture during aerial reconnaissance to provide evidence in case body sank before it could be recovered. Three others were found nearby.

A BROKEN SPEAR protrudes from right hip of Roger Youderian's body as i is dragged behind Indian canoe to burial site. Another spear was pulled from hi back before body was moved. Aucas had also used machetes on some victims.

THE NEWS IS TRAGIC AND DANGER LINGERS AFTER HASTY BURIAL

At his headquarters Saint's friends waited for his 4:35 p.m. call and then, when it did not come, began a frantic search. Flying over the area one friend saw his plane and a body nearby. While a group of missionaries, guides and soldiers prepared for a river reconnaissance, the U.S.A.F. Air Rescue Service based in Panama flew in Air Force Major Malcolm Nurnberg to try a helicopter rescue. Landing alongside the plane, Nurnberg searched the area without results. On his way out by air, however, he spotted four bodies downstream and reported their location to the ground party.

Next morning, five days after the men disappeared, Nurnberg and the ground crew met on the beach to recover the bodies and discovered they had been pierced by Auca spears. The fifth, which was found by Indian fishermen, disappeared into the river before it could be removed. A heavy tropical rain fell as the burial service began, closing down flying operations and forcing the men to spend a harrowing night in the heart of Auca territory, facing the danger of another attack. Next morning, after firing into the air to discourage attack, Nurnberg and his sad party crept warily through the jungle before the Aucas could add them to their kill.

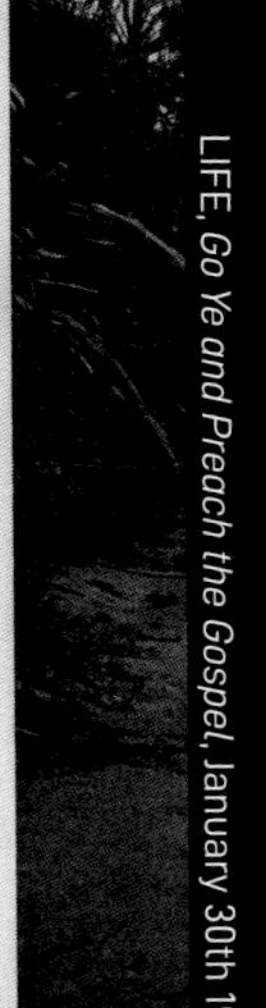

LIFE, *Go Ye and Preach the Gospel*, January 30th 1956

1970: Displacement

A revolving door of military dictatorships enact a series of water infrastructure laws that privilege supply to urban populations in cities from more remote river sources at the expense of rural areas. By 1972, General Guillermo Rodríguez Lara declares *Ley de Aguas* with Decree 369 (*National Water Law*) at the onslaught of major petroleum discoveries and a period of accelerated migration to cities: "to exercise rights over natural resources in the most decisive way in order to establish in a real and definitive way national sovereignty over territorial waters, land, and the subsoil." As peri-urban poverty explodes around the major cities of Quito and Guayaquil, derisively labeled as "slums" and "informal settlements" by the *United Nations Development Programme*, so do water supply problems. In one of the first, long-term water infrastructure project (*Pita-Tambo*), more than 1,500 rural Indigenous farmers in an area of 850 hectares are deprived of their traditional waters in the upper valley of Río Guayllabamba, thus triggering rural displacement. Dispossession of Indigenous Peoples (most often labeled as 'peri-urban migration') is now performed through national infrastructure planning and state strategies of resource extraction. Through the pressure of the metropolis exerted on hinterlands—*urbanism*—is by force a form of settler-colonialism.

Yann Arthus-Bertrand, *Guayaquil*, 1970

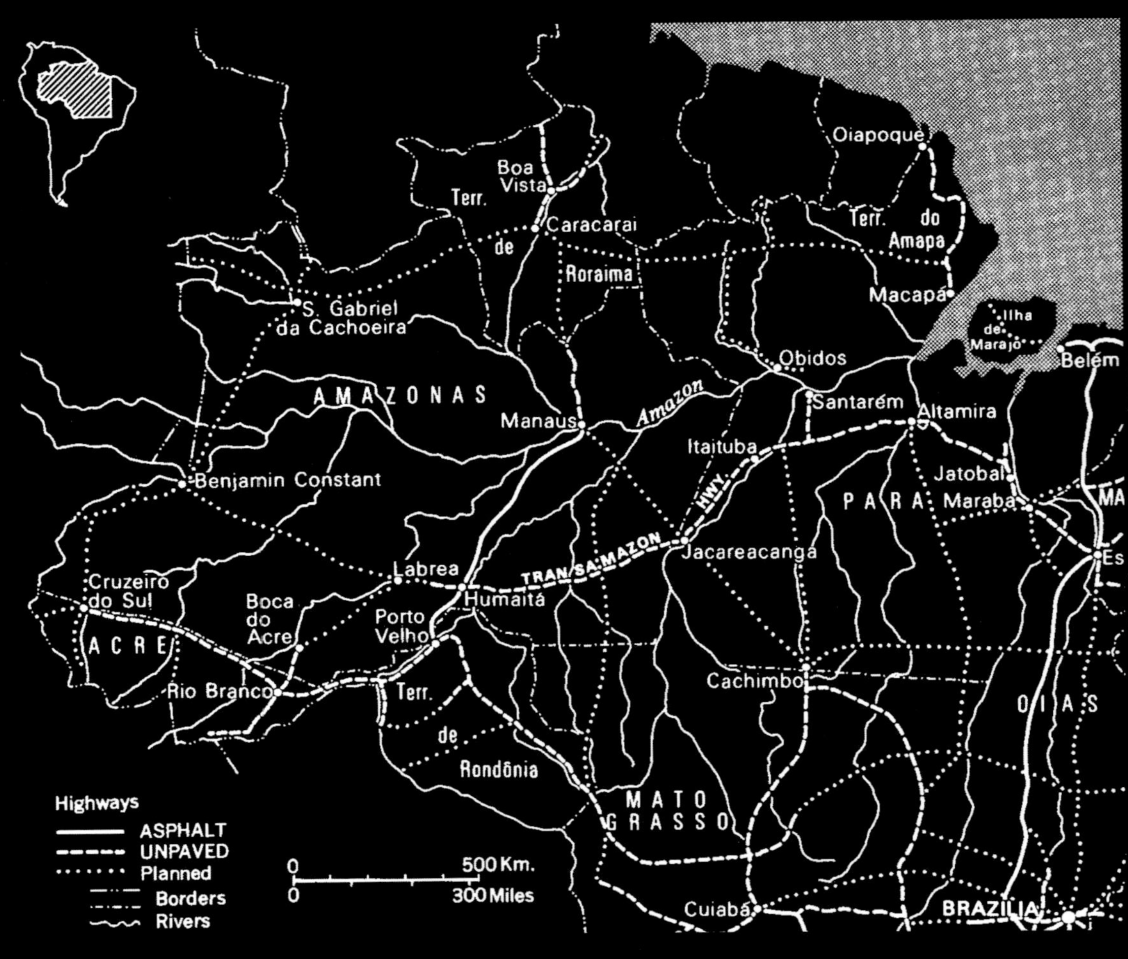
Oiapoque
Boa Vista
Terr.
Caracarai
de
Roraima
Terr. do Amapa
Macapá
Ilha de Marajo
Belém
S. Gabriel da Cachoeira
Obidos
AMAZONAS
Santarém
Altamira
Manaus
Amazon
Itaituba
Benjamin Constant
Jatobal
PARA
Maraba
MA
HWY
TRANSAMAZON
Jacareacanga
Es
Labrea
Cruzeiro do Sul
Humaitá
Boca do Acre
Porto Velho
ACRE
Cachimbo
Rio Branco
Terr.
OIAS
de
Rondônia
MATO GRASSO
Highways
ASPHALT
UNPAVED
Planned
Borders
Rivers
0
500 Km.
0
300 Miles
Cuiaba
BRAZILIA

1970: TransAmazônica

As an effort to unite the economies of Brazil, Colombia, Peru, and Ecuador in a single and continuous system of transcontinental trade based on resource extraction from the Amazon Rainforest, a 4,000-kilometer paved highway (BR-230) is proposed by Brazil's Ministry of Agriculture and the Institute of Colonization & Agrarian Reform (INCRA, *Instituto Nacional de Colonização e Reforma Agrária*, headquartered in the federal capital Brasília). While the project suffers from epileptic starts due to the exorbitant capital costs of highway construction, the State's master plan opens rampant levels of foreign investment that will irreversibly transform the region for the next half-century. At the turn of the millennium, the newly created investment portfolio of rapidly developing countries—the so-called BRIC economies (Brazil, Russia, India, China)—paves the real yet more distanced and unseen path towards accelerated destruction by foreign securities investment whose focus remains on the three "R"s of the Trans-Amazonian project: roads, rivers, and runways.

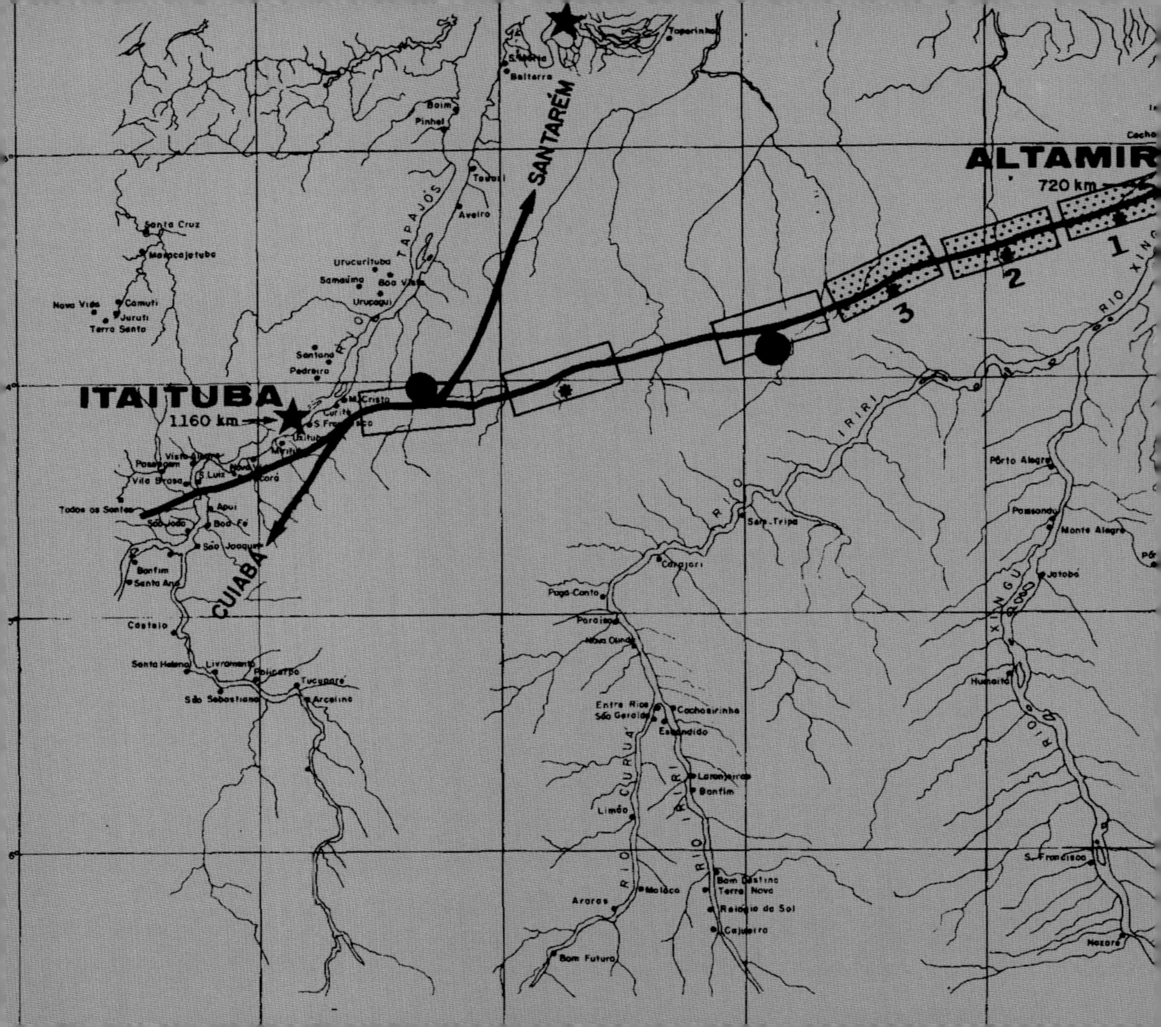

ITAITUBA
1160 km
SANTARÉM
CUIABÁ
ALTAMIR
720 km
1
2
3
RIO TAPAJÓS
RIO XINGU
RIO IRIRI
RIO CURUÁ
Santa Cruz
Maracajetuba
Nova Vida
Camuti
Juruti
Terra Santa
Urucurituba
Samaúma
Boa Vista
Urupagui
Santana
Pedreira
M. Cristo
S. Francisco
Curité
Todos os Santos
Passagem
Vila Brasa
S. Luiz
Apuí
Boa Fé
São João
São Joaquim
Bonfim
Santa Ana
Castelo
Santa Helena
Livramento
Policarpo
Tucuparé
Arcelino
São Sebastiano
Belterra
Boim
Pinhel
Aveiro
Toperinho
Pôrto Alegre
Passandu
Monte Alegre
Jatobá
Humaitá
S. Francisco
Nazaré
Pago-Conto
Paraíso
Nova Olinda
Carajari
Entre Rios
São Geraldo
Cachoeirinha
Laranjeiras
Bonfim
Limão
Bom Destino
Terra Nova
Relógio do Sol
Cajueiro
Malóca
Araras
Bom Futuro

INCRA, TransAmazônica: Esquema Diretor de Organização do Território, 1976

Manchete

Cr$ 4,00 • N.º 1.043 • RIO DE JANEIRO, 15 DE ABRIL DE 1972

VIAGEM FANTÁSTICA PELA TRANSAMAZÔNICA

Revista Manchete, *Amazônia*, 1973

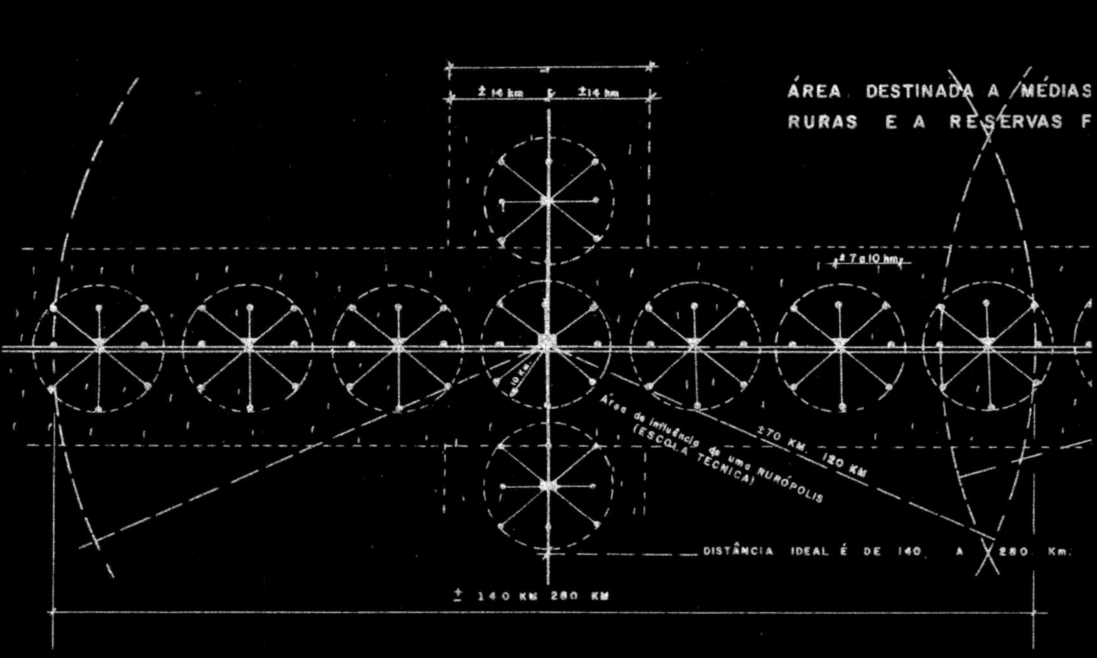
ÁREA DESTINADA A MÉDIAS
RURAS E A RESERVAS F
± 14 km
±14 km
± 7 a 10 km
10 Km
Área de influência de uma RURÓPOLIS
(ESCOLA TÉCNICA)
±70 KM. 120 KM
DISTÂNCIA IDEAL É DE 140 A 280 Km.
± 140 KM 280 KM

INCRA, *Rurópolis: Esquema de Planejamento Urbano-Rural para Colonização em Rodovias*, 1971

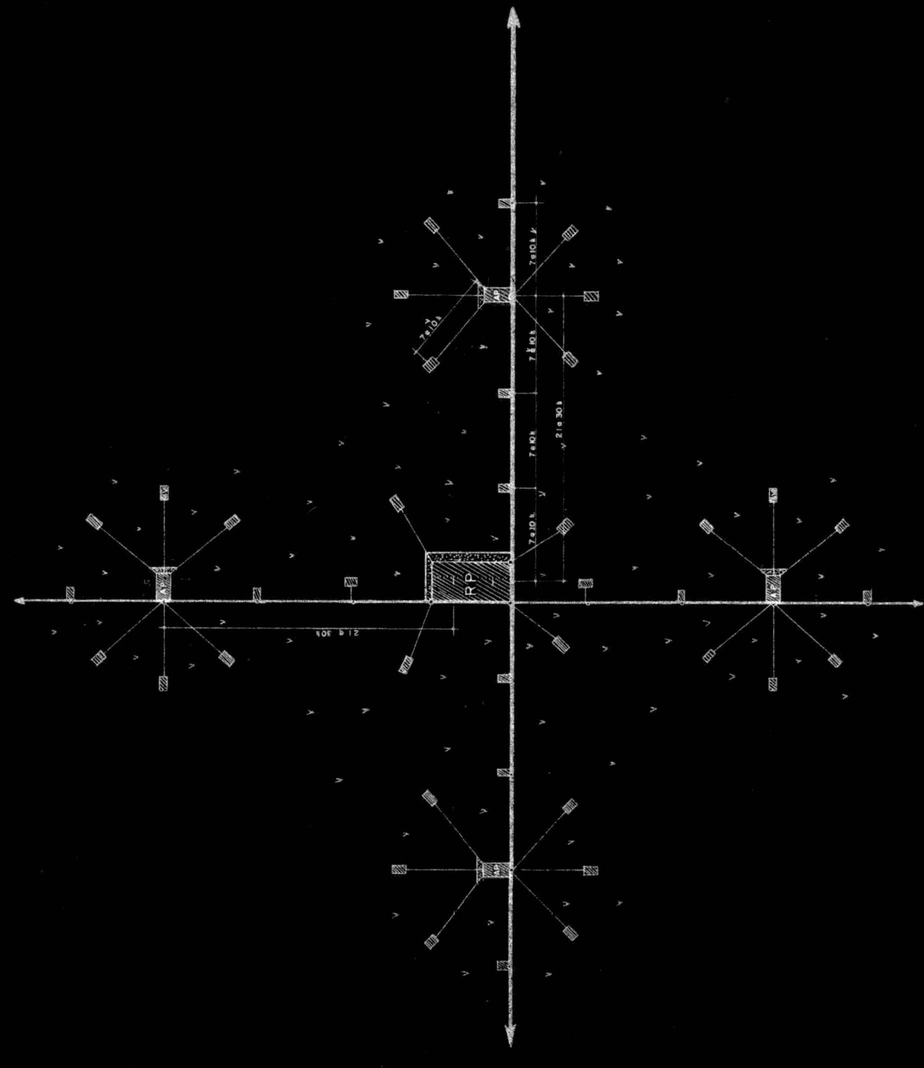

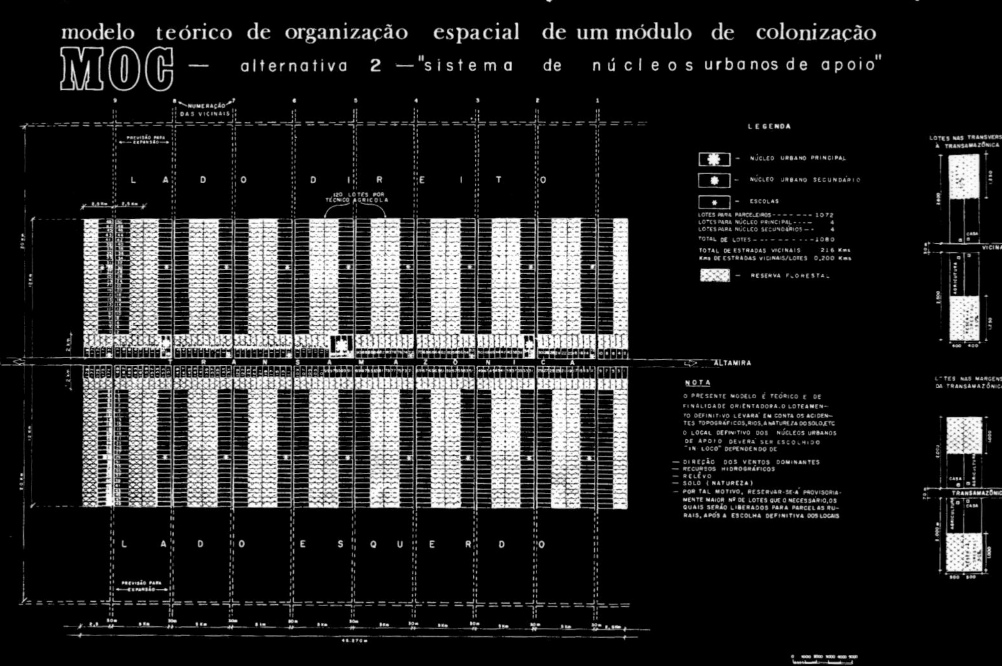

transamazônica
— ALTAMIRA —

MA·INCRA
MINISTÉRIO DA AGRICULTURA
INSTITUTO NACIONAL DE COLONIZAÇÃO E REFORMA AGRÁRIA
MÓDULO DE COLONIZAÇÃO
"MOC" – ALTERNATIVA 2
11

INCRA, *Rurópolis: Esquema de Planejamento Urbano-Rural para Colonização em Rodovias*, 1971

MA·INCRA

ESQUEMA TEÓRICO DE PLANEJAMENTO URBANO-RURAL PARA "ORGANIZAÇÃO TERRITORIAL DE UM MÓDULO DE COLONIZAÇÃO DAS TERRAS ALTAS DA AMAZÔNIA"

AUTOR: JOSÉ GERALDO DA CUNHA CAMARGO
ARQUITETO E URBANISTA

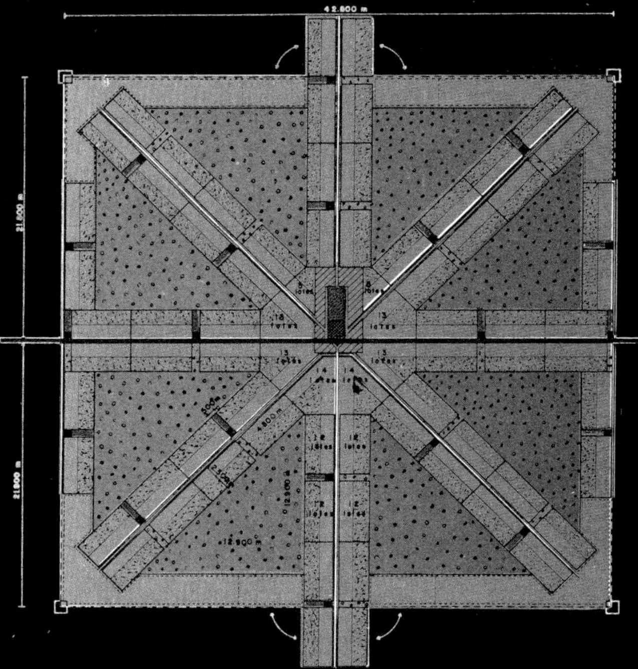

MÓDULO DE COLONIZAÇÃO (TEÓRICO) 183 184 ha

AGRÓPOLIS	ACRÉSCIMO / PROJETO	406 ha / 225 ha	
AGROVILA	ACRÉSCIMO / PROJETO	75 ha / 50 ha	125 ha x 20 = 2 500 ha
AGRICULT. FLORESTAL	1ª OCUPAÇÃO / 2ª OCUPAÇÃO		90 790 ha
AGRICULT. HORTIGRANJ.	1ª OCUPAÇÃO RESPECTIVA RESERVA		1.960 ha
RESERVA FLORESTAL	PRESERVAÇÃO DA FLORA E FAUNA (COMO ÁREA REPRESENTATIVA)		68 164 ha
ESTRADA	VICINAL - PROJETO		
RODOVIA			
AGRICULT. FLORESTAL	A SER PROJETADA		19 060 ha
AGRÓPOLIS	A SER PROJETADA		80 ha
ESTRADA	VICINAL - FUTURA		

RESUMO:

ÁREA DESTINADA À COLONIZAÇÃO.......115.020 ha......62.79 %
ÁREA DESTINADA À RESERVA FLORESTAL.......68.164 ha.....37.21 %
TOTAL (ÁREA DO MÓDULO DE COLONIZAÇÃO)...183,184 ha.....100 %

RES (PARCELEIROS) PREVISTO PARA
ULO DE COLONIZAÇÃO

NÚMERO DE FAMÍLIAS DE AGRICULTORES (PARCELEIROS) PREVISTO PARA A FASE DE IMPLANTAÇÃO DO MÓDULO DE COLONIZAÇÃO

RESIDENTES NAS AGROVILAS (PROPRIETÁRIOS DE LOTES DE 100 ha) = ...816 FAMILIAS
RESIDENTES NA AGROPOLIS (PROPRIETÁRIOS DE LOTES DE 100 ha) = ...91 FAMILIAS
RESIDENTES NOS LOTES MAIS PRÓXIMOS À AGRÓPOLIS (PROPRIETÁRIOS DE LOTE DE ± 25 ha) 78 FAMILIAS
TOTAL DE AGRICULTORES (PROPRIETÁRIOS) = 985 FAMILIAS

NOTA:
NESSE ESQUEMA A FORMA GEOMÉTRICA FOI USADA EXCLUSIVAMENTE PARA FACILITAR OS CÁLCULOS DAS ÁREAS E A DIDÁTICA DA IDÉIA. O ESQUEMA SERVIRÁ DE DIRETRIZ, MAS DEVERÁ SER ADAPTADO À TOPOGRAFIA, ÀS PLANTAS PEDOLÓGICAS E DE UTILIZAÇÃO DOS SOLOS, AOS ESTUDOS CLIMÁTICOS, ETC.

22 – Esquema Teórico de Planejamento Urbano Rural para organização territorial de um "Módulo de Colonização das terras altas da Amazônia"

0 1 2 3 4 5 6 7 8 9 10 11 12 13 14 15 km

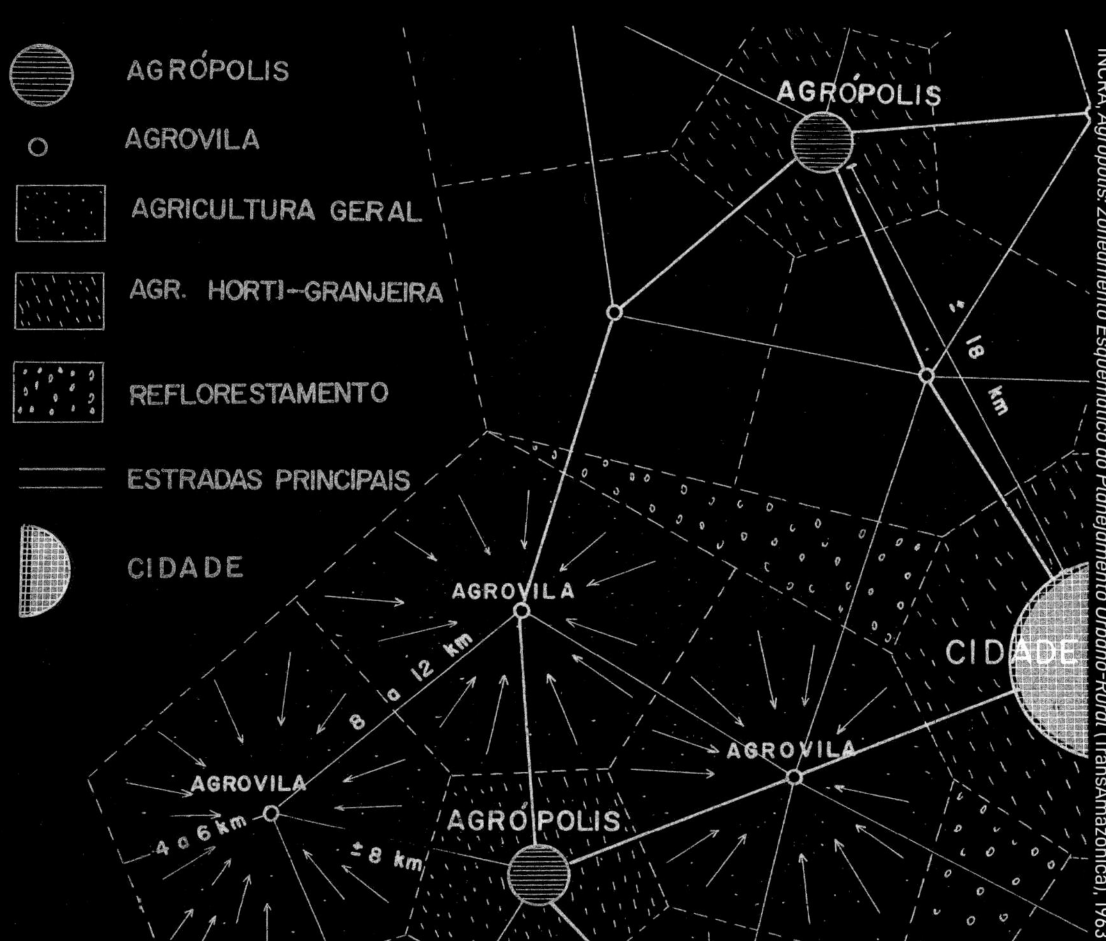

INCRA, *Agrópolis: Zoneamento Esquematico do Planejamento Urbano-Rural* (TransAmazônica), 1963

Pense num carro capaz de andar pela Transamazônica. Agora.
Em estrada pavimentada qualquer um passa.
Com postos de gasolina e oficinas por perto ainda é fácil.
Eu quero ver é andar agora pela Transamazônica com barro por baixo, mata por cima. Sem pôsto de gasolina, sem oficina, sem manutenção.
Ali, sòzinho, no peito e na raça.
É, amigão, o negócio é êsse aí. E nesse aí, só o Fuscão embarca.
Foi feito assim, uê. Forte, brabo, com torque para varar serra.
Motor 1500 que não cansa de correr, nem de subir, nem de viver.
Como você.
E a mecânica é garantida nas transamazônicas da vida, por êste mundo afora.
Em côres lindas, que combinam com o verde das nossas matas, o azul do nosso céu, o branco das nossas praias, certo?
É, amigão, a verdade dói, mas precisa ser dita - o melhor carro, para andar na Transamazônica amanhã, é o único carro capaz de andar na Transamazônica hoje.
VW 1500
PLANO DE LA CIUDAD LINEAL

Transamazonica a redescoberta do Brasil

TransAmazônica / Flávio Alcaraz Gomes, *TransAmazônica*, 1972

CORREIO
1,00 BRASIL
TRANSAMAZÔNICA
DES. PUNTAR

Casa da Moeda do Brasil, TransAmazonica Commemorative Stamp, 1971

1971: Dispossession by Proxy

As a weaponized affront on civil liberties of African-American Peoples at the height of the Civil Rights Movement in the United States and ensuing rise of the Black Panther Movement—later disguised by FLOTUS Nancy Reagan a decade later with her anti-drug *Just Say No* campaign that instigates international guerrilla warfare—the *US War on Drugs* goes into overdrive by waging war on communism through decades-long paramilitary attacks on drug cartels, smuggling ops, and cocaine processing facilities across the Andes while masking an anti-Communist Cold War. US-backed South American guerrilla armies hunting down narco-traffickers are the new face of American imperialism displacing the largest cartels from Colombia into smaller neighboring countries like Venezuela and Ecuador, while criminalizing traditional Andean practices such as the use of coca plant whose powerful alkaloid is well known for its performance-enhancing effect. Dubbed an intoxicant and demonized by Jesuits for its perceived idolatry as early as the mid-16th century, it was effectively banned by the Spanish Crown in the 17th century throughout the Chota-Mira Valley first before nationwide prohbition, irrespective of the legacy of coca as medicinal plant used by Andean Peoples since nearly 10,000 BCE.

TEXACO
TEXACO-GULF
LAGO AGRIO No1
POZO DE
DESCUBRIMIENTO
CONCLUIDO: 8-ABR. 1967

1972: Dispossession by Petrol

Ironically named *Nueva Loja* after the historically-rich Cinchona harvesting region where Spanish colonizers first set foot in South America, the Texaco Petroleum Company sets up base-camp in Northern Ecuador's Sucumbíos Province in the late 1960s after a major oil 'discovery' near the Aguarico River, homelands of the Kofan (Cofán) Peoples. Also known as *Lago Agrio* after the company's first gusher back in Texas called 'Sour Lake,' the region becomes a petrocapitalist hinterland; Texaco is its superintendent. To accelerate extraction, a new 500-kilometer Trans-Andean Pipeline is built running east-west from the Western Amazon to the Central Andean Mountains to the Pacific coast whose new terminus is the Port of Esmeraldas. Precursor to *Petroecuador*, the State creates a huge consortium made of Texaco and Shell—the *Corporación Estatal Petrolera Ecuatoriana* (CEPE)—to coordinate the auctioning of large blocks of Amazonian land. Overseen by then General Guillermo Rodríguez Lara after successive military dictatorships, Ecuador's extraction fervor launches the former banana republic into the age of petroleum. The frontier myth of Nueva Loja, the new boomtown, makes *terra nullius* of the strategically designated 'Amazon' as unoccupied wilderness. The 20-year agreement between the State and Texaco sees not only black gold flowing

across the Andes at a rate of 200,000 barrels a day but it encounters a major push-back: Indigenous resistance organizes around the ensuing environmental hazards and operational violence. Man-camps, resource despoliation, illegal logging, infrastructural floods, erosion, and unchecked pollution of waterways from spills and emissions are unseen, external effects of an economy dedicating 30% of the country's Gross Domestic Product (GDP) to oil exports. In what will be the largest oil spill in world history (twice the size of the 1989 Exxon Valdez Spill), the territories of Kichwa & Waorani Nations are dramatically impacted but General Rodríguez Lara will dig his heels in and proclaim, "we all become white when we accept the goals of national culture." According to Judith Kimerling in *Oil, Contact, & Conservation* (2013), "Ecuador, Texaco, and missionaries from the Summer Institute of Linguistics and Wycliffe Bible Translators (with funding from the Rockefeller Foundation) collaborated to pacify the Waorani Peoples and end their way of life... In addition to wells, pipelines, and production stations, Texaco built a 100-kilometer road into Waorani territory—which it named *Via Auca* (Kechwa for 'savage')—and settlers used the new road to colonize Waorani lands." Cured by petro-capitalism, oil extraction is aggrandized and naturalized as a national economic imperative by wasting the lands and territories of Indigenous Peoples.

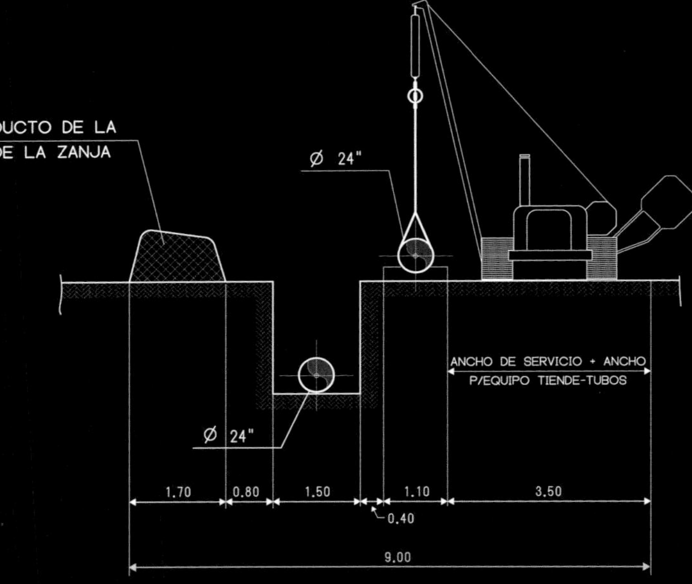

SISTEMA CONSTRUCTIVO RESTRINGIDO TIPICO INSTALACION DE TUBERIA ANCHO = 9.00

ESC ______ 1:75

Trans-Andean Crude Oil Pipeline under Construction (Pichincha), c.2010

Pacific Ocean
Pasto
Colombia
Esmeraldas
Tulcán
San Gabriel
Otavalo
Lago Agrio
Equator
Quito
Shushufindi
Coca
Latacunga
Rio Napo
ORIENTE
Manta
Portoviejo
Ambato
Rio Curaray
Rio Putumayo
Rio
Block 10
Riobamba
Bababoyo
Acuarico
Guayaquil
Salinas
Ecuador
1916 Treaty
Rio Tigre
Rio Napo
Cuenca
Machala
Rio Santiago
Rio Morona
Rio Amazonas
Iquitos
Loja
Talara
1830 Protocol
Rio Marañón
Brazil
Peru
LEGEND
Border of Ecuador prior to the 1942 Rio de Janiero
Ecuador

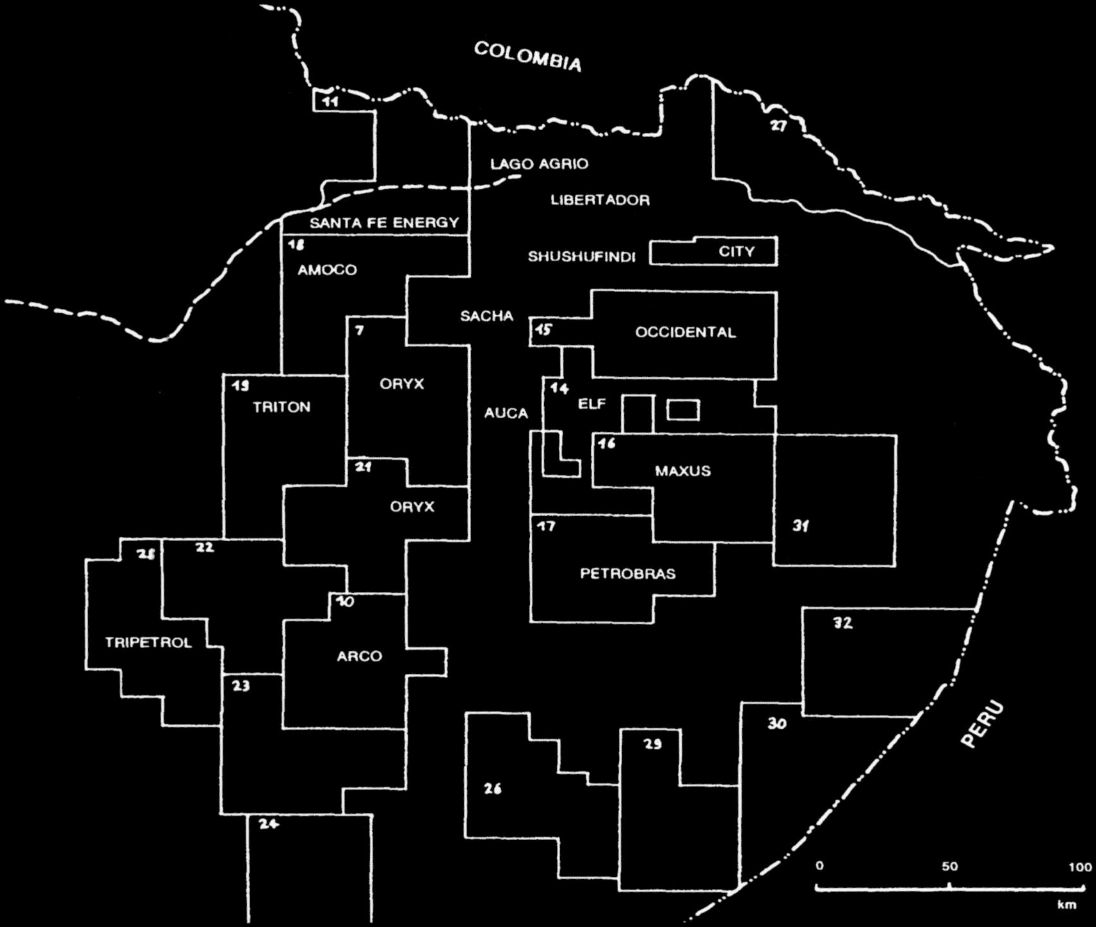

Major Oil Blocks & Petroecuador Fields 1967-1992 (Oriente Basin), 1995

COLOMBIA

11

27

LAGO AGRIO

LIBERTADOR

SANTA FE ENERGY

18

AMOCO

SHUSHUFINDI

CITY

SACHA

15

OCCIDENTAL

7

ORYX

19

TRITON

14

ELF

AUCA

16

MAXUS

21

ORYX

17

31

28

22

PETROBRAS

10

TRIPETROL

ARCO

32

23

30

PERU

29

26

24

0 50 100

km

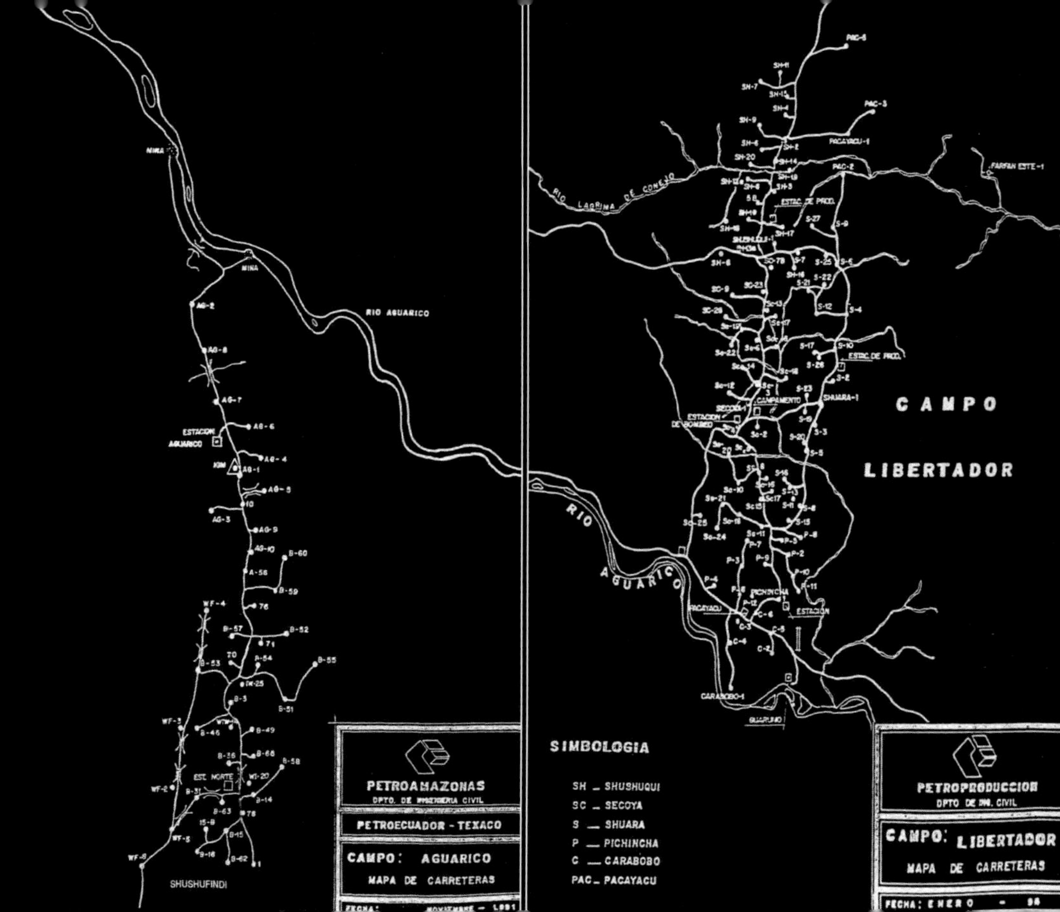

RIO AGUARICO
MINA
SHUSHUFINDI
PETROAMAZONAS
PETROECUADOR - TEXACO
CAMPO: AGUARICO
MAPA DE CARRETERAS
RIO LAGRIMA DE CONEJO
RIO AGUARICO
CAMPO LIBERTADOR
FARFAN ESTE-1
PACAYACU-1
SHUARA-1
SECOYA-1
CARABOBO-1
PICHINCHA
CAMPAMENTO
ESTACION DE BOMBEO
SIMBOLOGIA
SH _ SHUSHUQUI
SC _ SECOYA
S _ SHUARA
P _ PICHINCHA
C _ CARABOBO
PAC _ PACAYACU
PETROPRODUCCION
DPTO. DE ING. CIVIL
CAMPO: LIBERTADOR
MAPA DE CARRETERAS
FECHA: ENERO - 96

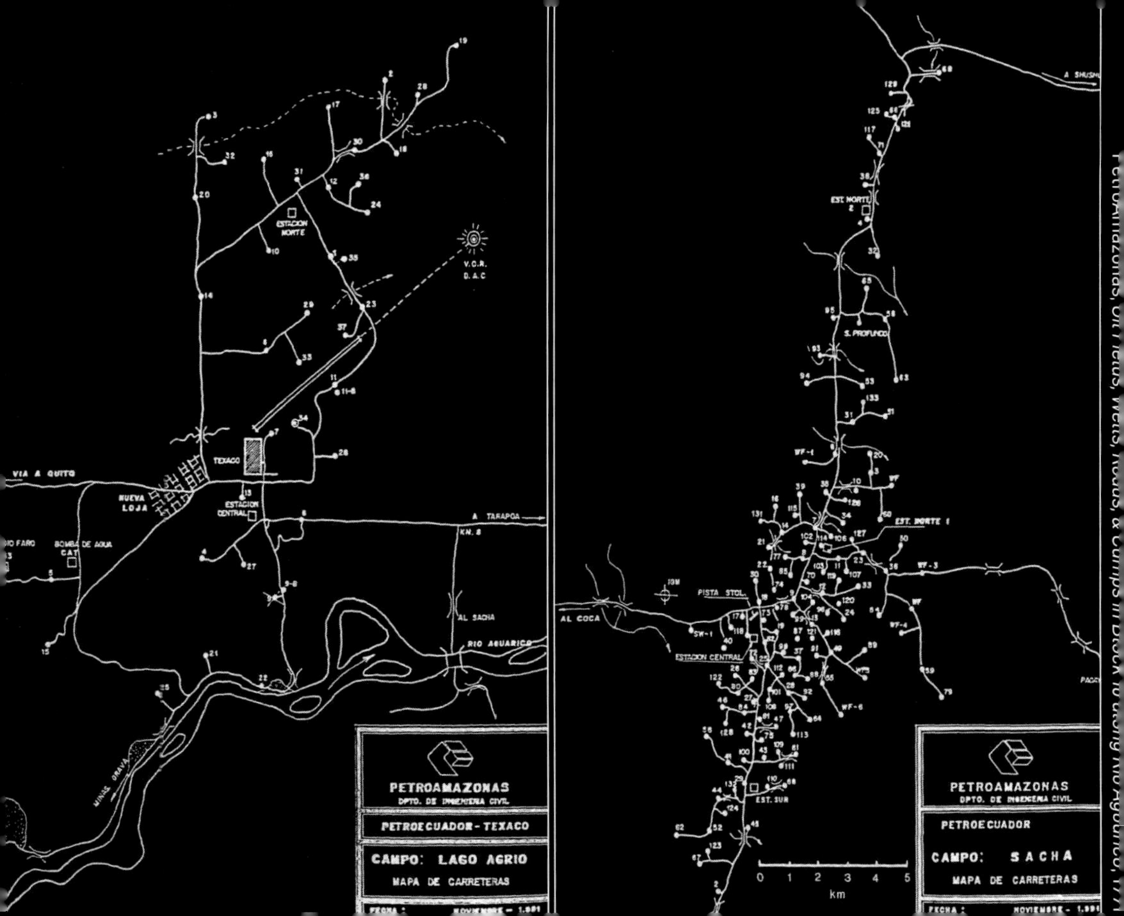
VIA A QUITO
NUEVA LOJA
TEXACO
ESTACION NORTE
ESTACION CENTRAL
V.C.R.
D.A.C
A TARAPOA
KM. 8
BOMBA DE AGUA
CAT
AL SACHA
RIO AGUARICO
MINAS GRAVA
PETROAMAZONAS
DPTO. DE INGENIERIA CIVIL
PETROECUADOR - TEXACO
CAMPO: LAGO AGRIO
MAPA DE CARRETERAS
FECHA: NOVIEMBRE - 1.991
EST. NORTE 2
S. PROFUNDO
EST. NORTE 1
PISTA STOL.
IGM
AL COCA
ESTACION CENTRAL
EST. SUR
0 1 2 3 4 5
km
PETROAMAZONAS
DPTO. DE INGENIERIA CIVIL
PETROECUADOR
CAMPO: SACHA
MAPA DE CARRETERAS
FECHA: NOVIEMBRE - 1.991

de Suc
" Lago Agric
RIO
AGUARICO
Sta Cecilia
Rio Pushino
UMBAQUI
1128
RIO
COCA

Texaco – Willbrosud, *Plan of Trans-Ecuadorian Pipeline* (detail), 1969

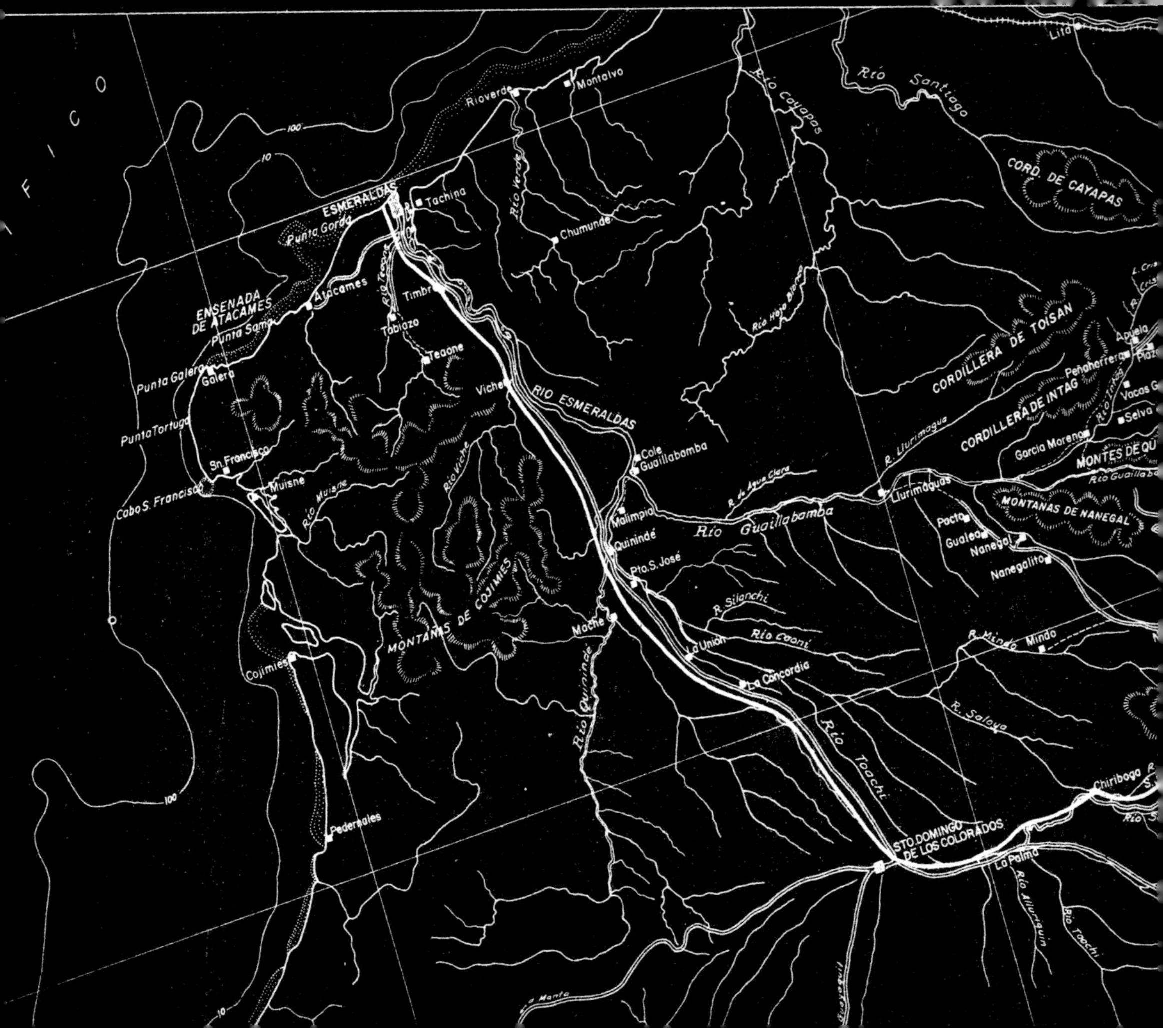

Lita
Montalvo
Rioverde
Río Santiago
Río Cayapas
100
10
CORD. DE CAYAPAS
ESMERALDAS
Tachina
Punta Gorda
Río Verde
Chumunde
ENSENADA DE ATACAMES
Atacames
Río Teaone
Tabiazo
Teaone
Punta Sama
Río Hoja Blanca
CORDILLERA DE TOISAN
Apuela
Peñaherrera
Punta Galera
Galera
Viche
RIO ESMERALDAS
CORDILLERA DE INTAG
Río Intag
Punta Tortuga
R. Llurimagua
Garcia Moreno
Cole
Guaillabamba
Sn. Francisco
Río Viche
Muisne
Río Muisne
Cabo S. Francisco
R. de Agua Clara
Llurimaguas
Río Guaillabamba
Malimpia
Río Guaillabamba
MONTAÑAS DE NANEGAL
Pacto
Gualea
Nanegal
Quinindé
Pto. S. José
Nanegalito
MONTAÑAS DE COJIMIES
R. Silanchi
Mache
La Unión
Río Cooní
R. Mindo
Mindo
Cojimies
La Concordia
R. Saloya
Río Quinindé
Río Toachi
Chiriboga
100
Pedernales
STO. DOMINGO DE LOS COLORADOS
La Palma
Río Alluriquín
Río Toachi
10

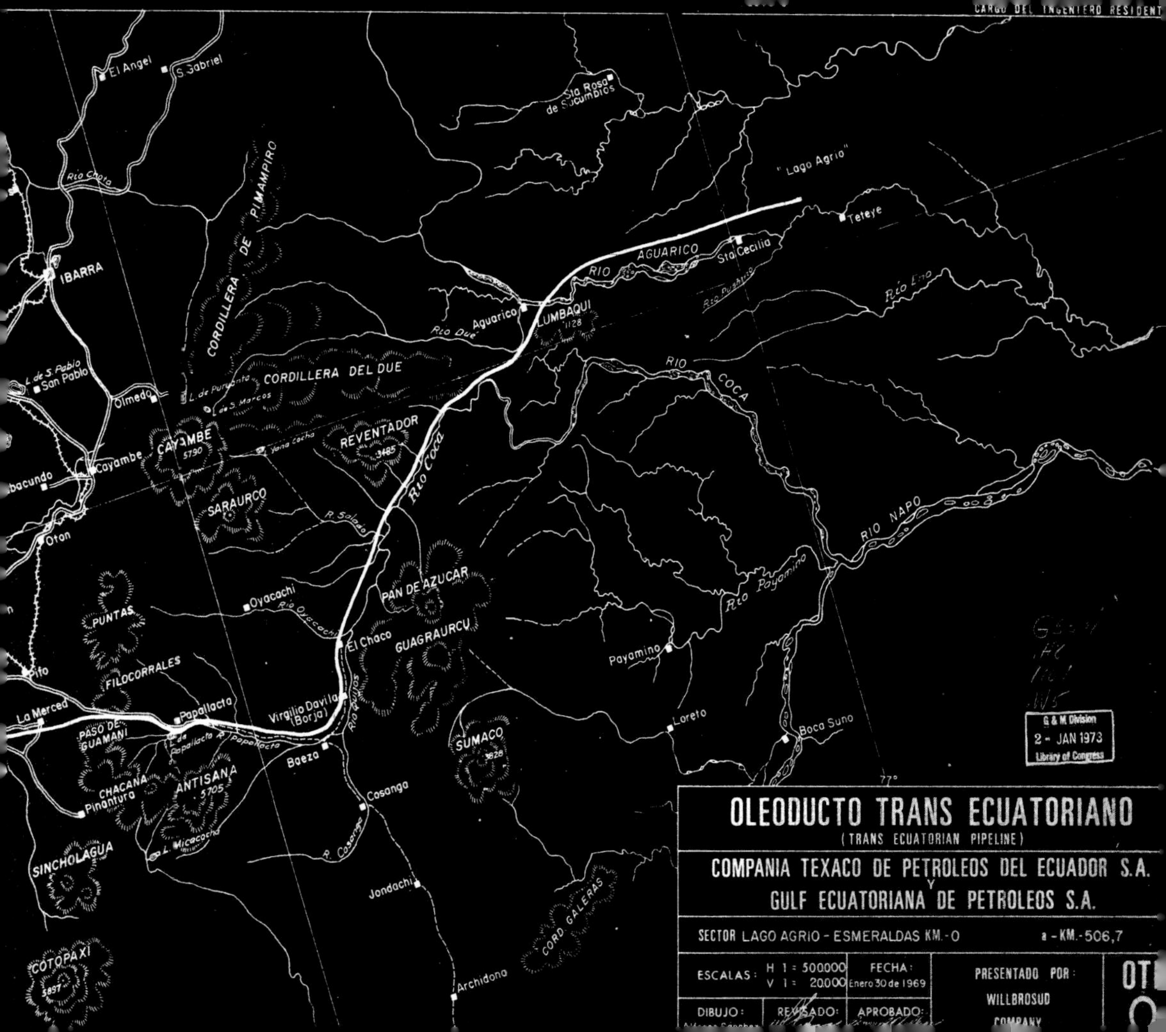
CARGO DEL INGENIERO RESIDENT
El Angel
S. Gabriel
Sta Rosa de Sucumbios
"Lago Agrio"
Teteye
Rio Chota
CORDILLERA DE PIMAMPIRO
IBARRA
AGUARICO
RIO
Sta Cecilia
Rio Pushino
Rio Eno
Aguarico
Rio Due
LUMBAQUI
1128
RIO COCA
L. de S. Pablo
San Pablo
CORDILLERA DEL DUE
L. de Puruanta
L. de S. Marcos
Olmedo
CAYAMBE
5790
Yana Cocha
REVENTADOR
3485
Rio Coca
Cayambe
bacundo
SARAURCO
R. Salado
RIO NAPO
Oton
PAN DE AZUCAR
Rio Payamino
Oyacachi
Rio Oyacachi
PUNTAS
El Chaco
GUAGRAURCU
Payamino
Pifo
FILOCORRALES
Virgilio Davila (Borja)
Rio Quijos
La Merced
Papallacta
Loreto
Boca Suno
PASO DE GUAMANI
L. de Papallacta
R. Papallacta
Baeza
SUMACO
3828
77°
CHACANA
Pinantura
ANTISANA
5705
Cosanga
L. Micacocha
SINCHOLAGUA
R. Cosanga
Jondachi
CORD. GALERAS
COTOPAXI
5897
Archidona
OLEODUCTO TRANS ECUATORIANO
(TRANS ECUATORIAN PIPELINE)
COMPANIA TEXACO DE PETROLEOS DEL ECUADOR S.A.
Y
GULF ECUATORIANA DE PETROLEOS S.A.
SECTOR LAGO AGRIO - ESMERALDAS KM.-0 a - KM.-506,7
ESCALAS: H 1 = 500000 V 1 = 20000
FECHA: Enero 30 de 1969
PRESENTADO POR: WILLBROSUD COMPANY
DIBUJO:
REVISADO:
APROBADO:
OT

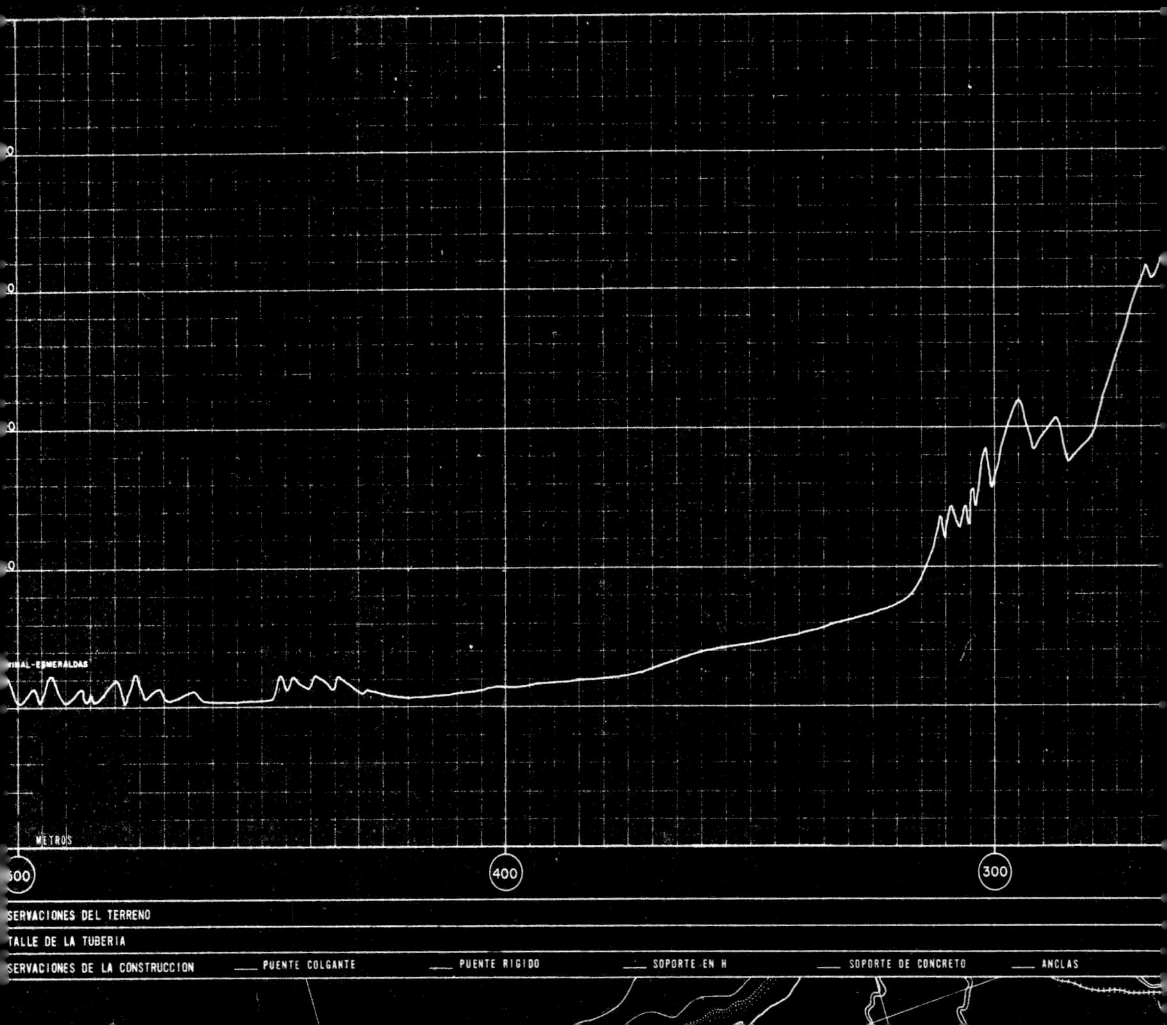

IBAL-ESMERALDAS
METROS
500
400
300
SERVACIONES DEL TERRENO
TALLE DE LA TUBERIA
SERVACIONES DE LA CONSTRUCCION
PUENTE COLGANTE
PUENTE RIGIDO
SOPORTE EN H
SOPORTE DE CONCRETO
ANCLAS

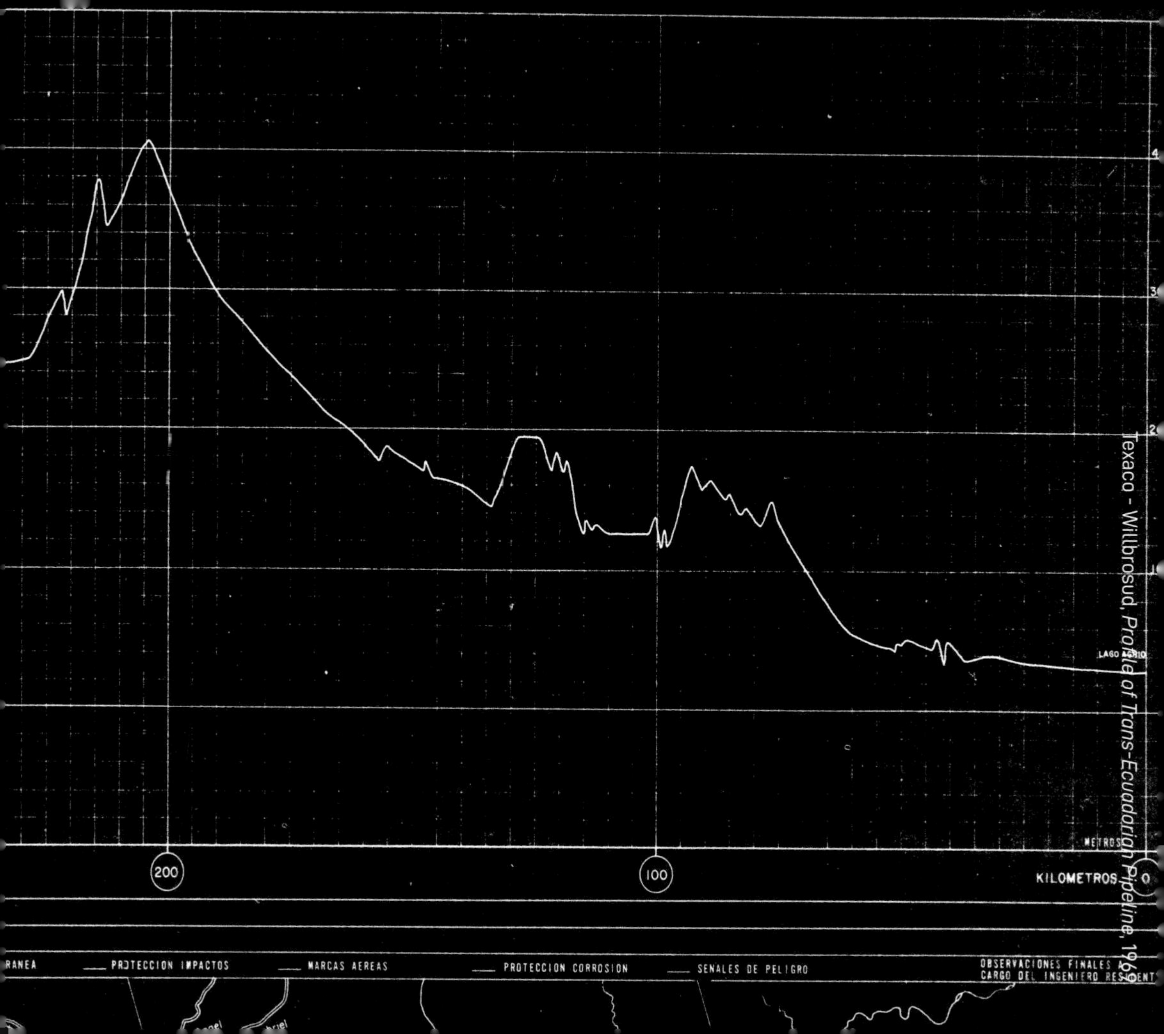

Texaco - Willbrosud, *Profile of Trans-Ecuadorian Pipeline*, 1969

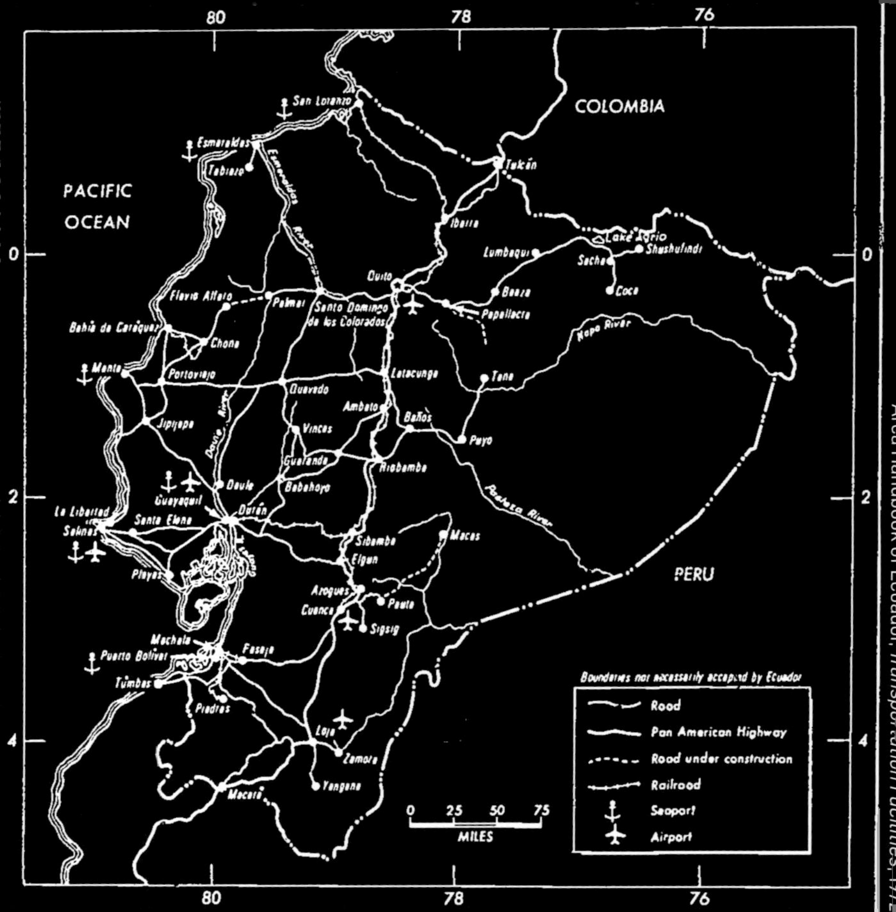

80
78
76
COLOMBIA
PACIFIC OCEAN
PERU
San Lorenzo
Esmeraldas
Tabiazo
Esmeraldas River
Tulcán
Ibarra
Lake Agrio
Shushufindi
Lumbaqui
Sacha
Coca
Quito
Baeza
Papallacta
Flavio Alfaro
Palmar
Santo Domingo de los Colorados
Bahía de Caráquez
Chone
Napo River
Manta
Portoviejo
Quevedo
Latacunga
Tena
Ambato
Baños
Puyo
Jipijapa
Vinces
Daule River
Guaranda
Riobamba
Daule
Babahoyo
Guayaquil
Durán
La Libertad
Salinas
Santa Elena
Pastaza River
Sibambe
Macas
Playas
Elgun
Azogues
Paute
Cuenca
Sigsig
Machala
Pasaje
Puerto Bolívar
Túmbes
Piedras
Loja
Zamora
Yangana
Macará
0
2
4
Boundaries not necessarily accepted by Ecuador
Road
Pan American Highway
Road under construction
Railroad
Seaport
Airport
0 25 50 75
MILES

BOTICAS DE TURNO

SU BOTICA, G. Avilés y Luque. Telfs. 528216 — 528211
CENTRAL, L. de Garaicoa 1.402. Telf. 518892
VENTRAL, L. de Garaicoa 1.402. Telf. 518392
ESPEJO, Machala 422. Telf. 392516
IDEAL, P. Moncayo 1132. Telf. 514411
NACIONAL, Ayacucho 2201. Telf. 380547
PANCHANA, Guaranda 1.204. Telf. 515683
S. FRANCISCO, 9 Octubre y P. Carbo. Telf. 515247
REX No. 3, 9 Oct. y Escobedo. Telf. 515713
PACY, Noguchi 231 y Calixto Romero

EL UNIVERSO

EL MAYOR DIARIO NACIONAL

AÑO 51 Nº 285 — Guayaquil — Ecuador — Lunes 26 de Junio de 1972

Edición Nacional
2 SECCIONES

Precio en Guayaquil: $ 1,60

INICIO Y FIN DEL OLEODUCTO: Obra de unidad geográfica de Oriente, Sierra y Costa Ecuatoriana. A la izquierda, los tanques de almacenamiento de la estación de Baeza, en el corazón de la selva amazónica. A la derecha, el puerto de Balao en la Provincia de Esmeraldas. Los dos oleoductos que llevan el petróleo hasta las boyas-atracaderos a 6 kms. de la playa. El oleoducto recorre 505 kilómetros del Oriente a la Costa.

Dr. Raúl Prebish, de ONU, llegó a Quito

QUITO, 25. — El doctor Raúl Prebish, Subsecretario General de la ONU, llegó ayer al país, en visita oficial de tres días. En el aeropuerto fue recibido por funcionarios de la Junta de Planificación y de la Cancillería. En la foto recibe el saludo del Embajador de Argentina, Ezequiel Federico Pereyra. — (Foto DE LA ROSA).

Hoy se instala la Comisión Para Desarrollo del Trópico

A partir de hoy se verificará en Guayaquil la III Reunión de la Comisión Asesora del Programa para el Desarrollo del Trópico Americano.

A este certamen internacional concurren Delegados de Venezuela, Colombia, Ecuador, Perú, Bolivia, Brasil y representantes del Instituto Interamericano de Ciencias Agrícolas (IICA). Este evento de alto nivel técnico se realizará en los salones del Hotel Humboldt, donde se aprecia un gran cartel de bienvenida colocado por los organizadores de esta reunión.

PROGRAMA

A partir de las nueve de la mañana se receptarán las inscripciones de los participantes. A las once de la mañana será la sesión inaugural. En este acto intervendrá el Ing. Agr. Gonzalo Gambarrotti, del Comité de Coordinación del Ecuador.

Sobre "los antecedentes del Programa Cooperativo, disertará, el doctor Luis A. Montoya, Secretario Ejecutivo del Programa para el Desarrollo del Trópico. Pertenece el doctor Montoya al staff del IICA, de la OEA.

La inauguración oficial de la reunión estará a cargo del Ministro de la Producción, economista Felipe Orellana Albán.

DELEGADOS DEL ECUADOR

La nómina de los delegados nacionales es la siguiente:

Ing. Mario León, de la Junta Nacional de Planificación; economista Luis Guerra, del Banco Nacional de Fomento; doctor Enrique Ampuero, Subdirector de INIAP; ingeniero Jacinto Varas, Director EET-Pichilingue; ingeniero Porfirio Lozano, del Programa Nacional del Banano y Frutas Tropicales; Oswaldo Yépez, del Ministerio de la Producción; Coronel Hernán Torres, del IERAC; mayor Fernando Chávez, del IERAC; ingeniero Jorge Gutiérrez del CEDEGE; ingeniero Augusto Bueno C., Director del Programa de Empresas Agrícolas; ingeniero Teodoro Landín F., del Programa Nacional del Arroz; ingeniero Jorge Andrade, del Programa Nacional del Arroz; ingeniero Walter Gómez V., del Programa Nacional del Arroz; ingeniero Bolívar Lupera, del Programa Nacional del Arroz; ingeniero Washington Naranjo, del Departamento de Extensión del Ministerio de la Producción; ingeniero Wilfrido Llaguno, del Programa Nacional de Granos y Forrajes; doctor Armando Cardozo, del IICA de la OEA; Oscar Valarezo Ayala, del Banco Nacional de Fomento de Guayaquil; Coronel Eudoro Naranjo, del Banco Nacional de Fomento de Guayaquil; ingeniero Sixto Cadena, de la Dirección de Planificación del Ministerio de la Producción; doctor Leonardo Paredes, Rector de la Universidad de Esmeraldas; ingeniero Enrique Suárez, de la Dirección de Planificación del Ministerio de la Producción; economista Héctor Garay H., Director del Centro de Coordinación Académica de la Universidad Central; doctor Antonio Andrade, Decano de la Facultad de Agronomía y Veterinaria de la Universidad de Guayaquil; doctor Fernando Santillán, Decano de la Facultad Forestal de la Universidad de Esmeraldas; ingeniero René Mendoza, del Programa Nacional del Arroz; ingeniero Heli Marín, de la Universidad de Esmeraldas; economista Holger Pazmiño, de la Universidad de Esmeraldas; ingeniero Jaime Cevallos Viteri, de la Comisión Nacional de Poza Honda; ingeniero

Pasa a la Pág. 5 Nº 1

Ceremonia de hoy en Balao

El Ecuador entra en la era del petróleo

Texto de
JAIME VELIZ LITARDO

Hoy, en una ceremonia que se cumplirá en la terminal petrolera de Balao, a 5 kilómetros de Esmeraldas, tendrá lugar la más tajante delimitación histórica de Ecuador, pues, con la apertura de las válvulas finales del Oleoducto Transecuatoriano, comenzarán a llenarse seis gigantescos tanques de acero con capacidad para 322.000 barriles de crudo cada uno, desde los cuales comenzará el embarque del petróleo, que generando ingentes divisas para el fisco, hará posible al Gobierno Nacional cumplir, en su totalidad, con los fines propios del Estado. Al mismo tiempo, este incesante y creciente flujo de divisas dó- [...] cres en el Banco Central para de allí salir al torrente circulatorio y crear mayor capacidad adquisitiva en el público.

FIN DE UNA HISTORIA Y COMIENZO DE OTRA

Hasta hoy, la historia del Ecuador ha sido un permanente suceder negativo en el cual, como oasis se han suscitado ligeros factores de progreso. La narración histórica nacional está llena de cuartelazos, de hombres ambiciosos de poder, de crímenes políticos, de persecuciones, de injusticias, de anarquía, caos, todo ello enmarcado por los déficit anuales de minúsculos presupuestos con que operaban los gobiernos.

En medio de aquello, como chispazos de esperanza se hacía presente el esfuerzo de [...] país, la acción de los guayaquileños José Joaquín de Olmedo y Diego Noboa para expulsar del poder político al militarismo extranjero que oprimía al naciente Ecuador, se hacía visible la visión de García Moreno, creando escuelas, normales, observatorios, escuelas politécnicas y —naturalmente— el penal panóptico que hoy lleva su nombre. Eloy Alfaro imprimiendo progreso mediante la liberación de instituciones y la humanización de las leyes y llevando a Quito el ferrocarril del sur. Esto, como excepción, puesto que la pobreza fiscal y la falta de recursos del Gobierno fueron siempre la norma sin excepción.

Al parecer, esta historia concluye para dar paso a un nuevo Ecuador, cuyo Gobier- [...] frondosa flora burocrática, emprender en obras públicas que represente una fuente considerable de trabajo, habrá, en suma suficientes medios de pago en poder del público, lo cual, en conjunción, promoverá un inusitado desarrollo social y económico, en todos los niveles.

UNA CLARINADA DE ESPERANZA

El 29 de junio de 1963 —exactamente hace 9 años— llegaron a Quito representantes de dos de las más grandes empresas petroleras del mundo, la Texaco Petroleum Company y de la Gulf Oil Company, quienes avizorando las posibilidades que ofrecía el nororiente ecuatoriano y formando un consorcio financiero para afrontar los gastos millonarios que la exploración exi-

El Universo, *The Port of Esmeraldas as Ecuador enter the Age of Oil*, 1972

SECRET ROUTINE

PAGE 001 OF 003

STATE/INR JCS/MC(DIA) CIA/NMCC
SWS NSA TREAS SDO
(HARD COPIES TO: NSC/S NFAC WHSITRM OCR).

THIS IS AN INFORMATION REPORT, NOT FINALLY EVALUATED INTELLIGENCE

DIST 14 FEB 78

1.5 (c)

1. IN MID-JANUARY 1978 ECUADOR AGREED TO PARTICIPATE IN CONDOR, A COUNTER TERRORISM ORGANIZATION COMPOSED OF THE INTELLIGENCE SERVICES OF SEVERAL SOUTH AMERICAN COUNTRIES. THE OVERALL RESPONSIBILITY FOR ECUADOR'S PARTICIPATION AND ACTIVITIES IN CONDOR LIE WITH THE ECUADOREAN JOINT COMMAND OF THE ARMED FORCES; HOWEVER, THE JOINT COMMAND HAS ASSIGNED VARIOUS INDIVIDUAL RESPONSIBILITIES TO THE ARMY, NAVY AND AIR FORCE. FOR EXAMPLE, THE ARMY THROUGH THE DIRECTORATE GENERAL OF INTELLIGENCE (DGI) IS RESPONSIBLE FOR INTELLIGENCE REPORTING AND THE EXCHANGE OF INFORMATION AMONG VARIOUS CONDOR MEMBERS. THE NAVY IS RESPONSIBLE FOR TELECOMMUNICATIONS AND THE AIR FORCE IS RESPONSIBLE FOR PSYCHOLOGICAL WARFARE. COMMENT:

1978: Operation Condor

In an effort to "eliminate Marxist subversion" and stamp out threats of Soviet influence, communism, and left-wing socialism in South American countries at the height of the Cold War, Ecuador joins in on the US-backed and CIA-operated, 'counter-terrorist' *OPERATION CONDOR*. Decades of epileptic presidential regimes dotted with the corrupt populist José María Velasco Ibarra (the longest serving President in Ecuador), the United States' decades-long relationship with Ecuador as co-guarantor of the 1942 Peruvian-Ecuadoran boundary (with Brazil, Argentina, and Chile) was one end of a long spear; decades of surveillance, intelligence-gathering, counter-intelligence, and covert operations based in Quito and Guayaquil in the fight against communism, namely power vectors from Colombia and Cuba. Following the US-financed, military-backed coup d'état that deposed Argentinian President Isabel Perón on March 24th, 1976, a right-wing military junta establishes a state of siege and martial law in cities across the country. Between 1976 and 1983, state-sponsored terrorism across Latin America will sanction the torture and murder of left-wing political dissidents and socialists will lead to the disappearance of over thirty thousand people whose whereabouts, to this day, remain unknown.

ECUADOR
AMERICA DEL SUR
OCEANO PACIFICO
OCEANO ATLANTICO
COLOMBIA
PERU
MUNICIPALITY OF METROPOLITAN DISTRICT OF QUITO
METROPOLITAN INSTITUTE OF HERITAGE
CENTER OF QUITO
PROPERTY: 375.25 HAS.
DATUM: WGS 84
N
01/42
GRAPH SCALE

1978: Conservation as Oppression

With the successful merger of universal heritage protection involving architectural sites *and* natural areas, the historic center of Quito (the cradle of Pre-Columbian culture) and the Galapagos Islands (Darwin's scientific wonderland) are recognized for their "exceptional universal value" and registered as the first World Heritage Site on the planet. The unspoken effect of eurocentric conservation based largely on the conservation of colonial histories practically guarantees the politicization of conservation of a handful of sites while ensuring the extractive destruction of many others far beyond the gaze of the unassumingly Promethean tourist. "World Heritage" designation is the perfect mirror and merger of two former and equally ambitious imperial endeavors: the *Venice Charter of 1961* on the protection of monuments (seated in Italy) and the *International Union for the Conservation of Nature* (seated in the US) on the protection of wilderness regions through the creation of national parks that converged at the first international *Conference on the Environment* at UNESCO in Stockholm in 1971. In the vein of other equally violent national park systems that rely on the dispossession of Indigenous lands, the creation of the World Heritage Site in the Amazon Rainforest poses as a late 20th century symbol of colonial conservation gone global.

Ecuador 79

QUITO Y LAS ISLAS GALAPAGOS, PATRIMONIO MUNDIAL

Febrero 1979

AEREO S/. 13.60

IMP. EN EL I.G.M. QUITO — ECUADOR

UNESCO World Heritage, *Commemorative Stamp: Quito & Galapagos Islands*, 1979

1978: Black, so What?

Out of her traumatic childhood experiences of racism, the Afro-Peruvian poet Victoria Santa Cruz (1922–2014) records a 4-minute performance titled *Me Gritaron Negra!* ("They shouted Black"), inspired by her father (playwright) and her mother (dancer), to overcome legacies of colonial erasure of Afro-Peruvian culture. Devalued and denied, Santa Cruz embraces the color of her skin, her body, and her ancestry, as sources of pride, regeneration, and emancipation—according to director Torgeir Wethal—by "setting her body in motion to the rhythm of clapping hands, constructing a powerful metaphor for emancipation by forcefully uttering the words 'Black, so What?'" According to scholar of Afro-Peruvian dance Katherine Aissa Porras, Victoria speaks of "ancestral memory" by, and through dance: "Rhythm is the great organizer. It is the key to our connections to the secrets of the organic cultures of the past. We can discover rhythms with the vehicle of the human body, never with the cold, colonizing intellect." Victoria's performance is a powerful setting space of emancipation akin to what historian Deonne N. Minto described as the imminent power of "black liberatory feminism" in Luz Argentina Chiriboga's 1992 *Drums Under My Skin*: "the release of the black female body, in particular, from imperial and patriarchal oppression will engender transformation."

1980: Metropolitanization III

Guayaquil, the port city in the Río Guayas estuary, where Cinchona bark was historically shipped off to Spain up until the 19th century, is now the largest city of the country with over 1 million inhabitants followed by the capital city of Quito. Concentrating the greatest wealth in the country (large landholders) alongside the largest poverty rates and largest slums (worker class) in Ecuador, half of the nation's population in the region live without access to potable water, regular electricity, or sanitary sewage. As the poorest country in South America, the rise of coastal slums (specifically in Guayaquil) increases dramatically after the 70s, following the national oil boom and infrastructure boom that sees the construction of highways such as the *Guayaquil-El Empalme Corridor* (E48 Highway), and the *Perimetral Highway* connecting to Guayaquil. With world oil prices dropping in the 1980s and worsening debt crisis (from suspended payments), the 1987 earthquakes will not only rupture the Trans-Ecuadorian and Poliducto (propane) pipelines along the Napo River region—that connects Quito to oil-producing Lago Agrio—but will expand the divide between élite minority (whites) and working class majority (Afro-Ecuadorian, Mestizx, Indigenous) hit the hardest by government austerity measures enforced by the US through the Inter-American Development Bank.

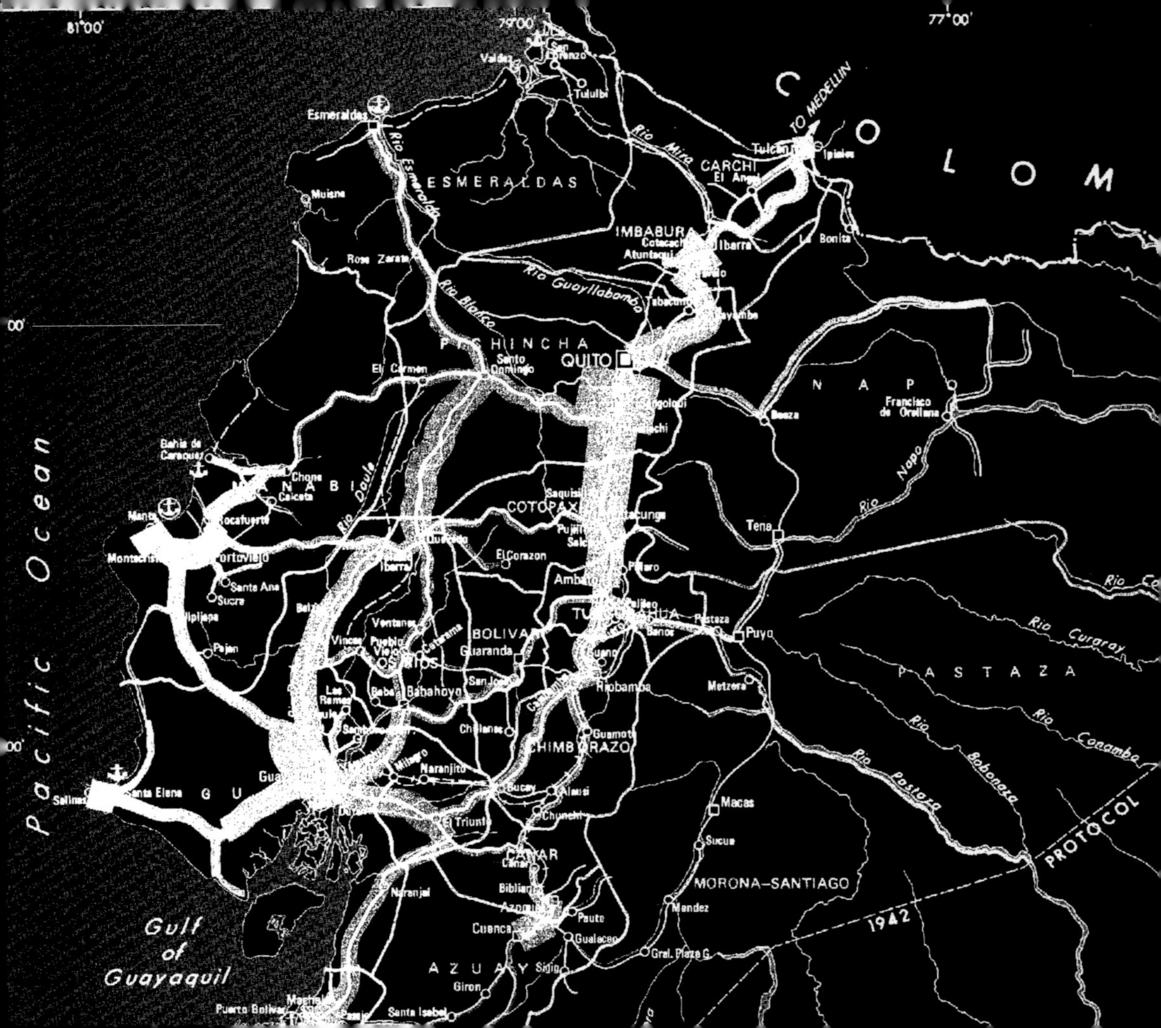

81°00'
79°00'
77°00'
Pacific Ocean
Gulf of Guayaquil
COLOM
TO MEDELLIN
Esmeraldas
Rio Esmeraldas
ESMERALDAS
Muisne
Rosa Zarate
Rio Blanco
Rio Mira
CARCHI
Tulcan
Ipiales
El Angel
IMBABURA
Ibarra
Cotacachi
Atuntaqui
La Bonita
Rio Guayllabamba
Tabacundo
Cayambe
PICHINCHA
QUITO
Santo Domingo
El Carmen
Tululbi
San Lorenzo
Valdez
Machachi
NAPO
Francisco de Orellana
Baeza
Rio Napo
Tena
Bahia de Caraquez
Chone
MANABI
Calceta
Manta
Rocafuerte
Montecristi
Portoviejo
Santa Ana
Sucre
Jipijapa
Pajan
Rio Daule
COTOPAXI
Saquisili
Latacunga
Pujili
Salcedo
Quevedo
El Corazon
Pillaro
Ambato
Pelileo
Banos
Pastaza
Puyo
Rio Curaray
PASTAZA
Rio Conambo
Rio Bobonaza
Rio Pastaza
Metzera
Ventanas
Vinces
Puebloviejo
Catarama
BOLIVAR
Guaranda
San Jose
Babahoyo
Baba
Las Ramas
Riobamba
Guano
Guamote
Chillanes
CHIMBORAZO
Milagro
Naranjito
Bucay
Alausi
Chunchi
Macas
Sucua
Salinas
Santa Elena
El Triunfo
CAÑAR
Cañar
Biblian
Azogues
Cuenca
Paute
Gualaceo
Naranjal
MORONA-SANTIAGO
Mendez
Gral. Plaza G.
AZUAY
Sigsig
Giron
Machala
Puerto Bolivar
Pasaje
Santa Isabel
1942
PROTOCOL

75°00' 73°00' SEPTEMBER 1975

ECUADOR

GUAYAQUIL SECOND PORT PROJECT

1972 HIGHWAY TRAFFIC FLOW

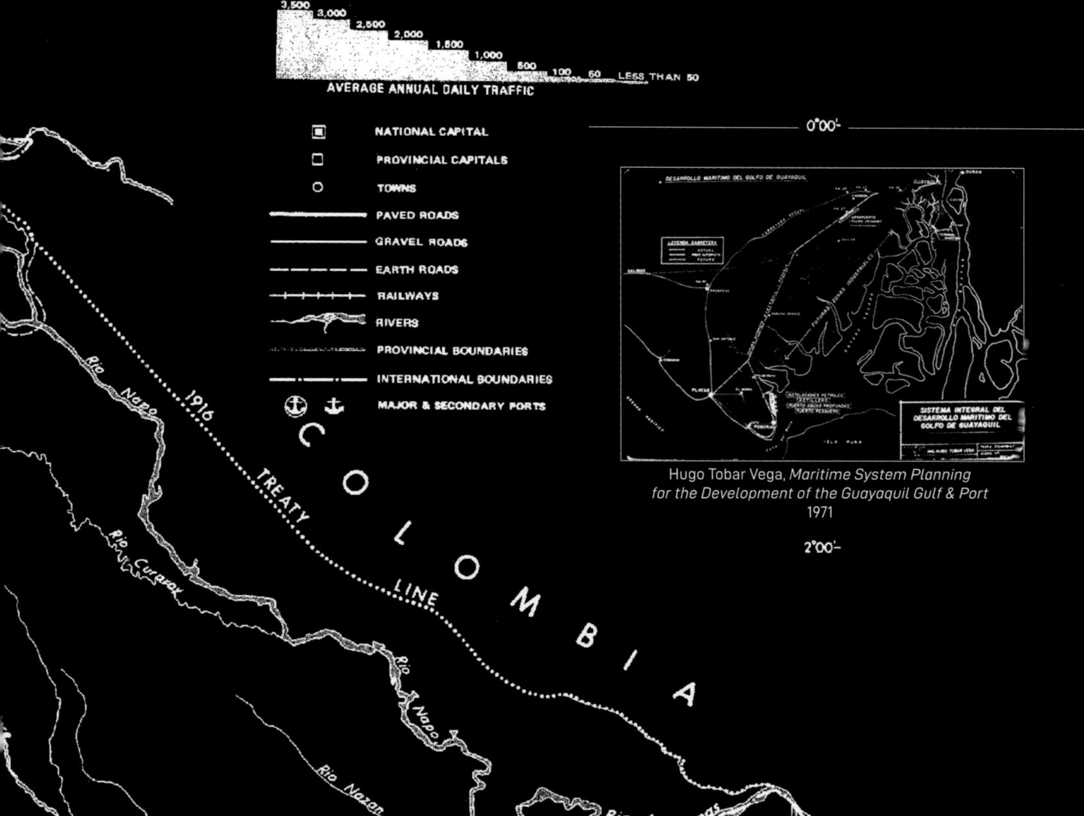

Hugo Tobar Vega, *Maritime System Planning for the Development of the Guayaquil Gulf & Port* 1971

World Bank, *Appraisal of a Second Guayaquil Port Project*, 1976

Yann Arthus-Bertrand, *Guayaquil*, 2009

1990: Solidarity & Resistance

From the Far North to the Far South, the first cross-continental gathering of Indigenous Peoples, *Encuentro Continental de los Pueblos Indígenas*, themed "500 Años de Resistencia" (*500 Years of Resistance*) takes place in Ecuador's capital of Quito, a second watershed event in the 500-year campaign to end Christopher Columbus Day occurring globally (and its quincentennial celebration planned in 1992) and history of *Indigenous Peoples Day,* following a proposal at the 1997 United Nations Conference in Geneva and the Native American solidarity movement at Alcatraz earlier in 1969. The meeting leads to the drafting of the *Quito Declaration* by over 150 Indigenous Nations from Abya Ala (colonized Latin American Nations) and from across the Turtle Island (colonized North America Nations). As a collective manifesto, its focus is on land and Indigenous sovereignty through the creation of 9 commissions for the conference, to establish an agenda of action items: women's rights, self-determination, 500-year history, education, governance, territory, law, human rights, and alliances. Subsequent pan-Indigenous meetings and conferences will take place to fulfill the prophecy of the *Eagle* and the *Condor*, the coming together of Indigenous Peoples from North and South as a Confederacy after five centuries of colonial oppression.

1990: The Declaration of Quito

The Continental Gathering "500 Years of Indian Resistance," with representatives from 120 Indian Nations, International and Fraternal organizations, meeting in Quito, July 17-20, 1990, declare before the world the following:

The Indians of America have never abandoned our constant struggle against the conditions of oppression, discrimination and exploitation which were imposed upon us as a result of the European invasion of our ancestral territories.

Our struggle is not a mere conjunctural reflection of the memory of 500 years of oppression which the invaders, in complicity with the "democratic" governments of our countries, want to turn into events of jubilation and celebration. Our Indian People, Nations and Nationalities are basing our struggle on our identity, which shall lead us to true liberation. We are responding aggressively, and commit ourselves to reject this "celebration."

The struggle of our People has acquired a new quality in recent times. This struggle is less isolated and more organized. We are now completely conscious that our total liberation can only be expressed through the complete exercise of our self-determination. Our unity is based on this fundamental right. Our self-determination is not just a simple declaration.

We must guarantee the necessary conditions that permit complete exercise of our

In this Gathering, it has been clear that territorial rights are a fundamental demand of the Indigenous Peoples of the Americas.

Based on these aforementioned reflections, the organizations united in the First Continental Gathering of Indigenous Peoples reaffirm:

1. Our emphatic rejection of the Quincentennial celebration, and the firm promise that we will turn that date into an occasion to strengthen our process of continental unity and struggle towards our liberation.

2. Ratify our resolute political project of self-determination and conquest of our autonomy, In the framework of nation-states, under a new popular order, respecting the appellation which each People determines for their struggle and project.

3. Affirm our decision to defend our culture, education, and religion as fundamental to our Identity as Peoples, reclaiming and maintaining our own forms of spiritual life and communal coexistence, In an Intimate relationship with our Mother Earth.

4. We reject the manipulation of organizations which are linked to the dominant sectors of society and have no Indigenous representation, who usurp our name for (their own) Imperialist interests.At the same time, we affirm our choice to strengthen our own organizations, without excluding or Isolating ourselves from other popular struggles.

self-determination; and this, In turn must be expressed as complete autonomy for our Peoples. Without Indian self-government and without control of our territories, there can be no autonomy.

The achievement of this objective is a principal task for Indian Peoples. However, through our struggles, we have learned that our problems are not different, in many respects, from those of other popular sectors. We are convinced that we must march alongside the peasants, the workers, the marginalized sectors, together with intellectuals committed to our cause, In order to destroy the dominant system of oppression and construct a new society, pluralistic, democratic and humane, in which peace Is guaranteed.

The existing nation-states of the Americas, their constitutions and fundamental laws are judicial/political expressions that negate our socio-economic, cultural and political rights.

From this point in our general strategy of struggle, we consider it to be a priority that we demand complete structural change; change which recognizes the inherent right to self-determination through Indian own governments and through the control of our territories.

Our problems will not be resolved through the self-serving politics of governmental entities which seek Integration and ethno-development. It is necessary to have an Integral transformation at the level of the state and national society; that is to say, the creation of a new nation.

5. We recognize the Important role that Indigenous women play In the struggles of our Peoples. We understand the necessity to expand women's participation In our organizations and we reaffirm that It Is one struggle, men and women together, in our liberation process, and a key question in our political practices.

6. We Indian Peoples consider It vital to defend and conserve our natural resources, which right now are being attacked by transnational corporations. We are convinced that this defense will be realized if it Is Indian People who administer and control the territories where we live, according to our own principles of organization and communal life.

7. We oppose national judicial structures which are the result of the process of colonization and neo-colonization. We seek a New Social Order that embraces our traditional exercise of Common Law, an expression of our culture and forms of organization. We demand that we be recognized as Peoples under International Law, and that this recognition be incorporated into the respective Nation States.

8. We denounce the victimization of Indian People through violence and persecution, which constitutes a flagrant violation of human rights. We demand respect for our right to life, to land, to free organization and expression of our culture. At the same time we demand the release of our leaders who are held as political prisoners, an end to repression, and restitution for the harms caused us.

Quito, Ecuador (July 1990)

Declaración de Quito y resolución del Encuentro Continental de Pueblos Indígenas, July 1990

1990: Mass Resurgence

On June 4th, 5th, and 6th, an uprising of Indigenous Nations from across Ecuador converge on the capital city of Quito in defense of *Pachamama* (*Mother Earth*, *Madre Tierra*), demanding from the Ecuadorian government to acknowledge historical forms of labor oppression and exploitation. With Indigenous women from different communities at the forefront of peaceful demonstrations and direct demands, communities across the countryside mobilize to form blockades in a coordinated effort to demonstrate a nearly unprecedented level of political strategy and territorial coordination with considerable effect on practically every major highway in the countryside showing the significance and impact of the late 1980s foundation of CONAIE, the *Confederation of Indigenous Nationalities of Ecuador.*

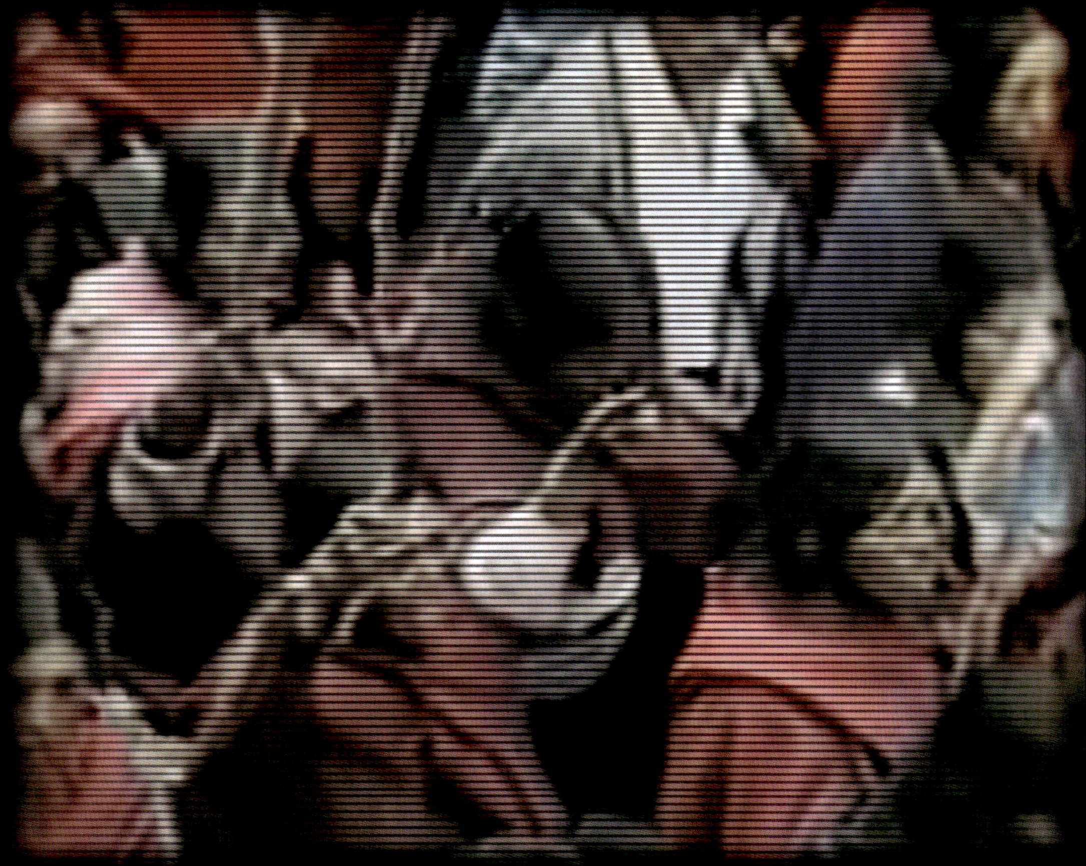

CONAIE, *Levantamiento Indígena Ecuador*, 4–6 de Junio 1990

CONAIE, *Levantamiento Indigena Ecuador*, 4–6 de Junio 1990

CONAIE, *Levantamiento Indigena Ecuador*, 4–6 de Junio 1990

1991: Plantation Logic 2.0

With the *Andean Trade Preference Act* (precursor to the 2002 *Andean Trade Promotion & Drug Eradication Act* of the Bush Administration), a neoliberal extension of the *War on Drugs* takes shape with sponsored substitution of coca crops in Andean drug-producing countries and subsidies to drug transit nations like Ecuador to curtail trafficking. The 1991 deal operates on a *quid pro quo* basis: for each "convicted trafficker," Ecuador receives 10,000 US dollars. With subsidies for alternative cash crops (cut-flowers), wholesale growers in Colombia and Ecuador are given unimpeded access to space, labor, and water needed to produce and distribute massive amounts of cheap flowers on the global market. As the two largest flower suppliers in the world, the burgeoning floriculture industry casts a shadow over water shortages and exploitation of cheap, migrant labor (namely Indigenous and Afro-Ecuadorian women entering the workforce at younger ages) in the high mountain, indoor plantations of greenhouses and rose farms. After 2 decades of economic austerity measures including the devaluation of the sucre and unabated inflation, the burden of foreign debt servicing to Ecuador's loan sharks (US, IMF, IADB) is unjustly imposed on a now widespread informal economy of service workers whose environmental dangers are ignored and externalized by the State.

Eitan Abramovich, *Interior of Industrial Rose Facility* (Nemocon, Colombia), 2015

1992: Conservation Con Job

Starting in 1972 after acknowledging worldwide ecological damages, the United Nations during the *1992 Earth Summit* in Rio de Janeiro made a guide consisting of *27 Principles for Sustainable Development* signed by 175 countries. Twenty years later, after the Kyoto and Paris Agreements, 'sustainable development' goals categorically fail. Its flexible mechanisms arguably re-arm the most controversial mining and oil companies to continue rampant extractive practices in the name of 'sustainability,' a buzzword coined in the *1987 Brundtland Report* "Our Common Future." Scholars Ana María Varea & Pablo Ortiz note in their 1995 book *Marea Negra en la Amazonia (Oil Slick in the Amazon)* that this new level of neoliberal speak is the "green panorama... an expression of the cultural hegemony of new capitalism and its ideology of safe management of global resources prompted by many western conservationists." With the imminent dollarization of the Ecuadorian economy and increasingly damaging effects of climate change (including El Niño) on the gradient of Andean, Amazonian, and coastal Pacific ecosystems, the deeper entanglement and tightening of capitalism and conservation will become practically irreversible for an economy exclusively dependent on oil extraction and environmental despoliation.

Chevron
¡Paga lo que debes!

1993: Ethnocide by Oil

In a class-action suit led by Indigenous Peoples from the Kofan, Quichua, Secoya, Siona, and Huaorani Nations, with the Ecuadorian State (*Petroecuador*, replacing CEPE) in an $18 billion lawsuit against the oil consortium led by Texaco. Now owned by Chevron after its acquisition later in 2001, Texaco Petroleum (TexPet) extracted over 1.5 billion barrels of crude oil from the Amazon Upper Basin during more than two decades of drilling between 1964 and 1992. By then, more than 300 hundred wells had been drilled across a region of over 1 million acres, with operations generating more than 3 million gallons of wastewater and sludge every day. At the same time that the suit against Chevron is filed and takes place over two decades of litigation and appeals, a class-action suit is brought forth by 3,000 former Ecuadorian banana workers who join nearly 30,000 other workers worldwide in a case against pesticide manufacturers and chemical companies (Dow, Shell, and Occidental) as well as their major buyers, the banana producing giants—Dole, Chiquita, and Del Monte. The organization of labor movements, Indigenous Nations, and allied environmental organizations form a converging movement and decentralized front against corporate colonialism of the North.

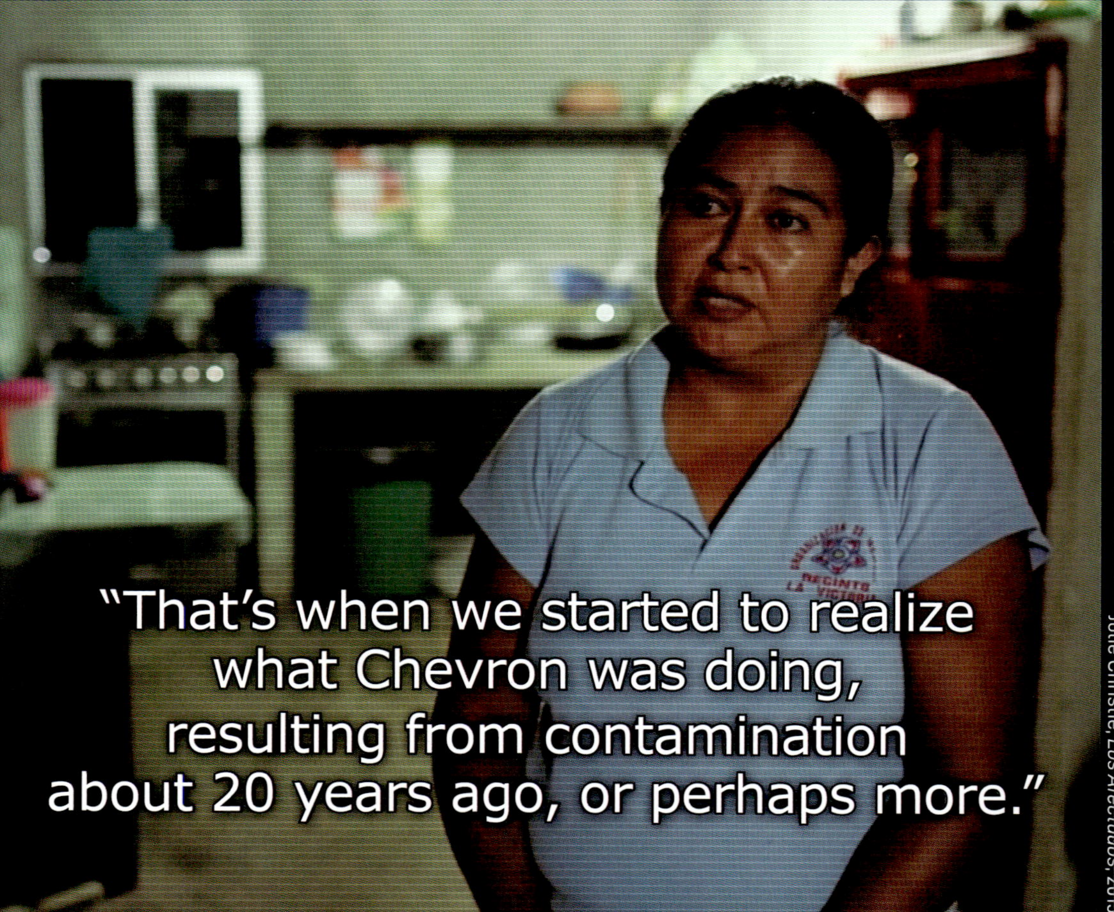
"That's when we started to realize
what Chevron was doing,
resulting from contamination
about 20 years ago, or perhaps more."

Lou Dematteis

Crude oil flowing into a lagoon next to a Texaco well in Shusufundi, Ecuador. Residents have accused Texaco of dumping about 3,000 gallons of oil a day into lagoons and are seeking more than $1 billion in damages.

Ecuadorean Indians Suing Texaco

By AGIS SALPUKAS

Maria Sánchez, who lives in the rain forest of Ecuador, said she cannot bathe in the river and lagoons near her house. She and her son are reluctant to walk on the road because oil stains her feet and clothing, she said tearfully at a news conference yesterday in New York, and she is also allergic to the gasoline used to

Indigenous people with Philadelphia lawyers.

said, however, that Texaco had spread oil from settling basins next to the wells on roads in the oilfields of

firm of Kohn, Nast & Graf of Philadelphia, conceded yesterday that they faced an uphill battle, but said they believed they had a chance of getting the case heard. A principal, Joseph C. Kohn, said the suit was being handled on a contingency basis.

Environmental groups have made Ecuador an example of the conflict in preserving the Amazon region while developing its rich resources, notably oil. Judith Kimerling, an environmen-

AMAZON.COM

1994: Domain Domination

After the failure of ill-conceived Cadabra™, Jeff Bezos trademarks the name of the world's longest river in conceiving a wholesale-to-retail empire that later becomes the world's largest transnational corporation: Amazon.com™. Fifteen years later, the Internet Corporation for Assigned Names and Numbers (ICANN) grants the online retail giant exclusive legal rights to the top-level internet domain name *.amazon* in spite of major objections from the eight countries that actually occupy the Amazon River region: Ecuador, Peru, Colombia, Venezuela, Guyana, Suriname, French Guiana, and Brazil. As it transitions from selling books to going far beyond its foundation as a bookstore near the turn of the millennium, Amazon.com's corporate logo sheds the river meander and any territorial referent from its identity. Instead, it focuses on the abstraction of the word amazon itself as if originating from nowhere and devoid of any historical basis, opting for a more generic, globalized identity that extends Bezos' vision for the company "to sell anything and everything, anywhere"... Thus, a few years later, San-Francisco-based design company Turner Duckworth conceives of the smile in 2001 (a smirk, really) pointing from the 1st to the 4th letter, as if drawing the contour of a new globe in the universe of total consumption of literally everything, from a to z.

amazno
#NoAmazonInLIC
I'D TAX THAT
FUCK BEZOS

Anti-Amazon Tagging in Prospective Warehouse City Locations across the U.S., 2017–2018

MERRELL 547 260 Mg Oral Tablet
Quinamm
Sanofi - aventis
NDC: 00068-0547

1995: Chemical Domination

Abusing the powerful, chemical properties of the quinine alkaloid isolated from the Cinchona plant, Marion Merrell Dow Pharmaceuticals is ordered to stop marketing over-the-counter drugs like Quinamm (and other products containing quinine sulfate) as remedies for nocturnal leg cramps. Citing a "lack of evidence of efficacy and dangerous side effects," the Food and Drug Administration (FDA) effectively bans its use other than for malaria during a ruling made on August 22nd following a study that tracked data since 1969. A few months later, in an entirely different case involving perceived patent infringement of quinine-based medication, Merrell Dow issues a blunt, condescending, and dispossessive message to the British High Court.

In *Merrell Dow Pharmaceuticals Inc. v. H.N. Norton & Co. Ltd.*, on October 27th, Lord Hoffman of the British House of Lords makes the case for the technological supremacy and corporate proprietorship of industrially produced synthetic quinine over Indigenous knowledge from traditional sources in the Andes: *"There is an infinite variety of descriptions under which the same thing maybe known. Things may be described according to what they look like, how they are made, what they do and in many other ways. Under what description must it be known in order to justify the statement that one knows that it*

Let your patients enjoy a world free from allergy suffering.

exists... The so-called Amazonian Indians have known for centuries, even for millennia, that Cinchona bark can be used to treat malarial and other fevers. They used it in the form of powdered bark. In 1820, French scientists discovered that the active ingredient, an alkaloid called 'quinine', could be extracted and used more effectively in the form of sulphate of quinine. In 1944, the structure of the alkaloid molecule ($C^{20}H^{24}N^{2}O^{2}$) was discovered... Does the Indian know about quinine? My Lords, under the description of a quality of the bark which makes it useful for treating fevers, he obviously does. I do not think it matters that he chooses to label it in animistic rather than chemical terms. He knows that the bark has a quality which makes it good for fever and that is one description of quinine. On the other hand, in a different context, the Amazonian Indian would not know about quinine. If shown pills of quinine sulphate, he would not associate them with the Cinchona bark. He does not know quinine under the description of a substance in the form of pills. And he certainly would not know about the artificially synthesized alkaloid.” In 1998, the Technical Board of Appeals reiterates a similar perspective, albeit anthropologically: “*The Amazonian Indian who treats himself with powdered bark for fever is using quinine, even if he thinks the reason why the treatment is effective is that the tree is favoured by the Gods.*”

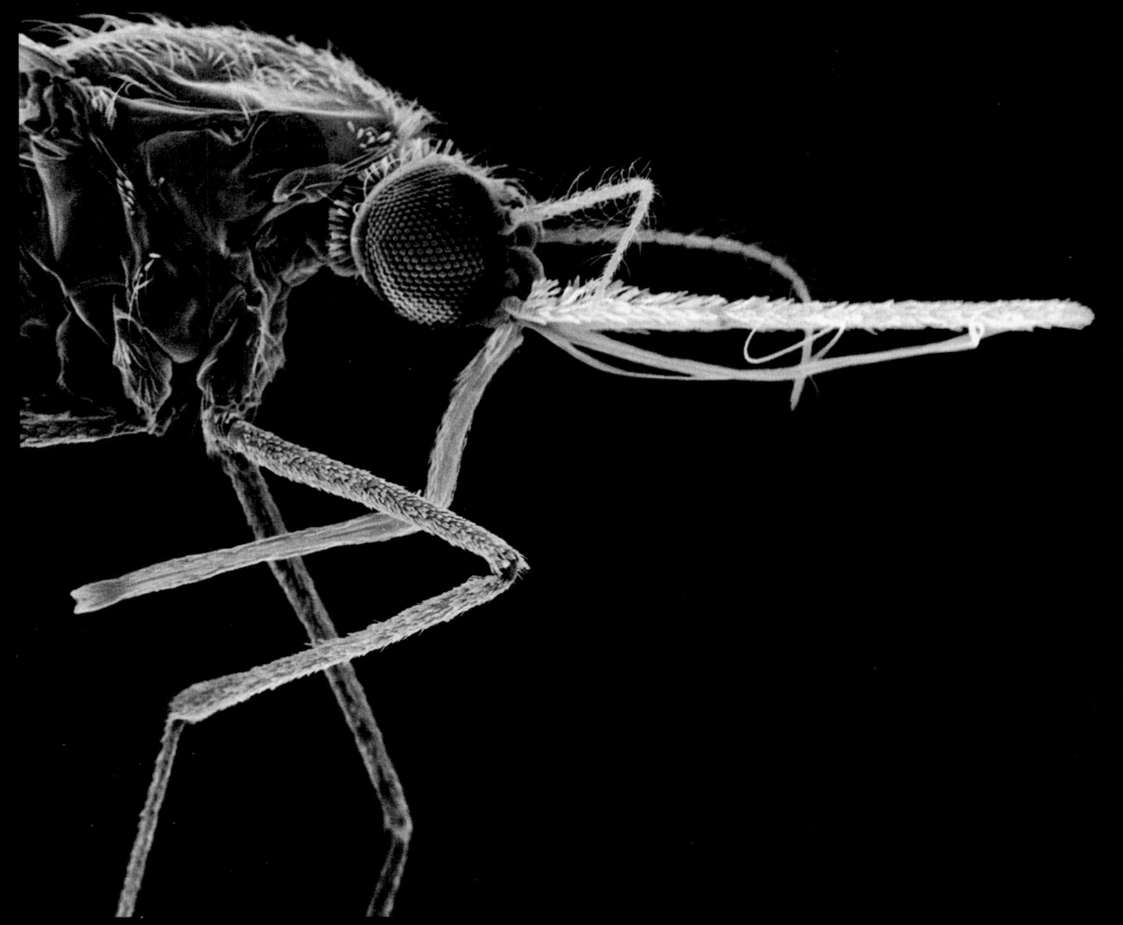

1998: Global Mutation

With the goal of cutting malaria deaths in half by 2010, the World Health Organization (WHO) announces *Operation Roll Back Malaria* (RBM) in 1998 to counter the second leading cause of death in the world after tuberculosis. According to the WHO's Fact Sheet No. 094, "*The geographical area affected by malaria has shrunk considerably over the past 50 years, but control is becoming more difficult and gains are being eroded. Increased risk of the disease is linked with changes in land use linked to activities like road building, mining, logging and agricultural and irrigation projects, particularly in 'frontier' areas like the Amazon and in South-East Asia. Other causes of its spread include global climatic change, disintegration of health services, armed conflicts and mass movements of refugees. The emergence of multi-drug resistant strains of parasite is also exacerbating the situation.*" While the global prevalence of the tropical parasitic disease is estimated between 300-500 million clinical cases annually, the burden of 1-2 million deaths is concentrated in sub-Saharan Africa. In spite of planned increases in international aid for its control, 90% of deaths from malaria occur in a handful of countries: Congo, Nigeria, India, Indonesia—colonial proxies for decades if not centuries of political instability, civil unrest, refugee flows, and climate change.

2001: Genetic Colonialism

Increasing food insecurity from climate change exposes dangers of dwindling crop diversity while promoting seed banking and genetic crop research. With funding from philanthrocapitalists such as Bill & Melinda Gates Foundation, a massive subterranean facility is constructed in Norway's Arctic region to store seed duplicates (at a constant, sub-zero temperature of -18° Celsius) to "protect 70% of the world's agricultural biodiversity that lies in the hands of small-scale farmers" against the dominant big four (rice, wheat, maize, potatoes). In 2004, Ecuador ascends to signatory country with Svalbard's 146 other member nations, yet the honor of contributing Cinchona seeds goes to Tanzania with *C. hybrida*. While the intention of open-source seed banking is to promote sharing and prohibit patenting of plant IP, biological sequencing skyrockets in spite of the 2009 *International Plant Treaty*. Agricultural activist Vandana Shiva will condemn privatization of botanical big data as "piracy of common genomic data of millions of plants bred by peasants... So much more than germ plasm, seeds are living, self-organizing entities, subjects of evolution, history, culture, and relationships... Seed imperialism boosts the corporate takeover of our seed, agriculture, food, knowledge and global health systems, manipulating information, and eroding democracies."

2004: Plantation Logic 3.0

With increasing resistance of the plasmodium parasite to synthetic quinine, recent scientific studies show the alkaloid extract from natural bark from Cinchona trees endemic to the Andean region of Loja are far superior to pharmaceutical substitutes. From India and Indonesia to Kenya and Guatemala, Cinchona cultivation makes a major comeback around the world except in Ecuador where the Saraguro Peoples are locked out of due to export restrictions imposed by Anglo-European countries, dollarization of its economy, and political instability. Home to the largest and most productive plantations in the world, the Kivu region in the eastern region of the Democratic Republic of the Congo (DRC) will surge in bark production in spite of geopolitical conflicts along borders of Rwanda, Burundi, and Uganda. Notwithstanding advances in plant inoculation, grafting techniques, and alkaloid separation, the Luxembourg-owned plantations operated by Pharmakina SA now produce nearly 50% of world demand for quinine, with over 100 tons of bark produced annually, much of which destined for German quinine manufacturer Buchler GmbH. Labor conditions and wages on plantations are virtually indistinguishable from the 19th century. And in spite of the abundance of quinine production, the DRC still maintains the second-highest rate of malaria deaths in the world.

Thomas Imo, *Quinine Production at Pharmakina* (Bukavu, DRC), 2004

Cinchona Bark Barge from Idgwi Island on Lake Kivu near the DRC-Rwanda Border, 2012

2007: Keep It In The Ground

Six months prior to the adoption of the *United Nations Declaration on the Rights of Indigenous Peoples* (UNDRIP) as a comprehensive framework to ensure and enforce the self-determination of Indigenous Peoples worldwide, Ecuadorian lawyer and activist Lourdes Tibán makes a bold proposal to the *UN Permanent Forum on Indigenous Issues* on the heels of a massive drilling project—Ishpingo-Tambococha-Tiputini Field (ITT)—in Yasuní National Park, headwaters of the Amazon: "Petrol, minerals, it's all beneath the earth, which leads to a tremendous problem."After decades of hyper-inflation, 7 presidents in less than a decade, $15 billion in foreign debt to the IMF and IADB, paralyzing interest rates, and an estimated 900 million barrels in Amazon oil reserves, Tibán emboldens a global movement to actively oppose resource extraction, "if the world truly is interested in saving the planet, the government has decided to sell the oil, but keep it in the ground." That same year, Ecuador paradoxically adopts the very first constitutional amendment in the world that recognizes nature's rights *Pacha Mama* (*Mother Earth*), "to exist, persist, maintain, and regenerate its vital cycles." Less than 4 years after Tibán's appeal, President Correa fails to garner international support and drilling goes commences in the ITT oil block in 2016; nonstop ever since.

TV

2008: Plurality Inc.

In spite of the proclamation of Ecuador as 'Plurinational State' reportedly overturning its 1830 Constitution that favored policies of a neoliberal élite and white minority, the Confederación de Nacionalidades Indígenas del Ecuador (CONAIE)—Ecuador's largest and most active organization of Indigenous Nations—maintains strong skepticism of the government's late-blooming socialist motives and leftist inclinations in its acknowledgment of 14 different Indigenous Nations within the boundaries of the nation-state. The Ecuadorian President Rafael Correa will co-opt the central pillar of *buen vivir* ("living well") advocated for decades by Indigenous Nations, in order to secure his own reelection and majority rule. In a 2004 manifesto on Indigenous governance, Lourdes Tibán's words serve as a predilection of longstanding, colonial conservatism: "*It is important to note that with the Spanish invasion, and later in the constitution of the Independent Republic and then in the Nation-State, attempts have been made to homogenize all our peoples and nationalities (Indigenous, Afro-descendants) under a single white-mestizo culture, to adopt a single language under a central, mandatory, and coercive legal order, without considering that Nations and Peoples that were already in existence here are diverse, heterogeneous in cultures, customs, and visions.*"

kindle

amazon

2011: Amazon Fire

In response to the ever-increasing market share and dominance of Apple's iPad in the market of tablet computers, AMAZON Inc. releases its first electronic ink reader, *Kindle Fire*. Released on November 15th, the first-generation tablet coincidentally enters the world stage precisely at the tail end of the tropical dry season when Amazonian forest fires are at their peak, running rampant throughout the region. In the next decade, the handheld device becomes the best-selling digital reader as part of an effort by the e-commerce giant to enter the emerging era of cloud computing. In a strange Andean turn of events, AMAZON's digital 'cloud forest,' AMAZON Web Services (AWS) becomes the largest segment of its new business enterprise. A year later, Australian WikiLeaks founder Julian Assange would seek refuge as a political asylum in 2012 with the Ecuadorian Embassy in London to escape extradition to Sweden and prosecution from the US following the release of classified documents regarding secret activities of American intelligence agencies. Less than a decade later, AWS is now part of an intelligence community and commercial cloud enterprise (C2E) as multi-billion dollar Cloud Service Provider (CSP) to 6,500 agencies of the U.S. Government including the State Department, the DOD (Department of Defense), and CIA (Central Intelligence Agency).

2014: Amazon on Fire

Following a massive settlement from a court case dating back to 1993, the Government of Ecuador's $9.5 billion judgment is reversed in a shocking turn of events that lets Chevron off the hook for the damage caused by now defunct Texaco in the *Lago Agrio Region* of northeastern Ecuador, home to pristine rainforests and over 100,000 Indigenous Peoples from 5 different nations across an area the size of Rhode Island. After 25 years of litigation in what would become the largest settlement in the history of human rights and environmental violations, the class-action attorney from New York Steven Donziger becomes the target of subsequent retaliation by Chevron who sell their assets to the federal government of Ecuador and flee the country. In a 2013 Strategy Research Report, U.S. Army Colonel John Conway labels the region as a strategic 'black spot': "Lago Agrio is a hidden ungoverned [lawless] territory in eastern Ecuador, a central node to the many security-related issues of Ecuador." The report overlooks an important historical connection: Nueva Loja as the 21st-century incarnation of a former boomtown to the south, Loja, where Cinchona plants once thrived in abundance but were exploited for 200 years by foreign powers between the 17th and 19th centuries to near extinction.

2014: Highway to Hell

In spite of the meager attempt at protecting a fraction of its landscape as *World Heritage Site* since its adoption in 2000, UNESCO's 'Amazon Conservation Complex" in Northern Brazil fails at protecting one of the planet's largest reserves of biodiversity. However, it does succeed in paving the way and produce an alibi for the unimpeded construction of the *Trans-Amazonian Highway Project* in its quest to connect the Atlantic with the Pacific Coast for European and Asian markets. Another massive project now lies on the horizon: the Manta-Manaus Multimodal Corridor. A 600-kilometer land route from the Ecuadorian Port of Manta on the Pacific Coast to the new port of Francisco de Orellana, and then along a 2,860-kilometer river route, starting from the Coca River, then along the Napo River through Peru and Brasil to the Port of Manaus on the Amazon River. As part of over 500 megaprojects in Latin America, the road towards 'integration' and connectivity' is uneven: extracting and transporting petroleum hydrocarbons, agricultural goods, fishing products, wood, and biofuels westbound along the Amazon towards Asia-Pacific markets. Atop a Brazilian truck cab reads in Portuguese: *isso é coisa de deus*, ("this belongs to God")... as if holy are the logistics of resource transport: the Christian mission of assimilating any and all parts of the Amazon.

Isso É Coisa De Deus
Constellation
GLOBETROTTER

Nelson Almeida, queueing on BR 163 highway in Northern Brazil, 2017

National Flag of Ecuador, 2014

2014: Driven Towards Extinction

As an ancient symbol of health and immortality, the Andean Condor (Vultur gryphus) not only covers a massive territorial range throughout the Andes Mountains across South America (with other varieties in Central America and as far north as California), but also represents over 4,000 years of history facing the perilous challenge of extinction from habitat loss and infrastructure collisions, poisoning from farmers, rampant poaching, and wildlife trade. As the national symbol of five countries including Colombia, Ecuador, Peru, Bolivia, Chile, the striking 3- to 4-meter wingspan raptor sits atop of Ecuador's coat of arms hovering above the state-space of mined mountains, denuded forests, and industrialized waters that threatens its very existence. Gold, blue, and red are more than national signifiers of resource richness, they are the tricolor strata of settler-colonialism that edigy the extraction of its hinterlands and exports through its global ports... As a naturalized national code, that extractive identity was engrained into settler imagination over two centuries ago at the precise moment that German naturalist Wolfgang von Goethe depicted in his 1810 Tableau "Heights of the Old and New World" the scavenger bird towering at extreme altitudes above Alexander von Humboldt's head when climbing Mount Chimborazo back in the early 19th century.

Pichincha Comunicaciones
@pichinchauniver

🔴 #ATENCIÓN | Moradores de #Cayambe rescatadon a una polluela de cóndor, que sufrió una fractura en el fémur. #Chitachaca, fue operada y se encuentra en recuperación. Se espera que dentro de tres o cuatro semanas pueda regresar a su nido.
@teleamazonasec

Translate Tweet

3:43 PM · Jul 7, 2020 · TweetDeck

Silvia Paralta, *Andean Condor*, 2016

VIDAS!
Productos para el cuidado
y tu aseo personal
Pharma
VIDAS!
CAJA 3

2016: Dispensing Dispossession

According to the World Health Organization, "malaria causes nearly 250 times more deaths in the world's poorest countries than in the richest." In a remarkable twist of fate, Indigenous Peoples of Ecuador along with Afro-Ecuadorian and Mestizx Peoples are now forced to line up at pharmacies across the country for their household supplies of quinine as a result of deforestation, pollution, territorial dispossession, IP secrecy, and international patent law, that remove citizens further and further away from access to traditional medicine from their original homelands where the Cinchona tree once flourished. Cinchona bark is now actively produced through plantations in Central America, Central Africa, and South Asia in coordination with quinine processing, tablet manufacturing, and product distribution based in Europe. With increasing intensities of El Niño events, warmer temperatures from climate change, the Intergovernmental Panel on Climate Change (IPCC) predicts the increasing prevalence of malarial infections as a result of the expanding range of malaria-carrying mosquitoes at increasingly higher and higher altitudes. In a few years to come, malaria transmission will be found at elevations exceeding 2,300m in the Central Andes, locations where inhabitants are more at risk and more susceptible due to a historic lack of immunity.

David Díaz Arcos, Plantas medicinales Quito y Mercado San Francisco, 2013

2016: Curandera Counter-Culture

Serving the Quito region since 1565, the 400-year old *Hospital San Juan de Dios* is restored into a major feature of the city's Spanish heritage and colonial museum with funding provided under the UNESCO World Heritage between 2009-2014. While its interior is lined with 16–17th century artwork depicting medical colonialism and indoctrination, its outside is ironically surrounded by traditional healers and herbalists, in the markets of San Roque and San Francisco. As thousand-year old practices, these medicinal traditions and healing practices (natural herbs, essential oils, sundries, concentrates) continue to be passed down through *curanderas* (healers/herbalists) as strategies of resistance to the invasion of global pharmaceuticals. "Traditional medical practitioners in the Ecuador highlands, those known as *curanderos* but especially the *limpiadoras* (*cleansers*)," as *The Journal of Ethnobiology and Ethnomedicine* reported in 2009, "make extensive use of magical plants in the treatment of supernatural folk illnesses such as *susto* (*soul loss*), *mal viento* (*evil wind*), *mal prójimo* (witchcraft), and *mal aire* (*bad air*). In most documentation on magical plant use over the past thirty years or so however, the rationale underlying the use of magical plants is poorly addressed (if at all) much less than plants used for treating naturalistic disorders."

A Niños y Adultos
PUESTO Nº 8

David Diaz Arcos, *Hierbas Medicinales* (Mercado San Roque, Quito), 2016

Se Cura El Espanto (Mercado san Roque, Quito), 2015

Colectivo Arquitectura Expandida, *Mercado San Roque a Quito*, 2015

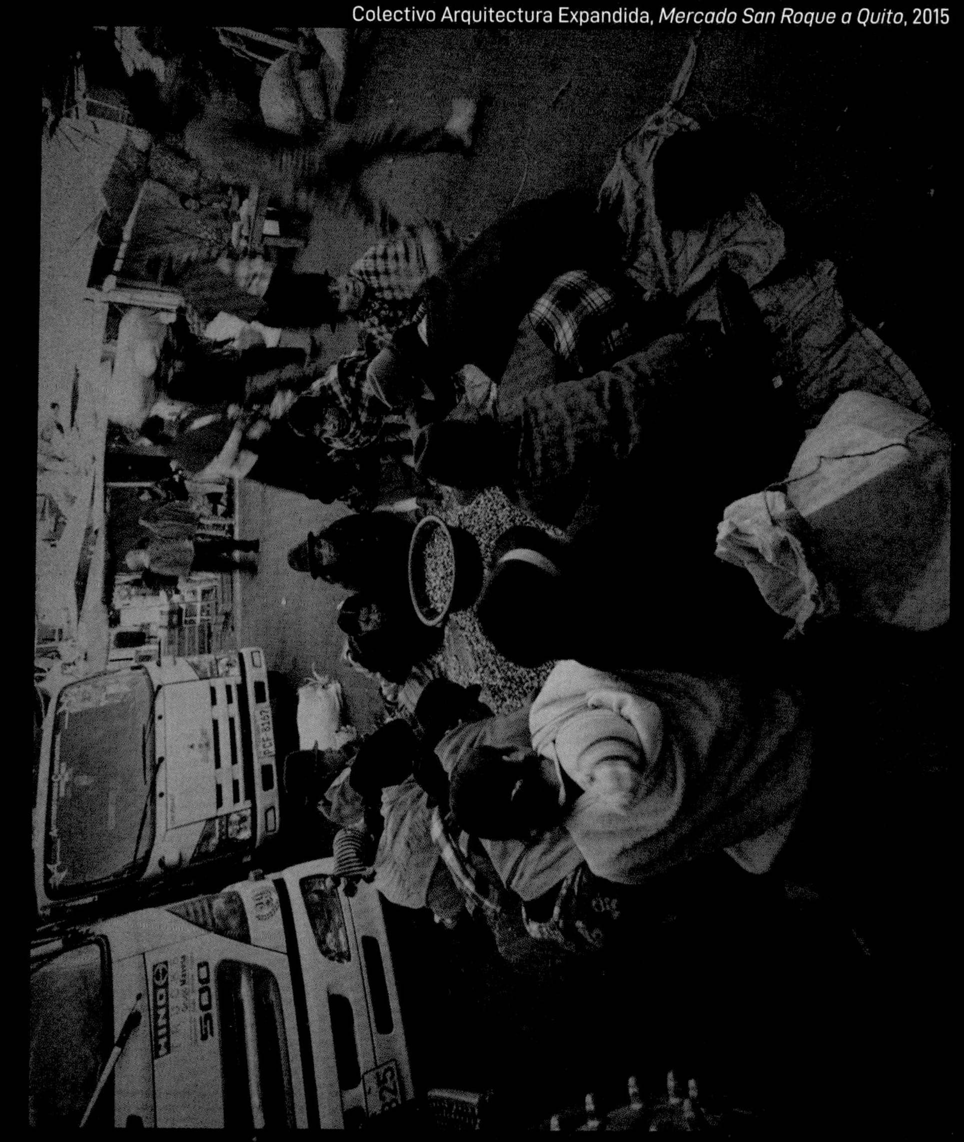

FIVE DOCUMENTARIES OF 2009
IAL BOARD OF REVIEW

ED! Intelligently and artfully made."
THE NEW YORK TIMES

dy of real world political action."
an, LOS ANGELES TIMES

exposes corporate inhumanity."
nan, NEW YORK DAILY NEWS

shot film. It captures the magic
beauty of the Ecuadorean people."
OPLE'S HISTORY OF THE UNITED STATES

the most powerful, emotion-provoking,
locumentary I have ever seen."
IFESSIONS OF AN ECONOMIC HIT MAN

Three years in the making, CRUDE tells the epic story of one of the largest and most controversial legal cases on the planet: the infamous $27 billion "Amazon Chernobyl" lawsuit pitting 30,000 rainforest dwellers in Ecuador against the U.S. oil giant Chevron.

Winner of 19 international awards, CRUDE takes you inside a riveting, high stakes drama steeped in global politics, the environmental movement, celebrity activism, human rights advocacy, multinational corporate power, and rapidly-disappearing indigenous cultures.

Photo: David Gilbert

sh, Spanish, A'ingae & Secoya w/English subtitles

ODUCTION IN ASSOCIATION WITH @RADICAL.MEDIA AND THIRD EYE MOTION PICTURE COMPANY
.AND ROBERT FRIEDMAN JON KAMEN TED SARANDOS FRANK SCHERMA JUSTIN WILKES
ATE PRODUCERS POCHO ALVAREZ EDWARD L. O'CONNOR JUAN DIEGO PÉREZ RENEE PURSE STUART ZWEIBEL
IGINAL MUSIC BY WENDY BLACKSTONE DIRECTOR OF PHOTOGRAPHY JUAN DIEGO PÉREZ
MICHAEL BONFIGLIO PRODUCED BY J.R. DELEON RICHARD STRATTON
. PRODUCER & 2ND UNIT DIRECTOR MICHAEL BONFIGLIO
ODUCED BY JOE BERLINGER

THIRD EYE

DVD VIDEO

A JOE BERLINGER FILM

CRUDE

FROM FILMMAKER JOE BERLINGER (*BROTHER'S KEEPER, PARADISE LOST, METALLICA: SOME KIND OF MONSTER*)

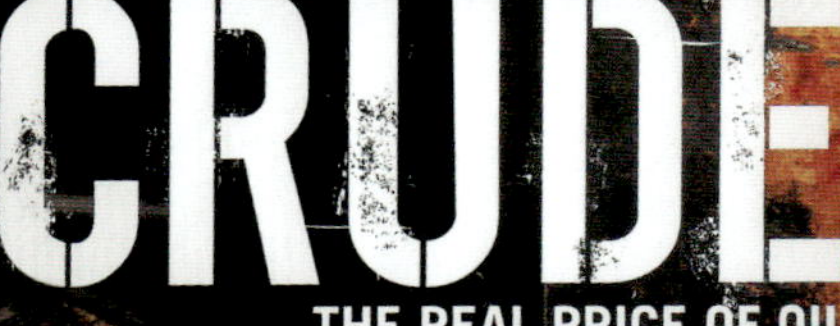

THE REAL PRICE OF OIL

"A legal THRILLER with RARE DEPTH and POWER."
-Stephen Holden, THE NEW YORK TIMES

"★★★★ ELOQUENT."
-Peter Travers, ROLLING STONE

"A GRIPPING account of corporate malfeasance."
-Tom Huddleston, TIME OUT LONDON

"CINEMATIC...SUPERB!"
-Scott Foundas, LA WEEKLY

Photo: David Gilbert

Joe Berlinger, *Crude: The Real Price of Oil* (film poster), 200

2016: Friction & Fiction on the Frontier

After nearly two decades, the $9.5 billion judgment for environmental damage is rendered by Ecuador's High Court in the case against Chevron in the Amazon. Overturning a counter-claim, the 2009 documentary film *CRUDE: The Real Price of Oil* features legal activist Steven Donziger in an exposé on the magnitude of environmental destruction by Chevron in Ecuador, ever since Texaco started operations in 1964. While the District Court of New York deems the original judgment of the Ecuadorian courts as "biased, coerced, and corrupt," the *International Court of The Hague* acknowledges falsified testimony and tainted evidence by Chevron. In its own propaganda media machine *The Amazon Post*, "Chevron Corporation will resist any enforcement effort and seek to hold anyone who would attempt to enforce the fraudulent judgment in another jurisdiction accountable to the full extent of the law." In spite of imminent defeat of the oil giant by Indigenous Peoples of Aguarico River and 30,000 farmers from Lago Agrio region, countless people are left penniless and landless; livelihoods destroyed by petrochemical pollution in the shadows of a new oil boom representing half of Ecuador's GDP. Late, in August 2019, Donziger will be unjustly and dubiously placed under house arrest for an unprecedented 600 days with charges of contempt by Chevron.

18 MIL M

Julie Christie, *Trans-Andean Pipeline Graffiti: "18 Billion Gallons of Toxic Water,"* 2015

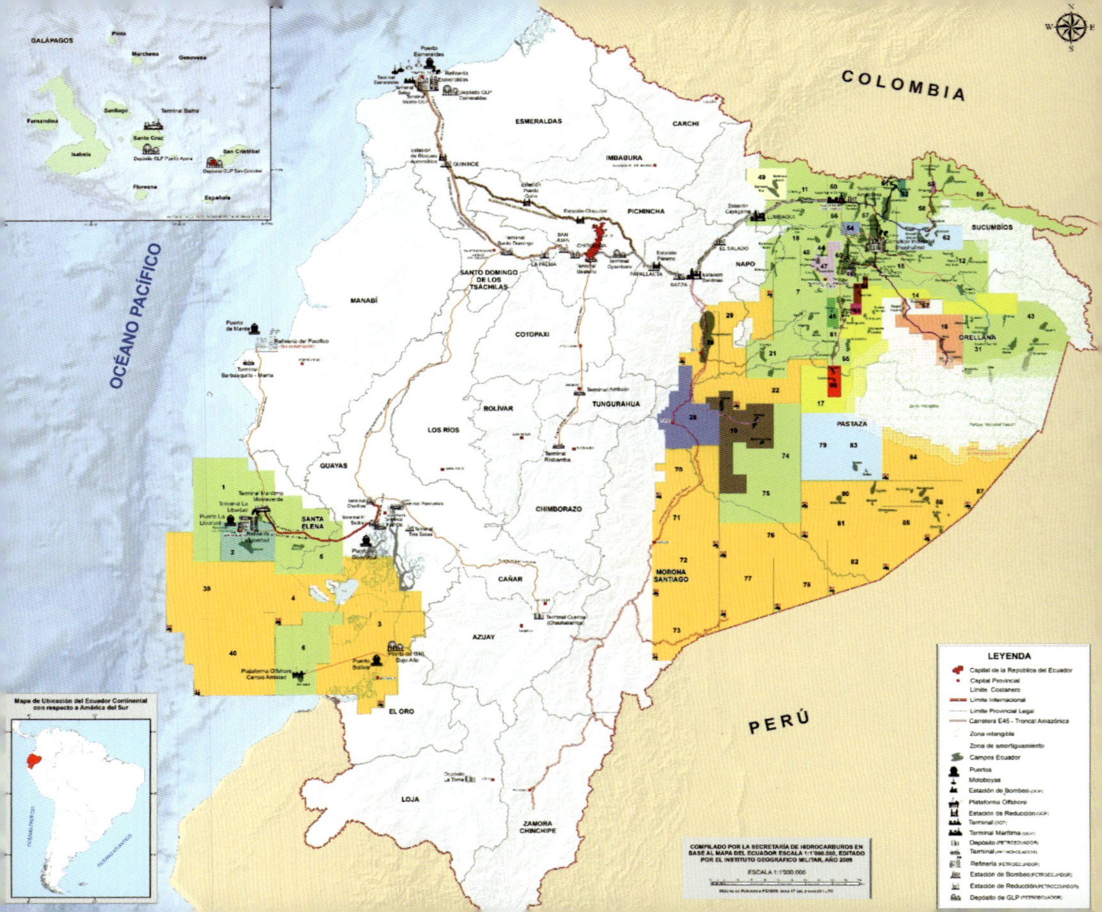

COLOMBIA
PERÚ
OCÉANO PACÍFICO
GALÁPAGOS
ESMERALDAS
CARCHI
IMBABURA
PICHINCHA
SUCUMBÍOS
NAPO
ORELLANA
SANTO DOMINGO DE LOS TSÁCHILAS
MANABÍ
COTOPAXI
TUNGURAHUA
PASTAZA
BOLÍVAR
LOS RÍOS
GUAYAS
SANTA ELENA
CHIMBORAZO
MORONA SANTIAGO
CAÑAR
AZUAY
EL ORO
LOJA
ZAMORA CHINCHIPE
LEYENDA
Capital de la República del Ecuador
Capital Provincial
Límite Costanero
Límite Internacional
Límite Provincial Legal
Carretera E45 - Troncal Amazónica
Zona intangible
Zona de amortiguamiento
Campos Ecuador
Puertos
Motoboyas
Estación de Bombeo
Plataforma Offshore
Estación de Reducción
Terminal
Terminal Marítima
Depósito
Refinería
Depósito de GLP
Mapa de Ubicación del Ecuador Continental con respecto a América del Sur
COMPILADO POR LA SECRETARÍA DE HIDROCARBUROS EN BASE AL MAPA DEL ECUADOR ESCALA 1:1'000.000, EDITADO POR EL INSTITUTO GEOGRÁFICO MILITAR, AÑO 2009
ESCALA 1:1'000.000

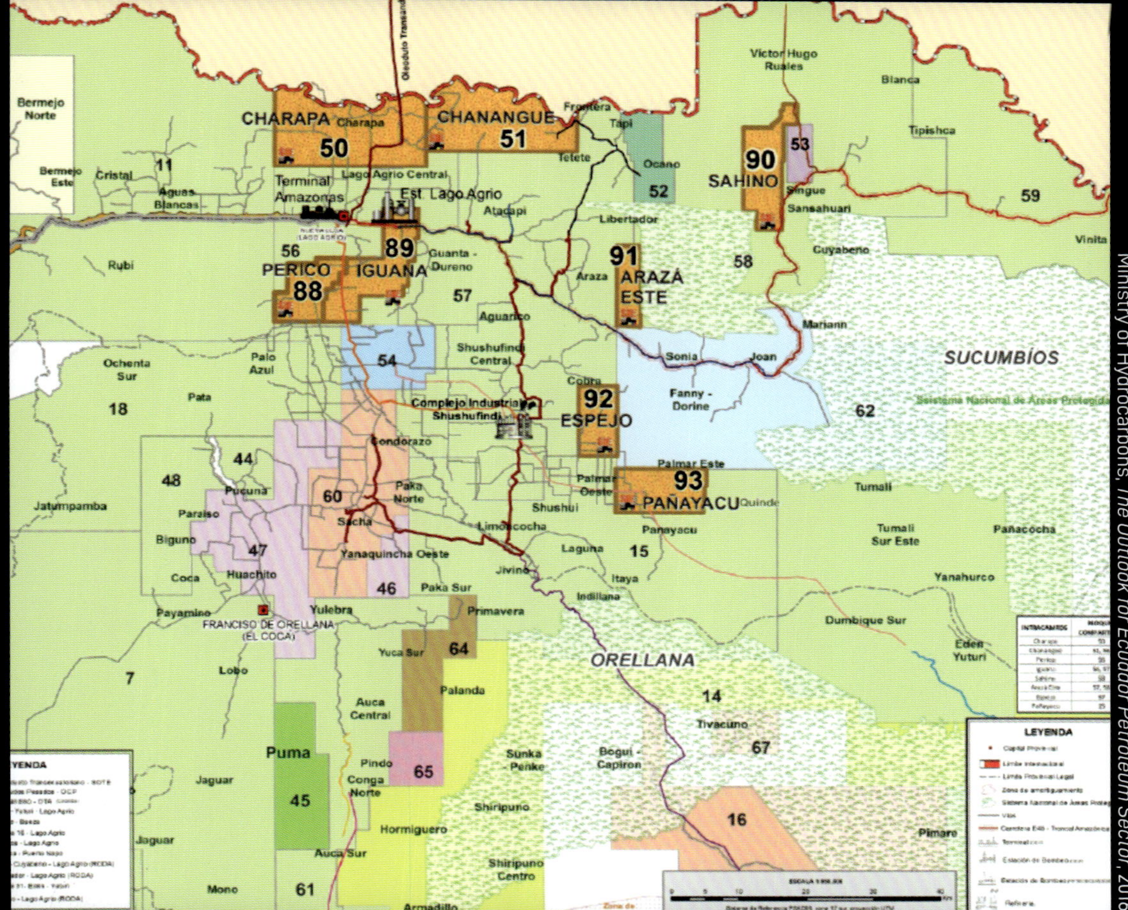

Ministry of Hydrocarbons, *The Outlook for Ecuador Petroleum Sector*, 2016

Chevron
CHEVRON-TE

Julie Christie, *Trans-Andean Pipeline Graffiti: "Chevron-Texaco Never",* 2015

Nicholas Ohl, Section of Trans-Ecuadorian Pipeline from Lago Agrio to Esmeraldas, 2016

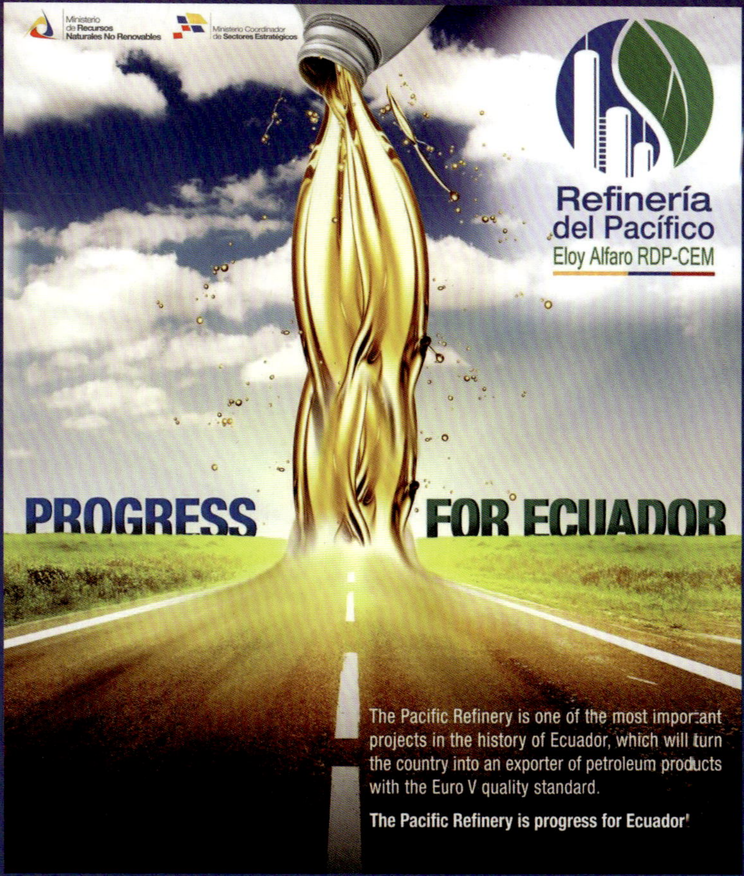

Ministerio de Energía y Recursos Naturales no Renovables, *The Oil & Gas Year: Ecuador Report*, 2013

2017: Scientist, Missionary, Raider?

With funding from the *Natural History Museum of Denmark*, Dr. Nina Rønsted and her team of ecologists from the University of Gothenburg venture to the Andean mountain range to seek out original colonial-era species of the Cinchona tree with the highest concentrations of quinine. Borrowing DNA of Cinchona plants released from the Botanical Collection at Kew Gardens in London, research of this international team reacts to the growing global resistance of the *anopheles mosquito* to synthetic pharmaceutical forms of quinine sparking a new round of neocolonial scientific expeditions. Accompanied by Swedish and Danish botanical experts, their 21st century quest across the Atlantic Ocean to South America for a rare variety of the Cinchona plant species is remarkably Humboldtian. After locating the illustrious *Cinchona parabolica* in an extremely remote part of the highlands of the Andes in Northern Peru (near the 16th century village of Cascarilla named after the Spanish term for 'Cinchona bark'), Dr. Rønsted will reflect upon collecting and packaging the precious sample for transport to Europe: "...guard it with your life." Reportedly, a success for "their" collection and "science in general." Dr. Rønsted confidently declares near the end of their high-altitude journey: "there are things out there that have never been discovered yet."

Dr. Nina Rønsted Retrieving Sample of Cinchona Parabolica For DNA Testing, 2017

Smithsonian National Museum of Natural History, *Cinchona micrantha*, 2017

2017: Errata, For The 1 Millionth Time?

Using conveyor belt technology, the *Smithsonian National Museum of Natural History* ceremonially digitizes its one-millionth specimen: the Cinchona plant, the neotropical species with 23 varieties. Its entry into the National Herbarium's database is its prize specimen, *Cinchona micrantha* Ruíz & Pavón L. (1799). With the assistance of Andean guides, elders, and herbalists (Kechwan, Aymaran), the species was originally collected by botanist Hipólito Ruíz López and pharmacologist José Antonio Pavón Jiménez on order of Catholic Monarch and King Charles III of Spain "for the profit... and promotion of botany throughout all his domains in America, and thus to make it possible to discover and increase the number of medicinal plants of commercial, industrial, artistic, and economic interest" according to their travelogue between Huánuco and Loja, from 1777 to 1789. However, the record at the National Herbarium will surreptitiously leave out the Cinchona plant's bloody history. Notwithstanding dangers of steep mountainsides, Indigenous bark collectors (cascarilleros) were flagrantly undercut and tricked as Ruíz would report in his 1792 treatise *Quinologia*: "miserable conditions, abuses, outrages, improper felling of trees; imperfect methods of packing" often precipitated by rush orders and predatory practices by Jesuit priests and Spanish merchants.

Matteo Nardone, Protesters outside Brazilian Embassy in Rome (Italy), 2019

2019: White Denial

During what was one of the worst years on record for climate change, wildfires season saw a year-to-year surge occurring in the Amazon Rainforest and biomes across Brazil, Bolivia, Paraguay, Peru, and Ecuador during that year's tropical dry season. Standing behind the remote and distanced conservation efforts of European environmental groups and hashtags such as #SOSAMAZONIA, Spanish and Portuguese organizations continue to tout the benefits, most for themselves, of resource conservation and natural preservation of 'their' Amazon. Appropriating rights to foreign lands and territories on which they have no historic claim nor legal basis, the anti-Indigeneity of green European organizations are masked by hashtags and buzzwords such as #EUROPAVERDE. The colonial hypocrisy of European and American conservation organizations will rest on striking, disingenuous statements made by the United Nations in favor of 'sustainable development,' or the weaponization of 'environmental justice' movements. Not surprisingly, a week before 'World Malaria Day,' World Health Organization Director Dr. Zsuzsanna Jakab coincidentally declared on April 20th, 2016 that "the European Region is the first in the world to have achieved interruption of indigenous malaria transmission."

Eraldo Peres, *Amazon Forest Fire Near Br-163 in the City of Porto Velho*, 2019

Amazon Watch, Sarayaku Land Defender Patricia Gualinga, Kichwa Nation of Sarayaku, 2012

2019: Holy Divestment

During the Special Amazon Synod in the Vatican City, the leader of the Sarayaku Peoples of the Kichwa Nation Patricia Gualinga, whose homelands are the Central Amazonian Rainforest of Ecuador along the Bobonaza River and threatened by a surge in oil exploration and extraction, demands of Pope Francis, the Vatican, and the Catholic Church to renounce resource extraction in their homelands and to completely divest from oil exploration, extraction, and other forms of mining: "Women are the keepers of the biological libraries of the Amazon, through our knowledge of traditional medicines... the Church has been comfortable with investing in the extractive industries, but they have to stop." Although his Holiness Pope Francis declared a few years earlier in his 2013 gospel of joy *Evangelii Gaudium* that "money must serve, not rule," the Vatican's Bank—Istituto per le Opere di Religione—reported in its annual 2019 filing a total of $3 billion in assets with nearly $30 million held in gold at the U.S. Federal Reserve.

Mitch Anderson / Amazon Frontlines, Nemonte Nenquimo & Comunidades Waorani / Sopeso, 2017

2019: Decentering the Settler-State

In a landmark victory for Indigenous rights of self-determination and territorial sovereignty throughout the Amazon Rainforest, Provincial Court judges in Pastaza region in favor of Waorani Peoples. Protecting over a half million-acre area of the Ecuadorian Rainforest from oil drilling and extraction, the ruling dramatically defeats the state oil consortium, Petroecuador, and its foreign oil interests. The case is anticipated to disrupt the state auction of another 7 million areas into 16 oil concessions during the prior year. The victory comes after the Ecuadorian Supreme Court accepted a different case presented in October 2018—from Kofan of Sinangoe Peoples—to develop a national system of jurisprudence to fight against systematic violations of the right to prior consultation and consent from Indigenous Peoples. Together, these major legal victories against oil extraction and mining industries come from combined efforts of Waorani and Kofan Nations, united with Kichwa, Sapara, Shiwar, Shuar, Sekopai, and Siona Nations in the face of similar right violations on their lands.

Mitch Anderson / Amazon Frontlines, *Nemonte Nenquimo & Comunidades Waorani Peoples*, 2019

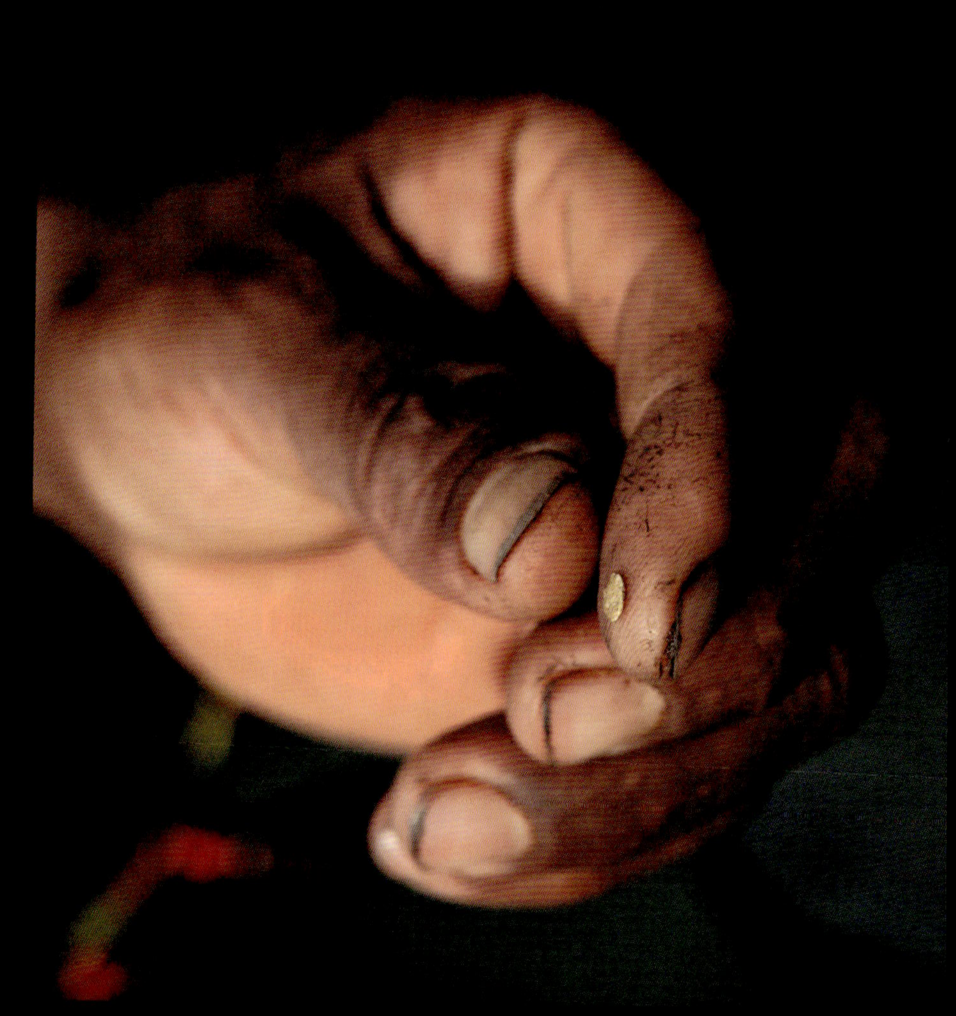

Jeronimo Zuniga, *Gold Flake Found by Indigenous Guardian of Koran Nation in Las Pizarras*, 2019

Jerónimo Zúñiga, *Indigenous Guardians Reviewing Hidden Camera Images Along Río Kofanes*, 2017

Mitch Anderson / Amazon Frontlines, *Nemonte Nenquimo & Comunidades Waorani Peoples*, 2019

da es
MAS

Mitch Anderson / Amazon Frontlines, *Nemonte Nenquimo & Comunidades Waorani Peoples*, 2019

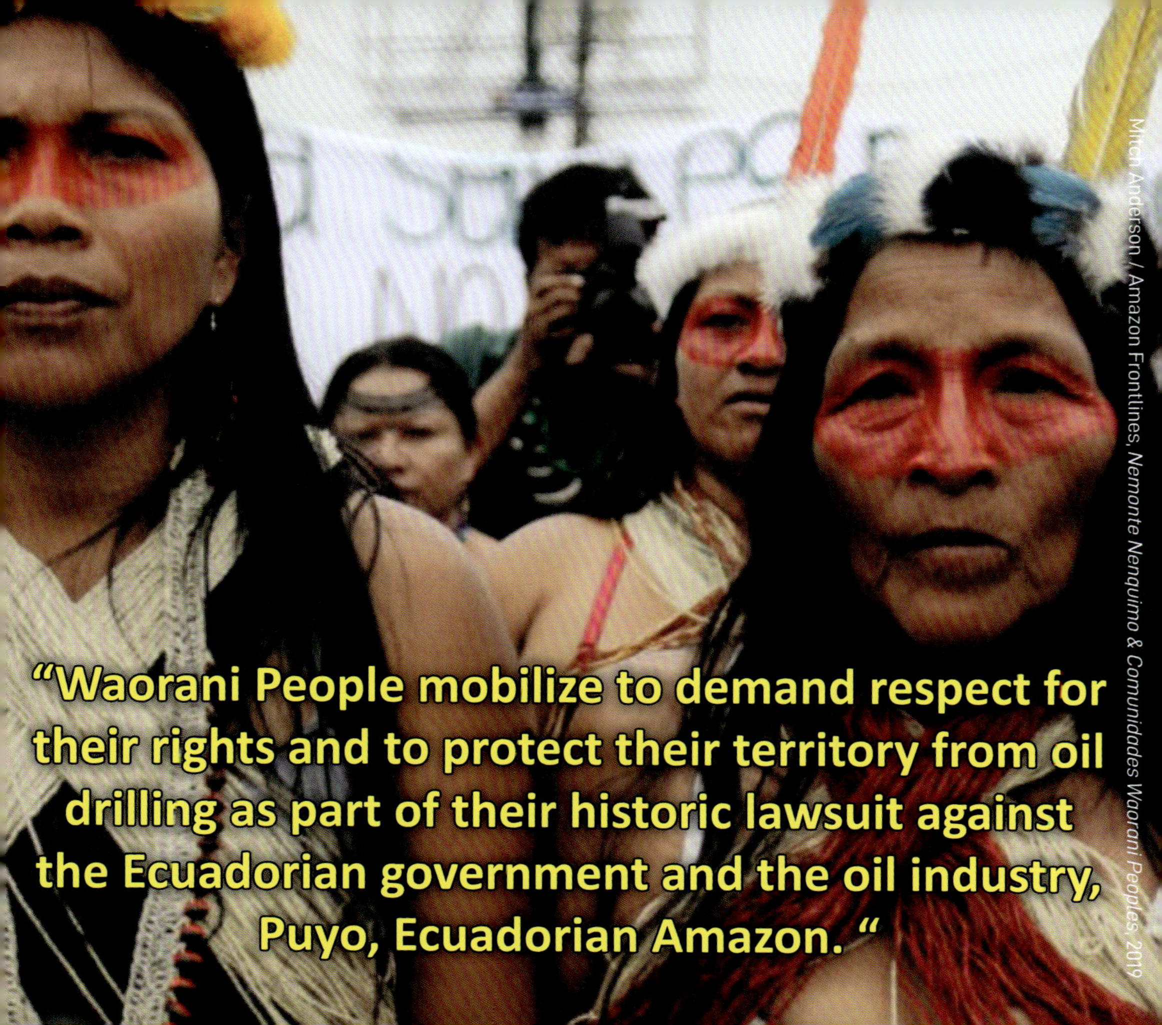
"Waorani People mobilize to demand respect for their rights and to protect their territory from oil drilling as part of their historic lawsuit against the Ecuadorian government and the oil industry, Puyo, Ecuadorian Amazon. "
Mitch Anderson / Amazon Frontlines, Nemonte Nenquimo & Comunidades Waorani Peoples, 2019

THE 100 MOST INFLUENTIAL PEOPLE
TIME

Jerónimo Zúñiga, *Indigenous Guardians of Kofan de Sinangoe patrolling illegal mining*, 2019

“Eight years of being
without your children,...”

2019: Over-Incarceration

In spite of the 2006 National Pardon for drug micro-trafficking, a staggering proportion of Afro-Ecuadorian women are still locked in a vicious cycle of poverty, under-education, and social inequality largely from over-incarceration and over-sentencing. Small felony drug charges (as micro-dealers or drug mules) in Ecuador disproportionately represent sanctions and regulations imposed two decades prior by US foreign intervention especially with the punitive Law 108 in Ecuador originating from the *1988 UN Convention Against Illicit Traffic in Narcotic Drugs*. Intended "to combat and eradicate the production, supply, improper use and illicit trafficking of narcotic and psychotropic substances," the policy's focus on crop eradication and drug criminalization contributed led to an all-time high of 80% total women prisoner population such at *El Inca* (*el Centro de Rehabilitación Social Femenino,* Quito)—the country's largest prison, where Mestiza, Indigenous, and Afro-Ecuadorian women were disproportionately incarcerated (over 50%) for minor drug offenses. Overwhelmingly pressured in the 1990s by US Drug War Policy on Ecuador, Law 108 (rooted in the prohibitionist *1961 UN Single Convention on Narcotic Drugs*) unjustly and unfairly sanctioned the tiny country that produces virtually no coca plantations, unlike its Colombian or Venezuelan neighbors.

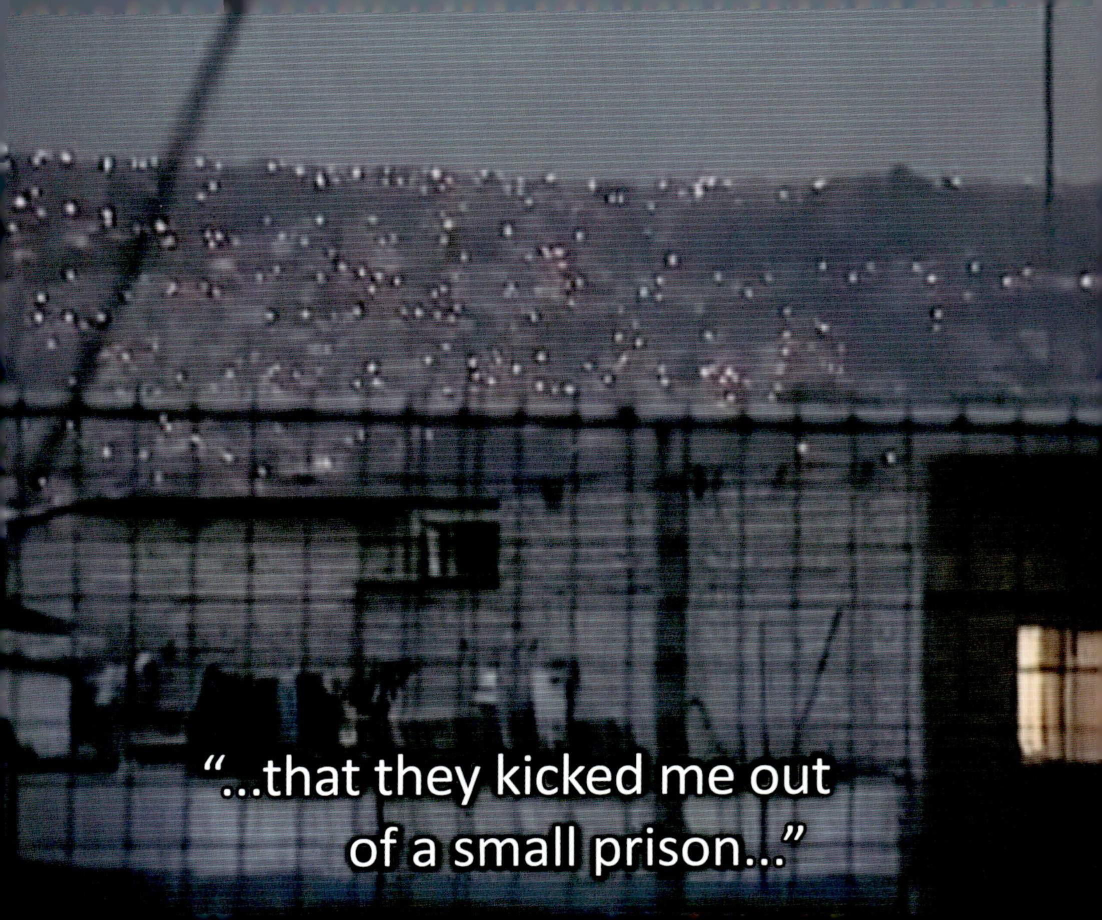
“...that they kicked me out
of a small prison...”

“...into a big prison like the city.”

Kristel Mucino, *Drugs & Prisons in Ecuador: The Human Face of Misguided Drug Laws*, 2019

Caroline Bennett, *Gender Violence in Ecuador*, 2017

2019: Femicide

Plagued by a rising epidemic of gendered-based violence against women, the United Nations reports that 14 out of the 25 countries in the world with the highest femicide rates are located in South America. Reflective of colonially inherited and industrially reinforced, heteropatriarchal patterns of male domination and male violence, only 2% of criminal offenses and human rights violations by men are in fact prosecuted. It is reported that even far less are reported based on official data. Exacerbated by the prison-drug war complex as Jill Harrison and Maureen Norton-Hawk assessed in their 2010 study, "The Care, Custody, and Control of Incarcerated Women in Ecuador:" "stories from incarcerated women are not unique but rather reflect a culture that has traditionally treated women as expendable objects to be used and eventually discarded. Every woman we met over the course of our investigation at *el Inca* recounted themes of poverty, isolation, abuse, sexual assault, and rape." Of the 14 countries in South America with the highest rates of violence against women in civilian society, the country that has the highest, per capita rate of violence against women—which includes Indigenous, Afro-Latina, and Mestiza women—in all of South America, is Ecuador.

María Carón & Raúl Ayala, *Mujeres Custodias de Nuestro Hábitat en Peligro* (Quito), 2017

Mona Caron & Raúl Ayala, *Mujeres Custodias de nuestro Hábitat en Peligro* (Quito), 2017

Quinine Bisulphate (300mg Tablet), 2014

2019: Stress & Strain

In spite of claimed advantages of its economies of scale, the price of pharmaceutical quinine still remains far out of reach for millions of malaria sufferers (especially in the Global South) even when taking into account supply and demand in mass production of the pill. The *League of Nations* is called in to assess the situation that has worsened since 1931, where over 250 million people are affected by malaria in the world today (second only to tuberculosis), with nearly 1 million deaths a year—the equivalent of one child every 30 seconds. Today, with the majority of the burden of malaria carried by South Asia and Africa, the bumper crop of political independence in the middle to late 20th century has yet to loosen the grip of racial capitalism that suppresses true forms of economic self-determination and territorial sovereignty, especially in the countries hardest hit: Nigeria, Congo, Mozambique, India, Mali, Ghana, Uganda, Tanzania, Cameroon, and Burkina Faso. Ironically, the list of hardest hit countries includes equatorial and tropical countries that currently hold plantations and maintain communities of labor in the growth, management, and development of Cinchona species, new and old. As a form of pharmacological dispossession, they are further literally and bodily removed—historically and botanically—from quinine's curative powers.

Eduardo Leon, *Indigenous Uprising* (Quito, Ecuador), 12 October 2019

2019: Indigenous Uprising

Protesting sanctions and austerity measures imposed by the *International Monetary Fund* (IMF) adopted by Ecuadorian President Lenín Moreno, a consolidated movement of urban Mestizos, working class groups, students, and rural communities of Indigenous Peoples converge and come together from across the Amazon Rainforest and Andes Mountain Regions with the leadership of *CONAIE* (Confederación de Nacionalidades Indígenas del Ecuador) on the streets of the nation's capital of Quito for a massive rally lasting two weeks in early October against the hike in fuel prices imposed by the Federal Government. In a cowardice manner of retreating, the office of the President and seat of the Republic's Government was temporarily relocated almost 300 miles away south to the Port City of Guayaquil. After public pressure and negotiations with CONAIE less than two weeks after the beginning of public protests and demonstrations, President Moreno agrees to withdraw from Decree 883 that sought to hike fuel prices and end four decades of fuel subsidies. Moreno's decree was based on a spiral of debt and economic poverty maintained by the IMF since the 1970s that has disempowered working classes and penalized rural (primarily Indigenous) populations heavily reliant on oil, gasoline, and diesel for transport, heating, and agriculture.

RESI
ENCIA

David Díaz Arcos, Indigenous Uprising (Quito, Ecuador), 12 October 201

Charles G. Ripley, *Moreno Traidor del Pueblo* (Quito, Ecuador), 2017

Ronaldo Schemidt, *Evo sin Pueblo* (La Paz, Bolivia), 2019

2019: Un Violador en tu Camino

Following the political uprisings in Quito led by Indigenous women in the Fall of 2019, thousands of women descend onto the streets of Santiago in the neighboring, Andean country of Chile to protest against socio-economic inequalities, chauvinism, and political elitism at the root of gendered-based violence running rampant across South America. After 43 days of intense demonstrations against state oppression and, in a display of transnational solidarity, the feminist group *Las Tesis from the* Port City of Valparaiso stages a live performance to mark the *International Day for the Elimination of Violence against Women* on November 25th. Spreading around the world, the pro-feminist performance denounces gender-based violence, police abuse, and state repression of women's rights and justice. On that day, Las Tesis' performance goes viral inspiring demonstrations worldwide, from Chile and Argentina to Italy and India, with their anthem: "Un Violador en tu Camino—A Rapist in your Path". Performed in unison facing state, judicial, and parliamentary buildings, arms are raised and crossed to signal a call to stop patriarchal oppression... then lowered, pointing directly at the architectures of the nation-state and to condemn its patriarchal agents: "El violador eres tú. The Rapist is You."

2019: Communitarian Feminism

Less than a month after the protests against IMF sanctions in Ecuador, the *Organization of American States* (OAS)—long considered a puppet organization of Washington DC—intervenes in the re-election of Bolivia's first Indigenous President Evo Morales, a firm advocate of economic sovereignty: "Our sin, our crime, is to have proven that Bolivia can develop without the capitalist system, without the International Monetary Fund." Following a series of events that lead to the coup against Morales in November 2019 and installation of interim right-wing President Jeanine Áñez (who would later be arrested in the wake of Senkata and Sacaba Massacres), Aymaran community leader Adriana Guzmán and staunch feminist activist aptly declares, "this is a coup against an Indigenous, sovereign government, along with the rural organizations and social movements. It is punishment so that we don't ever again think that it is possible to live outside of capitalism, that a good life could be possible—so that we never again think of self-determination, think that we can govern ourselves, organize ourselves. So that we accept the capitalist, neoliberal, patriarchal, colonialist system. That is the message". As part of *Feminismo Comunitario Antipatriarcal de Bolivia* and *Feministas de Abya Yala* who was radicalized by the *Gas Wars of 2003* in La Paz, Guzmán discusses the geopolitical significance of feminism in leading the movement against settler-colonial heteropatriarchy: "By thinking how we could end with patriarchy, with this patriarchy that is capitalist, that is racist, that is neoliberal and transnational, it is how we have formed communitarian feminism. This construction is fundamentally rooted in a political position, by making a platform that enables us to step up and understand this world, and to shape the world we want to live in. This platform is the place to find our memory and the possibility to recognize ourselves as Aymara Women. This platform has also enabled us to discuss if we want to return to live in the ways in which we lived before. It has been important to break with the linear logic of colonial time that argues about passing from the pre-modern to the modern, to the post-modern, from the uncivilized to the civilized, that talks about progress, development, evolution, from the un-evolved to the evolved. This is a colonial logic of time, but also a way to narrate your story. It is also hegemonic, it argues that the ones that arrived from Europe were evolved, civilized and had license to civilize. Nowadays is has become into ways to 'help' us through international cooperation, as well as with money to keep us 'evolving'... Seeing our history before 1492 has made us reflect that women were also oppressed, and there were types of oppression and violence that existed before the Spaniard invasion as well. We have called those oppressions Ancestral Patriarchy. This has been important to put into question the idea that by abolishing the colony, patriarchy will end as well. We sate the risk in this narrative of a patriarchal recycling in the process of Bolivian transformation because we have been watching 'colonialism,' 'decolonization,' but not *patriarchy*. What we argue is that in 1492 what happened is a patriarchal junction, patriarchy that arrived with invaders—*colonial patriarchy*—merged with the ancestral patriarchy. For that reason, in these territories of Abya Ayala, women live with a double patriarchy, and it is a double patriarchy that oppresses not just women, but also males, young children, and nature as well. Because there is a patriarchal merging it does not mean that women feel one kind of oppressions in their communities, and a different one in cities. The oppressions have merged, making us live double, and triple oppressions that become visible in different shapes and circumstances. This concept of the patriarchal juncture it has worked in Bolivia for the discussions to think about the country, to reposition the fights of our people. They can look at patriarchy from within communitarian feminism and fight for de-patriarchalization, as well as for decolonization, and autonomy. Autonomy of our bodies and sexuality, the autonomy of the body and sexuality of women."

Donald J. Trump
@realDonaldTrump

HYDROXYCHLOROQUINE & AZITHROMYCIN, taken together, have a real chance to be one of the biggest game changers in the history of medicine. The FDA has moved mountains - Thank You! Hopefully they will BOTH (H works better with A, International Journal of Antimicrobial Agents).....

10:13 AM · Mar 21, 2020 · Twitter for iPhone

103.5K Retweets **387.6K** Likes

Donald J. Trump @realDonaldTrump · Mar 21
Replying to @realDonaldTrump
....be put in use IMMEDIATELY. PEOPLE ARE DYING, MOVE FAST, and GOD BLESS EVERYONE! @US_FDA @SteveFDA @CDCgov @DHSgov

15.9K 29.9K 134.3k

Donald J. Trump (former US President), Hydroxychloroquine, 21 March 2020

2020: Hoax

Reacting to the global risk and international threat brought on by the pandemic spread of the COVID-19 coronavirus across the world, U.S. President Donald Trump calls for the immediate mobilization of a synthetic quinine derivative—*hydroxychloroquine*—as miracle cure for the life-threatening viral infection that is affecting Americans in the order of hundreds of thousands (especially service workers and People of Color) with nearly 150,000 deaths and 3 million cases of infection. Nearly every medical scientist and health professional admonish and overturn the careless, baseless, knee-jerk recommendation made by the President, a baseless if not dangerous remedy that was also endorsed and supported a few days earlier by Tesla CEO Elon Musk on March 16th, 2020: "Maybe worth considering chloroquine for C19?" The conjectural tweet advocating for the use of the malaria drug came on the heels of opposition to shelter-in-place and stay-at-home order effectively delaying the reopening of TESLA's manufacturing plants. Within the next six months, following a gross lack of leadership and downplay of health risks, the toll of the virus peaks at 1 million worldwide cases in 3 days by October 2020. By the Fall, the US President, the First Lady Melania Trump, as well as British Prime Minister Boris Johnson and Brazil President Jair Bolsonaro, all contract COVID-19.

Aldair Mejía, Indigenous Peoples from Peru Abandoning the City of Lima, 20

2020: Urban Exodus

In a show of solidarity and self-organization against economic justices and regional distrust of central governments, a coalition of Indigenous Peoples in Lima and from across the Andean country of Peru engage in a massive urban exodus, unilaterally decide to abandon the chronic poverty and unjust conditions of the city in order to return to their traditional homelands in rural areas. With similar conditions in Ecuador where the highest concentrations of viral infections are found in large cities linked to service sector work, essential infrastructures, and other areas of high transmission vectors, the lack of governmental support (services, equipment, compensation) during the global COVID-19 health crisis leaves the most vulnerable people, namely Indigenous Peoples and Afro-Latinx—especially elders and knowledge keepers—at considerable risk. Without any guarantees for subsistence nor health care in urban areas, the vacuum of health care support in the wake of the rapid spread of the virus (a humanitarian crisis really) forces even more people, in the tens of thousands, to flee the congested environments of the city and begin their journey home to ancestral lands and traditional communities in rural, and sometimes extremely remote areas in the valleys, hillsides, and mountains.

2020: Missionaries, Barred & Banned

On Friday April 17th, *The Guardian* newspaper reports that: "A Brazilian judge has banned a group of Christian missionaries from entering a vast Amazon Indigenous Reserve with the world's highest concentration of isolated tribes, citing risks from the COVID-19 pandemic as one of the main reasons. Indigenous leaders and activists hailed the decision as 'historic' and expressed hope that it could prevent a genocide in the Javari Valley, a remote reserve the size of Austria on Brazil's western borders." According to *The Guardian News Service*, "Federal judge Fabiano Verli banned three missionaries, Andrew Tonkin, Josiah McIntyre and Pastor Wilson de Benjamin, from the reserve, along with the controversial missionary group *New Tribes Mission of Brazil* (MNTB) which recently bought a helicopter to convert isolated peoples in the region." Offering little substantive evidence, *Missão Novas Tribos do Brasil* (MNTB) dismissed The Guardian's claims as conjecture and speculation in a newsletter posted by partner organization *Ethnos360 Aviation* on April 29: "MNTB is not entering any new people groups at this time, with or without the helicopter. Additionally, missionaries are not spreading coronavirus because mission personnel have been evacuated from the villages, where they have been working for years at the request of and by permission of the people."

Celso Roldán, *Peruvian botanical researcher Roque Rodríguez showing the red Cinchona bark*, 2016

2020: Un-Naming

Passed down by oral tradition across generations of Saraguro Peoples—long before written history—the Republic of Ecuador has never officially recognized the episteme of the Cinchona plant taken from Kechwan Lands whose original name is *yara chucchu cara chucchu* meaning "tree of intermittent fever," (*yara*: "tree", *cara*: "bark", *chucchu*: "cold of the fever", or *ayac-cara*: "bitter bark"). The global pharmaceutical industry has yet to request permission from the Saraguro Peoples to extract, process, use, sell, let alone patent *quinine* that Kechwan tradition in the Loja region calls *chahuarguera.* While adopted by José Antonio Pavón in the late 18th century during his travel to the Central Andes with Hipólito Ruiz López, the name would be dropped and supeseded by Linnean designation from 1742, *Cinchona officinalis*. Across centuries of extraction, falsification, simulation, industrialization and erasure, European and American scholars will continue to repeat errors, spread falsehoods, as conveniently whitewash tales of its bloody history, a plant whose sovereignty is not only to respected and honored drawing back to its traditional Kechwan lands in the Andes, near Loja. The legacy of the *fever tree*, as a current and present weapon of domination and exploitation on Idjwi Island on the far eastern border of the Democratic Republic of Congo, also requires reckoning.

Arjo Vanderjagt, *Efflorescence: Cinchona Pubescens Vahl v. Chahuaguea (Baños)*, 2019

2021: Un-Patenting

To this day and for the foreseeable future, international patent laws in the United States and Europe do not recognize what it refers to as "undocumented knowledge held abroad." Marginalizing and erasing traditional Indigenous knowledge, the legal recognition of Kechwan oral tradition that has made possible the production of quinine as the natural cure to eradicate malaria throughout the world has yet to be honored. Consent, we can be sure, was never granted to abuse and violate the plant's reproductive rights. And this legacy of erasure, at the intersections of science and colonialism, development and dispossession, conservation and extraction, must end. As Graham Dutfield observes in a 2001 article "'Trade-Related Intellectual Property Rights' Aspects of Traditional Knowledge," 2001: *"An indigenous person and a scientist may both know that quinine bark extract can cure malaria. But they are likely to describe what they know in very different ways that may be mutually unintelligible (even when communicated in the same language)... It might be countered that, since the indigenous peoples of western Amazonia do not really understand why quinine works, their quinine-based treatment is a technology that is not science-based. If that is so, however, one could infer that many western 'scientific' applications ought likewise to be 'downgraded' to*

Somos Raíces Fuertes

EL Tratado del Quino

Sara Sisa Bordados, *El Tratado del Quino*, 2021

technologies, since they are not based on a complete understanding of why they work... Although the indigenous people do not have the knowledge of quinine as a molecule or a chemical formula, they have another type of knowledge that is just as valid. When determining whether a proposed entity is patentable or not, it seems that prior art, although of another kind, should be considered as such and should have the capability to disqualify a patent candidate on grounds of lack of novelty." Notwithstanding the exhaustive royalties and reparations owed to the Saraguro Peoples over five centuries of colonial extraction in the use of *quinine,* no compensation has ever been granted to the Peoples of Kechwa Nations who've helped guide, cultivated knowledge, and provided access to Americans and Europeans between the 16th and 20th centuries. Thus, above and beyond the necessary land reparations, economic compensations, development restrictions, infrastructure adaptations, and massive conservation needed, not only should the patent and artifacts of the Cinchona plant be returned and its colonial name un-named, *Chahuarguera itself* needs to be returned—historically and politically—to its original lands and its original peoples to honor it, and protect it for future generations living in Andean and Amazonian lands. *Quina es la flora del pasado, presente y futuro.*

Pablo Escudero, *Blockades of Imbabura Region*, 2020

2020-21: Blockades

Following the global spread of the COVID-19 virus reaching pandemic levels in western countries, the accelerating rate of viral infection via global ports of entry in Latin American Nations, namely in the coastal city and global port of Guayaquil in Ecuador, prompt communities of Kichwan and Waorani Nations to adopt infrastructural measures of protection to safeguard communities by restricting access to their territory from foreigners. Forecast to extend across a period of two years, to account for multiple waves of infection prior to vaccine development, extra-territorial risks that may compromise the health and welfare of Indigenous communities, including their elders, are abated by blocking off access to transportation corridors, including roads, trails, and paths as unilateral signs of self-determination and declarations of sovereignty. These seemingly small, territorial interventions may offer a glimpse into the growing opposition to the politics of pacification, policies of assimilation, and infrastructures of extraction that will continue to invade and attempt to contaminate these lands for the foreseeable future.

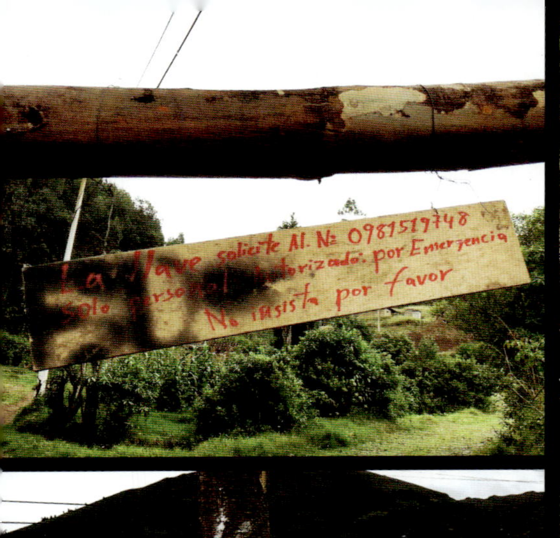
La llave solicite Al. Nº 0981519748
solo personal ...torizado: por Emergencia
No insista por favor

ESTIMADOS MORADORES
POR SEGURIDAD DE LA SALUD HAY UNA
ENTRADA Y SALIDA ES POR SIGXILOMA
DE 5am A 8Pm GRACIAS POR SU COMPRENSIÓN
LA DIRECTIVA →

Por EMERGENCIA SANITARIA
CORONAVIRUS. "PESILLO EN CUARENTENA"
PARA EL INGRESO LLAMAR A LOS TLF: Gobernadora
0980485269 o al 0999156102 Vicegobernadora
¡¡ Para registro y control medico!!

PARE

Pablo Escudero, *Blockades of Imbabura Region*, 2020

Pablo Escudero, *Blockade at Imbabura*, 2020

"The internal enemy—*colonization*—is within us all, from elites to the oppressed."

Silvia Rivera Cusicanqui

Amo la Montaña / I Love the Mountain

(2010)

Towards a Flora of the Future

by way of a conclusion

How can the re-reading of political history open pathways towards liberation from settler oppression? In what ways do alternative forms of representation—counter-mappings—help to dismantle dominant narratives of conquest? How can an alternative understanding of territorial relations help turn away from systems of capitalist domination? How can the territorial trope and counter-narrative of a plant—the Cinchona plant and the fever tree—open different levels of historical understanding and lead to restorative justice to reclaim suppressed sovereignties?

Historical and representational in scope, these questions capture the political aspiration of this book. As an inquiry, the book necessarily challenges the settler-colonial frameworks and the maps upon which those structures are inscribed and planned by the state. The book thus questions and confronts the semiotic structures embedded in the singularity and homogeneity of the image of the nation-state itself. Boundaries, categories, classifications, frames, scales, and data that typically legitimize nationalist histories and intimate national myths are then weaponized to construct settler-spaces and settler-surfaces and quash challenging or competing sovereignties. We specifically target the techno-spatial subtexts of nationalism that are inscribed in reference texts and maps; themselves entirely premised on racial erasure. A close reading of these references proves essential in exposing the nested motives of dispossession and attendant acts of dehumanization, entrenched across a range of scales: urban policies, provincial decrees, national laws, and international trade agreements. To challenge these frameworks to challenge the seemingly implacable image of its authority as displayed in the national flag and its projected permanence in its presentation of who it leaves in and who it leaves out.

Counter-Mappings as Counter-Narratives. If the visible authority of nation-state is symmetrically aligned with its heteropatriarchal image, then its public policies have disproportionately targeted Indigenous and Afro-Latinx women as subjects of control and objects of oppression. Through systems of subjugation and incarceration, gendered violence, and political erasure, the force of the nation-state politically extends and technocratically expands colonial forms of violence from the past five centuries. Between scales of the body and the territory, there are at least two underlying ways to characterize the systematic nature of the state's campaigns of territorial dispossession and racial domination. Not only are they unjust, but they are also inhuman. First, by depoliticizing the land-based organization of Indigenous Peoples and imposing technocratic systems of white supremacy. Maintained by the force of the state police and provincial property laws, these systems destroy ecologies through engineered infrastructures as much as they suppress identities through pedagogical curricula (both designed to eliminate barriers, open access, and plunder resources). The range of policies from carceral feminism to cultural assimilation is extensive and deeply entrenched in the ideologies of erasure, elimination, and assimilation.

The over-representation of Indigenous and Afro-Ecuadorian women in prisons as a result of over-incarceration of women for non-violent crimes or their under-representation in public governance systems as a result of occupational discrimination and under-education is pervasive. Second, by disembodying livelihoods and displacing Indigenous and Afro-Ecuadorian women leaving them relegated to urban peripheries and subjugated to the margins of cities (Quito and Guayaquil are major examples) by the eviscerating effects of metropolitan economies—under-education, hindering access to settler economies, and severing traditional support systems and kin. Together, these state-sponsored forms of aggression and the heteropatriarchal instruments of settler-colonialism have dismantled and disarmed political geographies of Indigenous governance and traditional ways of living by disempowering and deterritorializing the matriarchal foundations of Indigenous communities, including intergenerational relations of kin.

As sites of dispossession, the collective body-politic and bodies of Indigenous and Afro-Ecuadorian women also represent sites of resistance. In her 2013 book, *The Inheritance of Resistance: Indigenous Women Leadership in Ecuador*, French-Brazilian-Ecuadorian political scientist Manuela Lavinas Picq explains the historical depth of this campaign of gendered violence and erasure:

> "Indigenous women have a long history of political leadership that has led to their unexpected absence from contemporary politics. Their stories of rebellion reveal their inheritance of political resistance across generations. Women first contested against colonial armies, then against oppressive independent states, in positions of leadership, in courts, and through daily acts of resistance. However, official history hardly remembers the female leadership of Indigenous rebellions and has failed to record the significance of many more nameless women. They have been kept anonymous in the archives of the New World, erased from history records in selective processes of nation-making that reinforced the tale of impotent Indians facing powerful colonizers. Their experiences survived not only in the form of storytelling, but also in the inheritance of resistance. I explore stories of female leadership as a reminder that the politicization of Indigenous women predates feminist politics in the West. These stories subvert familiar understandings of Indigenous women as passive and propose new understandings of the present."

Therefore, the remembering of these women's names placing and re-telling of their fragmented histories within their political territories is central to the intergenerational project of resistance, whose intersections defy Western cartographic conventions, spatial subjects, and toponymic identities. Marginalized or obscured, the overlapping and gendered geographies of Andean lowlands and Amazonian headwaters are far from being peripheries, they are centers. This indeed resonates with words of Kofan land defender Alex Lucitante at the opening of this book:

> "Since the beginning of our life as a people, this territory has been our supermarket, our pharmacy, our hardware store. Our ancestors were born and buried here. Our connection to this place is deeper than the state's. We should be managing it and protecting it."

Yet these territories have most often been considered inconvenient and counterproductive, divided and treated as separate from settler spaces of the metropolis for one reason or another: either for their location, altitude, their climate, their identity, their organization, their topography, their ecology, or their inaccessibility. If the landscape of settler-colonial space is plotted and planned before it is transformed, then settler-imagery of the Andes and the Amazon as evacuated, unoccupied, and unpoliticized nature is a prerequisite in the planning and plotting of 'new' regions through an infrastructure straight lines, right angles, and sharp corners and below the surface of the state. The neutering and nationalization of nature is thus a precondition for the exploitation and extraction of carbon resources (oil, gas, minerals) on one hand, and the conservation of resources on the other, as the foil for dispossession. And yet, territorial flows challenge these settler-colonial delusions. Ecological processes that are deeply embedded in webs of life in the ground and water directly challenge the recognizable geometries of engineered infrastructures (especially megaprojects) that perpetuate the appearance of stability, precision, and permanence nation-state. Those challenges are dramatically exacerbated by environmental risks of climate change (with increasing prevalence of torrential rains and landslides or thermal shifts affecting agricultural crops) as well as industrial accidents (oil spills, river contamination, toxicity).

Identifiable in the eyes of white settlers, state citizens, and privileged élites, and omnipresent in the heteropatriarchy of planning bureaucrats, the enclosing lines of the nation-states of Brazil, Venezuela, Colombia, Ecuador, Peru, and Bolivia run parallel with the legibility and reproducibility of contemporary property boundary systems, as much as they align with the sharp edge of the 1494 Treaty of Tordesillas that divided the earth into two distinct halves between Spanish and Portuguese empires. To show how they fail, how they exclude, how they pollute, or how they harm is to challenge and confront the normativity and the nature of the nation-state propped up by its images and maps. In other words, the exercise of ground-truthing the distortions and manipulations of the settler-colonial space between the map and the territory is a form of spatial, archival activism. Exposing different scales and structures, this form of historiographic activism challenges the toponymic conventions of division, divisibility, and dissociation that violently wall-off and erase overlapping natural systems, land-based traditions, and accompanying territorial sovereignties of current and future generations.

A Landscape of Liberation. If the idea of the political concerns people, humanity and sovereignty of all beings, then the process of liberation from dispossession involves building relations between them through embodied presence; re-placed. As Enrique Dussel observed in *Filosofía de la Liberación* (1977), liberation is about "continued existence as coexistence, as surviving and flourishing with others, that is the source of the political."

Intrinsic to the image and imagination of this project, the political stands out from the enclosed lines of nationhood, from the austerity measures set by a national government, or from endless queues for domestic goods produced by foreign transnationals that capitalize on the dissociation between the map and the territory—between what is imagined and what is actualized. The dichotomies in political struggles for humanity, liberation, and sovereignty are therefore as much territorial and epistemological as they are cognitive and psychological. As psychiatrist Frantz Fanon from Martinique observed in his 1961 *Les Damnés de la Terre* (*The Wretched of the Earth*), the ontological facets of dispossession leave a mental mark in "the spirit of discouragement which has been deeply rooted in people's minds by colonial domination."

When weaving the political with the psychological—or the historical with the territorial—the process of counter-mapping the nation-state reveals the lives of peoples with other beings and entities that literally and figuratively lie outside the sharp edges of its boundaries; communities that are systematically impacted by the injustices of its policies as much as the violence of its ideologies. This is where the epistemological design of the book takes place. What else explains how one of the smallest nations in Latin America carries the burden of the highest rates of violence against women and girls as seen in Ecuador for the past decade? Or why has the US Dollar penetrated the national currency of Ecuador so persistently and for so long? The strategy of counter-mapping makes visible connections between political geographies, social histories, and cultural traditions that otherwise cannot be clearly understood in a legible, non-nationalistic, non-specialized, or non-disciplined way.

"They Shouted Black"

Rhythmic poem by Victoria Santa Cruz

(1978)

I was just seven years old,
Just seven years old...
What seven years old?!
I didn't' even reach five!

Suddenly, some voices on the street,
shouted at me, Black!
Black! Black! Black! Black! Black! Blaack!
Am I Black? I said
Yes!
What does it mean to be Black?
Black!
And I didn't know the sad reality it hide
that might be behind Black!
And I felt Black,
Black!
Just like they said,
Black!
I stepped back,
Black!
Just as they wanted,
Black!
And I hated my hair and my thick lips,
And I sadly looked at my toast skin,
And I stepped back,
Black!
I stepped back...
Black! Black! Black! Black!
Black! Black! Blaaack!
Black! Black! Black! Black!
Black! Black! Black! Black!

And time passed by,
and always bitter
I kept carrying on my back
my heavy burden
and it was heavy!...

I straightened my hair,
I powdered my face,
And in my groins always echoed,
the same words
Black! Black! Black! Black!
Black! Black! Blaaack!
Until one day I stepped back almost falling,
Black! Black! Black! Black!
Black! Black! Black! Black!
Black! Black! Black! Black!
Black! Black! Black!
So what?
So what?

Black!
Yes
Black!
I am
Black!
Black
Black!
Black I am

Black!
Yes
Black!
I am
Black!
Black
Black!
Black I am

From here on out I don't want to
straighten my hair
I don't want to
And I will laugh at those
that in order to avoid—according to them
that in order to avoid a bad experience
call Blacks 'colored folks'
and what color is that?
BLACK
How beautiful it sounds!
BLACK
What rhythm does it have!
BLACK BLACK BLACK BLACK
BLACK BLACK BLACK BLACK
BLACK BLACK BLACK BLACK
BLACK BLACK BLACK
Finally
Finally, I understood
Finally
I no longer step back
Finally
I don't back down anymore
Finally
And I confidently move forward
Finally
I move forward and wait
Finally
And I blessed the sky because God wanted
that deep black was my color
And I understood
Finally
I have the key
BLACK BLACK BLACK BLACK
BLACK BLACK BLACK BLACK
BLACK BLACK BLACK BLACK
BLACK BLACK
Black I am!

Translation: Katherine Aissa Porras, 2012

The representation of these communities and connections certainly does not lie in the categories of official maps or the codes of state images, but rather in their critique and confrontation. By challenging the legibility of the visual identifiers of the state itself, answers lie—albeit imperfectly—in challenging representations of maps and their narratives. Unlike Humboldt's revered 'Tableau' and travel log across the Andes in his 1809 illustrious Essay on the Geography of Plants depicting the flora of Chimborazo volcano as the quintessential peak of colonial conquest, or Frederick Edwin Church's 1949 painting *Heart of the Andes* as the pinnacle of picturesque art at the Hudson River School of Painting, the format of this book does not try to capture history in some kind of grand, global narrative or as a kind of cosmography. Rather, it attempts to rebuild and reconceive different histories and overlapping geographies through cycles and patterns of struggle and conflict led by Indigenous & Afro-Ecuadorian women who lie between the lines of or are left out entirely from settler-colonial narratives.

Transgression & Transfiguration. By displacing and decentering western colonial narratives, the multimedia approach of this book makes space for new narratives from alternative bodies and deep-seeded traditions by re-centering what was marginalized, suppressed, or erased. This focus is committed to the core of understanding of who the oppressed are, for the process of liberation is contingent on centering the politically disempowered and economically disadvantaged, as liberation theologist (and pastor in the shadow of violence) Gustavo Gutiérrez articulates in his 1972 *A Theology of Liberation: History, Politics, and Salvation*, and who, later in 1990, stated:

> "It is impossible to construct a nation and a fatherland for all when there is marginalization and injustice for the majority."

This book is an attempt to identify marginalized histories and build alternative worlds around these peripheries, to see and seek out new geographies that not only shed light on oppression but also on the landscapes of liberation that lie beyond it.

Towards these ends, boastful victorious characterizations of imperial conquest and illustrious narratives of explorations and discoveries that uphold settler-colonial idolatry of

Euro-American history are confronted and requestioned here. We challenge the overt patriarchy and domination that covertly masks oppression and dispossession by placing the minority of settlers in positions of power. That dominant white minority permeates all facets of settler society: government, education, business, public services, and the arts. And as these counter-mappings unfold, alternative histories emerge. The buried legacies of Indigenous or Afro-Ecuadorian women across hundreds of years comes to light: from Afro-Ecuadorian midwife and freed slave from Guayaquil, María del Tránsito Sorroza in the 17th century, to Kichwa activist and founder of Federación Ecuatoriana de Indios, Rosa Elena Tránsito Amaguaña Alba in the 20th century. Today, Andean activist Adriana Guzmán speaks clearly of this longstanding confrontation against settler-colonial patriarchy from the south, in Bolivia, through a radical, Indigenous practice of communitarian feminism:

> "a platform to understand the colonial world differently and shape the space we want to live in... as Aymara Women."

Aligned with Guzmán's *communitarian feminism*, the poetry of Afro-Peruvian singer, songwriter, and performer Victoria Santa Cruz from the central Andes is especially significant. Embodied in Santa Cruz's performative art and poetry are the strategies of resistance and reclamation; a Black woman who, as a young girl coming of age, suffered through years of colonial trauma into her adulthood from racist bullying and cultural shaming based on her skin color.

Santa Cruz's lyrical prose not only embodies autonomy of mind and sovereignty of being but, as a Black "who no longer backs down," she pledges her own political independence in strategies of refusal through her words and plays. In the 1978 performance, *Me Gritaron Negra* (*They Shouted Black*), Santa Cruz responds to the racialization of her being and the subjugation of her body in the colonial world by building an alternative one through her voice, her lyrics, her rhythm, her body, her resonance. As Peruvian and Afro-Latina scholar Lady Rojas Benavente explains in her 2006 review of Santa Cruz's performance almost four decades earlier, reflecting on her legacy of poetic resistance:

Metro Ecuador, *Massive cleanup of Quito led by Indigenous Peoples after protests*, October 14th 2019

"the anaphoric and cumulative repetition of 'Black' throughout Santa Cruz's poem is a rhetorical strategy that reinforces the use of language, demonstrating how different positions are taken by the dominator or dominated as subjects that consitute social relations of power... In this way, she inverts the pejorative dehumanizing sense of Blackness, and replaces it with values of humanity and rebirth that drive her to unleash all creative possibilities... The affirmation and actualization of herself—that is, the need to recognize her otherness and the desire to accept herself as the subject of her history—guides her in the personal and collective search for the richness that she has inherited from her African culture."

Bearing energy, the ancestral past and the carrying of tradition can power both resistance to oppression and reclamation of self. Afro-Ecuadorian author Luz Argentina Chiriboga's 1992 novel *Drums Under My Skin* located that agency in the story of a young mulatta girl (Rebeca) from the historically Black coastal Esmeraldas encountering the frictions with metropolitan mestizo culture and historically colonial forms of white supremacy and heteropatriarchy: "I was no longer ashamed of that painful past I once mistakenly tried so hard to hide. I can feel part of my grandmother now, her resonance, I can her drums beating under my skin." And furthermore, as Afro-Latinx and Black historian Gabriella Davis explains in her 2019 McNair Scholarship work, "Ecuador is Black, Afro-Ecuadorian Literary Resistance in Drums Under My Skin":

"By understanding how various marginalized Black Ecuadorian identities move throughout oppressive spaces, a deeper, complete appreciation of the beauty in embracing all forms of Blackness can truly disrupt racist sexism in Ecuador..."

... essentially, racist sexism so intrinsic to colonial heteropatriarchy and white supremacy that, in themselves, need to be broken and dismantled. In re-reading Chiriboga's oeuvre, Davis makes another important observation regarding this liberatory project:

"Author Argentina Chiriboga herself is from Esmeraldas, a city in Ecuador that is historically and socially known as Black. Her knowledge of this space allows her to write the Esmeraldan memory of resistance into her work. She also places lo negro, or Blackness, within Ecuador by textually remembering Black traditions and consciousness in order to break the ideological structure of mestizaje. However, she is not simply making room for Blackness in Ecuador; rather, she makes it the center of everything."

Taken together, Guzmán and Santa Cruz's words and works pay it forward by looking back: their retroactive stanzas also read like projective scripts. Like a declaration, they both reclaim the histories and territories of Andean space. On one hand, that space is transitive and topographic, fluvial and botanical, inclusive of coast and mountains, rivers and oceans, low and high altitudes, rejecting settler-colonial cartographies and categories that historically define and divide 'the' Andes, 'the' Amazon, and 'the' Coast. On the other hand, that space is emancipatory, where they imagine alternative worlds through new geographies and freedoms steeped in once suppressed and outlawed traditions, now liberated from the stronghold of colonization, gendered violence, and patriarch. Here, that Andean landscape is both Indigenous and Black feminist space.

These counter-narratives map out views from the margins of empire, like edge epistemologies drawing a view from the outside of the nation-state to wedge itself from within and without the specter of settler-colonialism. These counter-mappings are anticolonial and employ a logic of the periphery and embody the edge. "Border thinking," as Madina Tlostanova and Walter Mignolo observed in 2012, "emerges in the process of delinking from the colonial matrix and escaping from its control... a specific epistemic response from the exteriority of Western modernity, a response from the outside created from the perspective of the inside."

And if these narratives of oppression are sometimes difficult to discern, they are most often visible in the reoccurring patterns of repression and domination. Confronting these same narratives requires a decentering of dominant ones, as revolutionary Cape Verdean and Guinea-Bissau agronomist Amílcar Cabral observed in a 1970 speech, dedicated to the life of anthropologist and the leader of the Mozambique Liberation Front Dr. Eduardo Mondlane in the aftermath of his assassination by state agents:

> "History teaches us that, in certain circumstances, it is very easy for the foreigner to impose his domination on a people. But it also teaches us that, whatever may be the material aspects of this domination, it can be maintained only by the permanent, organized repression of the cultural life of the people concerned. Implantation of foreign domination can be assured definitively only by physical liquidation of a significant part of the dominated population."

Timeline as Treatise. Not unlike the political uprisings that recently took place in mid-October 2019, a group of 120 different tribal nations from across the Americas gathered in Quito (Ecuador) on Tuesday, July 17th, 1990. Invoking the spatiality of the urban as grounds for settler confrontation, the unprecedented gathering, referred to as Levantamiento (Uprising), sought to oppose the quincentennial worldwide celebrations of Christopher Columbus underway by a multitude of settler-colonial governments and settler organizations across Iberoamerican territories. The first of many cross-continental gatherings that would soon follow, Levantamiento was a massive opposition to the sesquicentennial celebrations of Columbus' arrival on the shores of the Americas planned for 1992: the advent of foreign, Christian, colonial European powers that began in the year 1492, with the landing (crashing) of Christopher Columbus on the shores of Hispañiola Island in the Caribbean Ocean. The rassemblement of tribal nations and Indigenous Peoples was opposing the 'mission civilisatrice' of Europeans and the Doctrines of Discovery issued in the papal bulls of the Catholic Church with two objectives: either assimilating non-Christians (so-called 'savages') through subjugation and slavery (for purposes of labor exploitation, knowledge extraction, economic domination) or exterminating them (for political control and historical supremacy in the case of resistors). Both aimed to access and extract any and all possible resources—including lands—as their property. Part reclamation and part reparation, the ensuing 1990 Quito Declaration thus clearly proclaimed itself as a counter-colonial challenge to the years 1492 and 1992:

> "Our struggle is not a mere conjunctural reflection of the memory of 500 years of oppression which the invaders, in complicity with the 'democratic' governments of our countries, want to turn into events of jubilation and celebration. Our Indian People, Nations, and Nationalities are basing our struggle on our identity, which

shall lead us to true liberation. We are responding aggressively and commit ourselves to reject this 'celebration.'"

Mirroring the 2019 uprisings in Quito, the intercontinental gathering in the summer of 1990 was a historical encounter. Not only did it establish a point of contact with settler-space in the capital city of Quito but marked a point of reference in settler-history by bringing Indigenous leaders from Andean and Amazonian tribal nations together in the sacred ground of volcanos that surround the Ecuadorian capital. Woodland Cree Elder Rosie Cecile Auger, a renowned healer, warrior, and medicine woman from Driftpile First Nation, Treaty 8 Territory in Alberta (Canada), who spoke at the 1990 meeting on the sloping terrain that flanks the Pichincha Volcano:

> "I feel very sad that people here are so oppressed. But I have great faith that with our ceremony, this gathering, that we will conquer and remove that fear, and begin to live from our own spirits and our own minds, ourselves... not being afraid of anything because the great gift we have as Aboriginal Peoples is our cultures, our traditions, our spiritual ways, all these ways have been here for thousands of years."

In this zone of contemporary contact, the gathering sought to confront settler-history as told by the so-called victors and to challenge settler-space inscribed in the maps, metes, boundaries, and lines that delineate the contours of the Spanish Empire. The 1990 Levantamiento was a challenge to the presence of settlers, and the lands they live on, after more than five centuries of contested occupation. Essentially, if the dominant conflicts and battles between nations (with their ensuing forms of resistance) are always over land, then dominant images of nations are not only manufactured as sites of invention, but they can also be reclaimed as spaces of intervention. The power that nation-states vehemently control to narrate and to represent themselves is also the power to misrepresent and to misstate.

The Indigenous uprising and assembly at the 1990 Levantamiento reflect on a battle between nations whose story is unfinished and narrative incomplete. The voices through which these stories are presented are fundamental to the communities represented. If, as the Brazilian educator Paulo Freire asserted in his 1968 *Pedagogy of the Oppressed*, "the coding of an existential situation is the representation of that situation, showing some of its constituent elements in interaction. Decoding is the critical analysis of the coded situation."

In other words, decoding is the process of delineating time and unraveling dominant narratives. Decoding is not just a process of understanding but a strategy of protest and opposition, a method and action seeking to reconnect with old narratives and reweave new ones. As a process of re-understanding and reclaiming history, decoding thus takes on a critical, analytical proposition in this book to achieve at least three aims: to deconstruct the western narrative, to dismantle the dark nature of dispossession, and to delineate a space of dialogue that opens the imagination to see the other side of the anticolonial project.

It is precisely the misunderstanding of these histories (diachronically and synchronically) and misinterpretation of the massive insurgence of Indigenous nations in 2019, that descended upon the nation's capital in the October-November uprisings. Major national news media outlets (Teleamazonas, El Telégrafo, El Comercio, El Universo, Ecuavisa), let alone the global media organization, barely reported on what would challenge the pro-nationalist narrative of state dissidents and rioters. The massive clean-up effort of protest spaces in the capital city of Quito, the collective effort and shared responsibility known as "la minga" is one of those. As Indigenous demonstrators retreated from the city and returned to their home territories after the demonstrations, a huge infrastructural project of restoration took place in streets and public spaces of the city region with the effort of over 10,000 people working together in the days following the demonstrations, involving everything from street cleaning to wall repainting, broken glass repair to garbage removal.

A Territorial Turn. It is here that not only does the process of dismantling take shape but where the rebuilding becomes more visible. It is a process that moves away from the project of reform, to turn away from the dominant and oppressive structures of settler-colonialism, and to redirect energy towards community-building. This is the main goal of this book: to create space for alternative world-building by functioning as a treatise—a pact. Through the multitude of seemingly bureaucratic and administrative permissions from authors, photographers, and institutions inherent in the reproduction of images, to the conversations behind the information, data, and facts established by this timeline in its creation, this book will always be accountable to these histories and their legacies—past, present, and future. As an agreement, the timeline is a kind of living document that warrants continuous scrutiny and revision; but it also lead up to actualization and action since history not only lies in a paper world. Toward this end, this anticolonial space is brought to light and to life through the intergenerational significance of strategies of resistance and of refusal through protests, demonstrations, blockages, and blockades.

It is precisely for this reason that the book concludes with a series of photographs taken by Mestizo farmer and architect Pablo Escudero in the Central Andean Province of Imbabura, outside of the nation's capital Quito. Taken with a handheld mobile phone, the images may seem rather quotidian even unintentional, but their immediate depiction of blockades that took place in the early days of the global COVID-19 pandemic quarantine, during the countrywide lockdown that took place across the central mountainous region of the Andes is extremely timely. More than just logs haphazardly thrown over dirt roads, paved streets, or even highways, the banality of these interventions are remarkable assertions of self-determination and territorial sovereignty. More than mere oppositions to the hostility of asphalt, the images taken on a long and uninterrupted walk, document historical expressions of spatial blockades to the dominant global order of capitalism and imposed structure of settler-colonialism that requires continuous and uninterrupted flow for its operation. Invoked practically overnight as a result of surging viral spread during the early days of COVID-19's pandemic, these minute interventions are territorial expressions of self-determination in the wake of a global capitalist world whose infrastructures and systems have infiltrated practically and almost nearly all aspects of daily lives and bodies across the Americas—north, south, and central. Nearly. Almost. The blockades may seem to be actions of remote, peripheral, even marginal actors in the countryside of metropolitan centers and urban agglomerations; but as images they represent something much, much more. As economic blockages and flow stoppages, they are the activation of political autonomies. The blockades are demonstrations of sovereignties that have existed for millennia and thus, as spatial-material actions (not merely linear boundaries), they represent the exercise of territorial sovereignties and rights to self-governance. When considered as an amalgamation of coordinated actions taken by Indigenous communities exercised upon the surface of the settler-colonial state, the scale of these blockages is of nearly unprecedented proportion in the history of the nation of Ecuador.

Unlearning & Unbuilding. To conclude with these conflicted and challenging contexts, this book can be understood as a proposal to unlearn present histories to make room for different ones. We believe it is a cultural project that we propose as an intergenerational process—a shift that recognizes movements already and well underway. In their 2012 book *Learning to Unlearn: Decolonial Reflections from Eurasia and the Americas,* Madina V. Tlostanova and Walter D. Mignolo explain this intergenerational change as a process of,

> "learning to unlearn to relearn... to forget what we have been taught, to break free from the thinking programs imposed on us by education, culture, and social environment, always marked by the Western imperial reason... this is a crucial principle in the curriculum of Amawtay Wasi, The Intercultural University of the People and Nations of Ecuador."

In its translation of research into action, the experimental and confrontational approach of this project remains contingent and precautionary. As Colombian anthropologist, Arturo Escobar writes in his 2008 *Territories of Difference,* "the challenge is to translate these insights into political strategies that incorporate multiple modes of knowing while avoiding the modern dream of organizing (the people) in logocentric, reductionist ways."

If timelines can be understood as treaties—as agreements between generations—then the role of understanding and acknowledging those spatial blockades as geopolitical blockages makes the seemingly passive act of reading and re-reading their forms into an active way of being and relating. In other words, the blockades are not only expressions of resistance, they are exercises of the sovereign. Nevertheless, the blockades are also invitations to recognize, respect, and potentially remake relations anew between more than just nations, but between generations. As both a pact and an agreement—not dogma nor doctrine—the readings of these blockades (much like the re-readings in this book) offer a way of turning away from the metropolitan mirage of the settler-colonial center towards reconnecting and relating to one another through alternative territories and temporalities.

If this book seems like a proposal or sounds like a declaration, we signal readers to look very closely at how it is organized as a codex: a way to re-read and decipher the present by re-learning an unfinished and suppressed past(s) to avoid misreading and misguiding the future. The book can thus be read as an open-ended declaration of independence from the system of settler-colonialism by facing the structures of white supremacy that uphold it, to dismantle it. And if the book reads like a reciprocal confrontation or rhetorical re-encounter with the present, then it should be engaged like the process of treaty-building: one that privileges the ancestral (that which precedes the current generation, and yet still exists), underscores the anticolonial (that which resists extraction and privileges relational being with all forms of life), and honors the territorial (through land repatriations and economic reparations to descendants of the dispossessed and exploited). As a part of the process of world-building, the timeline can work as a declarative counter-map that traces the contours around a set of different, alternative, perhaps even new relations. Like treaty-making, that process of world-building goes hand-in-hand with the process of historical reclamation. Long periods of time can be represented to eventually re-see, re-learn, re-understand, and reclaim that history itself—a search for the truth entrenched in the past—is a human responsibility to reconsider, much like a cypher, how to reshape the present. For, out of the civilizing mission that the botany of violence has emerged can also become the flora of the future.

* * *

Works Cited & Selected Readings between Dispossession & Liberation

Acosta, José de and Diego de Alcobaza. *Confessionario para los Curas de Indios con la Instrucion Contra sus Ritos: y Exhortacion para Ayudar a bien Morir...* Lima: Antonio Ricardo, 1585.

Acosta, José de. *The Natural and Moral History of the Indies, Vol.1.* Reprinted from English Edition of Edward Grimston, with an Introduction by Clements R. Markham. London: Hakluyt Society, 1880/1590.

Acosta Solis, Misael. "La Cinchona o Quina: Planta Nacional del Ecuator." *Revista De La Academia Colombiana De Ciencias Exactas, Físicas Y Naturales* Vol.17, No.65 (1989): 305–311.

______. *Cinchonas del Ecuador.* Quito: Mayo, 1946.

Adi, Hakim. "The New Scramble for Africa." *E-International Relations*, April 15, 2013.

Agee, Philip. *Inside the Company: CIA Diary*. New York: Stonehill, 1975.

American Medical Association. *Memorial to Congress: Cultivation of the Cinchona Tree in the United States.* Philadelphia: Collins, 1870.

Anderson, C. Milton (U.S. Agricultural Attaché). "Funds from Oil, Other Sources to Boost Ecuador's Agriculture." *Foreign Agriculture* Vol.12, No.38 (September 23, 1974): 8–10.

Andrade, José M., Hernán Lucero Mosquera, and Chabaco Armijos. "Ethnobotany of Indigenous Saraguros: Medicinal Plants Used by Community Healers 'Hampiyachakkuna' in the San Lucas Parish, Southern Ecuador." *BioMed Research International* (July 4, 2017).

Apiani, Petri. *Cosmographia: Per Gemmam Phrysium*. Antverpiae: Apud Ioannem VVithagium, 1524.

Aranda, Ricardo. *Colección de Las Tratados Convengiones, Capitulaciones, Armisticios Y Otros Actos Diplomaticos y Politicos Celebrados desde la Independencia Hasta el Dia Precedida de una Introduccion que Comprende la Epoca Colonial*. Lima: Imprenta Del Esatado, 1890.

Archivos de Indias de Bogotá. *Carta del Barón Alejandro de Humboldt Dirigida Desde Lima al Virrey del Nuevo Reino de Granada*, No.356 (1802); *Expediente Sobre el Comercio y Desarrollo de la Quina de Loja* No.352 (1778).

Armijos, Chabaco, Iuliana Cota, and Silvia González. "Traditional Medicine Applied by the Saraguro *yachakkuna*: a Preliminary Approach to the Use of Sacred and Psychoactive Plant Species in the Southern Region of Ecuador." *Journal of Ethnobiology and Ethnomedicine* No.10 (2014): 20.

Asher, Kiran. "Spivak and Rivera Cusicanqui on the Dilemmas of Representation in Postcolonial and Decolonial Feminisms." *Feminist Studies* Vol.43, No. 3 (2017): 512–24.

Asthana, Roli. "Involuntary Resettlement: Survey of International Experience." *Economic and Political Weekly* 31, No.24 (1996): 1468–75.

Austrich, Ricardo R. "El Real Jardin Botánico de Madrid and the Glorious History of Botany in Spain." *Arnoldia* Vol.47, No.3 (1987): 2–24.

Avery, Kevin J. *Church's Great Picture: The Heart of the Andes*. New York: The Metropolitan Museum of Art, 1993.

Bado, Sebastiano. *Anastasis Corticis Perúviae, seu Chinae Chinae Defensio, Opus in Tres Libros Distinctum & in eis Documenta Medicinae, & Philosophice.* Genua: Petri Joannis Calenzani, 1663.

Bacon, Francis. The Essays, or Councils, Civil and Moral. London: John Haviland, 1625.

Baez, Eduardo. *Cruelty and Utopia: Cities and Landscapes of Latin America*. New York: Princeton Architectural Press, 2005.

Baker, Peter and Maggie Haberman. "Trump Tests Positive for the Coronavirus." *The New York Times*, October 2, 2020.

Bales, Kevin & Trodd, Zoe. *Anti-Slavery Usable Past*. Nottingham: University of Nottingham Rights Lab, 2020.

Barbieri, Alisson F., Roberto L.M. Monte-Mor, and Richard E. Bilsborrow. "Towns in the Jungle: Exploring Linkages Between Rural-Urban Mobility, Urbanization and Development in the Amazon." In *Urban Population-Environment Dynamics in the Developing World: Case Studies and Lessons Learned,* edited by Alex de Sherbiniin et al., 247–279. Paris: CICRED, 2009.

Bárcena, Alicia. "ECLAC: At Least 2,795 Women Were Victims of Femicide in 23 Countries of Latin America and the Caribbean in 2017." Gender Equality Observatory for Latin America and the Caribbean Press Release (Economic Commission for Latin America and the Caribbean). November 15, 2018.

Batisse, Michel and Gerald Bolla. *The Invention of "World Heritage."* English translation by Robert Grauman and Raymond Johnson. Paris: History Club, Association of Former UNESCO Staff Members, 2005.

Baynard, Chris W., James M. Ellis, and Hattie Davis. "Roads, Petroleum and Accessibility: The Case of Eastern Ecuador." *GeoJournal* Vol.78, No.4 (2013): 675–95.

BBC (Latin America News Desk). "Bolivia: Ex-interim President Jeanine Áñez arrested over 'coup'." *BBC*, March 13, 2020.

Becker, Marc. "Indigenous Communists and Urban Intellectuals in Cayambe, Ecuador (1926–1944)." *International Review of Social History* 49 (2004): 41–64.

_____. *Indians and Leftists in the Making of Ecuador's Modern Indigenous Movements*. Durham: Duke University Press, 2008.

_____. *Indigenous and Afro–Ecuadorians Facing the Twenty–First Century*. Newcastle Upon Tyne: Cambridge Scholars Publishing, 2014.

_____. *The FBI in Latin America: The Ecuador Files.* Durham, North Carolina: Duke University Press, 2017.

_____. *The CIA in Ecuador*. Durham: Duke University Press, 2020.

Beckerman, Paul and Andrés Solimano, eds. *Ecuador: Crisis and Dollarization*. Washington, DC: World Bank, 2001.

Benítez Bastidas, Nhora M. and Jorge I. Albuja León. "Legado de Personajes Afros y Afrodescendientes a la Memoria Social del Ecuador y el Turismo Cultural Como Estrategia de Visibilización." *Revista Iberoamericana de Ambiente y Turismo* Vol.10, No.1 (2014): 89–127.

Bhabha, Homi K. *Nation and Narration*. London: Routledge, 1990.

Biney, Ama. "No European could be great without a colony…" In *The Berlin Conference of 1884-1885 / Africa's Great Civilizations hosted by Henry Louis Gates, Jr.*, edited by PBS and WETA, 00:29–4:08. Video, 6:57 mins. Arlington: Public Broadcasting Service (PBS), 2019.

Borchart de Moreno, Christiana Renate and Segundo E. Moreno Yáñez. *Crónica Indiana del Ecuador Antiguo.* Quito: Proyecto EBI–GTZ: Ediciones Abya–Yala, 1997.

Borisevich, D.V. et. al. *Geography of Malaria*, 1966. Moscow, 1968.

Bouchardat, Apollinaire and Auguste Delondre. *Quinologie: des Quinquinas et des Questions qui dans l'État Présent de la Science et du Commerce s'y Rattachent avec le Plus d'Actualité*. Paris: G. Baillière, 1854.

Bowman, Isaiah. "The Ecuador–Peru Boundary Dispute." *Foreign Affairs*, October 11, 2011.

Bradley, D.J. "Malaria: Old Infections, Changing Epidemiology." *Health Transition Review* Vol.2, Supplement. National Center for Epidemiology and Population Health. The Australian National University (1992): 137–153.

Breedlove, Byron, and Paul M. Arguin. "Portrait of the Coveted Cinchona." *Emerging Infectious Diseases Journal – CDC* Vol.21, No.7, (July 2015): 1280–1281.

Brewster, Claire, Catherine Davies, and Hilary Owen. "Capítulo Seis: Las Mujeres, la Guerra y la Independencia Hispanoamericana (Women, War, and Spanish American Independence)." In *South American Independence: Gender, Politics, Text*, 131–158. Liverpool: Liverpool University Press, 2006.

Brockway, Lucile H. "Science and Colonial Expansion: The Role of the British Royal Botanic Gardens." *American Ethnologist* Vol.6, No.3, August, 1979.

_____. *Science and Colonial Expansion: The Role of the British Royal Botanic Gardens.* New Haven and London: Yale University Press, 2002.

Bru de Ramón, Juan Bautista, et. al. *Colección de Laminas que Representan los Animales y Monstruos del Real Gabinete de Historia Natural de Madrid,* Tomo I. Madrid: Andres de Sotos, 1784.

Bruce-Chwatt, L. J. "Three Hundred and Fifty Years of the Peruvian Fever Bar," *British Medical Journal* Vol.296 (May 28, 1988): 1486–1487.

Bruntland Commission. *Our Common Future: Report of the World Commission on Environment and Development.* Oxford: Oxford University Press, 1987.

Bryant, Sherwin "Slavery and the Context of Ethnogenesis: African, Afro-Creoles, and the Realities of Bondage in the Kingdom of Quito, 1600-1800." PhD Diss., Ohio State University, 2005.

Bruce-Chwatt. "Three Hundred and Fifty Years of the Peruvian Fever Bark." *British Medical Journal* Vol.296 (May 28, 1988).

Bureau tot Bevordering van het Kinine-Gebruik. *Chininum: Scriptiones Collectae*. Amsterdam: Bureau Tot Bevordering Van Het Kinine-Gebruik, 1923, 1924–25.

_____. *Malaria en Kinine*. Amsterdam: Bureau Tot Bevordering Van Het Kinine-Gebruik, 1926.

_____. *Kinine-Formularium.* Amsterdam: Bureau Tot Bevordering Van Het Kinine-Gebruik, 1935.

Cabrera, José María León and Clifford Krauss. "Deal Struck in Ecuador to Cancel Austerity Package and End Protests." *The New York Times*, October 13, 2019.

Cacuango, Dolores. *La Federación Indígena del Ecuador*. Cayambe: FEI (Hoja Volante, Leonardo J. Muñoz), 1944.

Calancha, Antonio de la. *Coronica Moralizada de la Orden de San Agustín en el Perú*. Barcelona: Pedro Lacavalleria, 1638.

Calik, Muhammed Ali. "Bolivia proved developing without IMF possible: Morales." *Anadolu Agency*, August 2, 2020.

Capa, Cornell. "'Go Ye and Preach the Gospel' Five Do and Die." *LIFE Magazine* Vol.40, No.5 (January 30, 1956): 10–19.

Casas, Bartolomé de las and Theodor de Bry. *Narratio Regionum Indicarum per Hispanos Quosdam Devastatarum Verissima.* Frankfurt: Sumptibus Theodori de Bry & Ioannis Saurii typis, 1598.

_____. *Narratio Regionum Indicarum per Hispanos Quosdam Devastatarum Verissima.* Oppenheim: Hieronymi Galleri, 1614.

Castillo, Elvia Duque. *Aportes Del Pueblo Afrodescendiente: La Historia Oculta De América Latina*. iUniverse, 2013.

Cavender, Anthony P., and Manuel Albán. "The Use of Magical Plants by Curanderos in the Ecuador Highlands." *Journal of Ethnobiology and Ethnomedicine* Vol.5, No.3 (2009): 1-9.

Castillo, Evlia Duque. *Aportes Del Pueblo Afrodescendiente: La Historia Oculta De América Latina*. Bloomington: iUniverse, 2013.

CDC Bulletin. "Central Amazon Conservation Complex." UNESCO World Heritage Centre, 1944.

Cepek, Michael. "A Trip Through Ecuador's Cofán Community and Its Disappearing Homeland." *Pacific Standard,* March 8, 2017.

Center for Economic and Social Rights. "Rights Violations in the Ecuadorian Amazon: The Human Consequences of Oil Development." *Health and Human Rights* Vol.1, No.1 (1994): 82–100.

Césaire, Aimé. *Discours sur le Colonialisme* Paris: Présence Africaine, 1950.

Château de Versailles, "Science and Curiosities at the Court of Versailles." Versailles: Établissement Public du Musée et du Domaine National de Versailles, 2011.

Charles V (Holy Roman Emperor). "Leyes y Ordenanzas Nuevamente Hechas por su Majestad para la Gobernación de las Indias y Buen Tratamiento y Conservación de los Indios." Madrid: Francisco Sanchez, 1542.

Chauca, Roberto. "Missionary Hydrography and the Invention of Early Modern Amazonia." *Colonial Latin American Review* Vol.27, No.2 (2018): 203–225.

Chaumeton, François Pierre. *Flore médicale*. Paris: C.L.F. Panckoucke, 1833.

Chevron Corporation. "The Facts: Chevron in Ecuador & Plaintiffs' Strategy of Fraud." *The Amazon Post*, April 15, 2021.

Chevron Corporation and Texaco Petroleum Company vs. the Republican of Ecuador. "A Rejoinder to Criticisms of the Expert Opinion of Kenneth J. Goldstein, and Jeffry W. Short. Regarding the Environmental Contamination from Texpet's E&P Activities in the Former Napo Concession Area, Oriente Region, Ecuador." PCA Case No.2009–23. December, 2013.

ChevronToxico. "The True Story of Chevron's Ecuador Disaster." 2000.

Chifflet, Jean-Jacques. *Pulvis Febrifugus Orbis Americani.*

Lovanii: 1653.
Chiriboga, Luz A. *Bajo la Piel de los Tambores: Novela/ Drums Under my Skin*. Quito: Editorial Casa de la Cultura Ecuatoriana, 1991.
Chiriboga, Oswaldo R. "Indigenous Corporal Punishment in Ecuador and the Prohibition of Torture and Ill Treatment." *American University International Law Review* Vol.28, No.4 (2013): 975–1016.
Cielo C, Sarzosa NC. "Transformed Territories of Gendered Care Work in Ecuador's Petroleum Circuit." *Conservation & Society* Vol.16, No.1 (2018): 8–20.
"Cinchona Plantation in Java." Budget Films, c.1950.
Clark, A. Kim, and Marc Becker. *Highland Indians and the State in Modern Ecuador.* Pittsburgh: University of Pittsburgh Press, 2007.
Clements, Robert Markham. *Travels in Peru and India While Superintending the Collection of Chinchona Plants and Seeds in South America, and Their Introduction into India*. London: John Murray, 1892.
Cobo, Bernabé. *Historia general de las Indias.* Written in 1653.
_____. With notes and illustrations by D. Marcos Jiménez de la Espada. *Historia del Nuevo Mundo.* Seville: E. Rasco, Bustos Tavera, 1890.
_____. *Biblioteca de Autores Espanoles: Desde la Formacion del Lenguaje Hasta Nuestros Dias.* Madrid: Derechos Reservados, 1964.
Comité Ejecutivo de la Federación Indígena. "Manifiesto que el Comité Ejecutivo de la Federación Indígena dirige al Pueblo Ecuatoriano." Cayambe: FEI (Galo Ramón), 1945.
Commisión de Transición hacia el Consejo de las Mujeres y la Igualdad de Género. *Re/construyendo historias de mujeres ecuatorianas*. Quito: Trama Ediciones, 2010.
Confederación de Nacionalidades Indígenas del Ecuador (CONAIE). "Levantamiento Indígena del Inti Raymi, 1990." Video Partes 1–5. Quito: CONAIE, 1990.
Congreso Nacional del Ecuador. "Ley 108: Registro Oficial No. 523." El Plenario De Las Comisiones Legislativas, 17 de Septiembre. Quito: Congreso Nacional del Ecuador, 1990.
Connolly, Elizabeth. "A Dynamic Equilibrium: Doctors and Patients in Seventeenth Century England." PhD Diss., University of Adelaide, February, 2017.
Connelly, Frances S. *The Sleep of Reason: Primitivism in Modern European Art and Aesthetics, 1725–1907.* University Park, PN: Penn State Press, 1999.
Connett, Christina Findlay. "Cartography as a Strategy of Empire in 'Historia General de los Hechos de los Castellanos en las Islas i Tierra Firme del Mar Oceano by Antonio de Herrera y Tordesillas.'" PhD Diss., Universitat de València, 2014.
Contini, Elisio. "A Colonização na Transamazônica: um Enfoque Analitico do Plano Governamental, seus Resultados e Problemas." Master's Thesis, Escola Brasileirade Administração Públic, 1976.
Conway, John A. (Col). "Lago Agrio (Nueva Loja), Ecuador: A Strategic Black Spot?" Strategic Research Report & Thesis, Master of Strategic Studies Degree. US Army War College, 2013.
Cowan, J. M. "Cinchona in the Empire: Progress and Prospects of its Cultivation." *Empire Forestry Journal* Vol.8, No.1 (July, 1929): 45–53.
Crawford, Matthew James. "An Empire's Extract: Chemical Manipulations of Cinchona Bark in the Eighteenth–Century Spanish Atlantic World." *Osiris* Vol.29, No.1 (2014): 215–29.
_____. *The Andean Wonder Drug: Cinchona Bark and Imperial Science in the Spanish Atlantic 1630–1800.* Pittsburgh: University of Pittsburg Press, 2016.
Cretineau-Joli. *Historia, Religiosa, Política y Literaria de la Compañía de Jesús,* Tomo I. Barcelona: Libreria Religiosa, Imprenta de Pablo Riera, 1853.
Crowder, Nicole. "Guardians of Life: The Indigenous Women Fighting Oil Exploitation in the Amazon." *Washington Post*, November 3, 2014.
Cunha, Cheston B, and Burke A Cunha. "Brief History of the Clinical Diagnosis of Malaria: from Hippocrates to Osler." *Journal of Vector Borne Diseases* Vol.45, No.3 (2008): 194-199.
Cusicanqui, Silvia Rivera. *Un Mundo Ch'ixi es Posible: Ensayos Desde un Presente en Crisis*. Buenos Aires: Tinta Limón, 2018.
_____. "Amo la Montaña/I Love the Mountain." *Afterall: A*

Journal of Art, Context and Enquiry Vol. 44 (2017): 144-149.

_____. *Sociología de la Imagen: Miradas Ch'ixi Desde la Historia Andina*. Buenos Aires: Tinta Limón, 2015.

_____. "Sociología de la Imagen: Miradas Ch'ixi Desde la Historia Andina." Lecture, Auditório Virginia Gutiérrez , Posgrados Ciencias Humanas, Universidad Nacional de Colombia (August 22, 2009).

Cuvi, Nicolás. "The Cinchona Program (1940–1945): Science and Imperialism in the Exploitation of a Medicinal Plant." *Dynamis* Vol.31, No.1 (2011): 183-206.

Cuvi, Nicolás. *Ciencia e Imperialism en América Latina: la Misión de Cinchona y las Estaciones Agrícolas Cooperativas (1940–1945).* PhD Diss., Universitat Autònoma de Barcelona, 2009.

Dauchy, Serge et al., eds. *The Formation and Transmission of Western Legal Culture*, Studies in the History of Law and Justice Vol.7. Switzerland: Springer, 2016.

Dávila, Pedro Francisco and Jean Baptiste Louis de Romé de L'Isle. *Catalogue Systématique et Raisonné des Curiosités de la Nature et de l'Art qui Composent le Cabinet de M. Davila,* Tome I-II. Paris: Briasson, 1767.

Davis, Gabriella, "Ecuador is Black: Afro-Ecuadorian Literary Resistance in Drums Under My Skin." *Student Scholars Day Oral Presentations*, Grand Valley State University, 2020.

Davis, Erik M. "The United States and the Congo, 1960-1965: Containment, Minerals and Strategic Location." Master's Thesis, University of Kentucky, 2013.

Deaderick, William H. and Lloyd Thompson. *Endemic Diseases of the Southern States.* Philadelphia: W. B. Saunders Company, 1916.

Deb Roy, Rohan. "Quinine, Mosquitoes and Empire: Reassembling Malaria in British India, 1890-1910." *South Asian History and Culture* Vol.4, No.1 (2013): 65-86.

_____. *Malarial Subjects: Empire, Medicine and Nonhumans in British India, 1820–1909*. Cambridge: Cambridge University Press, 2017.

_____. "The Untold Story of Modern Science is one of Empire and Colonial Exploitation." *Quartz India*. April 9, 2018.

Debret, J.B. *Voyage Pittoresque et Historique au Brésil*, Tome I. Paris: Firmin Didot Fréres, 1834.

Delbourgo, James, and Nicholas Dew. *Science and Empire in the Atlantic World.* London: Routledge, 2008.

Dematteis, Lou, and Kayana Szymczak. *Crude Reflections: Oil, Ruin and Resistance in the Amazon Rainforest*. San Francisco: City Lights Books, 2008.

Denisova, Natalia K. "Filosofía de la Historia de América: Los Cronistas de Indias en el Pensamiento Español." PhD Diss., Fundación Universitaria Española, 2017.

Dickason, Olive P. *The Myth of the Savage: and the Beginnings of French Colonialism in the Americas.* Edmonton: The University of Alberta Press, 1997/1984.

Diestelkamp, Edward, Brent Elliott, and Melissa Thompson. "A World Under Glass: the Architectural, Horticultural and Social History of Glasshouses." *Occasional Papers from the RHS Lindley Library* Vol.17. London: The Royal Horticultural Society, 2019.

Divale, William, and Marvin Harris. "Population, Warfare, and the Male Supremacist Complex." *American Anthropologist* Vol.78, No.3 (1976): 521–538.

Drayton, Richard. *Nature's Government: Science, Imperial Britain, and the "Improvement" of the World.* New Haven: Yale University Press, 2000.

Drekonja, Gerhard. "Ecuador: How to Handle the Banana Republic Turned Oil State." *Boletín de Estudios Latinoamericanos y Del Caribe* No.28 (1980): 77–94.

Durán Calisto, Ana María. "For the Persistence of the Indigenous Commune in Amazonia." *E-Flux Architecture*. February 5, 2019.

Dutfield, Graham. "TRIPS–Related Aspects of Traditional Knowledge." *Case Western Reserve Journal of International Law* Vol.33, No.2 (2001): 233–275.

Enciso, Martín Fernández de. *Suma de Geografia que Trata de Todas las Partidas e Provincias del Mundo.* Seville, 1519.

Ecuador – Indigenous and Afro–Ecuadorian Peoples Development Project (English). World Development Sources, WDS 1998–1. Washington DC: World Bank Group.

Edwards, Sandra G. "A Short History of Ecuador's Drug Legislation and the Impact on its Prison Population." In *Transnational Institute: Systems Overload – Drug Laws and Prisons in Latin America*, edited by Pien Metaal and Coletta Youngers, 50–59. Washington DC: Washington Office of Latin America, 2011.

Elliot, Elizabeth (Auca Missionary Foundation). *Through the Gates of Splendor.* Gospel Communications International Series. Video, 36 mins. Worcester: Vision Video, 1961.

El Tiempo. "Desde los Márgenes, Mujeres en Pie de Lucha." *El Tiempo*, March 8, 2018.

_____. "Mujer Afro, la Historia por Contar." *El Tiempo,* July 21, 2018.

El Universo (Redacción). "La CONAIE, 33 Años de Historia de un Movimiento Clave en Ecuador." *El Universo,* October 12, 2019.

_____. "Mujeres del 15 de noviembre de 1922." *El Universo*, November 15, 2013.

Emck, Paul. *A Climatology of South Ecuador: With Special Focus on the Major Andean Ridge as Atlantic-Pacific Climate Divide.* PhD Diss., Naturwissenschaftlichen Fakultäten der Universität Erlangen-Nürnberg, 2007.

Endara Tomaselli, Lourdes. *El Marciano de la Esquina: Imagen del Indio en la Prensa Ecuatoriana Durante el Levantamiento de 1990.* Colección Antropología Aplicada No.14. Quito: Universidad Politécnica Salesiana, Centro Cultural Abya Yala del Ecuador, 1998.

Encyclopedia Brittannica, 3rd Edition, Vol.9. Edinburgh: A. Bell and C. Macfarqunar, 1797.

Escudero, Lola. "Viajes, Ciencia e Ilustración. Las Expediciones Científicas Españolas en el Siglo XVIII." *Boletín 22 – Sociedad Geográfica Española*, March 18, 2020.

Espinosa, Carlos. "Colonial Visions Drama, Art, and Legitimation in Peru and Ecuador." In *Native Artists and Patrons in Colonial Latin America*, edited by Emily Umberger and Tom Cummins, 84–106. Tempe: Arizona State University, 1995.

Espinosa, Emilio Lamo de and Enriquez de Navarra. "Proceso Formativo de la Lay de Reforma y Desarrolo Agrario." Inaugural Conference of les *Jornadas Nacionales de Derecho Agrario*, 1974.

"Etymologia: Quinine." Emerging Infectious Diseases. National Center for Biotechnology Information.

Eyal, Sara. "The Fever Tree: From Malaria to Neurological Diseases." *Toxins* Vol.10, No.12 (November 23, 2018): 491.

Ezpeleta, José de. *Copia de Real Orden Adicionando Instrucciones para el Acopio de Quina en Loja y otras Provincias de Quito*. Bogotá: Biblioteca Nacional de Colombia, 1796.

Fajardo, S.J. Jose del Rey. "Marco Conceptual Para Comprender el Estudio de la Arquitectura de las Misiones Jesuíticas en la América Colonial." *Apuntes* Vol.20, No.1 (2007): 8–33.

Falchetti, Sirlei Ana. "Transformações Socioculturais e Espaciaisno Norte do Estado de Mato Grosso – Umprocesso de Colonialidade." *Tempo da Ciência* Vol.18, No.36 (2011): 49–71.

"Farewell to a Feminism Icon: Ketty Romo-Leroux." *El Universo.* June 2, 2019.

Federated Malay States Survey Department. "Malaya, showing Distribution of Agricultural Staff, Plantations, Reserves." *The Malayan Agricultural Journal* Vol.15, No.5 (May 1927): 210.

Ferguson, A.M. & J. "Cinchona Cultivation in Ceylon." *The Tropical Agriculturist* (March 1, 1882): 745.

Fernández–Muro, Mateo, et. al. "Shifting Urban Ecologies of San Roque Quito Ecuador." Master's Thesis, Parsons School of Design, 2016.

Flückiger, Friedrich A., and Frederick Power. *The Cinchona Barks: Pharmacognostically Considered.* Philadephia: P. Blakiston, Son & Co., 1884.

Food and Agriculture Organization of the United Nations. *International Treaty on Plant Genetic Resources for Food and Agriculture*. Geneva: FAO, 2001.

Fosberg, Francis Raymond. *Columbian Cinchona Manual.* Bogotá: Foreign Economic Administration, 1944.

_____. "Cinchona Plantation in the New World." *Economic Botany* Vol.1, No.3 (1947): 330–333.

Fraser, N. "Recognition or Redistribution? A Critical Reading of Iris Young's 'Justice and the Politics of Difference.'" *Journal of Political Philosophy* Vol.3 (1995): 166–180.

Franciscus. "'Querida Amazonia': Post–Synodal Exhortation to the People of God and to All Persons of Good Will." *The Vatican*, February 2, 2020.

Frenkel, Stephen, and John Western. "Pretext or Prophylaxis? Racial Segregation and Malarial Mosquitos in a British Tropical Colony: Sierra Leone." *Annals of the Association of American Geographers* Vol.78, No.2 (1988): 211-228.

Gallagher, Fergal. "Tracking Hydroxychloroquine Misinformation: How an Unproven COVID-19 Treatment Ended Up Being Endorsed by Trump." *ABC News*, April 22, 2020.

Gallup, John L. and Jeffrey D. Sachs. "The Economic Burden of Malaria." Supplement to *American Society of Tropical Medicine and Hygiene* Vol.64, No.1 (January 2001): 85-96.

Garavito, Natalia Tejedor, et. al. "A Regional Red List of Montane Tree Species of the Tropical Andes: Trees at the Top of the World." Richmond: Botanic Gardens Conservation International, 2014.

García Salazar, Juan. *Cimarronaje en el Pacifico Sur: historia y tradición. El caso de Esmeraldas, Ecuador.* Master's Thesis, Johns Hopkins University, 1989.

García, Salazar Juan. *La Poesía Negrista En El Ecuador / Black Poetry in Ecuador*. Esmeraldas: Banco Central del Ecuador, 1982.

The Gardens Trust. "John Claudius Loudon... and Greenhouse Technology." *The Gardens Trust*, May 27, 2014.

Gherardy, Juan G. "Ecuador: A Low-Threat Environment For Drug Trafficking." Master's Thesis, Naval Postgraduate School, March 2016.

Goetschel, Ana María. *Educación de las Mujeres, Maestras y Esferas Públicas. Quito en la Primera Mitad del Siglo XX.* Quito: FLACSO, Ediciones Abya Yala, 2007.

_____. *Re/Construyendo Historias de Mujeres Ecuatorianas.* Quito: Trama Ediciones, 2010.

Gomes, Flávio Alcaraz. *Transamazonica a Redescoberta do Brasil*. São Paulo: Livraria Cultura Editora, 1972.

Gondard, Pierre and Hubert Mazurek. "30 Años de Reforma Agraria y Colonización en el Ecuador (1964–1994): Dinámicas Espaciales" in *Dinámicas Territoriales: Ecuador, Bolivia, Perú, Venezuela, Estudios de Geografía* Vol.10 (2001): 15–40, 147.

Goodland, Robert J. A. "Environmental Ranking of Amazonian Development Projects in Brazil." World Bank Reprint Series, Number 198, March, 1980. *Environmental Conservation* Vol.7, No.1 (Spring 1980): 9–26.

Gorkom, K. W. van. *Kina.* Haarlem: De Erven Loosjes, 1896.

_____. *Over Malaria en Muskieten*. Malang: A.J. Jahn, 1901.

Goss, Andrew. *The Floracrats: State-Sponsored Science and the Failure of the Enlightenment in Indonesia.* Madison: University of Wisconsin Press, 2011.

Gosse, Philip Henry. *Wanderings Through the Conservatories at Kew.* London: Society for Promoting Christian Knowledge, 1856.

Government of West Bengal. "Directorate of Cinchona and other Medicinal Plant." Kolkata: Department of Food Processing Industries & Horticulture, 2021.

Gracia de Tolva, Juan Francisco de. "Traslado de una carta de Juan Francisco de Gracia de Tolva." Madrid: Catalina del Barrio y Angulo, 1624.

Gramiccia, Gabriele. *The Life of Charles Ledger (1818-1905): Alpacas and Quinine.* London: Palgrave, 1988.

Guaman Poma de Ayala, Felipe. *Nueva Crónica y Buen Gobierno.* c.1615.

Gubernatis, Angelo de. *La Mythologie des Plantes ou les Légendes du Régne Végétal, Tome* II. Paris: C. Reinwald, 1882.

Haggis, A. W. "Fundamental Errors in the Early History of Cinchona: Part I-II," *Bulletin of the History of Medicine* Vol.10, No.3 (October 1941): 417–469.

Haisell, Simon. "Indigenous Modernity and its Malcontents: Family, Religion and Tradition in Highland Ecuador." PhD Diss., University of Essex, March 2017.

Hamerly, Michael T. and Miguel Díaz Cueva. "Bibliography of Ecuadorian Bibliographies." *Ecuadorian Studies / Estudios Ecuatorianos* No.2 (December 2002).

Hamilton, Dom Adam. *The Chronicle of the English Augustinian Canonesses Regular of the Lateran, at St. Monica's in Louvain (Now at St. Augustine's Priory, Newton Abbot, Devon) A Continuation, 1625 to 1644.* London: Sands & Co., 1906.

Handelman, Howard. "Ecuadorian Agrarian Reform: The Politics of Limited Change." *South America* No.49 (1980): 1–19.

Hanratty, Dennis M., ed. *Ecuador: A Country Study.* Washington DC: Federal Research Div., Library of Congress, 1991.

Harner, Michael J. ed., *Music of the Jívaro of Ecuador.* Ethnic Folkways Library Record, Album No. FE4386. New York: Folkways Records and Service Co., 1973.

Harrison, Jill and Maureen Norton-Hawk. "The Care, Custody, and Control of Incarcerated Women in Ecuador." *Societies Without Borders* Vol.5, No.1 (2010): 21-48.

Harvey, Eleanor Jones. "Church's Cosmos." *Capturing the Cosmos: Frederic Church Painting Humboldt's Vision of Nature.* Exhibition. New York: Olana State Historic Site, 2016.

Hegen, Edmund Eduard. "Highways into the Upper Amazon Basin: A Study of Trans–Andean Roads in Southern Colombia, Ecuador, and Northern Peru." PhD Diss., University of Florida, June, 1962.

Henao, Luis Andres And Marcelo De Souza "Brazil's Bolsonaro Causes Global Outrage over Amazon Fires," *Toronto Star*, August 26, 2019.

Herrera y Tordesillas, Antonio de. *Descripción de las Indias Occidentales.* Madrid: Rodriquez Franco, 1730 (originally published in 1601).

Hettler, Jörg, et. al. *Environmental Problems of Petroleum Production in the Amazon Lowland of Ecuador*. Berliner Geowissenschaftliche Abhandlungen, Reihe A: Geologie und Paläontologi. FU Berlin: Selbstverlag Fachbereich Geowissenschaften, 1996.

High, Casey. "Remembering the Auca: Violence and Generational Memory in Amazonian Ecuador." *The Journal of the Royal Anthropological Institute* Vol.15, No.4 (2009): 719–36.

Hippocrates, W. H. S. Jones, E. T. Withington, Paul Potter, Wesley D. Smith, and Heraclitus. *Hippocrates: De Morbis Popularibus (Of Epidemics).* Cambridge: Harvard University Press, 1923.

Hirschkind, Lynn. "The Enigmatic Evanescence of Coca from Ecuador." *Ethnobotany Research and Applications* Vol.3 (2005): 97–106.

Hitt, Russell T. *Jungle Pilot: The Life and Witness of Nate Saint.* London: Hodder and Stoughton, 1960.

Hodge, W. H. "Wartime Cinchona Procurement in Latin America." *Economic Botany* Vol.2, No.3 (Jul/Sep 1948): 229–257.

Holland, Clifton L. "Encyclopedia of Religious Groups in Latin America and the Caribbean: Religion in Ecuador." Latin American Socio-Religious Studies Program, PROLADES, May 19, 2010.

Holland, J. H. "Ledger Bark and Red Bark." *Bulletin of Miscellaneous Information* (Royal Botanic Gardens, Kew) No.1 (1932): 1-17.

Holloway, Thomas H. "Review: Developing the Amazon by Emilio F. Moran." *The American Historical Review* Vol.87, No.5 (1982): 1507–1507.

Homassel-Hecquet, Marie-Catherine. *Histoire d'une jeune fille sauvage, trouvée dans les bois à l'âge de dix ans.* Paris: no publisher, 1755.

Honigsbaum, Mark. *The Fever Trail: In Search of the Cure for Malaria.* New York: Farrar, Straus and Giroux, 2001.

Howard, John Eliot. *Examination of Pavon's Collection of Peruvian Barks Contained in the British Museum.* London: C. Whiting, 1853.

_____. *Illustrations of the Nueva Quinologia of Pavon.* London: Lovell Reeve & Co., 1862.

_____. *Quinology of the East Indian Plantations.* London: Lovell Reeve & Co., 1869.

Howes, Rebecca Gail, "Antonio Preciado and the Afro Presence in Ecuadorian Literature." PhD Diss., University of Tennessee, 2013.

Humboldt, Alexander von. "Über die Chinawälder in Südamerika." *Der Gesellschaft Naturforschender Freunde zu Berlin Magazin für die neuesten Entdeckungen in der gesammten Naturkunde* (Januar-März 1807): 57-68.

_____. Political Essay on the Kingdom of New Spain. London: Longman, Hurst, Rees, Orme, and Brown, 1811.

Humboldt, Alexander von and Bonpland Aimé. *Essay on the Geography of Plants (1807),* edited by Stephen T. Jackson. Chicago: University of Chicago Press, 2009.

_____. *The Institutions & Monuments of the Ancient Habitants of America.* London: Longman, Hurst, Rees, Orme & Brown J. Murray & H. Colburn, 1814.

Humboldt, Alexander von. *Kosmos – Entwurf einer physischen Weltbeschreibung.* Stuttgart: J. O. Cotta'fcher Berlag, 1845.

_____. *Aspects of Nature in Different Lands and Different*

Climates with Scientific Elucidations. Philadelphia: Lea and Blanchard, 1849.

_____. *Personal Narrative of Travels to the Equinoctial Regions of America during the years 1799–1804*. London: Henry G. Bohn, 1853.

_____. *Cosmos: A Sketch of a Physical Description of the Universe*, Vols I-II. London: Henry G. Bohn, 1864.

Humboldt, Alexander von, Elise C. Otté, and Henry G. Bohn. *Views of Nature: Or, Contemplations On the Sublime Phenomena of Creation; With Scientific Illustrations*. London: H. G. Bohn, 1850.

Hummerstone, Robert G. "Cutting a Road Through Brazil's 'Green Hell'." *The New York Times*, March 5, 1972.

Hyde, Jessica. "The Lawless Frontier at the Heart of the Burning Amazon," *Pulitzer Center*, September 17, 2019.

Hyer, Travis. "Considering Ecuador's New Water Law Through the Lens of Indigenous Rights Under International Law." *Willamette Environmental Law Journal* Vol. 63 (2015): 63–95.

"Informes Nacionales sobre la Aplicación del Tratado Internacional sobre los Recursos Fitogenéticos para la Alimentación y la Agricultura (TIRFAA), Ecuador." May 11, 2016.

Instituto de Género, Derecho y Desarrollo. *Derechos de las mujeres de Pueblos Originarios Guía para cursos de capacitación*. Rosario: INSGENAR, 2011.

Irfan, Umair. "Why It's Been So Lucrative to Destroy the Amazon Rainforest." *Vox*, August 30, 2019.

Jacobs, Frank. "Amazonia or Bust!" *The New York Times*, June 19, 2012.

Jahn Verri, Fernanda. *O Planejamento Urbano Integradoe a Atuação do Serfhau no Riogrande do Sul (1964–1975)*. Master's Thesis, Universidade Federal do Rio Grande do Sul, 2014.

Jäger, Heinke. "Biology and Impacts of Pacific Island Invasive Species. 11. Cinchona pubescens (Red Quinine Tree) (Rubiaceae)," *Pacific Science* Vol.69, No.2 (1 April 2015): 133–153.

Jaramillo Arango, Jaime. "Estudio Crítico Acerca de los Hechos Básicos en la Historia de la Quina." *Revisa de la Facultad Ciencias Medicas* Vol.1, No.2 (April 1950): 61–128.

_____. "A Critical Review of the Basic Facts in the History of Cinchona." *The Journal of the Linnean Society* Vol.53, No.352 (1949): 272-311.

Jarcho, Saul. "The Hunt for a Manuscript on Cinchona." *Perspectives in Biology and Medicine* Vol.31, No.3 (1988): 437-439.

The Journal of the Linnean Society, Botany Vol.14. London: Taylor and Francis, 1875.

Juan, Jorge. *Observaciones Astronomicas y Fhisicas Hechas de Orden de S. M. en los Reynos del Perú*. Madrid: En la Imprenta Real de la Gazeta, 1748.

Jussieu, Joseph de. *Description de l'Arbre à Quinquina*. Paris: La Société du Traitement des Quinquinas, 1737.

Kalisyaa, Luc Malemo, Margaret Salmon et al. "The State of Emergency Care in Democratic Republic of Congo." *African Journal of Emergency Medicine* Vol.5, No.4 (December 2015): 153-158.

Kane, Joe. *"With Spears from All Sides" The New Yorker*, September 27, 1993.

Kaufman T. and E. Ruveda. "The Quest for Quinine, Those Who Won the Battles and Those Who Won the War." *Natural Products Synthesis*, (Angewandte Chemie, 2005): 854–885.

Keefe, Patrick Radden. "Reversal of Fortune." *The New Yorker*, January 2, 2012.

Kennon, Isabel, and Grace Valdevitt. "Women Protest for Their Lives: Fighting Femicide in Latin America." *New Atlanticist*, February 24, 2020.

Kenny-Troya, Alexandra. *Elites y la Nación en Obras: Visualidades y Arquitectura del Ecuador, 1840–1930*. Universidad de Cuena, C.C.E. Núcleo Del Azuay, 2015.

Kerbosch, Mathieu. "Some Notes on Cinchona Culture and the World Consumption of Quinine" *Bulletin of the Colonial Institute of Amsterdam* (December 1, 1939): 36–51.

_____. *Het Kina-Monopolie van Nederlandsch-Indië (Nota voor het Ministerie van Overzeese gebiedsdelen, 1945)*, No.106, Kerbosch Collection, KITLV, Leiden.

Kimerling, Judith. "Oil, Contact, and Conservation in the Amazon: Indigenous Huaorani, Chevron, and Yasuni." *Colorado Journal of International Environmental Law and Policy* Vol.24, No.1 (2013): 44–115.

King, George. *A Manual of Cinchona Cultivation in India.* Calcutta: Office of the Superintendent of Government Printing, 1870.

King, George, and Royal College of Physicians (London). *A Manual of Cinchona Cultivation in India.* Calcutta: Office of the Superintendent of Government Printing, 1876.

King, A.F.A. "Insects and Disease, Mosquitoes and Malaria." *Popular Science Monthly* Vol.23 (September, 1883): 644–658.

Klohn, Axel M. and Philippe Chastonay. "Guaman Poma de Ayala's 'New Chronicle and Good Government.' A Testimony on the Health of the Indigenous Populations in XVIth Century Peru." *Hygiea Internationalis: An Interdisciplinary Journal for The History of Public Health* Vol.11, No.1 (2015): 147–161.

Koenig, Kevin. "The Chevron Tapes: Secret Videos Reveal Company Hid Pollution in Ecuador." *Amazon Watch*, April 8, 2015.

Konkel, Frank. "The Details about the CIA's Deal with Amazon." *The Atlantic*, July 17, 2014.

Korol, Claudia. "Adriana Guzman, Aymara y Feminista Comunitaria: El Golpe de Estado en Bolivia es Racista, Patriarcal, Eclesiástico y Empresarial." *Pagina 12*, November 15, 2019.

Kristenson, Olle. "Pastor in the Shadow of Violence: Gustavo Gutiérrez as a Public Pastoral Theologian in Peru in the 1980s and 1990s." PhD Diss., Uppsala Universitet, 2009.

Kumar, Prakash. "Planters and Naturalists: Transnational Knowledge on Colonial Indigo Plantations in South Asia." *Modern Asian Studies* Vol.48, No.3 (2014): 720–53.

Kurtenbach, Ralph. "News of Missionary's Death Underplayed Amid Vigilance in Ecuadorian Village." *Reach Beyond*, July 24, 2015.

La Condamine, Charles Marie de. *Journal du Voyage fait par Ordre du Roi, À l'Équateur servant d'Introduction Historique à la Mesure des Trois Premiers Degrés du Méridien.* Paris: De l'Imprimerie Royale, 1735.

_____. *Sur L'Arbre du Quinquina.* Amsterdam: Histoire de l'Académie Royale des Sciences, 1738.

_____. *Relation Abrégée d'un Voyage fait dans l'Intérieur de l'Amérique Méridionale*. Paris: La Veuve Pissot, 1745.

_____. *Mesure des Trois Premiers Degrés du Méridien dans l'Hémisphère Austral.* Paris, 1751.

La Fontaine, de Jean. *Les Amours de Psyche, Oeuvres Complètes,* Paris: P. Dupont, 1826.

Laignel-Lavastine, M. & Louis Girault. "Contribution à l'Étude du Rôle du Service de Santé Militaire: Conquête de l'Algérie 1830-1847." *Bulletin de la Société Française* Tome 33 (Paris: Le Secrétaire Général, 1939): 196-202.

Lambert, Aylmer Bourke. An Illustration of the Genus Cinchona; comprising *Descriptions of all the Official Peruvian Barks.* London: John Searle, 1821.

Laplace, Pierre-Simon. *Exposition du Système du Monde.* Paris: Courcier, 1808/1795.

Lara, Guillermo Rodriguez (General). *Reglamento de la Leydeaguas: Decreto Supremo No.40 / Registro Oficial No.233*. Quito: Instituto Ecuatoriano de Recursos Hidraulicos, 1973.

Laubert, Charles Jean. *Recherches Botaniques, Chimiques, Pharmaceutiques sur le Quinquina*. Paris: Panckoucke, 1816.

Laurence, William L. "Second Answer to Japan: Commercial Output of Ersatz Anti–Malaria Medicine is Not Yet Certain." *New York Times*, May 4, 1944.

Lawrence, Christopher. "Fever in the Tropics." *Livingstone Online*. Adrian S. Wisnicki and Megan Ward, dirs. University of Maryland Libraries, 2015.

Legg, Charlotte Ann. "The Medical Press and the Settler Colonial Politics of Persuasion in French Algeria, 1850–1914." *History* Vol.104, No.359 (2019): 105-124.

León Pinelo, Antonio de and Juan de Solórzano Pereira. *The Recopilación de Leyes de los Reynos de las Indias.* Madrid: Julian de Paredes, 1624.

Lejeune, Jean-François. "Dreams of Order: Utopia, Cruelty, Modernity." In *Cruelty and Utopia: Cities and Landscapes of Latin America*, edited by Eduardo Baez, 30–49. New York: Princeton Architectural Press, 2003.

Lévi–Strauss, Claude. *Totemism.* Translated by Rodney Needham. London: Merlin Press, 1991 (originally published by Presses Universitaires de France, 1964).

Linnaeus, Carl. *Species Plantarum*. Holmiæ, Impensis Laurentii Salvii, 1753.

Lind, Amy. *Gendered Paradoxes: Women's Movements, State Restructuring, and Global Development in Ecuador*. University Park: Penn State Press, 2010.

Lindestolpe, Johan. *Tanckar om Frossan, Och Kin-kina Barken.* Stockholm: J.G. Matthiae for J.L.S Horn, 1717.

Lindquist, Arthur W. and W.C. McDuffie. "DDT-Oil Sprays Applied from an Airplane to Control Anopheles and Mansonia Mosquitoes." *Journal of Economic Entomology* Vol.38, No.5 (October 1945): 545–548.

Little, Ruby R. *Histology of Barks of Cinchona and Some Related Genera Occurring in Colombia*. Washington DC: Foreign Economic Administration, Cinchona Section, 1945.

Livy-Bacci, Massimo. "The Depopulation of Upper Amazonia in Colonial Times." *Revista de Indias.* Vol.76, No.267 (2016).

Londoño López, Por Jenny. "Manuela Sáenz: 'Mi Patria es el Continente de la América.'" *Cuadernos Americanos* Vol.3, No.125 (2008): 67–85.

Long, Kathryn T. "'Cameras 'Never Lie'": The Role of Photography in Telling the Story of American Evangelical Missions." *Church History* Vol.72, No.4 (2003): 820–851.

Lopez, Oscar. "Lago Agrio: The Bitterness of a Judgment." *Cornell International Law Journal Online*, 2013.

López de Gómara, Francisco. *Historia General de las Indias.* Antwerp: Potjuari Bellero, ala enfena de Halcon, 1552.

López Ruiz, Sebastián José. *Conservación y propagación de los arboles de quina*. Bogotá: Biblioteca Nacional de Colombia, 1796.

"Lorenza Avemañay, Mujer Ilustre del Cantón Guamote." *Diario Regional Los Andes*, September 22, 2019.

Loudon, J.C. *Remarks on the Construction of Hothouses.* London: J. Taylor, 1817.

Liu, Cuirong, and James Beattie. *Environment, Modernization and Development in East Asia: Perspectives from Environmental History*. Houndmills: Palgrave Macmillan, 2016.

Luciano, Pellegrino A. "When Quinine Was King: A Note on the Global Ecology of Health." *Practicing Anthropology* Vol.37, No.2 (2015): 31-34.

Luna, Fernando Juan. "A Calculated Relationship: Rafael Correa and the Indigenous Movement." Undergraduate Thesis, Texas A&M, 2017.

Luttikhuis, Bart and A. Dirk Moses. "Mass Violence and the End of the Dutch Colonial Empire in Indonesia." *Journal of Genocide Research* Vol.14, Nos.3-4 (2012): 257-276.

Lyell, Charles. *Principles of Geology*. London: J. Murray, 1837.

Macdonald G. *The Epidemiology and Control of Malaria.* London: Oxford University Press, 1957.

MacLeod, Roy M. *Science and the Pacific War: Science and Survival in the Pacific, 1939–1945*. Berlin: Springer Science & Business Media, 1999.

Maehle, Andreas–Holger. "Peruvian Bark: From Specific Febrifuge to Universal Remedy." In *Drugs on Trial: Experimental Pharmacology and Therapeutic Innovation in the Eighteenth Century. Clio Medica* Vol.53 (1999): 223–309.

Magrin, Graciela O., José A. Marengo et al. "Central and South America". In *Fifth Assessment Report of the IPCC,* edited by Vicente R. Barros et al., 1499–1566. New York: Cambridge University Press, 2014.

Maier, Georg. "The Boundary Dispute Between Ecuador and Peru." *American Journal of International Law* Vol.63, No.1 (January, 1969): 28–46.

Markham, Clements R. *Peruvian Bark: A Popular Account of the Production of Chinchona Cultivation into British India.* London: John Murray, 1880.

Marquez, Ophelia and Lillian Ramos Navarro World, eds. "Compilation of Colonial Spanish Terms and Document Related Phrases." Midway City: SHHAR Press (Society of Hispanic Historical and Ancestral Research), 1998.

Martin, Paul M.V., and Estelle Martin-Granel. "2,500-year Evolution of the Term Epidemic." *Emerging Infectious Diseases* Vol.12, No.6 (2006): 976–80.

Martínez, Elizabeth Sutherland. *500 Años del Pueblo Chicano = 500 Years of Chicano History in Pictures*. Albuquerque: SouthWest Organizing Project, 1991.

Masterson, Karen M. *The Malaria Project: The U.S. Government's Secret Mission to Find a Miracle Cure.* New York: Berkley Press, 2015.

Mathias Peter and Nikolaï Todorov, et. al. *History of Humanity: Vol.VI, The Nineteenth Century*. Paris: UNESCO, 2008.

Mattison, Richard V. ed. *The Monthly Review of Medicine and Pharmacy* Vol.III. Philadelphia: Keasbey & Mattison, 1880.

Mbaya, Henry. "Social Capital and the Imperatives of the Concept and Life of Ubuntu in the South African Context." *Sciptura* Vol.106 (2011): 1–8.

McFarlane, Anthony. "The "Rebellion of the Barrios": Urban Insurrection in Bourbon Quito." *The Hispanic American Historical Review* Vol.69, No.2 (1989): 283-330.

Milman, Oliver. The Lawyer Who Took on Chevron – And Now Marks his 600th Day under House Arrest." *The Guardian*, March 28, 2021.

Mission Aviation Fellowship. "How Five Martyrs Transformed the Waodani People of Ecuador." Kent: MAF, 2021

Means, Philip Ainsworth. "The Rebellion of Tupac–Amaru II." *The Hispanic American Historical Review* Vol.2. No.1 (Feb. 1919): 1–25.

Melo, Mario. "Los Derechos de la Naturaleza: Un Paradigma Emergente Frente a la Crisis Ambiental." 2009.

Menezes, Elaine Cristina de Oliveira. "Industrialização e Meio Ambiente no Estado de Santa Catarina. Estudo de Caso sobre a Evolução e os Impactos Socioambientais do Segmento Têxtil-Vestuarista na Microrregião do Alto Vale do Itaja." Universidade Federal de Santa Catarina, Florianópolis, 2009.

Menezes, Fernando Dominence. "Enunciados sobre o Futuro: Ditadura Militar, Transamazônica e a Construção do 'Brasil Grande.'" Master's Thesis, Universidade de Brasília, 2007.

Mera, Juan León. *Cumandá: Un Drama entre Salvajes*. Quito: Imprenta del Clero, 1877.

"Mercado San Roque." *La TV Ecuador*, February 7, 2015.

Mignolo, Walter D. *The Darker Side of Western Modernity: Global Futures, Decolonial Options*. Durham and London: Duke University Press, 2011.

______. "The Geopolitics of Knowledge and the Colonial Difference," *The South Atlantic Quarterly* Vol.101, No.1 (2002).

Ministry of Hydrocarbons. "The Outlook for Ecuador Petroleum Sector New Investments Opportunities." Houston: Rice University Baker Institute for Public Policy, 2018.

Minto, Deonne N. "Toward a Black Liberatory Feminism: Erna Brodber's Myal and Luz Argentina Chiriboga's Bajo la Piel de los Tambores." In *Sisters in the Spirit: Transnational Constructions of Diaspora in Late Twentieth-Century Black Women's Literature of the Americas*. PhD Diss., University of Maryland, 2007: 147–190.

Missão Novas Tribos do Brasil (MNTB). "Q&A Regarding News Reports." McNeal: Ethnos 360 Aviation, 2020.

Moens, J.C.B. *De Kinacultuur in Azië, 1854–1882*. Batavia: Ernst & Co. 1882.

Moran, Emilio F. "Deforestation and Land Use in the Brazilian Amazon." *Human Ecology* Vol.21, No.1 (1993): 1–21.

Moran, Emilio F. *Developing the Amazon*. Bloomington: Indiana University Press. 1981.

Moreno, Yánez S. E. *Sublevaciones Indigenas en la Audencia e Quito*. Quito: Ed. de la Pontificia Universidad Católica del Ecuador, 1985.

Moszynski, Peter. "5.4 Million People have Died in Democratic Republic of Congo since 1998 because of Conflict, report says." *BMJ British Medical Journal* (Clinical Research Edition) Vol.336, No.7638 (2008): 235.

Murgueytio, Reinaldo. "Los Problemas de la Educación Indígena." *Revista Ecuatoriana de Educacion* Vol.1, No.3. (April/June, 1948): 66–76.

Murúa, Martín de. *Historia General Del Piru, 1616*. Facsimile of J. Paul Getty Museum Ms. Ludwig XIII 16. Los Angeles: The Getty Research Institute Publications Program, 2008.

"Mujeres Indígenas Hoy: 5 de Septiembre – Día Internacional de La Mujer Indígena." *Bartolinas*, September 5, 2010.

Mutis, Jose Celestino. *El Arcano de la Quina*. Madrid: Ibarra, Impresor de Camara S.M., 1828.

Naciones Unidas. *Boletin De Planficacion 6*. Santiago: Instituto LatinoAmericano de Planificacion Economica Y Social, 1978.

Nakajima, Hiroshi (Director-General). "The World Health Report 1998: Life in the 21st Century, A Vision for All." Geneva: World Health Organization, 1998.

National Aeronautics and Space Administration (NASA). "Mapping the Amazon." NASA Earth Observatory, September 26, 2019.

Netto, F. Ferreira, and W. Andrew Archer. "The Problem of the Amazon." *The Scientific Monthly* Vol.61, No.1 (1945): 33–44.

Newson, Linda A., ed. *Cultural Worlds of the Jesuits in Colonial Latin America.* London: University of London Press, Institute of Latin American Studies, 2020.

Ning, Lom Bryan-Bill. "Quinine and the Cinchona Plant: Gain or Bane for Africa?" *Hektoen International*, Spring, 2019.

Noboa, Fernando Jurado. "La Mujer Indígena en los Levantamientos Indígenas Coloniales y a Partir de 1768 / The Indigenous Woman in the Colonial Indigenous Uprisings and since 1768." *Sarance* No.45 (2020): 68–75.

"Nosotras." *La Jornada del Campo* No.78 (March 17, 2014).

Nunn, Nathan and Nancy Qjan. "The Columbian Exchange: A History of Disease, Food, and Ideas." *The Journal of Economic Perspectives* Vol.24, No.2 (Spring 2010): 163–188.

NY Times, "Makes Quinine Here of South American Bark: Company's Price on the Product Equals Dutch Monopoly's." *The New York Times*, March 23, 1941.

Our American Network (OAN Reporting Staff). "Elisabeth Elliot: Through Gates of Splendor." *Our American Stories*, Audio Recording, September 24, 2019.

O'Malley, John W., Gauvin Alexander Bailey, Steven J. Harris, and T. Frank Kennedy, eds. *The Jesuits: Cultures, Sciences, and the Arts, 1540–1773.* Toronto: University of Toronto Press, 2016.

Ortis Alarcón, Érica Paola and Gladys Marlene Yuquilema. *El Rol de la Mujer Indígena Dentrode los Movimientos sociales de los Cantones Riobamba, Guamote y Colta de la Provincia de Chimborazo Durante los Años de 1800 a 1880.* Universidad Nacional de Chimborazo, May 30, 2014.

Ossenback. Gabriela. "Políticas Educativas en el Ecuador, 1944–1983." *Estudios Interdisciplinarios de América Latina y el Caribe* Vol.10, No.1 (1999): 37-60.

Overmyer-Velazquez, Rebecca. *Folkloric Poverty: Neoliberal Multiculturalism in Mexico.* University Park: Penn State Press, 2010.

Pan American Union. "No.1609: Charter of the Organization of American States, signed at Bogotá, on 30 April 1948." Geneva: United Nations, 1952.

Parker, Lynn, and Kiri Ross-Jones. *The Story of Kew Gardens.* London: Arcturus, 2013.

Pepperell, Tallulah. "Pedro Franco Dávila" *The Sloane Letters Project*, August 18, 2017.

Pérez T., Aquiles R. *Las Mitas el la Real Audiencia de Quito.* Quito: Imp. del Ministerio del Tesoro, 1947.

Petroamazonas. *The Oil and Gas Year, Ecuador*. Petroamazonas EP: Ecuadorian National E&P Company, 2013. Philip, Kavita. "Imperial Science Rescues a Tree: Global Botanic Networks, Local Knowledge and the Transcontinental Transplantation of Cinchona." *Environment and History* Vol.1, No.2 (1995): 173–200.

Picq, Manuela L. "The Inheritance of Resistance: Indigenous Women's Leadership in Ecuador." In *Indigenous and Afro-Ecuadorians Facing the Twenty-First Century*, edited by Mark Becker, 71–94. Newcastle, UK: Cambridge Scholars Publishing, 2013.

______. *Vernacular Sovereignties: Indigenous Women Challenging World Politics.* Tucson: University of Arizona Press, 2018.

Planchon, Gustave and Douglas C. Harrod. *Des Quinquinas.* Paris: Savy, 1864.

Podgorny, Irina. "Bureaucracy, Instructions, and Paperwork – The Gathering of Data about the Three Kingdoms of Nature in the Americas, 1770–1815." *Nuevo Mundo Mundos Nuevos. Nouveaux Mondes Mondes Nouveaux – Novo Mundo Mundos Novos – New World New Worlds*, February 19, 2019.

Pomet, Pierre. *Histoire Générale des Drogues.* Paris: Jean-Baptiste Loyson & Augustin Pillon, 1694.

Ponce Leiva, Pilar. "Un Espacio para la Controversia: la Audiencia de Quito en el Siglo XVIII." *Revista de Indias* Vol.52, Nos.195-196 (1992): 839–865.

Porras, Katherine Aissa. "Afro-Peruvian Dance: An Embodied Struggle for Visibility and Integration." Master's Thesis, University of Hawaii at Manoa, 2012.

Porras de Campo, Ángel Esteban. "Introduction to the Study of 'Cumandá', by Juan León Mera." Biblioteca Virtual Miguel de Cervantes, 2011.

Pratt, Mary Louise. "Humboldt and the Reinvention of América." In *Amerindian Images and the Legacy of Columbus*, edited by René Jara and Nicholas Spadaccini, 584–606. Minneapolis: University of Minnesota Press, 1992.

______. *Imperial Eyes: Travel Writing and Transculturation.* London: Routledge, 1992.

Prieto, Andrés I. "*Missionary Scientists: Jesuit Science in Spanish South America, 1570–1810.*" Nashville: Vanderbilt University Press, 2011.

Proaño, Nancy Morán. "El Lucimiento de la Fe, Platería Religiosa en Quito." In *Arte de la Real Audiencia de Quito, siglos XVII-XIX: Patronos, Corporaciones y Comunidades*, edited by Alexandra Kennedy, 145–161. Hondarribia: Nerea, 2002.

Quijano, Anibal, and Michael Ennis. "Coloniality of Power, Eurocentrism, and Latin America." *Nepantla: Views from South* Vol.1, No.3 (2000): 533–580.

Radcliffe, Sarah A. "The Geographies of Indigenous Self-Representation in Ecuador: Hybridity, Gender and Resistance." *Revista Europea de Estudios Latinoamericanos y del Caribe / European Review of Latin American and Caribbean Studies* No.63 (1997): 9–27.

Radford, Robin and Anthony Radford. "The Great Cinchona Robberies: Philanthropy not Theft—The Story of Quinine Production in Papua New Guinea." Adelaide: South Australian Medical Heritage Society, 2014.

Radford, Anthony J., H. Van Leeuwen, and S.H. Christian. "Social Aspects in the Changing Epidemiology of Malaria in the Highlands of New Guinea." *Annals of Tropical Medicine & Parasitology* Vol.70, No.1 (March 1976): 11–23.

Rahier, Jean Muteba. *Blackness in the Andes: Ethnographic Vignettes of Cultural Politics in the Time of Multiculturalism.* London: Palgrave Macmillan, 2014.

Rahier, Jean Muteba. "Marc Becker: Indians and Leftists in the Making of Ecuador's Modern Indigenous Movements." *Estudios Interdisciplinarios de América Latina y el Caribe* Vol.21, No.2 (2010): 186–188.

Rapoport Delegation on Afro-Ecuadorian Land Rights. "Forgotten Territories, Unrealized Rights: Rural Afro-Ecuadorians and Their Fight for Land, Equality, and Security." *Afro-Descendants: Collective Land Rights in Latin America.* University of Texas, Rapoport Center for Human Rights & Justice, 2009.

"La Real Audiencia de Quito: Características, Funciones y Más." *Hablemos de Culturas*, April 12, 2019.

La Real Sociedad Española de Historia Natural. *Anales de Historia Natural.* Madrid: Don S. De Uhagon, Tesorero, 1875.

Rebok, Sandra. "Humboldt's Exploration at a Distance." In *Worlds of Natural History*, edited by Emma C. Spary, Helen Anne Curry, James Andrew Secord, and Nicholas Jardine, 319–334. Cambridge: Cambridge University Press, 2018.

Refoyo, Enrique. "Ecuador: Protests, Loans, and Decree 883." *United World*, October 17, 2019.

Rego, Renato Leão. "De Londres à Amazônia: A Integração Cidade-campo Como Esquema de Colonização e criação de cidades novas: do Norte Paranaense à Amazônia Legal." *R.B. Estudos Urbanos E Regionais* Vol.17, No.1, (April, 2015): 89–103.

______. "Shaping an Urban Amazonia: 'A Planner's Nightmare.'" *Planning Perspectives* Vol.32, No.2 (April 3, 2017): 249–70.

______. "Unidade de Vizinhança: um Estudo de Caso das Transformações de uma Ideia Urbanística." *Revisto Brasileira de Gestão Urbana* (*Brazilian Journal of Urban Management*) Vol.9, No.3 (2017): 401–413.

______. "Palmas, the Last Capital City Planned in Twentieth-Century Brazil." *Urbe. Revista Brasileira de Gestão Urbana* 12 (April 17, 2020).

Reilly, Alexa. "'Our Territory is Not for Sale:' Indigenous Led Anti-Extraction Social Movements in the Ecuadorian Amazon." *The Yale Review of International Studies*, February 2020.

Report on the Administration of British Burma during 1874–1875. Rangoon: The Government Press, 1876.

Réveil, Oscar et al. *Le Règne Végétal.* Paris: L. Guérin, 1872.

Riding, Alan. "Hundreds Killed In Ecuador Quake; Serious Economic Damage." *The New York Times*, March 10, 1987.

Rodas, Chaves G. "J. de. Moranville y el Primer Dibujo Universal de la Quina o Cascarilla." *Bulletin de l'institut Francais d'etudes Andines* Vol.32, No.3 (2003): 431–440.

Roersch van der Hoogte, Arjo. "Colonial Agro-Industrialism: Science, Industry and the State in the Dutch Goden Alkaloid Age, 1850-1950." PhD Diss., Utrecht University, 2015.

Rojas, Ángel F. *La Novela Ecuatoriana.* México: F.C.E., 1948.

Rojas Benavente, Lady. "'Me Gritaron Negra': de Victoria Santa Cruz Gamarra, Etnicidad en el Perú de los 50 y Poesía de Resistencia", *Actual, Revista de la Dirección General de Cultura y Extensión. Universidad de los Andes* 62-63 (May-December 2006): 85-96.

Roll Back Malaria. *The Global Malaria Action Plan for a Malaria–Free World.* The Roll Back Malaria Partnership, 2008.

Romo-Leroux, Ketty. *Legal and Social Situation of Women in Ecuador*. Guayaquil: University of Guayaquil, 1975.

_____. *Women: Hard Fight for Equality*. Department of Publications of the University of Guayaquil, 1983.

_____. *Women's Movement in Ecuador.* Department of Publications of the University of Guayaquil, 1997.

_____. *Manuela Sáenz, The Great Truth*. Ecuador: Offset Graba, 2005.

Rosati, Hugo A. "Guerras, Rebeliones y Milenarismos Indígenos." Instituto de Historia de la Pontificia Universidad Católica de Chile, 1996.

Ross, Ronald. "The Malaria Expedition to West Africa." *Science New Series* Vol.11, No.262 (1900): 36–37.

Ross, Ronald. "Researches on Malaria, Nobel Lecture, December 12, 1902." *Nobel Lectures, Physiology or Medicine 1901-1921* (Amsterdam: Elsevier, 1967): 24-116.

Roth, Klaus and Sabine Streller. "From Pharmacy to the Pub—A Bark Conquers the World." *Chemistry Views.* Chemie in Unserer Zeit/Wiley–VCH, May 7, 2013.

Royal Botanic Gardens (Kew). "Introduction of Cinchona to India." *Bulletin of Miscellaneous Information* No.3 (1931): 113–117.

Rubenstein, Steven. "Colonialism, the Shuar Federation, and the Ecuadorian State." *Environment and Planning D: Society and Space* Vol.19, No.3 (2001): 263–293.

Ruggiero, Diana M. "'Más Allá Del Fútbol': Teaching Highland Afro-Ecuadorian Culture and Engaging Race and Racism through Documentary Film." *Hispania* Vol.98, No.3 (2015): 594–606.

Ruiz, Hipólito and José Pavón. *Quinologia, o Tratado del Árbol de la Quina ó Cascarilla.* Madrid: En la Oficina de la Viuda é Hijo de Marin, 1792.

_____. *Suplemento á la Quinologia.* Madrid: Imprenta de la Vidua e Hijo de Marin, 1801.

_____. *Fruits, Seeds and Barks from the Royal Botanical Expedition to the Viceroyalty of Peru*. Madrid: Real Jardín Botánico-CSIC, 1777–1816.

Said, Edward W. *Culture and Imperialism*. London: Chatto & Windus, 1993.

Sallares, Robert et al. "The Spread of Malaria to Southern Europe in Antiquity: New Approaches to Old Problems." *Medical History* Vol.48, No.3 (2004): 311–328.

San Sebastián, Miguel. "Oil Development in the Amazon Basin of Ecuador: The Popular Epidemiology Process." PhD Diss., London School of Hygiene & Tropical Medicine, 2001.

San Sebastián, Miguel and Anna-Karin Hurtig. "Oil Exploitation in the Amazon Basin of Ecuador: A Public Health Emergency." *Revista Panamericana de Salud Pública/ Pan American Journal of Public Health* Vol.15, No.3 (2004): 205–211.

Sax, Sarah. "Inside Indigenous Women's Fight to Protect The Amazon." *Bustle*, September 23, 2019.

Schaumann, Caroline. "Who Measures the World? Alexander von Humboldt's Chimborazo Climb in the Literary Imagination." *The German Quarterly* Vol.82, No.4 (2009): 447–468.

Seeley Harris, Alice. *Congo Atrocity Lantern Lecture: 'A Young Man (Mola) and Child (Yola) with Severed Limbs.'* Antislavery International/Panos Pictures, 1903.

Segundo, Moreno. *Sublevaciones Indígenas en la Audiencia de Quito desde Comienzos del Siglo XVIII hasta finales de la Colonia.* Quito: Universidad Andina Simon Bolivar, 2014.

Serrano, Claudia. "Mujeres Negras e Indígenas: Resistencia, Valor y Dignidad." *Webislam*, August, 25, 2008.

Seligmann, Linda J. "To Be in Between: The Cholas as Market Women." *Comparative Studies in Society and History* Vol.31, No.4 (1989): 694–721.

Sheldon, Jennie Wood, Michael J. Balick, Sarah A. Laird, and George M. Milne. "Medicinal Plants: Can Utilization and Conservation Coexist? The Role of Plants in the Pharmaceutical Industry." *Advances in Economic Botany* Vol.12 (1997): 55–60.

Shiva, Vandana. "One Empire over Seed: Control Over the

World's Seed Banks." In *Gates to a Global Empire*, edited by Carla Ramos Cortés, 7–9. Mantasa: Navdanya International, 2020.

Smith, Nigel. "Brazil's Transamazon Highway Settlement Scheme: Agrovilas, Agropoli, and Ruropoli." *Association of American Geographers, Proceedings* Vol.8 (1976): 129–132.

Smith, Paul J. *Representing the Other: "Race", Text, and Gender in Spanish and Spanish American Narrative*. Oxford: Clarendon Press, 1992.

Smithsonian National Museum of Natural History and the U.S. National Herbarium. "Botany Digitizes Its 1,000,000th Herbarium Specimen." *Quarterly Newsletter from the Botany Department (NMNH)*, March 29, 2017.

Snowden, Frank M. *The Conquest of Malaria, Italy, 1900–1962*. New Haven and London: Yale University Press, 2006.

Southgate, Douglas, Robert Wasserstrom, and Susan Reider. "Oil Development, Deforestation, and Indigenous Populations in the Ecuadorian Amazon." *Latin American Studies Association*, Rio de Janeiro, Brazil, June 11-14, 2009.

Spenlé, Virginie. "'Savagery' and 'Civilization': Dutch Brazil in the Kunst and Wunderkammer." *Journal of Historians of Netherlandish Art* Vol.3, No.2 (2011).

Spruce, Richard. *Notes of a Botanist on the Amazon & Andes.* Edited and condensed by Russel Wallace. London: Millan and Co., 1908.

Steere, William Campbell. "The Botanical Work of the Cinchona Missions in South America." *Science* Vol.101, No.2616 (February 1945): 177–178.

Sternberg, George M. "Malaria" *Popular Science Monthly* Vol.58 (February 1901): 360–371.

Sumner, Judith. *Plants Go to War: A Botanical History of World War II*. Jefferson, NC: McFarland & Co., 2019.

Talbor, Robert. *The English Remedy or Talbor's Wonderful Secret for Cureing of Agues and Feavers.* London: F. Wallis, 1682.

Tardieu, Jean-Pierre. "Los Negros y la Minería." In *El Negro en la Real Audiencia de Quito*, Siglos XVI–XVIII, 135–65. Lima: Instituto Francés de Estudios Andinos, 2015.

Taylor, Norman. "Quinine: The Story of Cinchona." *The Scientific Monthly* Vol.57, No.1 (1943): 17–32.

Telles, Ana Clara. "Mothers, Warriors and Lords: Gender(ed) Cartographies of the US War on Drugs in Latin America." *Contexto Internacional* Vol.41, No.1 (Jan/Apr 2019): 15–37.

Thwaites, Reuben Gold. *The Jesuit Relations and Allied Documents: Travels and Explorations of the Jesuit Missionaries in New France, 1610–1791,* Vol.I (1610–1613). Cleveland: The Burrows Brothers Company, 1896.

Tibán, Lourdes Guala and Raúl Ilaquiche. *Kichwa Runakunapak Kamachik: Manual de Administración de Justicia Indígena en El Ecuador*. Copenhagen, Denmark: IWGIA, 2004.

Tinbergen, Jan, Antony J. Dolman, Jan van Ettinger, and Club of Rome. *Reshaping the International Order: A Report to the Club of Rome.* New York: Dutton, 1976.

Transnational Institute. "Ecuador: Overview of Drug Policies, Drug Law and Legislative Trends." Amsterdam: TNI, 2016.

Todd, Anthony. *The London Dispensatory,* 4th Edition. London: Longman, Rees, Orme, Brown, and Green, 1826.

Torti, Francisci. *Mutinensis Philosophiae, & Medicinae Doctoris*. Francofurti et Lipsiae: Fleischeriana, 1756.

Turrion, Maria Luisa et al. "Organización Administrativa del Ramo de la Quina." In *Medicina y Quina en la España del Siglo XVIII*, edited by Juan Riera Palmero, 35–44. Salamanca: Europa Artes Gráficas S. A., 1997.

Ulloa, Bayardo E. *Riobamba: Apuntes del Pasado.* Casa de la Cultura Ecuatoriana. Riobamba: Editorial Pedagógica Freire, 2003.

United Nations. *Economic Bulletin for Latin America* Vol.9, No.1 (March, 1964).

______. *UN Single Convention on Narcotic Drugs, 1961 as Amended by the 1972 Protocol*. Geneva: United Nations, 1972.

______. *UN Convention Against Illicit Traffic in Narcotic Drugs and Psychotropic Substances, 1988*. New York: United Nations Treaty Collection, 1994.

______. *UN Declaration on the Rights of Indigenous Peoples*, September 13, 2007.

UN Economic Commission for Latin American & the Caribbean (ECLAC). "Note for Equality N° 27: Femicide, The Most Extreme Expression of Violence Against Women" (El Feminicidio, la Expresión más Extrema de la Violencia

Contra las Mujeres). *Gender Equality Observatory for Latin America and the Caribbean.* November 15, 2018.

UNESCO. "America: 1492–1992: Trayectorias Históricas y Elementos de Desarrollo." *Revista Internacional de Ciencias Sociales* No.134 (December, 1992).

_____. "Convention Concerning the Protection of the World Cultural and Natural Heritage: World Heritage Committee, 14th Session." Banff, 7–12 December 1990.

UNESCO (World Heritage Center). "40th Anniversary Celebration of Quito and Galápagos as World Heritage." December 3, 2018.

Urdang, George. "The Legend of Cinchona." *The Scientific Monthly* Vol. 61, No.1 (1945): 17–20.

US Army Corps of Engineers (USACE). "Water Resources Assessment of Ecuador." September, 1998.

US Central Intelligence Agency (CIA). "Detailing Operation Condor in Ecuador." Information Report, February 14, 1978.

US Department of State (DOS). "Historical Summary of the Ecuador/Peru Border Dispute." *CIA*, October 28, 1976.

_____. "U.S. Relations with Ecuador (Document 306)." Washington DC: Department of State, 1959.

US Food and Drug Administration. "Stop to Marketing Quinine for Night Leg Cramps." *FDA Consumer* Vol.29, No.6 (July-August 1995): 2.

US Mission to the Organization of American States (OAS). "History." Washington DC: OAS, 2021.

Valen, Dustin. "On the Horticultural Origins of Victorian Glasshouse Culture." *Journal of the Society of Architectural Historians* Vol.75, No.4 (2016): 403–423.

Van Gorkom, Karel W. *The Cultivation of the Chinchonas or Peruvian Bark Trees in Java, with notes by C. Hasskari and by C.R. Markham on the Introduction of Chinchona into India.* London: Eyre and Spottiswoode, 1870.

Van de Sandt, Joris J. "Behind the Mask of Recognition: Defending Autonomy and Communal Resource Management in Indigenous Resguardos, Colombia." PhD Diss., Universiteit van Amsterdam, 2007.

Van Leeuwenhoek, Anthony. "Microscopical Observations on the Cortex Peruvianus." *Philosophical Transactions* No.25 (1706): 2446–2455.

Varea, Ana María, & Pablo Ortiz-T. *Marea Negra en la Amazonia: Conflictos Socioambientales Vinculados a la Actividad Petrolera en el Ecuador.* Quito: Abya Yala, 1995.

Vasquez, Marcela Enríque. "The Illusion of Getting a Job: Women's Work on Flower Plantations (A Case from Ecuador)." Master's Thesis, University of Florida, 2005.

Veale, Lucy. "A Historical Geography of the Nilgiri Cinchona Plantations, 1860–1900." PhD Diss., University of Nottingham, 2010.

Veloso, José Mariano da Conceição. *Quinografia Portuguesa ou Collecção de Varias Memorias Sobre Vinte e Duas Especies de Quinas.* Lisbon: João Procopio Correa da Silva (Santa Igreja Patriarcal), 1799.

Viatori, Maximillian. "Indigenous Threats and White Counterfactuals: The Semiotics of Race in Elite Print Media Coverage of Ecuador's 1990 Indigenous Uprising." *Anthropological Theory* Vol.14, No.4 (2014): 387–404.

Vidal, John. "Chevron Hits out at British Documentary on Oil Pollution in Ecuador." *The Guardian* (Environment), June 17, 2015.

Villena Sánchez–Valero, Miguel, et. al. *El Gabinete Perdido. Pedro Franco Dávila y la Historia Natural del Siglo de las Luces.* Madrid: Consejo Superior de Investigaciones Cientificas, 2009.

Voeks, Robert, and Charlotte Greene. "God's Healing Leaves: The Colonial Quest for Medicinal Plants in the Torrid Zone." *Geographical Review* Vol.108, No.4 (2018): 545–565.

Vriese, W.H. de. *De Kina-Boom uit Zuid Amerika Overgebragt naar Java, Onder de RegerAng van Koning Willem III.* \'s Gravenhage: C.W. Mieling, 1855.

Walls, Laura Dassow. *The Passage to Cosmos: Alexander von Humboldt and the Shaping of America.* Chicago: University of Chicago Press, 2009.

Warren, Martin and Maurice Shelton. *Dr. Warren's Epistle to His Friend, of the Method and Manner of Curing the Late Raging Fevers, and of the Danger, Uncertainty, and Unwholesomeness of the Jesuit's World Heritage Properties.* London: H. Woodfall, 1733.

Washington Office on Latin America. "Drugs and Prisons in Ecuador: The Human Face of Misguided Drug Laws."

Washington DC: WOLA, 2011.
Wasserstom, Robert and Donald Southgate. "Deforestación, Reforma Agraria y Desarrollo Petrolero en Ecuador, 1964–1994." *Natural Resources* Vol.4 (2013): 34–44.
Weddell, Hugh Algernon. *Histoire Naturelle des Quinquinas.* Paris: Victor Masson, 1849.
Weil, Thomas E., et. al. *Area Handbook for Ecuador.* Washington DC: American University, 1973.
Weiss, Wendy. "Debt and Devaluation: The Burden on Ecuador's Popular Class." *Latin American Perspectives* Vol.24, No.4 (1997): 9–33.
Wellcome, Henry S. "A Visit to the Native Cinchona Forests of South America." *The Monthly Review of Medicine and Pharmacy*, 1880.
______. "The Cinchona Forests of South America." *The Scientific Monthly* Vol.71, No.3 (1950): 205–208.
Wellcome Library. *Cinchona Tercentenary Celebration and Exhibition at Wellcome Historical Medical Museum.* London: The Wellcome Foundation, 1930.
Wemytewa, Edward (A:Shiwi Nation). "Message to Organizacion Nacional Indigena de Colombia (ONIC) y Coordinadora Andina de Organizaciones Indigenas (CAOI), 'V Continental Summit of Indigenous Peoples and Nations of Abya Yala' & 'II Continental Summit of Indigenous Women.'" November 5, 2013.
Widener, Patricia. "Oil Conflict in Ecuador: A Photographic Essay." *Organization & Environment* Vol.20, No.1 (March 2007): 84–105.
WikiLeaks. "Amazon Atlas: Map of Amazon's Data Centers." *WikiLeaks*, October 11, 2018.
Williams, Sheila. "The Pope-Burning Processions of 1679, 1680 and 1681." *Journal of the Warburg and Courtauld Institutes* Vol.21, nos.1/2 (1958): 104–18.
Wolfe, Sidney. "Quinine Sulfate," Letter to Dr. David Kessler, Commissioner, US Food and Drug Administration. *Public Citizen*, September 8, 1994.
The World Bank Group. "Project Appraisal Document on a Proposed Loan in the Amount of US $25 Million to the Republic of Ecuador for an Indigenous and Afro-Ecuadorian Peoples Development Project." *The World Bank Report* No.17217–EC. December 15, 1997.
World Health Organization (WHO). *Geographical Distribution of Arthropod–Borne Diseases and Their Principal Vectors.* Geneva: World Health Organization, 1989.
______. "Malaria." *World Health: Magazine of the World Health Organization.* September-October, 1991.
______. *World Health Statistics: Annuaire de Statistiques Sanitaires Mondiales.* Geneva: WHO, 1983.
______. "Epidemiological Assessment of Status of Malaria, 30 June 1966." *Weekly Epidemiological Record / Relevé épidémiologique hebdomadaire* Vol.42, No.7 (1967): 89.
Worrall, Simon. "Amazon Warriors did Indeed Fight and Die Like Men," *National Geographic,* News, October 28, 2014.
Wright, William. *Description of the Jesuits' Bark Tree [Cinchona Jamaicensis, Seu Caribbeana] of Jamaica and the Caribbees.* London, 1778.
Wroblewski, Michael. "Inscribing Indigeneity: Ethnolinguistic Authority in the Linguistic Landscape of Amazonian Ecuador." *Multilingua* Vol.39, No.2 (March 26, 2020): 139–68.
Wulf, Andrea. *The Brother Gardeners: Botany, Empire, and the Birth of an Obsession.* New York: Vintage, 2008.
Yanchatipan Simbana, Diana Cristina. *Personajes Afroecuatorianos en la etapa colonial del Ecuador y su influencia en los procesos de Independencia.* Quito: UCE, 2014.
Youngers, Coletta. "Reducing Female Incarceration: The 2008 National Pardon in Ecuador." In *Innovative Approaches to Drug Policy and Incarceration*, 1–3. Washington DC: Washington Office on Latin America, 2017.
Zaitchik, Alexander. "How Conservation Became Colonialism" (with photos by Mitch Anderson & Jerónimo Zúñiga/ Amazon Frontlines). *Foreign Policy* No.229 (July 2018): 56-63.
Zeuske, Michael. "La Invención de Humboldt." *Revista Equatoriana de Historia* No.51 (January/June 2020): 205-211.
Zéndegui, Guillermo de., et. al. *Colonial Art of Ecuador: Organization of the American States.* New Orleans: Roger Thayer Stone Center for Latin American Studies, 2012.
Zimmerer, Karl S. "Humboldt's Nodes and Modes of Interdisciplinary Environmental Science in the Andean World." *Geographical Review* Vol 90, No.3 (July 2006): 334–360.

AGAINST NOMENCLATURES

Un-Naming Colonial Categories from Plant to Pill, Places to Peoples

Amazon: name of the region, also called 'Amazonia' or 'Amazonica,' including the river and forest lands that cross the states of Brazil, Guyana, Suriname French Guiana, Venezuela, Colombia, Ecuador, Peru, and Bolivia. *[2014: Amazon on Fire]*

Amazonas: name of the river and delta, over 6,000 kilometers long, with a watershed whose headwaters extend into Ecuador, Peru, and Colombia. Upstream tributaries include: Putumayo, Caquetá, Vaupés, Guainía, Morona, Pastaza, Nucuray, Urituyacu, Chambira, Tigre, Nanay, Napo, and Huallaga. These tributaries flow downstream into the Marañón and Ucayali rivers, then into the main Amazon River towards the delta with the Atlantic ocean. *[1532: Avenge of the Amazonas]*

TransAmazon: name of the road network crossing the river and forest region of the Amazon River. *[2014: Highway to Hell]*

Aymara: nation of Indigenous Peoples in the Central Andes and Altiplano regions of South America, across Peru, Bolivia, and Chile (south of, and interconnected with Kechwan Lands). *[2019: Communitarian Feminism]*

Cinchona: name of febrifuge plant attributed by Linnaeus in 1742. The name is the improper spelling of 'Chinchona' (after the disputed story of the Countess of Chinchón); a misspelling that has persisted for over 300 years. Based on the University of Melbourne's *Multilingual Multiscript Plant Name Database*, other terms historically used for the Cinchona plant include: *Arból de la Quina, Bois-aux-Fièvres, Calisaya Bark, Cascarilla, China Bark, Cinchona calisaya, Cinchona carabayensis, Cinchona ledgeriana, Cinchona officinalis, Cinchona pubescens, Cinchona succirubra, Chinarinde, Chinarindenbaum, Chinin baum, Cinchonine, Écorce du Pérou, Écorce de Quina, Écorce de Quinquina Rouge, Fever Tree, Fieberrinde, Fieberrinden-baum, Jesuit's Bark, Kina-Kina, Ledgerbark, Peruvian Bark, Poudre des Jésuites, Pulvis Cardinalis, Pulvis Partum, Quina, Quina-amarela, Quina-do-Amazonas, Quina-quina, Quineira, Quinine, Quino, Quinquina, Quinquina Gris, Quinquina Jaune, Quinquina Rouge, Red Bark, Red Cinchona Bark, Yellow Cinchona, Yellowbark.* The Cinchona plant is endemic to the mid-altitudes of the central region of the Andes mountain range of South America (Colombia, Ecuador, Peru, Bolivia). *[1663: Errata, Cinchona or Chinchona]*

Cinchonology: science and study of the Cinchona plant (also *Quinologie*, *Quinologia*). *[1742: Maiming by Naming]*

Febrifuge: a medicine served to reduce or dispel a fever. *[1712: Fever Tree]*

Kechwa: one of several Indigenous nations of the central Andes (in reference to its people). The distinction is with local Afro-Ecuadorians (of African descent) and Mestizx Peoples (white, mixed European descent) in the plurinational state and constitution of Ecuador (also *Quechua*). *[2019: Indigenous Uprising]*

Kinabureau: abbreviated term designating the Dutch Cinchona Bureau, a transoceanic consortium of three Dutch companies—Nederlandsche Kininefabriek (NKF), Amsterdamsche Chininefabriek (ACF), Bandoengsche Kininefabriek (BKF). The consortium was formed in 1913 to consolidate and monopolize the global production, trade, and sale of Cinchona from plantation to market, via Amsterdam. To promote the use of Cinchona in the fight against malaria, the Kinabureau created a propaganda office called the 'Bureau Tot Bevordering van Het Kinine-Gebruik, Amsterdam' (*Office for the Promotion of Quinine Use*), located in the Netherlands. The Kinabureau closed in 1961. *[1932: Corporate Colonialism]*

Loja: one of the earliest regions identified by Jesuit missionaries and European explorers (mainly from Spain and France) where the Cinchona plant was stolen from and eventually over-harvested by the 18th century. Home since time immemorial to Saraguro Peoples, this region was once part of the Vice-royalty of Peru (thus, 'Peruvian Bark' or 'Jesuit's Bark' as it was called by Jesuits early on) from the late 16th century to the early 19th century, when Ecuador gained independence. *[1650: Jesuit's Bark]*

Quichua: Indigenous language spoken by

People of Kechwan Nations and tribal communities (also *Kichwa*, Kechwa, *Kichua*). *[1930: Indoctrination]*

Quinine: name of the naturally occurring alkaloid (one of many) in the bark of the Cinchona plant and only known natural cure for malaria on the planet. It is a bitter compound that is ground from the harvested bark. It was historically mixed with water, served as a tonic to reduce severe fevers and to cure malaria. It was isolated and identified as an alkaloid in the mid 19th century and chemically synthesized a century later. Found in different varieties of the plant species, quinine's diverse biological resistance as a naturally occurring chemical compound and alkaloid, persists amidst the growing prevalence of virulent strains of malarial-carrying anopheles mosquitoes (also *Quinquina*). *[1944: Jungle Fever]*

Quina: Latin designation for the bark of the Cinchona plant. *[1628: Errata, Quina-Quina?]*

Quino: alternative term designating the complete tree of the Cinchona plant. Not to be confused with 'Quina' or 'Quina-Quina' (referring to the bark), 'quinine' (referring to the alkaloid and bark extract), Quinoa (grain of a different plant from Southern Andes), or Quito (capital city of Ecuador). *I.* Contrasting and contradicting the use of the Latin-derived and Spanish-designated word 'Cinchona' (whose errors in the Anglo-American scientific world are described at length in this book), the earliest use of the term 'Quino' is Don Hipólito Ruiz' *Relación Histórica del Viage que Hizo a los Reynos del Perú y Chile* (1777) and later in his *Quinologia: O Tratado del Árbol de la Quina ó Cascarilla, con su Descripción y la de Otras Especies de Quinos* (1792). This epistemological analysis is described in great detail in two, mid-20th century articles: W.A. Haggis' "Fundamental Errors in the Early History of Cinchona" (1941) and Jaime Jaramillo-Arango's "Basic Facts in the History of Cinchona" (1949). In the future process of *un-naming* the Cinchona plant as this book proposes, this epistemological strategy hinges on peeling away several layers: a) scientific nomenclature; b) colonial appellation derived from empires; and c) logistical toponymies or typographic errata that ensued during the past 500 years of colonial discovery, extraction, domination of the plant. *II.* As a historical anti-thesis, 'Quino' potentially opposes the European and imperial indoctrination and institution of the Latin binomial attributed by Linnaeus with the 'Cinchona' species in the 18th century; a baseless term that was the result of a spelling mistake glossed over for centuries and originally premised on an imperial lie (fake news of the 16th century) in the imperial, romanticized fantasy and debunked claim of the Countess of Chinchón from Spain in 17th century Latin America. *III.* As a sentient being, 'Quino' not only resists its specialized, botanical identification as a singular and individuated scientific species, 'Quino' also challenges the Latin, secular, epistemological nomenclature of 'Quina,' a specialized term that reduced the entire body and being of plant down to a single part, the bark, exclusively intended for extraction. *IV.* As a self-pollinating tree with hermaphrodite flowers, Quino proclaims its rightful identity as a non-binary, bisexual being. Androgynous, its identity challenges its gendered categorization historically attributed by Latin-based, gendered languages of Christian, imperial origins for colonial purposes...to which the fullest and most accurate (if not respectful) term would possibly be 'Quinx.' As part of a territory, *Quinx* could be understood as a declaration of sovereignty. Quinx approximates and approaches the preexisting, original, oral, Andean, linguistic identification of the plant to which it relates traditionally, culturally, and regionally. *V.* Thus, if the fever tree (árbol de la fiebre) is not be claimed nor colonized again, its identify should not reflected in any scientific term whose variations have been defined by, confined to, shackled by any one single language, or even limited to the written word. Alternatively, perhaps its enduring nature is best expressed when spoken—[*Qui/no*]—where the pronunciation is a practice itself; a performative act of cultural transmission and a pattern of sharing knowledge that honors the sovereignty of the seed, the plant, and its territorial traditions for generations to come. *[2021: Un-Patenting]*

ARCHIVAL ACTIVISM

This project involving a book and an exhibition is the result of important contributions from independent artists, photographers, journalists, archivists, librarians, collectors, community elders, and community organizations. They all made themselves, including their work and their archives, unconditionally accessible amidst extreme occupational health risks, turbulent live-work schedules, family & community pressures, and logistically complex environments of COVID-19. The global pandemic saw the shutdown of institutions and organizations, small and large, which not only made the nature of archival research, interviews, and ground-truthing considerably more complicated, the ensuing lockdown orders and quarantine measures in different regions posed a unique challenge for a project of this scale and scope. The authors wish to extend deep gratitude and respect to all the contributors who kindly shared their time and experience in the process of making this book a collective effort.

Image Credits: Cover: 300mg Quinine Sulphate Tablet/Pharmakina | Front Flap: © Eduardo León. Back Flap, Left: © Abby Ross. Black Flap, Right: © Celso Roldán/AFP. 1: 300mg Quinine Sulphate Tablet (actual size)/Pharmakina. 6: © John Philips/Getty Images. 8-9: David Rumsey Map Collection. 14: © David Diaz Arcos. 24: Hans Weiditz/National Library of Medicine. 26: National Central Library of Rome. 28-31: Biblioteca Universitaria Estense. 32: John Carter Brown Library. 34-35: Getty Academic Institute. 36: Charlotte Mary Yonge/University of Michigan. 38-41: US Library of Congress/Jay I. Kislak Collection. 42: David Rumsey Map Collection. 44: Adapted from Burgess/New York Times, 2012. 46-49: Barry Lawrence Ruderman Antique Maps. 50-51: Antonio De Ulloa and Jorge Juan/Complutense University of Madrid/Hathitrust Digital Library. 52: Francisco Hernandez/John Carter Brown Library/Mexico Incunables Collection. 54-57: © Diego Grandi/The National Palace of Mexico/The Diego Rivera Foundation. 58-61: The First New Chronicle and Good Government (1615)/Det Kongelige Bibliotek. 62-65: Andrés Sánchez Gallque/ Leibsohn, Dana, and Barbara E. Mundy/Vistas: Visual Culture in Spanish America (1520-1820). 66: Antonio Vázquez de Espinosa/Wellcome Collection. 68: Fray Antonio de la Calancha/John Carter Brown Library. 70: Francis A. Countway/Library of Medicine. 72: Ricardo Palma/Koninklijke Bibliotheek. 74a: Giovanni Giacomo de Rossi/Getty Research Institute. 74b: Laurentius Beyerlinck/Getty Research Institute. 76: Vicente Albán, Courtesy of Museo Arqueológico Nacional. 78: Tonino Clemente/Centro Cultural Afroecuatoriano. 80: La Médecine Populaire (1881). 82-83: Biblioteca Brasiliana Guita e José Mindlin/New York Public Library. 84-87: Courtesy of Herzog August Bibliothek Wolfenbüttel. 88: Science Museum Group Collection. 90: The Linnean Society of London. 92: Gaudentio Brunacio/Complutense University of Madrid Library. 93: Courtesy of the National Central Library of Rome. 94-97: Henri Testelin/Château de Versailles Collections. 98: John Carter Brown Library. 100: Wellcome Collection. 102: © Ministerio de Cultura y Deporte/Archivo General de Indias. 104-107: Charles Marie de La Condamine/Wellcome Collection. 110: John Carter Brown Library. 112: Royal Society (London)/Philosophical Transactions (1706-1707). 114-117: John Carter Brown Library. 118-119: Francisco Requena/ Banco de la República. 120: US Library of Congress/Law Division. 122: Wellcome Library. 124: Carolus Linnaeus/Bibliothèque Interuniversitaire de Santé/Universidad de Valladolid. 126: Juan Bautista Bru de Ramón/ Universidad de Valladolid. 128: Diego de Villanueva/ Museum of the Royal Academy of Fine Arts of San Fernando. 129: Miguel Colmeiro/Dumbarton Oaks. 130: © GraficArt Fotografía. 132: "Baltazara y Manuela Chivisa (1778, Chimborazo): Las Hermanas Mártires" by Marcela Costales (1951-2020) in "Mujeres Patriotas y Precursoras de la Libertad: En El Bicentenario 1809-2009" (Quito, Ecuador: IECAIM, 2009): p.20/Instituto Ecuatoriano de Investigaciones y Capacitación de la Mujer (IECAIM), 2009 & Universidad Andina Simón Bolívar. 134: Museo del Prado. 136: Gustav Puhlman/Hathitrust Digital Library. 138-143: Paulus Minguet/ Biblioteca Nacional de Espana. 144: R. Christobel/Wellcome Collection. 146: 200 Bolivianos Currency Bill (2016)/ Banco Central de Bolivia. 148: © Antonio Huillca Huallpa, La Sentencia de Muerte a Túpac Amaru II, Jalado por 4 Caballos. (Bestias y jinetes que no pudieron romperle las extremidades de su cuerpo), Cusco, 18 de mayo 1781. "Oleo Sobre Lienzo", 130 X

90 cm. 2007. Courtesy of Salvador Huillca & Mel Alumine Huillca. 149: © Antonio Huillca Huallpa. Martirio de la Sra. Gregoria Apaza (Esposa del Lider Andrés Tupac Amaru) y Bartolina Sisa (Esposa del Lider Tomás Catari). Ambas del Alto Perú, Fueron Ejecutadas en la Plaza de las Piñas el 5 de noviembre 1782. Por haber defendido las tierra de América y por la Justicia Social para los pueblos. "Oleo Sobre Lienzo," 130 x 90 cm. 2009. Courtesy of Salvador Huillca & Mel Alumine Huillca. 150-153: Biblioteca Nacional de España/The Hispanic Digital Library. 154: The Punch (February 17, 1785) T. Smith Publisher/The Metropolitan Museum of Art/The Elisha Whittelsey Collection/The Elisha Whittelsey Fund, 1959. 156: J. Denis/Wellcome Collection. 158-161: The Illustrated London News (December 6, 1862): p.592/ The University of Michigan. 162: George Henry/California Digital Library. 164-167: © Pablo Escudero. 168: Libreria de Fernando, Madrid (1891). 170-173: Alexander von Humboldt/David Rumsey Map Collection. 174-175: Johann W. von Goethe & Alexander von Humbolt/David Rumsey Map Collection. 176-177: Friedrich Georg Weitsch/Stiftung Preußische Schlösser und Gärten Berlin-Brandenburg. 178-181: Roger Sculp/David Rumsey Map Collection. 182-185: Julius Schrader/Metropolitan Museum of Art. 188-189: Alexander von Humboldt/University of Michigan/ Hathitrust Digital Library. 190: Ernest Board/Wellcome Collection. 192-193: Louis Figuier, The Vegetable World (London: Cassell, Petter, and Galpin,1869)/Missouri Botanical Garden. 194: Adapted from Burgess/New York Times, 2012. 196-197: Manuel Villavicencio/US Library of Congress/Geography and Map Division. 198: Iconografía del Libertador/Ediciones Lerner/Colección Guillermo Hernández de Alba de Bogotá,1967. 200: Clements R. Markham, Peruvian Bark (London: John Murray, 1880). 202-203: H.A. Weddell, Histoire Naturelle des Quinquinas (Paris: Victor Masson, 1849). 204: Oscar Réveil, Le Règne Végétal (Paris: Guérin,1870-72)/Biodiversity Heritage Library. 206: Clements R. Markham, Peruvian Bark (London: John Murray, 1880). 208: © Wellcome Collection. 209: © Wellcome Collection. 210: Casa Nacional de Moneda/Banco Central de Reserva del Perú/ Oleg Muzyka. 212: Philip Henry Gosse, Wanderings through the Conservatories at Kew (London, Society for Promoting Christian Knowledge 1856)/Biodiversity Heritage Library. 214-215: Edward Walford, Plans of Kew Gardens (London,1888)/ University of California. 216: US Library of Congress (LC-DIG-stereo-1s0458)/The Robin G. Stanford Collection. 218-219: The Metropolitan Museum of Art (acquired by Purchase, Gift of William H. Huntington, by exchange, 1979). 220-227: Bureau Tot Bevordering van Het Kinine-Gebruik/Wellcome Collection. 228: © National Institute of Agrarian Reform (INDA) Archives/ Santiago del Hierro. 230: Archivo Leibniz-Institut für Länderkunde. 232-233: Manuel Jesús Serrano/Instituto Nacional de Patrimonio Cultural/Manuel Jesús Serrano Collection. 234: Robert Koch, Die Ätiologie der Milzbrand-Krankheit, 1876 (Leipzig: J.A. Barth, 1910)/Robert Koch Institute. 236: Alphonse Laveran, Du Paludisme et de son Hématozoaire (Paris: G. Masson, 1891)/ Bibliothèque Nationale de France/Gallica. 238: Unknown Photographer/Wellcome Collection. 240: Boston Public Library/ Norman B. Leventhal Map Center. 242: Álbum do Centenário de Brusque, 2010/Brusque Memória. 244: Chininum (Amsterdam: Bureau for Increasing the Use of Quinine, 1925)/Wellcome Library. 246-247: Arthur Mee (ed.), Harmsworth Popular Science (London: Educational Book Company, 1911)/Wellcome Library. 248: Bureau Tot Bevordering van Het Kinine-Gebruik (Kinabureau)/Stichting Nationaal Museum van Wereldculturen (SNMVW) TM-60018886. 250: Kinabureau/SNMVW TM-60018892. 251: Kinabureau/SNMVW TM-10012678. 252: Kinabureau/SNMVW TM-10012673. 253: Kinabureau/SNMVW TM-60016810. 254: Kinabureau/Wellcome Collection. 255: Kinabureau/SNMVW TM-10012676. 256: Kinabureau/Wellcome Collection. 257: Kinabureau/SNMVW TM-60041399. 258: Cambridge University Library/John Abercromby Alexander Collection. 259: Kinabureau/SNMVW TM-10012682. 260: Kinabureau/SNMVW TM-10012685. 261: Kinabureau/SNMVW TM-10012782. 262-263: Kinabureau/SNMVW TM-10012775. 264: Archivo Nela Mériguet Martínez. 266: Eduardo Kingman, Historia Illustrada del Ecuador III (Libresa/Vistazo, 2010). 268: Kinabureau/SNMVW TM-10012686/Bureau for Propagating the Use of Quinine/US National Library of Medicine. 270: Wellcome Library/Cinchona Tercentenary Exhibition. 272: Fanny Arregui de Pazmiño & Rogelia Carrillo de Landázuri/Talleres Gráficos/Nacionales/Biblioteca Ecuatoriana Aurelio Espinoza Pólit. 274: Southern Development Bank/ National Numismatic Collection/National Museum of American History. 276: Adapted from Burgess/New York Times, 2012.

278-283: Misael Acosta Solís, Cinchonas del Ecuador (Quito: Publicaciónes Científicas, 1946). 284: US Army Medical Department, Preventive Medicine in World War II-Vol. VI: Communicable Diseases/Office of Medical History (1963). 286: Rolf Blomberg/Archivo Blomberg. 288: US National Archives/Federal Register Vol.9 No.7/Library of Congress. 290: US War Department Special Services Division/National Library of Medicine. 292-297: © 1956 LIFE Magazine/Wheaton College Archives. 298-301: © Yann Arthus-Bertrand. 302: Instituto Nacional de Colonização e Reforma Agraria (INCRA). 304-305: José Geraldo D.C. Camargo, Urbanismo Rural (Brasilia: Gráfica Gutenberg, 1973)/Cornell University Library. 306-307: © Editora Manchete/ Fundação Biblioteca Nacional. 308-313: José Geraldo D.C. Camargo, Urbanismo Rural (Brasilia: Gráfica Gutenberg, 1973)/Cornell University Library. 314a: © Editora Manchete/Fundação Biblioteca Nacional. 314b: La Ciudad Lineal No.68 (Madrid, 1897)/ Biblioteca Nacional de España (Hemeroteca Digital). 315a: Instituto Nacional de Colonização e Reforma Agraria (INCRA). 315b: Flávio Alcaraz Gomes, Transamazônica; A Redescoberta do Brasil (Sao Paolo: Livraria Cultura Editora, 1972). 316-317: © Casa do Moeda do Brasil. 318: © Jeffrey B. Russell Photography. 320: © Luis G. Mejia C. 322: EP Petroecuador/Grupo Conduto. 324-325: EP Petroecuador/OCP. 326-327: Dr. Bernd Lehmann. 328-329: © PetroAmazonas/Journal of American Association of Petroleum Geologists. 330-335: US Library of Congress/Geography & Map Division. 336: US Government Printing Office. 337: © C.A. El Universo. 338: US Freedom of Information Act Collection. 340: UNESCO World Heritage. 342: Natural History Magazine. 343: UNESCO World Heritage/Correos del Ecuador/Philatelic Association of Ecuador (AFE). 344: © 1970 Victoria Santa Cruz. 346: Antonio Ubilla. 348-349: World Bank Report No. 947a-EC (April 20, 1976)/Latin America and Caribbean Projects Department. 349 (inset): Hugo Tobar Webb. 350-351: © Yann Arthus-Bertrand. 352: Tonantzin Land Institute/Tupac Enrique Acosta and Elizabeth Betita Martínez, 500 Años de la Mujer Chicana (Albuquerque, NM: Southwest Organizing Project, 1991). 354-355: © Confederación de Organizaciones Indígenas del Ecuador. 356-363: © Confederación de Nacionalidades Indígenas del Ecuador (CONAIE Archives/CONAIE Communications Administration). 364: © Meridith Kohut/Getty. 366-367: © Eitan Abramovich/AFP. 368: © C-SPAN. 370: © Cancillería del Ecuador. 372: Brass Moustache Films/Mark Donne. 373: © NY Times. 374: US Patent & Trademark Office No.75277670. 376-377: © Kurt Schlosser/© Andrey Sitnik/© Taylor Soper/ © Douglas Fruehling/Washington Business Journal. 378: Micromedex. 380: © 1991 Sanofi-Aventis. 382: © Lauren Holden/ Wellcome Collection. 384: © Matthias Heyde/Landbruks, OG Matdepartementet CC. 386: © Abby Ross. 388-389: © Thomas Imo/Photothek. 390-391: © JAG Images. 392: © Alfredo Cárdenas/Diario El Universo. 394: Asamblea Montecristi/Ecuador TV. 396: Scan Courtesy of Pierre Bélanger. 398: Moises Saman. 400: Lalo de Almeida. 402: © Tarciso Schnaider. 403: © Nelson Almeida (fotógrafo)/Historia AFP de Allison Jackson. 404: © Presidencia de la República del Ecuador. 406: Teleamazonas & Pichincha Comunicaciones. 407: © Silvia Peralta. 408: © Ecuavisa. 410-414 © David Diaz Arcos. 415: Colectivo Arquitectura Expandida. 415: © LA TV Ecuador. 416: © Eduardo León. 417: © Frente de Defensa y Modernización del Mercado San Roque. 418: © Joe Berlinger. 421: Brass Moustache Films/Mark Donne. 422-423: © Ministry of Hydrocarbons. 425: Brass Moustache Films/Mark Donne. 426: © 2010 Nicholas Gill. 427: Ministerio de Energía y Recursos Naturales no Renovables, Secretaría de Hidrocarburos & Ministerio de Sectores Estratégicos. 428: "Finding new compounds" (00:22:37) Film Still/Tobias Bagge. 430-431: "Guard it with your life" (00:19:52) Film Still/Tobias Bagge. 432: © Smithsonian Institution. 434: © Matteo Nardone. 436: © Nelson Almeida/AFP. 437: © Planet Labs Inc. 438-439: © Eraldo Peres/AP. 440: Patricia Gualinga/Amazon Watch. 442-444, 448-453, 455: Amazon Frontlines. 445-447, 454, 456-457: Alianza Ceibo/Alex Lucitante. 458-461: Kristel Mucino/ Washington Office on Latin America. 462: © Caroline Bennett. 464-466: © Mona Caron. 468: Adapted from Micromedex. 470: © Eduardo León. 472-473: © David Diaz Arcos. 474: © Charles G. Ripley. 475: © Ronaldo Schemidt/AFP. 476: © David Pellicola. 478: Adriana Guzmán/Koman Ilel. 482: @realDonaldTrump/Courtesy of Pierre Bélanger. 484: © Aldair Mejía/La República. 486: Mongabay. 488: © Celso Roldán/AFP. 490: © Arjo Vanderjagt. 492: © LA MINGA/OPSYS. 494-501: © Pablo Escudero. 508: Victoria Santa Cruz, "Me Gritaron Negra" (1970)/Music MGP/Katherine A. Porras, 2012. 511: © Metro Ecuador.

Special Thanks to: Tupac Enrique Acosta, David Diaz Arcos, Yann Arthus-Bertrand, Alexander Arroyo, Jean-Marc Bélanger, Mónica Belevan, Joe Berlinger, Hernán Bianchi-Benguria, Dirk Brinkman, Mona Caron, John Curl, Fabiola Cuvi, Tiffany Kaewen Dang, Henrietta Danker, Lou Dematteis, Ana María Durán Calisto, Enotrius, Pablo A. Escudero, Verónica Escudero, Ingeborg Eggink, Reid Farnsworth, Ali Fard, Daniela Fuentes Moncada, Jacob Geitner, Gordon Goff, María Guagalango, Patricia Gualinga, Christine D. Helmlinger Stewart, Salvador Huillca, Emanuela Innelli, Dr. Trevor Kemp, G. Mathias Kondolf, Gabriel Kozlowski, Sanford Kwinter, Dr. Bernd Lehmann, Ana Maria León, Eduardo León, Alex Lucitante, Olivier Martí, Miho Mazereeuw, Nina Mazereeuw, Scott McCreary, Ran Mei, Ivan Mejia, Nela Meriguet, Gabriel Moreno, Diana Mosquera, Oleg Muzyka, Matteo Nardone, Nemonte Nenquimo, Liesbeth Ouwehand, David Pellicola, Sophie Pinchetti, Alejandra Pinto, Katherine A. Porras, Jeremy Rosenberg, Abby Ross, Jeff Russell, Octavio Santa Cruz, Roi Salgueiro Barrio, Hashim Sarkis, Santiago Serna, Samantha Sigmon, Sara Sisa Bordados (Verónica Montesdeoca, Giss Simbaña, Erika Simbaña, Rosita Tasiguano, Rosario Tashiguano, Catalina Toapanta, Rebeca Uyana) & Manos de Colores (Daniela Fuentes Moncada), Andrey Sitnik, Silvercrowncoin, Fanke Su, Gloria Irene Taylor, Robert Wright, Robert Twiss, Hugo Tobar Webb, Ana Victoria Vásconez, Janie Day Whitworth, Patricia Yallico, and Yuri111.

Acknowledgements: Aldair Mejía, Alfredo Cardenas, Amazon Frontlines, American Association of Petroleum Geologists, Antropología e Historia del Perú, Apawki Castro, Archive.org, Archivo General de Indias, Biblioteca Nacional de Colombia, Biblioteca Nacional Digital Brazil, Carmen Montoya, Caroline Bennett, Celso Roldan,Centro Cultural Afroecuatoriano, Charles G. Ripley, Christine Van Luys, Cornell University, David Rumsey, Diana Tanchatipan, Douglas Fruehling, Emily Banas, Enrique Quispe Cueva, Faviano Kueva, Graham Foundation for Advanced Studies in the Fine Arts, HathiTrust Digital Library, Historical Archives from the Municipality of Loja, Instituto Ecuatoriano de Investigaciones y Capacitación de la Mujer, Isis Maria/Mídia NINJA, Ivan Mejia, Jair Alfredo Villao Palma, Jean Huets & Noma Petroff, John Carter Brown Library, Jose Rubio, JSTOR Global Plants, Karno Books, Ketty Romo-Leroux, Koman Ilel, Kurt Schlosser, Lalo de Almeida, Library of Congress, Marc Becker, Maritza Eliana Balcazar, Mark Donne, Mel Alumine Huillca, Mercado San Francisco, Mercado San Roque, Museo de la Ciudad de Quito, Museo Nacional de Arqueología, Naturalis Biodiversity Center, Néstor Llorca, Noël Ibrahimu, Pharmakina BV, Photographic Archives of the Instituto Nacional de Patrimonio Cultural del Ecuador, Planet Labs, Rafael Vélez Mantilla, Santiago del Hierro, Sebastián Dueñas Oviedo, Stichting Nationaal Museum van Wereldculturen, Taylor Soper, Tobias Bagge, Tres Mañuelas, Tropenmuseum, Universidad Andina Simón Bolívar, University of Virginia Libraries, Wellcome Library, Wheaton College, and WOLA Advocacy for Human Rights in the Americas.

About the Authors: *Pierre Bélanger* is a settler designer, landscape architect, and urban planner from Montréal and Ottawa with binational citizenship (US, CAN), currently in Boston, traditional lands of the Massachusett Peoples, territory of Wampanoag, Aquinnah, and Nipmuc Nations. They coordinate *#The1492Project*, an initiative dedicated to the removal of Columbus monuments across the Americas and the dismantling of structures of white supremacy. *Ghazal Jafari* is a designer of Persian and Azeri descent and territorial scholar in exile. Originally from Tehran (IR), her practice focuses on spatial and environmental justice, immigrant narratives, women resistance movements, and non-Western spatial discourses. She is founding director of *MIYAN RUDAN* (*Between Rivers*), a long-term initiative based along the Karun River watershed, borderlands of Iran and Iraq. *Pablo Escudero* is a farmer, architect, and urbanist from the Andean region of Pichincha in northern Ecuador and US Fulbright Scholar living on traditional territories of Kichwa People beginning PhD studies at UC Santa Cruz on Alexander von Humboldt. He is founding director of *LA MINGA Collective* based in Quito (EC) focusing on territories of conflict located at the intersection of the Amazon and the Andes. Together with Tiffany Kaewen Dang, Hernán Bianchi-Benguria, and Alexander Arroyo, they are founding members of *OPEN SYSTEMS*, a non-profit organization dedicated to systemic change by raising awareness of geopolitical conflicts at the intersection of environmental injustice, territorial dispossession, spatial inequality, climate change, and sovereignty.

This book and accompanying exhibition are dedicated to the memory of *German Amaguaña Matango* (1964–2020) from Imbabura (Ecuador), lands of Kichwa Nations.